Mark Urban is Diplomatic and De[...]
Newsnight and the author of the N[...]
bestseller *Task Force Black*. His previo[...]
were ground-breaking histories of earlier campaigns told through
the lives of men in those regiments. He held a gap-year
commission in the 4th Royal Tank Regiment and subsequently
served in the Territorial Army. As a television journalist Mark has
covered many of the world's conflicts during the last twenty-five
years. He lives in London with his wife and children.

Praise for Mark Urban

'As dashing and unconventional as the legendary unit itself'
Andrew Roberts, *Literary Review* (for *Rifles*)

'A superb study of the unit that effectively created the modern
British Army's infantry tactics' Nicholas Fearn, *Independent on
Sunday* (for *Rifles*)

'A real treat ... a deeply researched, beautifully crafted and
captivating volume ... A riveting slab of derring-do and high
adventure' Frank McLynn, Daily Express (for *Rifles*)

'A ground-breaking, often chilling account ... remarkable' *Sunday
Times* (for *Task Force Black*)

'With unparalleled access, Urban paints a picture of how our
finest fighting men could be truly effective ... An essential
record' *The Times* (for *Task Force Black*)

By Mark Urban

SOVIET LAND POWER

WAR IN AFGHANISTAN

BIG BOYS' RULES: THE SAS AND THE SECRET
STRUGGLE AGAINST THE IRA

UK EYES ALPHA: INSIDE BRITISH INTELLIGENCE

THE MAN WHO BROKE NAPOLEON'S CODES:
THE STORY OF GEORGE SCOVELL

RIFLES: SIX YEARS WITH WELLINGTON'S
LEGENDARY SHARPSHOOTERS

GENERALS: TEN BRITISH COMMANDERS WHO
SHAPED THE WORLD

FUSILIERS: HOW THE BRITISH ARMY LOST AMERICA
BUT LEARNED TO FIGHT

TASK FORCE BLACK: THE EXPLOSIVE TRUE STORY OF THE
SAS AND THE SECRET WAR IN IRAQ

THE TANK WAR: THE BRITISH BAND OF BROTHERS –
ONE TANK REGIMENT'S WORLD WAR II

THE
TANK WAR

THE BRITISH BAND OF BROTHERS –
ONE TANK REGIMENT'S WORLD WAR II

Mark Urban

For Craig and Tom

ABACUS

First published in Great Britain in 2013 by Little, Brown
This paperback edition published in 2014 by Abacus

A CIP catalogue record for this book
is available from the British Library.

ISBN 978-0-349-00014-5

Typeset in Bembo by M Rules
Printed and bound in Great Britain by
Clays Ltd, St Ives plc

Papers used by Abacus are from well-managed forests
and other responsible sources.

Abacus
An imprint of
Little, Brown Book Group
100 Victoria Embankment
London EC4Y 0DY

An Hachette UK Company
www.hachette.co.uk

www.littlebrown.co.uk

From this day to the ending of the world,
But we in it shall be remembered –
We few, we happy few, we band of brothers;
For he to-day that sheds his blood with me
Shall be my brother

William Shakespeare,
Henry V, IV, iii, 58–62

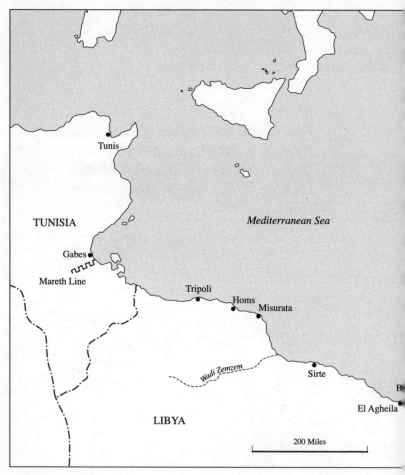

NORTH AFRICA

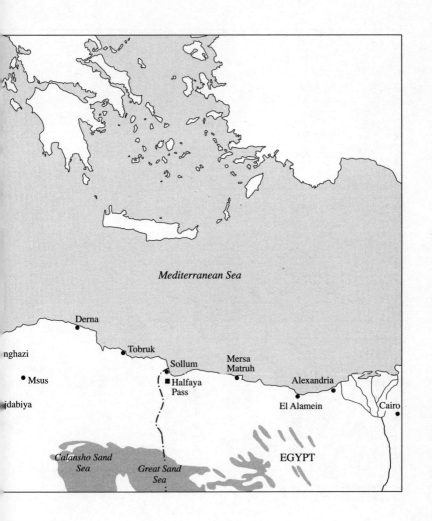

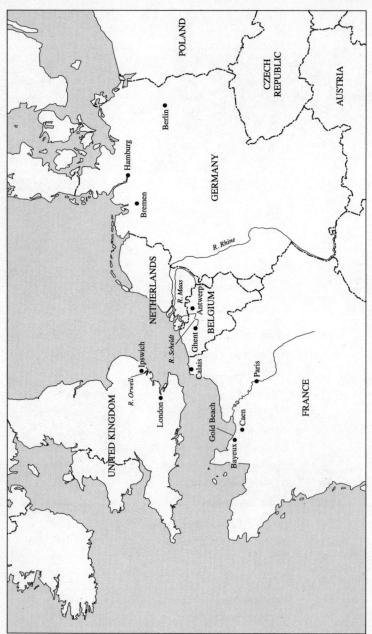

NORTH-WEST EUROPE

Contents

Introduction

The Second World War was a vast struggle that produced a literature to match. It covers everything from the experience of individuals in combat to the technology of weapons, the strategy of the protagonists and the personalities of leaders. This rolling barrage of words evolved in well-defined stages: the initial attempts to catalogue the experience of war, often in heroic or even propagandistic terms; the revisionism or myth-busting that followed; and the more recent attempts at a synthesis of these approaches.

Having written books about specific units of the British army in the American War of Independence of 1775–83 (*Fusiliers*) or the Napoleonic campaigns of 1809–15 (*Rifles*), it had for a long time been my ambition to apply the same treatment to a group of men in the Second World War. I just assumed somebody would get there first.

Starting in earnest with research in 2010, I realised that the treatment I had in mind had still not been used. There are, of course, many regimental histories out there. But how many talk about people running away? Or measure the claims of the Commanding Officer or the War Diary against those of the enemy they were fighting that day? The period in which many of these unit accounts were written was not one when people were ready to talk about certain issues, or to open certain archives.

My quest was not simply limited to matters of frankness: there were issues even more basic to the telling of a story. Many accounts of the war have relied on interviews with survivors, but it is odd how few have trawled for letters written home at the time of the fighting. Not many compare the official reports filed by a battalion, resting in the archives, with the accounts of those there at the time, or those of nearby or enemy units either. All of these approaches have been used before piecemeal but in general, on the rare occasions when they have been fused together (to excellent effect) they tend to relate to a particular battle or episode.

The question then was which unit should I choose? The principles that applied when writing my earlier books were that the unit should have played a significant part in the war from beginning to end, fighting in most of its key battles, and that its members should have left behind a substantial number of accounts. If the chosen group was part of one of history's celebrated divisions or brigades then so much the better. It is a measure of the scale of the Second World War, and the constant churn of the British army, that very few battalions or regiments satisfied these criteria. Some that had been heavily engaged in France in 1940 did not return to the fray until 1944, or ended up in a strategic backwater. Others that fought valiantly around Caen or at Arnhem near the end had not even been raised in the early years of the conflict.

My attention turned to a couple of the battalions of the Royal Tank Regiment. Some of them were in action during the abortive 1940 French campaign, and had then fought through the desert, Italy, Normandy and all the way into Germany. The 3rd RTR, for example, had produced some excellent memoirs by officers but, as will become clear here, the real beating heart of a tank regiment was its non-commissioned officer cadre, the people who commanded the majority of its tanks. Having found an extraordinary trove of writing and recollection from men of this kind, I settled on the 5th Battalion, aka 5th Tanks, 5th Royal Tank Regiment or 5th RTR. They had done all of these things, belonged for most of the war to the 7th Armoured Division or Desert Rats, and had left a profusion of accounts. Indeed, counting up the books, unpublished memoirs, letters, dispatches, audio recordings and my own interviews with survivors, I was able to tap into the experience of more than seventy members of the battalion.

There were a number of advantages to writing about a tank unit. In the first place its men, wrapped in steel, tended to live longer on a battlefield swept with machine guns and shrapnel than those on foot. This meant that it was possible to find a group of soldiers within the battalion who had fought through the whole war or much of it, telling the story in part through their experience. Such survivors were very rare indeed in the infantry.

In choosing an armoured unit there was another, even more important advantage. Nothing better symbolised the triumph of Germany during the early war years than the supremacy of its panzer force. The early fortunes of the Royal Armoured Corps symbolised too the failure of Britain to rearm quickly enough, and the squandering of its expertise in tank warfare gained during the First World War as the first country to use such machines on a large scale. The British tank man therefore faced an awful challenge when setting off to war in 1940. His road to victory would involve mastering technology, tactics and of course his own fear when confronted with an apparently unstoppable enemy.

Some time after starting my research, I realised that I must hurry because the survivors of the 5th RTR, who formed a vital resource, were passing away with alarming speed. Indeed, between first toying with the idea of writing this book in 2009 and setting pen to paper more than two years later, I would estimate the number of living veterans from the unit fell by almost half. A dozen of them helped me, for which I am truly grateful. At times I found their recall staggering. They could give me something precious that I could never have writing about earlier wars, the sense of how someone central to the story spoke or moved, how a particular battlefield smelt or sounded. I relied less on them for empirical fact – better drawn from records – or in calibrating the emotional temperature of the battalion at certain times, something best done with contemporary letters and diaries.

In understanding the realities of living on a tank, it helped that I had, long ago and for a short time, served as a junior officer in the 4th Royal Tank Regiment. Experience as a journalist on the world's more recent battlefields, where I have seen many a burning tank or twisted wreck, was also useful. But this bond of experience did not encourage me to write up the 5th RTR as a band of heroes or supermen. My previous books in this pattern have been described by reviewers as 'warts and all' accounts, and that is exactly what I have tried to do here: to be unflinchingly honest. This requires flagging up more good things than the habitual reader of Second World War books might imagine. The wartime generation of Britons was sometimes too stoical or modest to shout about its finer moments, and in the decades since many a historical reputation has been made by rubbishing British forces or extolling the skill of their German enemy. On occasion, though, honesty also requires me to write about men leaping terrified from their tanks or gunning down those holding white flags, things an earlier generation of writers, often veterans themselves, thought best to gloss over.

What I hope emerges is a full and frank account of a group of men who fought together for years, through dozens of battles and across thousands of miles. Their odyssey was as epic as that of any warrior band of antiquity. I did not choose the 5th RTR in order to make them look like some kind of elite. In many ways they were a normal, if highly professional, outfit and they could stand for any one of several regular armoured units – RTR or cavalry – that existed when the Second World War broke out. These battalions provided the human capital for the great and belated expansion of that British tank force needed to confront an enemy that had secured a huge head start. The 5th Tanks were, then, average men who did extraordinary things.

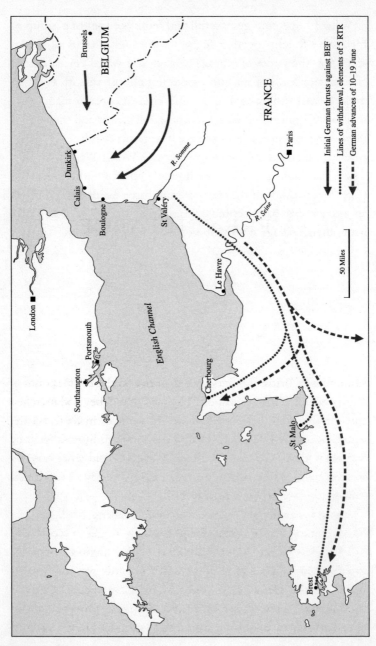

FRANCE, MAY–JUNE 1940

Initial German thrusts against BEF
Lines of withdrawal, elements of 5 RTR
German advances of 10–19 June

50 Miles

BELGIUM
Brussels

FRANCE
Paris

R. Somme
R. Seine

Dunkirk
Calais
Boulogne
St Valéry
Le Havre

English Channel

London
Portsmouth
Southampton

Cherbourg

St Malo

Brest

1

A FRENCH FARCE

Hundreds of British soldiers lay exhausted on the cobblestones of Brest's quayside that afternoon, 16 June 1940. They had marched into the harbour, having left scores of vehicles in fields on the outskirts of town. Many had for weeks endured little sleep, they had been under German air attack repeatedly and what was, for most of them, a first taste of war was ending bitterly. One felt that 'our emotions had been torn to bits'.

An old steamer lay in the harbour, a sitting duck for any Stuka that came over. Everyone just wanted to get on board and quickly away home. Many scanned the skies, anxiously expecting the reappearance of the Luftwaffe. The tide was too low for their ship, the *Manx Lass*, to dock, so men were being taken out on a lighter, a few dozen at a time. As if this process was not already taking an agonising amount of time, the French harbour master was insisting the vessel could not sail until all the paperwork had been done. In the attitude of the Cherbourg authorities, or indeed of the War Office that had sent them over, the gulf between peacetime procedure and the total war practised by their German enemy could hardly have been more absurd.

The soldiers who sat waiting their turn noticed little boxes being passed around. As each man received his, he saw it was a punnet of fresh strawberries. Some French dockers had taken pity on the Tommies, purloining the fruit from a cargo that was about to be shipped. Many of the British were ravenous as well as tired, so the strawberries tasted delicious.

Two weeks earlier, Britain had removed more than three hundred thousand troops from the beaches at Dunkirk. The soldiers in Brest were members of an armoured division that had been sent over after the initial dispatch of the British Expeditionary Force. However, Germany's blitzkrieg against Belgium and France had moved so swiftly that the British reinforcements had never been able to link up with the main force.

Many of those awaiting the lighter out to the *Manx Lass* were soldiers of the 5th Royal Tank Regiment. They had not brought any tanks to Brest, though: their fighting vehicles were scattered all over northern France. During a week of headlong retreat the battalion, in common with the rest of the British armoured division, had literally gone to pieces.

On the quayside were lorry drivers, spare tank crews and fitters from the battalion. The 5th's Commanding Officer was also there. Inland, a small party of volunteers was moving among the vehicles abandoned at the gates of the town, sabotaging them. Some, armed with hammers, attacked the distributors in the lorries' engines; others put sand in petrol tanks. There were orders against torching the vehicles, but columns of black smoke arced up into the sky. Fuel dumps were being lit, and other stores too.

The dozen or so tankies disabling the vehicles enjoyed their work. There was something thrilling in so much wanton destruction. In some of the wagons they found abandoned bottles of booze or trinkets, and helped themselves. Eventually, though, word came that Jerry was getting too close. They jumped on a truck and drove as fast as they could for the harbour.

Aboard the *Manx Lass* at last, Frank Cheeseman, a fitter from 5th Tanks, opened fire with his Bren gun as a German plane lined up to attack them. There was a brief cacophony of shooting but no harm done by either side, and as the lone attacker flew off the stress and exhaustion washed over the young soldier; he broke down crying.

The steamer had already gone when the truck carrying the sabotage team roared into the docks in the darkness of early evening. The tank soldiers jumped clear of the wagon, set its accelerator running and watched in delight as the vehicle sped off the dock, sailing through the air before landing in the harbour with an almighty splash. They ran up the gangway of a Royal Navy destroyer that had come into Brest to pick up the last remaining stragglers. Soon they too were underway, disappearing into the darkness.

Just as the rescue vessels sailed from Brest, another column of the 5th Tanks roared into the Channel port of Cherbourg, 150 miles to the north-east. Seven tanks made their way through the streets, and down to the docks. At this point the Commanding Officer and others evacuated at Brest had no idea what had become of the regiment's last working tanks and their exhausted crews.

The mixture of light tanks and cruisers that arrived at Cherbourg were the last runners from three different armoured squadrons, armed with more than fifty tanks, which had landed in France. Their crews had driven for more than fifty hours without halt in order to make it there. They too had feared air attacks as they rushed up the Cherbourg peninsula, the snapping Germans at their heels. Although the battalion's brief French campaign had been plagued with breakdowns among its British-made tanks, these seven had all completed the last road march of more than two hundred miles. They had nursed the machines, tending to their mechanical peculiarities, stopping every hour to tighten the tracks or find water for leaky radiators.

It hadn't been easy; indeed, at times their march north had assumed a desperate air. On one occasion, with the tanks' fuel supply close to exhaustion, they had pulled in at a petrol station where a forbidding *madame* guarded the pumps. She had initially insisted that there was nothing left to give them, and anyway she didn't have the keys to the locks on the pumps. One of the 5th Tanks soldiers drew his pistol and put it to the woman's head, telling her that 'if she did not find the keys by the time he counted five he would blow her brains out'. The keys were produced by the time he reached 'two' and the soldiers pumped hundreds of gallons into their vehicles. They left her with a receipt signed 'Winston Churchill'.

The army had absorbed hundreds of thousands of conscripts since the war started, but most of this squadron arriving in Cherbourg were regulars, seasoned tank soldiers highly trained in the operation of their war machines. One RTR officer noted: 'My soldiers were of a high standard in every respect, in intelligence, in behaviour, and in their willingness to tackle anything. The soldier of the Royal Tank Corps was in those days the cream of the army.'

Sergeant Emmin Hall had joined eight years earlier. A barrel of a man, tall too, Hall had served on the North West Frontier – what are now the tribal areas of Pakistan – and radiated the quiet authority of a veteran. A miner's son from Nuneaton in Warwick-shire, Hall was the product of unhappy family circumstances, both his brothers and his mother having died when he was young. Escaping his stepmother and hard-drinking father as soon as he could, Hall had joined the army in 1931. Having served in the regular army on a 'six and six' (a contract for six years' full-time service followed by six in the reserves), Hall had been recalled to the colours in 1939 as war became inevitable. Wearing three stripes, and aged twenty-seven by the time of the Cherbourg evacuation, Hall had begun to see the 5th Tanks as his real family and, looking out for the younger men, made sure his tank was the last of the seven to be loaded.

As the war machines were lifted by crane from the quayside to a waiting ship, the drivers watched anxiously. Some took a smoke, others wondered if there was still time for a drink before they embarked. Among the latter was Jake Wardrop, who had joined the 5th in 1937, training as a driver. Wardrop, who had celebrated his twenty-fifth birthday during the late campaign, had rescued his guitar from the tank and was intent on a sing-song before they left. A hard man in the best Glasgow tradition, ready to respond to an insult with his fists, Wardrop was also well read and a perceptive observer of the human condition. Members of his squadron remember 'cat-like eyes', an intense stare, someone who quickly sized up officers and rankers alike.

The drinkers among the regiment had found the campaign convivial enough: the crews had been able to buy wine, beer, calvados or brandy in many of the villages they passed through. They had also bought or taken their food as well, since the army system of supply never kept up with them. One member of the 5th Tanks insisted, 'I never ever had a meal cooked by the army whilst I was in France – we lived off the land.'

Charlie Bull was also on the quayside. He had joined the army not long after Sergeant Hall, also on a 'six and six'. He had finished his six years of regular service in1938, returning to his native Tutbury in Staffordshire, but the coming of war saw him called up and returning to his old battalion. If Wardrop had an air of danger about him, Bull was harder to read. On the surface he was a stolid, stout Englishman who went through most things uncomplainingly. There was something John Bull about Charlie, an Englishman who craved roast beef and ale, and who could be relied upon to maintain bluff good humour in the face of adversity. Beneath this exterior, though, was a man of more elemental passions, a Jack the Lad in the dance hall who had a taste for fancy cars, women and fine clothes. His life had already been marked by confrontations with authority: while Emmin Hall, from the same start, had gained promotion to sergeant, Bull's problems with peacetime discipline left him a private soldier. For him, the war would offer the chance of redemption.

Bull had found the brief campaign bewildering. Like many, he had been unnerved by the sporadic air attacks when screaming Stuka dive-bombers had dropped on their columns, often without warning. Having come through this ordeal, Charlie wanted to let his mother, the great pole of stability in his life, know all about it.Writing to her back in Staffordshire, the tank driver tried to sum up his feelings about what they had just come through: 'We had a pretty rough time while we were there, as we had to be on the move all the time, we didn't get much sleep either, but I think I liked it, and wouldn't mind going again. I got the wind up once or twice, especially when I could hear bombs whistling down all over the place.'

With the evacuation of this squadron and several hundred soldiers from Cherbourg on 17 June, the regiment's departure was largely complete. But it was not quite as simple as withdrawing from Brest and Cherbourg. Other men had fetched up in other ports. Lieutenant Brian Stone, a 5th Tanks reservist called up at the start of the war, had been evacuated from Saint-Malo, with the remnants of a group from A Squadron. The lieutenant, who was twenty-one years old, had gone from a private school to work at the head office of Shell in London a couple of years before. An avid reader and lover of classical music, plays and poetry, with blond wavy hair, he was as far from the Blimpish military archetype as it was possible to be. Yet he hungered for adventure, and with war approaching Stone knew where he might find it, so he joined the Territorial Army. Once evacuated and back in Britain, Lieutenant Stone was keen to get back to his unit in order to convince the regular army men who ran the show that he was worthy of the command of tanks.

Few of the battalion's five hundred plus souls remained in France. Just six men had been killed during the brief campaign. They had died during the one formal engagement that they had fought, on 28 May, advancing on the little town of Saint-Valéry-sur-Somme. There the tanks had been thrown forward in an attack that was supposed to be supported by French infantry. The allies failed to materialise, so the armour was soon hit by the Germans defending the place. A few tanks were knocked out before the operation was called off, with just one of the British commanders claiming a kill.

Parties of the 5th, in common with the other remnants taken away in that evacuation from France, landed in ports all along the southern coast of England and Wales. Other members of the battalion were scattered even further afield, but whose fate would be closely tied to the men returning from France.

Gerry Solomon had volunteered for the tanks soon after the outbreak of war. He had endured three months of square-bashing – parade-ground drill under bawling instructors from the cavalry – before being sent for further training as a driver/mechanic. Tall, earnest and motivated, Solomon represented the wartime volunteer, that great tide of humanity being pressed into khaki. Such was the shortage of weapons and scale of Britain's mobilisation during those early months of war that their training had focused largely on military basics such as map-reading and physical fitness. When his future colleagues were reassembling themselves as a battalion in Warminster, Trooper Solomon was sitting in a classroom being taught at a civilian garage. It had been pressed into the war effort in order to teach the new recruits about ignition systems, crankshafts, and clutch plates. He was nervous about how the returning veterans – most of them regular soldiers – would react to a civilian like him, turning up as a tank driver/mechanic, without ever having taken a spanner to a real tank, let alone driven one.

The state of flux in which regiment, army, nation and industry found itself that summer of 1940 extended even to where the war should be prosecuted. With the fall of France, attention had moved from helping allies on the Continent to self-preservation. Precautions against invasion were under way everywhere, from sowing mines on possible landing beaches to hoisting barrage balloons over London. But even at this moment of supreme national peril, Britain could not forget that it was a global empire whose colonial possessions might become targets for Germany's allies, Italy and Japan.

In Egypt, on 10 June, a British garrison that had been idling away the days joined the war. Italy had entered the fray and every-one at Headquarters in Cairo knew that this would soon mean war on the desert border with Libya, where a substantial Italian colonial garrison was based. Egypt was, at this time, the one place outside England where the British army had significant numbers of tanks. British commanders were busily trying to put as much of their garrison on tracks or wheels – mechanising and motorising regiments – as they could, recognising that a war in North Africa would involve large distances and rapid movement.

A FRENCH FARCE

Lieutenant Arthur Crickmay, having joined the 5th Royal Tank Regiment at the outbreak of war, had been posted to the 6th RTR in Egypt late in 1939. Crickmay, aged twenty-four in the summer of 1940, was something of a dandy, whose careful attention to his clothes and the trim of his moustache masked an underlying diffidence or shyness. Like Trooper Solomon he hailed from Suffolk, and like Lieutenant Stone his family was far from wealthy. As the months of phoney war had ticked by, Crickmay was cheered to find his pay went far in Cairo, where he brushed up his squash game at the Gezira Sporting Club, acquired a Chrysler for touring about and ate well at numerous watering holes.

Crickmay may have embraced the social or sporting preferences of an English gentleman but he was no dilettante in the business of war. During several desert exercises with the 6th he had become proficient in the tricky business of navigation across often featureless sands, returning from one two-hundred-mile round trip to rescue a stranded tank crew with a sense of exultation at his achievement. An architecture student when the war broke out, he was intelligent, well read and technically proficient – a man ideally suited to the command of a troop of tanks. Returning from a desert exercise in May 1940, Crickmay wrote home, 'actually I enjoyed myself a great deal . . . I seem to have been a soldier all my life'.

While Brian Stone had yet to prove himself to the point at which he would be given command of a troop of tanks (usually three or four vehicles) Crickmay had already made his mark with the regular officers who ran his battalion. The two men represented a new generation, drawn into this branch of the army because it embodied technology and modernity. There was also a definite class aspect to choosing the Royal Tank Regiment. While Britain's cavalry had begun to mechanise in the 1930s, its officers generally had the money to ride to hounds and shun those they regarded as social climbers. One officer who joined the RTR at that time comments of its commissioned element on the eve of war:

> The officers of the Royal Tank Corps were an odd mixture in those days. Some had been the pioneers of tanks during the First World War. They were of all kinds and tended to be men of character. Some were officers who had joined since the war, because they saw the corps as the arm of the future ... The younger officers tended to be more homogeneous in origin, mostly promising games players who had an interest in motor cars or motor cycles and little or no private income – very much the same material as those who joined the RAF.

Lieutenants Stone and Crickmay fit neatly into that category. Indeed, as a teenager Crickmay had amazed his family by converting an old motorbike into a four-wheeled motorised buggy. But whereas a dashing young man who joined the Royal Air Force might find himself at the controls of a Hurricane or Spitfire, those who became tank soldiers were equipped with decidedly less exciting machines. The returnees from France knew that many of their tanks had broken down and been left by the wayside.

Solomon, Stone or Crickmay had volunteered for tanks because they knew that Britain had invented this form of warfare. What they could not have appreciated was the degree to which that early lead had been squandered during the inter-war years. That was just starting to become apparent on the battlefield. Tank production and design had been run down to the point that, in 1930, the entire country had manufactured just sixteen. When rearmament started in earnest, from 1936 onwards, the threat of air attack led ministers to give priority to the RAF. In the meantime, other countries – including Germany and the Soviet Union – had made great strides in the development of their armoured forces.

The balance of power, as it applied to the tank forces that many generals in 1940 considered to be the essential element of modern land warfare, had therefore tilted decidedly against Britain. Yet the British General Staff remained convinced that it understood this vital branch of war as well or better than any other, and the Royal Tank Regiment had staked its name on excellence in this very field.

By the late summer of 1940, the 5th Royal Tank Regiment was being equipped with replacement tanks. Daily its men, based in southern England, watched the German aircraft flying up to bomb London. The Battle of Britain had been joined in earnest, but even before its outcome was clear, and the threat of invasion passed, rumours of foreign service were sweeping the battalion. The fates of Arthur Crickmay, Brian Stone, Emmin Hall, Jake Wardrop, Charlie Bull and Gerry Solomon were becoming linked by the destiny that awaited their unit. Some became as close as brothers, others were on little better than nodding or saluting terms, but they would all play significant parts in the 5th Battalion's odyssey. Two of these six would not survive the road to victory, and two more would be taken out of the war by serious injury. Along the way they would all be promoted, two would be decorated for bravery and one banished from the regiment for fomenting a revolt. The path that awaited the men of the 5th Tanks was one of unequal contests, disappointment and intense personal danger. But it was also one that would be crowned with triumph.

2

ARRIVALS AND DEPARTURES

The flotsam of the 5th Tanks washed up in Thursley Camp in Surrey. While some places the army called 'Camp' were in fact settled towns with a long history of being garrisoned, Thursley was one in the real sense of the word, with lines of tents, soldiers standing guard and the constant throb of vehicles arriving or leaving. The settlement had been placed in a dip below the Thursley village common, a few miles from the leafy vistas of the Devil's Punch Bowl, a popular spot with picnickers on the old London to Portsmouth road. It was to this picturesque setting that Trooper Gerry Solomon reported in September 1940, in his own words 'relieved' at not being sent to a cavalry regiment, 'anxious' about how the veterans of France would regard him, and 'hungry' for action.

Having presented himself at Regimental Headquarters, itself

tented, the new recruit awaited his fate. At twenty-four, Solomon was more mature than many of the recruits the pre-war regular army was used to receiving. By the time war broke out, he had been working for several years as a grocer's clerk, pedalling his bike around the more genteel parts of Ipswich, taking orders for produce. He was also a more sober character than the old sweats who had drunk their way through the brief campaign in France, being the grandson of a Methodist minister and one of five boys raised by a devout mother.

The advent of national service produced a huge expansion of the army, drawing in a wider spectrum of society than those who ran it were used to dealing with. Many recruits realised that war was coming, and by volunteering hoped to have some control over their fate. 'I didn't want to get into the infantry,' said Solomon, who had heard enough from his father about their suffering in the trenches during the Great War. 'That definitely weren't me. If I want to go into action, I want to ride into action.' His reaction was typical of many soldiers who volunteered for this branch even before the war; they had heard about the slaughter of the Somme or Ypres, and knew that a British invention, the tank, had broken the stalemate. They wanted to be part of that.

A year into the war, the arrival of wartime volunteers such as Solomon was still a novelty for a battalion like 5th RTR. So far, its manpower had been based on pre-war professional soldiers (like Trooper Wardrop from the Cherbourg column), and reservists who were either recalled regulars like Sergeant Hall and Charlie Bull or greenhorns with a modicum of training such as Lieutenant Brian Stone. In time, the war volunteers and conscripts would form a majority within the battalion, but in late 1940 many saw them as alien creatures, basically civvies who hadn't a clue what they were doing. As Stone had discovered in France, there was a sense in both the officers' mess and the barrack room of regular army men not wanting to let the new-comers play in their war, something that they had waited years for.

For the battalion, then, the first question with a new arrival was where to put him. The 5th Tanks, in common with other armoured regiments at the time, had five major components: the fighting squadrons labelled A, B, and C; the headquarters squadron; and the 'echelon'. HQ Squadron included the colonel's immediate staff, people like the medical officer, the fitters (who repaired stricken vehicles), the padre and the regimental sergeant major, as well as some troops of vehicles. The echelon was its wheeled transport, equipped with trucks to move shells, petrol, rations and people up to the tanks. In practice, this transport was broken down into a main group that dealt with bringing supplies to the battalion, and forward groups (one for each fighting squadron) that took them onwards to the tanks.

Trooper Solomon was not a properly trained armoured vehicle driver. Indeed, until he arrived at Thursley he had not even been in a working tank. There simply weren't enough to equip the newly mobilised units and training bases. The non-commissioned officers would also want to get some sense of the man before they assigned him to one. Solomon was therefore sent to A Squadron but entered in the books as 'L.O.B.' – Left Out of Battle. He entered that pool of soldiers, which included Lieutenant Brian Stone, who would get their chance to crew a tank when some unfortunate man became a casualty. Both Stone and Solomon found themselves assigned in September 1940 to A Squadron's transport packet, manning the trucks that brought up supplies. Solomon looked at Stone, with his blond wavy hair, blue eyes and passion for high culture, and wasn't quite sure about him: 'We found him a little effeminate.'

After France, with the threat of German invasion high, the 5th

Tanks were placed in a home defence role. They sent guards out to various points, and Trooper Solomon was detailed to drive out in a lorry to change over the men on duty or to bring supplies. By late September, however, the armoured battalion had begun to regain its purpose. New tanks arrived throughout July and August, and it was now time for the squadrons to begin exercising with them on the local heathland. Crews melded together once more, and the unit regained its pride as a group of professional tank soldiers.

On Saturday nights some of the officers would walk up the hill from the camp to Admiral Robert Hamilton's house, not far from the common. He was a Great War sailor whose nieces had told the 5th's commanding officer that they would happily entertain some young subalterns each week.

The boys and girls would meet, eat sandwiches, drink beer and play records in the admiral's sitting room. There was dancing and good-natured flirting. One of the women remembers the tank officers first arriving just a few weeks after the evacuation of France: 'They were all very stressed, but we obviously didn't realise what they had been through.' With time the mood became more relaxed. Lieutenant Stone was a regular at these parties, as was his firm friend in A Squadron, Lieutenant Deryck MacDonald, who soon became enamoured of one of the admiral's nieces. While their soldiers enjoyed big bands on the radio or in nearby Guildford, the young officers' Saturday night assemblies in Thursley resounded to light-hearted French ballads.

Sport provided another release from daily training and the expectation of further action. Within the Royal Tank Regiment the various battalions tended to specialise in different sports. Among the men of the 5th, the boxing team held particular status. Jake Wardrop was a boxer – constantly out running and sparring with his teammates. In matters of organised violence, as in music, the officers' tastes were generally for something a little more subtle, with rugby being a particular favourite. The rugby team contained all ranks, and its fixtures against other regiments were, as for the boxing team's matches, occasions for fierce rivalry and unit pride. Charlie Bull's idea of sporting recreation, however, was less aggressive. He and quite a few others spent free Sunday afternoons at the Guildford Lido, swimming, enjoying the summer weather and eyeing up women.

The waifs and strays evacuated from Cherbourg returned to their original squadrons. So Wardrop went back to C, as did Sergeant Emmin Hall. Charlie Bull, meanwhile, was in B Squadron. All three men served on tank crews.

In joining the RTR Gerry Solomon donned its distinctive black beret, and also the black overalls (called denims by the soldiers) which were used when working on the vehicles. The officers carried long sticks – ash plants – instead of the swagger sticks of other regiments, a tradition that went back to the Western Front, when tank commanders walked ahead of their lumbering vehicles, prodding the mud with the ash plants to make sure it was firm enough to take the tanks' weight.

The inter-war years of cuts to the army and economic depression followed by rearmament had left scars on those of its armoured branch. These emerged in the constant arguments among officers about the best tactical use of tanks, and in the other ranks a jeering contempt for the newly mechanised cavalry. Until the mid-1930s, the Royal Tank Corps had maintained a near monopoly on the crewing of armoured fighting vehicles, reserving unto itself the right to regulate their employment on the battlefield in much the same way as the Royal Engineers might opine over where to build a bridge or the Royal Artillery advise a divisional commander on the best type of barrage to neutralise his enemy.

Starting in 1936, the army decided that it must do something urgently to boost the strength of its tank force. War clouds were gathering and Germany, France and Russia had all surged ahead of Britain in the creation of armoured divisions, which, bound by tradition, retained dozens of regiments of horsed cavalry across the empire. The Tank Corps had started to expand – but only slowly. It had fielded six battalions, each with forty to fifty tanks, when the decision to accelerate mechanisation was reached. Another two regular units (the 7th and 8th RTR) were raised before the outbreak of war. By the time the 5th were at Thursley Camp a further twelve units of RTR, created on a Territorial or reserve basis, had formed or were in the process of gathering. Many experienced officers and NCOs were drawn out of the 5th and other regular battalions to help with this mobilisation. Nonetheless, even as early as 1936 those running the army had decided that the expansion required could not be handled by the Tank Corps alone. Their decision testified to the political clout of cavalry generals within the British set-up, since other countries such as the US and Canada managed to form their armoured divisions from scratch, without mechanising cavalry or indeed even having a professional cadre such as the Royal Tank Corps to fall back on.

The Imperial General Staff, however, had decided that catching up demanded the mechanisation of the cavalry. The British army's equestrian tradition was such that, even as the machine age powered forwards, many in the mounted arm were loath to lose their horses. The 1936 manual prepared by the army for the substitution of hay-fed chargers with petrol-driven ones tried to minimise the shock, noting that 'the principles of training in field operations given in Cavalry Training (horsed) are, in general, applicable to Armoured Car Regiments'. What would the relationship be between them and the Tank Corps? The top brass knew they might make poor bedfellows, since they had spent years competing for resources, bad-mouthing one another time and again.

The answer, in 1939, was the formation of the Royal Armoured Corps, in which the erstwhile horse soldiers and the Royal Tank Corps were pushed together with much ill feeling. The wearers of the black beret were to be styled the Royal Tank Regiment, it being one element of the Royal Armoured Corps. At the same time that the new corps was formed, twelve cavalry regiments were earmarked for the first wave of mechanisation.

Among the old sweats in Thursley Camp there was still much use of Tank-Corps terminology: calling men like Solomon 'private' instead of 'trooper', referring to 'companies' rather than 'squadrons', or 'sections' rather than 'troops'. The rejected language was that of the cavalry. Although members of the unit slowly changed their lexicon, the use of the word 'battalion' to describe the 5th RTR persisted until the end of the war. It did so stubbornly, despite the Royal Armoured Corps edict that such bodies of the old Tank Corps would simply become 'regiments' of the RAC, a cavalry term used by the likes of the 11th Hussars or King's Dragoon Guards.

The question of which word to use was one of those awkward issues of British military identity. In most armies, a regiment is a group of battalions, but the cavalry had retained the term even when the body of men and machines in question (say six hundred and fifty, respectively) was closer in size and command terms to a foreign battalion. In keeping with the professional armoured soldiers' desire to differentiate themselves from the equestrian fraternity, this account will refer to the 5th Tanks as 'the battalion'. One of its members, who had experienced the formation of the Royal Armoured Corps, said that the tankies felt demoted, 'from a high and mighty corps to a regiment', adding, 'We didn't like the cavalry. "Donkey bashers", we called them.' Stories abounded of RTR men sent to help newly mechanised cavalry regiments, only to discover that most of their vehicles weren't working. The general view was that they might know how to groom a horse, but were clueless as to the maintenance of such a complex piece of machinery.

Gerry Solomon had experienced none of the unpleasantness of 1938, but through his training in Tidworth, where there was a mixed staff of cavalry and tankie instructors, he soon acquired the sense that the RTR was the place to be. Like many recruits, he noticed that those from the cavalry were more preoccupied with 'bull' such as the minutiae of dress, parade-ground drill and deference towards those in command. He also had the feeling that, although many regiments were at last forsaking their beloved horses, their cavalry spirit was more likely to get them killed: 'I got the impression, somehow or other, that the cavalry . . . couldn't forget that they didn't have horses and would go charging in.' Arriving in the 5th Tanks, recruits were told it operated on the principle of 'shit and efficiency' – it didn't matter what things looked like; what was vital was that they worked properly.

The sense that they were better than erstwhile horse soldiers – smarter, more technically proficient and well led – was all very fine but did not sit easily with the late events in France. Some other battalions of the RTR had distinguished themselves just before Dunkirk with an effective counter-attack against the advancing Germans at Arras. But as far as the 5th Tanks was concerned, it had been a dismal campaign in which the battalion had been scattered with just a single claimed kill of an enemy tank. At Thursley the Commanding Officer, Lieutenant-Colonel Dinham Drew, therefore drove his men hard to put the regiment back on its feet and restore its confidence. Infractions of discipline were swiftly punished, earning him the nickname 'Detention' Drew. He drove his young officers too, drilling them in the manoeuvres needed to bring a squadron into battle.

In addition to moulding his men, the colonel also had to over-see the re-equipment of the regiment, and the tanks that arrived in Thursley had plenty of peculiarities. Just as the army struggled to create new regiments, so industry strived to step up production massively, while embracing the technological changes needed to meet the Germans.

The 5th RTR had been built to a strength of fifty-two tanks. Four of these were being kept by the commanding officer and others in battalion headquarters, and sixteen went to each of the three squadrons. A Squadron, which had a reconnaissance role in the field, had been given tanks called A9s. B and C Squadrons were equipped with A13s. There were similarities between these two types, which both represented the evolution of what the army termed 'cruiser' tanks: they shared a main gun, the two-pounder, and were lightly armoured. However, the steel plate on the front of the A9 was just 14mm thick, which was only enough to stop a rifle shot or shell splinters. The A13 had started with similar armour but been upgraded to 30mm. The A13 weighed in at thirteen tons and the A9 at twelve. They were designed for quick, decisive strokes rather than slugging it out.

Getting to grips with the tanks for the first time, those who had come through the wartime training system would have been struck by the cramped interiors of the A9 and A13. The War Office had decreed that the tanks should fit on standard railway flatcars, and this made them narrower than some continental designs. When squeezed from the top down, because a lower profile meant a smaller target, this compressed the available space within the armoured shell. For this reason the V12 Nuffield engine in the back of the hull was very hard to work on, and the turret, for example of the A13, particularly small. Three men had to fit inside it: commander, gunner and wireless operator or gun loader. The gunner had no hatch of his own in the turret roof and could only observe the world through the narrow aperture of his gun-aiming telescope as he was bounced about. The wireless operator and commander had their own hatches, but these were a tight squeeze for some of the battalion's boxers or other big men who had to push one shoulder down through the hatch before the other. As those who had just been in France could testify, the design of these tanks added to the difficulty of maintaining them, and created a sense of claustrophobia, particularly if you worried about being able to get out quickly.

During the tactical debates of the inter-war years the army had ruled that there should be two types of tanks, cruisers like those given to the 5th RTR and 'infantry' tanks. The latter, as the name implied, were designed to support foot soldiers in battle. Consequently they were heavily armoured and slow-moving. The cruisers, by contrast, were to form armoured divisions that would be used for the more exciting stuff – racing forward to block a gap in friendly lines, or to exploit one in the enemy defences. The British theorists also expected the cruisers to do most of the tank-to-tank fighting, but the enemy could not be expected to adhere to these tactical distinctions decreed by the British General Staff. So when the Arras battle took place, in May 1940, it pitted British infantry tanks against German armour with results that were cheering but a little inconvenient for those who believed in having two different types of vehicle. The Matilda – the infantry tank – was much better armoured than the cruisers, with frontal protection almost three times as thick as that of the A13, and the Germans encountered considerable difficulties knocking out Matildas. The tank had proven a success even if the campaign as a whole had not.

All three tanks – Matilda, A9 and A13 – shared the same gun, the two-pounder or 37mm tank gun. This weapon had been designed to drive a small metal projectile, weighing two pounds and roughly the size of a small pear, through the armour of an enemy tank. The whole round, comprising the projectile and a brass case containing an explosive charge that sent it down the barrel, was about eighteen inches long; it could easily be picked up with one hand. Knocking out an enemy tank with a slug this small required a gun that could shoot it at high speed, and in this respect the two-pounder, which sent its shell down range at 2700 feet per second, was good for its time (the mid-1930s). The combination of a two-pound shot and this speed of travel was sufficient to pierce 50mm of armour angled at 30 degrees at a thousand yards. If it penetrated the enemy vehicle the shot might pass through a man, disable a vital piece of equipment or, since it was often red hot, cause the explosion of ammunition or fuel inside. Gunnery instructors appreciated that this might not happen on the first shot; it might take many hits to knock out the enemy tank.

The crews preparing their tanks for deployment from Thursley Camp had been taught that the two-pounder was their weapon of choice for dealing with enemy armour. If they came up against infantry, anti-tank guns or other resistance they were instructed to use the machine guns mounted on their tanks. There was no high-explosive shell for the two-pounder gun, a consequence of Tank Corps dogma that deemed a gun firing armour-piercing rounds only was sufficient to do battle with enemy ones, and of the practical difficulty of packing much power into so small a shell. The crews in any case were confident that their two-pounders could sort out the Italian tanks in Libya – and in this particular matter their optimism was not misplaced.

As for the build of these tanks, it had something in common with Bristols, Morgans and Rileys, the great British sports cars of the day: there was a good deal of engineering ingenuity in them. The A9 had a power traversing system to help the gunner lay his weapon more quickly onto the target – one of the first tanks so equipped. The A13 had a new kind of suspension that allowed it to travel more quickly and comfortably across country. British tanks also embodied, like their sports-car counterparts, craftsmanship. They were built by British engineers – often in the same plants that built railway locomotives or ships – and each vehicle arrived in Thursley from the factory with a highly polished brass plate giving its serial number and manufacturers' details.

The War Office contracted big industrial concerns as part of the mobilisation of British industry. A9 tanks were made by Harland & Wolff and Vickers-Armstrong; the A13 by Nuffield Aero, as well as the London, Midland & Scottish railway works. Tank production was also underway at several other factories that had previously made rolling stock or civilian vehicles. Many of the engineers were unused to working on tanks, and so production brought myriad challenges of fitting together components from suppliers they had not previously dealt with. 'Concessions', the permitted variations in the shape of parts, were generous, a fault that 'cost millions of lost man hours', according to Major George MacLeod Ross, one of Britain's leading tank designers. Contrasting British methods with what he saw a couple of years later in America, MacLeod Ross wrote:

> We still pursued our love affair with 'craftsmanship', which may be defined as, 'the ability to fit two things together which do not fit'. There was no place for craftsmanship in an American production plant, even the presence of a vice or a bench in such factories was regarded as a sign of incompetence. Accuracy was invariably the enemy of craftsmanship.

The fitters in 5th Tanks knew all too well what he was talking about. A complex machine like a tank was only as strong as its weakest component. Within weeks of getting their vehicles, soldiers were reporting frequent breaks in the tracks on the A9 as well as all sorts of problems with the fan belts and engine cooling on the A13. These issues of reliability might have been overcome by deploying large numbers, but shifting production beyond the scale of a cottage industry proved problematic. During the first year of the war, by pressing so many new plants into service, Britain managed to produce about 1300 tanks – a respectable total, and one comparable to Germany's. But the British made a dozen different types, half of which were already obsolete, whereas the Germans concentrated production on a smaller number of more effective models. Crucially, they also insisted upon building to exacting engineering tolerances, reaping their reward in superior reliability.

While training in Surrey the 5th had put on a number of demonstrations, one of them for some American visitors. The US army had gone even further than the British in its disarmament years, disbanding entirely its nascent tank corps. Even though the United States was officially neutral at this time, the country was rapidly re-establishing both armoured regiments and mass-production facilities, while the British government was negotiating to buy weapons from American factories. The US army saw the RTR as natural partners in the business of tank soldiering.

By October 1940 the feeling in southern England was that the country had weathered the worst that the Luftwaffe could do. Hitler had postponed the invasion of Britain, while the war was spreading worldwide. Italian forces were operating in East Africa, as well as launching bombing raids on Egypt, Palestine and Malta. Japan, meanwhile, aligned itself with Germany and Italy. The 5th Tanks had reformed itself and rediscovered a well-practised confidence in its tactical exercises.

On 5 October the regiment was assembled in Thursley Camp for a short, sharp address. Colonel Drew told them the battalion had been ordered on overseas service. The men would be entitled to 'embarkation leave' of a few days each. Charlie Bull reported to his mother, 'We are under orders to move again any time now, don't know where we are going of course, but we are being issued with tropical kit', but was simply observing the security instructions imposed on soldiers heading overseas. Where they were heading was in fact common knowledge within the battalion.

The men were issued with such items as the sola topi or pith helmet, and khaki drill shorts. The removal of several dozen NCOs and officers in order to form a new RTR battalion meant some last-minute promotions. Bull got his first tape, becoming a lance corporal, but Stone and Solomon remained Left Out of Battle in A Squadron.

As departure time drew near, the young subalterns made their way up to Admiral Hamilton's house on Saturday nights for one last time. Fond farewells were taken and the girls tried to lighten the mood with their choice of records. Charles Trenet's 'J'Attendrai'– 'I Will Wait' – played. Brian Stone had not found love at these parties even if he had enjoyed them enormously, but his friend Deryck MacDonald had fallen in a few weeks for Brenda Pitt, the admiral's niece, and they promised to write to one another.

By the end of October the young officers and most of the rest of the battalion were awaiting embarkation in two northern ports. Most of the men were leaving from Liverpool, while the tanks, trucks and most of the drivers were to go from Glasgow on the *Clan Chattan*. After waiting briefly on the Clyde, the *Clan Chattan*'s convoy formed up and sailed out to sea. For Glaswegian Jake Wardrop the departure was particularly evocative. 'I pointed out Dumbarton Rocks, the Gairloch, and Loch Long to the Englishmen,' he wrote in his diary. 'I was off to the war and far away too.' Trooper Solomon stood on deck, watching Britain disappear on the murky horizon. There were no regrets. 'I was full of the spirit of adventure,' he said, 'I wanted to get in the action.'

3

THE DESERT

During the final days of 1940, Arthur Crickmay found himself sitting in a small tank, looking down at the town of Bardia in eastern Libya. It was very cold, as only desert nights could be, so he was wrapped up in a coat, sweater, gloves and woollen balaclava. For a man who had happily discussed with his mother the elegant cut of flannels or the most stylish way to button a coat, being wedged into the tiny turret of a Mk VI in this get-up, constrained by radio wires, headphones and goggles, was too much. 'Trussed up like a mummy,' he later wrote, 'I almost cried with frustrated agitation.' He had been fighting hard for six months, since the outbreak of the desert war, had endured many dangers and had seen extraordinary things. Hundreds of miles behind him, new regiments, including 5th Tanks, were arriving. The desert army was swelling, so experienced hands like Crickmay were at a premium. What had they learned during those early months of desert war?

The Italians had launched the campaign from Libya, which was one of their colonies, in June 1940, fielding 215,000 troops compared to the fighting force of 50,000 under British command in Egypt. With their enemy also commanding air superiority, the dice were loaded against Egypt's defenders in all respects but one: as the Italians pushed into Egypt, British supply lines had shortened as those of the invaders had extended. A cruiser tank took around seventy gallons of petrol, and it could easily burn it up in as many miles, or one day's fighting. The distances from rail head to front line could be measured in hundreds of miles, and if you ran out of petrol and water your war would come to a halt very quickly.

Geography thus imposed its own imperatives on the struggle. Distances were great and habitation sparse; what life there was confined itself largely to the coast. While logistical considerations might have dictated sticking close to the North African littoral, exploiting what ports, roads and railways there were, the enterprising general could simply hook inland and bypass any defence of these places. Along most of the coastline was a flat coastal plain fifteen to thirty miles wide. Beyond that the ground rose abruptly, creating a high escarpment up to a plateau. There were places on the long road from Alexandria to Tripoli where there were exceptions to these topographical rules, and these variations in this otherwise monotonous landscape created exceptional conditions for attack or defence. The area of Sollum and Halfaya, where the upland escarpment bulged all the way to the sea, placing a wall-like obstacle across the coastal plain was one, and it was here that the Libyan–Egyptian frontier had found its natural place.

Lieutenant Arthur Crickmay, although callow in years and lacking seniority, understood the desert better than many of his brother officers. He had travelled to the Middle East three years earlier,

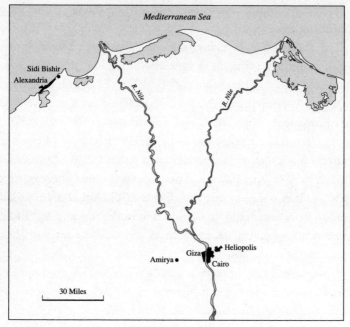

THE NILE DELTA

while still a student, exploring the way through Egypt and northern Libya with a friend. Then, during early exercises he had polished his desert navigation skills to the point at which other officers had come to rely upon them. These abilities saw him posted to the reconnaissance section of 6th RTR, where by late 1940 he bore witness to a remarkable reversal of fortunes. The Italians, despite their great superiority in men and equipment, had been beaten and thrown back. Starting on 8 December, the British had launched what was meant to be a short-term counter stroke, moving westwards inland, bypassing the Italians at Sidi Barrani on the Egyptian coast and threatening their line of communication with Libya. Lieutenant Crickmay spoke for many when he observed that 'we never dreamt how far we should eventually go. The Italian army seemed a huge and menacing thing in those days.'

Having deployed into the field in April 1940, Crickmay had already learned many of the lessons of soldiering in this wilderness that his comrades in 5th Tanks were about to undertake. Of course, the old hands tried to impart some of these pearls of hard-earned wisdom, but often their words were ignored or drowned out in the general flow of bumf and bombast from headquarters.

The young lieutenant knew all about the savage variance of climate that boiled you one month and froze you the next. He also knew about the problems of supply, which could push a man to his physical limits within days. In France, the 5th had been able to forage for food and drink in villages but here, with the exception of the odd Bedouin trading in eggs or poultry, there were almost no possibilities to find food or water if the system failed. Crickmay wrote to his mother:

The chief discomforts are a lack of water and monotony of grub. Bully [beef] and biscuits are the order of the day and most people suffer through desert sores through lack of green veg and fresh meat. I had a septic ulcer for about five weeks, which interferes with our main pleasures i.e. eating and drinking. Sleep of course is the other pleasure.

During his rare moments of leave, Crickmay had zoomed back to Cairo and happily blown twenty-five pounds in a weekend, drinking and eating to excess. While he was there he also tried to find clothes that would stand up to the rigours of desert soldiering, having discovered that leather shoes in particular soon fell apart in the heat.

For many of those who had found themselves serving during the early months of the desert war, the physical discomforts heightened a sense of isolation. Long periods of waiting for something to happen produced so much time to chat to crewmates that they could soon learn every intimacy of each other's lives. It also heightened a sense of being a tightly knit group cast adrift on a sea of uncertainties. In a letter home of September 1940, Crickmay wrote, 'I sometimes think we are the legion of the lost and doomed to sit in the desert for so many years that they eventually forget we are here', but the events of December suddenly galvanised everything. The men serving in the desert had not only been extremely busy, but had become the focus of national attention back home, where Egypt seemed to offer some rare good news in an otherwise dismal panorama of war setbacks.

The Italians had been tumbled back to the Libyan border. The escarpment at Halfaya gave them a natural line of defence, which the British had promptly stormed and, in the last days of 1940, were pushing into Libya. The British were by now close to Bardia, where Crickmay watched large numbers of Italian prisoners trudging into captivity.

On 27 December, the tanks of 5th RTR were unloaded in Alexandria. The British War Cabinet had decided to reinforce the army in Egypt, so the quaysides were a scene of constant activity for weeks. The opinions of the British soldiery who stepped blinking into the Egyptian sunlight were frequently harsh. Many remarked on the squalor of the scene, the pushiness of the locals and the strangeness of the food. One 5th Tanks man recorded that their port of disembarkation was 'dirty, filthy, smelly'. Another, a corporal in A Squadron who had served with the Tank Corps on the North West Frontier, later said of his first impressions of Egypt: 'I didn't like it at all – I never liked it – it was scruffy.' In time, they would come to dream of a few days in Cairo or Alex, just as Lieutenant Crickmay did.

By the end of 1940 there were hundreds of thousands of British servicemen and women in Egypt. There was an extensive network of airfields, bases and transport facilities that ran from Cairo, down the Nile valley to Alexandria and the sea, an area known collectively as 'the Delta'. The British had taken Egypt in 1882 but had allowed a nominally independent government to remain, under a king. When arguments between traders and British soldiers turned ugly there were nationalistic undertones on both sides. British soldiers often referred to the Egyptians as 'wogs', 'darkies' and 'gippos'. The Egyptians, in turn, felt that many of the perspiring infidels were violent and stupid. The locals felt occupied, while British soldiers often resented having to stand to attention when the Egyptian national anthem was played, regarding many Arabs as sympathetic to the enemy.

Despite these tensions, the British had made themselves comfortable during their decades in Egypt. There was an elegant Cairo social scene centred on Shepheard's Hotel and the Gezira Sporting Club. The drink flowed and there were plenty of pretty daughters in the ex-pat community, or bored wives of fellow officers. Officers from the RTR soon learned their place within a distinct social hierarchy – one in which many in the cavalry and many others looked down on them as 'oily rags' and upstarts. At the Gezira Sporting Club this division showed itself in the preference of the smart set for polo and other equestrian sports, while the RTR man, with his more slender means, enjoyed cricket, rugby or racket games. While the tank officers often felt this difference keenly, the cavalry affected indifference to them, as one wrote in his memoirs:

The horse still prevailed as the ruler of the cavalry and Horse Artillery life – out of working hours. This tended to keep the officers of the cavalry and the Tank Corps apart in their social life, which was unfortunate. The horse soldiers had always been sufficient unto themselves; by the time they had played polo and talked about it, they had no particular wish – or indeed energy – left for seeking conversation on the more pedestrian pursuits of cricket, football or golf.

For the 5th Tanks, the pleasures or indeed the social humiliations of the Cairo social scene would have to wait. The voyage out had been so comfortable that the battalion's officers felt the men needed to be thrown into some hard work, and soon. Both of the ships that carried them to the Middle East were commercial liners that had been taken up a short time before. Only the dancing girls and cabaret artistes had been offloaded before they became troop ships: the soldiers were waited upon by stewards, ate fine food and drank copious amounts of alcohol. 'Each day we bought six bottles of beer . . . sat on deck and drank them and ate our ice cream,' Trooper Wardrop reported in his diary. 'The weather was lovely and the tan was improving daily.' Wardrop saved a bottle of rum and, once ashore, 'on Hogmanay I was on guard and we killed it as the clock was striking'.

The early days of 1941 were a period of intense activity, as tanks were modified in the workshops and painted in desert colours, and exercises began on the training grounds near camp. Those running 5 RTR soon found themselves having to organise a swap with the 3rd, which had also come over as part of their brigade. The 5th handed its A9 tanks over to the 3rd, and got A13s in return, so that each battalion had one main type of vehicle. It made logistical sense, and the 5th weren't complaining because they felt the later, heavier model was the better tank, but it was just a small taste of the endless chopping and changing by those in command that would characterise the months to come. Each new brainwave meant hours or days of hard work for the men. For A Squadron, who had manned the A9s before they went to the 3rd, this meant forgetting much of the preparation they had undergone at Thursley Camp and learning the peculi-arities of a new wagon.

The soldiers got down to the job with alacrity, with good news from the front about further advances into Libya creating 'a festive atmosphere'. But as the British pushed further into Libya, this caused worry as well as celebration for Lieutenant-Colonel Drew, the Commanding Officer. He knew that many of the A13s in his regiment had motored several hundred miles; the machines they had received from 3rd Tanks were particularly worn out. Given the standard of 'craftsmanship' of these machines, it was reckoned unwise to go more than a thousand miles between major engine overhauls. The way they had been put together, these tanks simply shook themselves apart if not regularly serviced. Yet it was about five hundred miles from 5th RTR's camp to where the army was fighting. The first couple of hundred could be done by train, but the battalion faced the prospect of driving hundreds further before it could even come into action.

During the early months of the desert war, the forces available to British commanders had been so small that the 7th Armoured Division represented their only striking force. Apart from them, there was the 4th Indian Division and a score of infantry battalions from New Zealand and elsewhere. Even before the outbreak of war the army had appreciated the mobility that would be required for such a small force to operate across such large distances of wilderness, and had hence placed a high priority on the formation of the armoured division.

It was initially put together by Major-General Percy Hobart, known throughout the tank corps as 'Hobo'. A pioneer of Great War vintage, Hobo had been one of the most vocal and forceful advocates of tanks during the inter-war years. Now, in Egypt, he was at last allowed a practical field for his theories about armoured warfare. One of those who worked with the general as he brought the new formation up to scratch described Hobart as 'a merciless trainer, who drove us all hard and overlooked no detail, his intensity matched by his keen interest in all ranks under his command'.

Hobart had also gone to extremes in the years before the outbreak of war, arguing a decisive role for armour on the battlefield. He and his fellow Tank Corps visionaries did not see the role of their beloved machines either in bludgeoning their way through enemy defences or in slugging it out in positional contests. Rather, they envisaged a war of swift strokes, of rushing into gaps and exploiting enemy weaknesses. For this reason they became convinced that armoured formations should not be slowed down by large numbers of infantry or artillery. Ideally, they would have these fellow combat arms mounted in armoured, tracked vehicles too, although this was not something British industry could manage during the war.

The tank corps theorists often expressed their thoughts in naval terms; they considered the type of change they were trying to bring about was as big as that faced by the Royal Navy when it moved from sailing ships to ironclads a century earlier. The first tanks, when sent to the Western Front in 1916, were initially called land ships, and it was easy to see the terrain they moved across, particularly in the desert a quarter of a century later, as a sea of sand.

As 5th RTR prepared to go 'up the blue', as soldiers in Egypt described the wilderness battlefield of Libya, they practised manoeuvres in a distinctly naval fashion. Groups of tanks would deploy from 'line astern' to 'line abreast'. Their aerials flew pennants denoting the place of each machine within its troop, squadron and regiment.

The 1939 *Army Tank Brigade Training Instruction* portrayed the weight of fire of an armoured squadron as almost like a naval broadside and, noting experience of war at sea, insisted that 'all our manoeuvre should be designed as to bring our maximum strength in gun-power into action against isolated parts of the enemy'. In an engagement where two forces of tanks, coming up some transport route in a long snake, ran into each other the British tank man's job was to manoeuvre swiftly past the head of the enemy column, bringing fire onto its flanks before, if possible, turning to cut the column somewhere in the middle, applying the maximum of friendly fire to bear but allowing the enemy to use the minimum number of tanks possible. Hobo and others borrowed one of Nelson's terms for this tactic, calling it 'crossing the T'. It followed that in a war of bold movement British tank men had to be able to fire on the go. The 1939 *Instruction* insisted this would give them a major advantage, since 'the Germans have not trained much in shooting from moving tanks, and up till quite recently it was known that their tanks stop to shoot'.

Hobart had also insisted that radio communications allowed tank forces to disperse and come together on the battlefield in a much more dynamic way than other arms. The early desert battles seemed to vindicate this notion, because the preponderance of Italian airpower forced the British to spread out. Radios were the essential enabler in allowing the tanks to act together. Hobart's arguments had been calculated in part to bring the Tank Corps through the difficult spending battles of the inter-war years and contained a good deal of hyperbole. His emphasis on the independence of his beloved armoured forces and the resentment of the wider army about Hobo's debating tactics made him many enemies. He was removed from the command of the 7th Armoured Division before he could bring it into action, for in Egypt, as in Whitehall, Hobo upset too many people.

When the 5th RTR moved up the blue many did carry forward Hobart's thinking. Lieutenant-Colonel Dinham Drew was a Great War Tank Corps veteran, as were a couple of his majors. They were steeped in these ideas about how to fight, and reports from the front only enhanced their confidence that their doctrine was well founded. The taking of the Halfaya Pass and the Italian positions beyond it in mid–December had shown the value of boldness. Pat Hobart, the RTR major who had taken the Italian position at Sidi Omar (and nephew of Major-General Hobart), reported:

> We drove around to avoid the enemy shelling ... then formed up in line and advanced at full speed on the fort in what I imagined to be the best traditions of the *arme blanche* [i.e. the cavalry] ... in we went with every gun and machine gun firing. My orders to the squadron were to drive straight through the perimeter, doing as much destruction as possible, out the other side, and then to return again.

Then, in February, even more dramatic news filtered into the camps of Cairo and Alexandria. The Italians had been driven westwards down the coast, towards Benghazi. In this part of Libya the littoral bulges up to the north, where a massif, the Jebel Akhdar (meaning 'green mountain'), creates a separate land of verdant valleys that can be bypassed by cutting across the desert to the south. This is precisely what the 7th Armoured Division did, taking an ancient route across the sands known to desert caravan leaders as the Trigh al Abd.

On 5 February 1941 British troops reached the coast near a place called Beda Fomm, cutting off the Italian army's withdrawal route. Tanks from the 1st RTR, 2nd RTR and 3rd Hussars were soon in action. It was here that they encountered much of the motorised transport and armour that the Italians had managed to save from their ill-fated campaign in Egypt. The British tanks moved swiftly into firing positions, engaging first the head then the flanks of the enormous enemy column. Within a few hours 2nd Tanks, for example, had knocked out forty-six enemy tanks. The rout of the Italian army had begun.

By 23 February victors of Beda Fomm were reappearing in

Cairo. The armoured division, or at least most of it, was being withdrawn to refit. This was to become a pattern of the desert campaign: the exhaustion of men and machines caused a cyclical rotation of armoured battalions so they could be rebuilt back in the Delta before being sent 'up the blue' once more. The Italians had been decisively beaten, and the British army had advanced five hundred miles in just a few months. It was time for a different formation – a hastily assembled amalgam of mainly virgin units – to take over. The 5th Tanks were part of this, and Lieutenant Crickmay's battalion, 6th RTR, was plucked out of the 7th Armoured Division in order to be kept at the front, providing a little veteran backbone to this new outfit.

The 5th Tanks had left Cairo late in January, their armour being taken to the Egyptian port of Mersa Matruh by train, the echelon's lorries and most of the men by road. From then on there was no choice but to push the tanks forward under their own power, up and over the Halfaya Pass and across the border into Libya, past Bardia and Tobruk. The first tank train had left Cairo on 27 January and they reached El Adem, an aerodrome south of Tobruk, ten days later.

There, machines were moved about within the unit. The A13s brought out from Britain ended up in C Squadron whereas the others, particularly A Squadron, got clapped-out machines from other regiments. People were shifted too, and to his delight Trooper Solomon was moved from the Left Out of Battle contingent to driving a tank belonging to the officer commanding A Squadron. Others lounged about, getting a run into Tobruk for a beer and a swim, or reading in between working on their tanks.

The army in late March found its front at El Agheila, hundreds of miles to the west, one of those places where a rare change in the coastal geography presented a defensible position – in this case, a bottleneck between the Mediterranean and some inland salt flats impassable to tanks. The 5th prepared to move up to this front, dispatching recce parties along the desert route that reached the coast near Ajdabiya, just south of Beda Fomm and east of El Agheila. One of these, under Lieutenant Deryck MacDonald, got so badly lost that the RAF were sent to scan the desert, without luck. The hapless young officer and his recce party eventually turned up a few days later.

During the stop at El Adem the regiment had tried to bring its A13s up to scratch with much maintenance. Mindful that many of them were passing the mileage where engines were normally over-hauled the Battalion Technical Officer had been sent off to Cairo to obtain more motors. Some staff type there seemed to promise them, but the order to move forward again came before anything could be done. On 21 March the road move, nearly three hundred miles along the Trigh al Abd, began. For Solomon and other new men it was an education in the physical hardships of tank soldiering. They spent long hours being bounced and kicked by the hard surfaces of the moving machine they served. They were caked in buckets of sand thrown up by the tracks of the vehicle in front, and if they came sharply to a halt, were often engulfed in a sand cloud of their own making.

Each day began with the sun shining behind the tanks as they travelled westwards. Most had absolutely no idea where they were. There was no roadway, so they simply followed the tracks through the sand. It didn't take long for the breakdowns to start, the first vehicle spluttering to a halt with an ignition problem. The fitters who stopped to repair it found the engine took hours to cool down, and 'by the time we did move off the desert was horribly empty'. Each squadron had one truck with four or five trained mechanics on board. In addition, the Battalion Technical Officer had several specialists helping him. But the small staff of experts proved inadequate on this, their first proper desert march. There were simply too many vehicles breaking down. 'We passed many tanks, but fortunately we had nothing to do with them, because they were write-offs,' said one of the 5th's fitters.

The move to Ajdabiya proved a gruelling learning experience in many ways. Crews that did manage to get underway again after repairs soon discovered that if they had not been paying careful attention to their map reading, noting the distances between way-points and the few landmarks that appeared, they got hopelessly lost. Many men cheerfully quaffed their water ration, assuming that the half-gallon allowed per man per day would be replenished by some unseen echelon every morning. By the third day some were so thirsty that they were leaving seat cushions from their vehicles out at night, having discovered that dew formed on them and the rubber could be wrung out into a tin. It tasted disgusting, but if the alternative was a thumping headache, dry mouth and nothing to drink, what choice was there?

Having limped into the forward area, with leading elements arriving on 6 February, the battalion tried to pick up the pieces. Many tanks had been left along the desert road, and it did not appear the brigade, division or army had any plan or troops detached to recover them. Others, who had got lost en route, appeared in odd places over the following days. A Squadron was sent forward with other reconnaissance troops to man outposts at the front of the army while the rest of the 5th tried to prepare for battle.

In truth, though, their country had hardly given them the tools for the job. Many of the A13s were by this time approaching two thousand miles on their engines, twice the recommended period between overhauls (one had reached 2002 miles). The tracks had an estimated life of two thousand miles, after which the metal pins that held them together became so stretched that they would frequently break.

Sitting down in his tent on the last day of March 1941 Major Southon, the Battalion Technical Officer, was a man full of woes.

He made notes of the state of the equipment under his care, scanning the returns given in by each of the squadron fitter sergeants. Of the fifty-three tanks on the regiment's books, just twenty-seven were at the correct end of the desert road and in working order. The rest were scattered between there and Tobruk, hundreds of miles to the east, where the nearest properly equipped workshops were located. Next to twenty of the tanks listed on his 'Tank State 30/3/41', the Technical Officer wrote 'engine u/s'. It meant 'unserviceable'.

The arrival of the 2nd Armoured Division at the front had started what was meant to be a period of consolidation and re-organisation for the British army. The 7th Armoured Division was re-equipping back in the Delta; thousands of troops had been diverted to fight in other places, from Greece to East Africa; and the general assumption in London was that the Italians had received such a sound beating, losing half of Libya and 130,000 prisoners in the process, that they would be unable to act for many months. This drubbing of the Italian army sent into Egypt had, however, been declared unacceptable by the Axis leadership. Hitler had ordered German reinforcements to North Africa. Elements of two panzer divisions had started to unload in Tripoli early in February. On the 6th a commander had been appointed for the expeditionary force, which had been christened the Deutsche Afrika Korps (German Africa Corps). The man in charge was referred to by Trooper Wardrop in his diary as 'the big bad policeman': General Erwin Rommel.

The new German commander had already made a name for himself in France. In Africa, he soon realised there were 'hitherto undreamed-of possibilities' for armoured warfare. 'It was the only theatre where the principles of motorised and tank warfare could be applied to the full,' he wrote, 'the only theatre where the pure tank battle between major formations was fought.' Rommel nurtured strategic grand designs for his small armoured corps too: he could see the possibility of driving through the British in Egypt and on to the oilfields of Arabia.

Lieutenant Crickmay and the rest of 6th RTR, meanwhile, found their problems multiplying. Deprived of the chance to head back to the Delta with the remainder of 7th Armoured Division, they had handed over their tanks to another unit before being kitted out with captured Italian M13s. Some four hundred Italian tanks had been captured in the late offensive, and given the shortage of functional British vehicles it was decided to equip some British and Dominion battalions with them. There were all manner of disadvantages to this arrangement, not least the high chance of being shot at by your own side or bombed by the RAF. The Australian garrison of Tobruk was so worried about this possibility that it painted large white kangaroos on its ex-Italian vehicles. Crickmay also found that many of the vehicles had dead Italians or their body parts still inside, and 'the smell never left those wretched machines'.

The use of these captured vehicles, and the fate of those who had crewed them, were unpleasant reminders of the volatility of war in the desert. For the tank crewman, a reversal of fortunes could easily mean oblivion. Heading back to their battle positions Crickmay and the others in 6th RTR took a dim view of the preparations made by the untried armoured division they now served. 'The plan for defence was impracticable, if you could call it a plan,' he wrote in his post-war memoir. 'When eventually the attack came, we got no orders, there was a chaotic muddle.' By 1 April 1941 Crickmay and the others were thrown into a desperate fight. Galvanised by the arrival of Rommel, the Axis forces had bounced back far sooner and with greater violence than anyone in British headquarters had expected.

4

FIRST BLOOD

During the afternoon of 2 April 1941, the tanks of C Squadron moved into position, between Ajdabiya and Brega. Orders had been changing all day: the battalion was to withdraw; it was to form a rear guard for the brigade; it was to be every battalion for itself. For three days they had been pressed hard by the enemy, moving back steadily from the El Agheila position. The first blows had fallen on a composite force using the working tanks of A and B Squadrons and some armoured cars manned by the cavalry. They had been bombed by Messerschmitts and Stukas, they had seen and engaged the advancing Italians and they had fallen back.

Trooper Jake Wardrop sat in the driver's seat of his A13, nursing it into position alongside the other C Squadron tanks. They were facing west, with the Mediterranean a few miles to their right. The town of Adjabiya, just behind them, was an important junction. Turn north, following the coast, and the road took you to Benghazi. Go east, directly through the desert, and you would eventually reach Tobruk via the Trigh el Abd. It was exactly the same route as the 5th Tanks had travelled in the opposite direction a couple of weeks earlier. The men of C Squadron were feeling pleased with themselves – the drivers in particular. Despite all the breakdowns, they still had fourteen working tanks and their Officer Commanding, Major Winship, was proud of them for it.

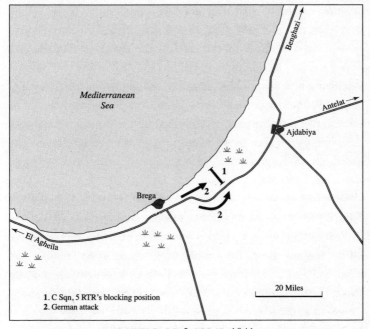

BATTLE OF 2 APRIL 1941

The major was well known to Wardrop and Sergeant Hall; he had commanded the makeshift squadron evacuated from Cherbourg the previous year. Winship was a dyed-in-the-wool Tank Corps man, with service dating back to the Great War, a fine embodiment of the fighting traditions of the tribe. They all

43

remembered when, back in France, Winship had thrown aside the steel helmet issued to him by the army, shouting out to his assembled squadron, 'If I am going to get killed, I will be wearing the Tank Corps beret.' Every man had then followed this lead, throwing their tin hats into a heap by the roadside.

Now it had come to a fight, Winship's C Squadron had drawn itself up along a line of dunes, the commanders directing their drivers into 'turret-down' positions, stopping the tanks in such a way that the ground concealed everything bar the commander's position on top of the turret from an approaching enemy. When they spotted their prey they would shift into 'hull-down' positions – driving closer to the crest of the slope, so that the gun could engage the enemy beyond, but the hull of the tank remain shielded from hostile fire. It made the vehicle a much smaller target. While they usually drove forward into a hull-down position, in this instance they had reversed up the slope with the guns traversed to the rear, over the engines, so they could drive off all the faster when the time came to put some distance between themselves and the enemy.

Wardrop knew that the other squadron had already had some fighting and he was excited. He was not afraid of a scrap, both in the boxing ring or in his tank. One of four children, he had grown up in Glasgow, raised by a father who was an engineer. Jake had tried working as an apprentice technician at a dentist's and as a painter before joining up in 1937. Once in the army he generally managed to channel his aggression in constructive ways. Jake and his mate Stan Skeels, another boxing team member who served in C Squadron, became notorious in the battalion for brawling – 'a beer and the whiff of a barmaid's apron was all it took'. But for all his brawn and his skill with his fists, Wardrop was also razor sharp, an optimist with a subversive wit.

George Stimpson made up the final member of this C Squadron trio. Barely five feet tall, Stimpson was no fist fighter, but was a keen footballer who hailed from Banbury. 'Little George', as Wardrop called him, had also joined the regular army before the war and been on one of the crews evacuated from Cherbourg. Stimpson had already learnt that Skeels and Wardrop would defend him to the last if a fight broke out on one of their drinking expeditions.

The three friends had found themselves facing a court martial soon after arriving in Egypt. They had been caught by the sergeant major, an old regular-army stickler, having a rowdy sing-song in their tent at Amirya, back in the Delta. The men refused Lieutenant-Colonel 'Detention' Drew's suggested punishment of twenty-eight days in jail, opting instead for a full court martial. It was a gamble, but one they won since they had been able to prove that their alleged offence had taken place before 'lights out', clearing themselves in the process. After this courtroom victory, Wardrop noted in his diary, 'Although I could have managed quite well without the incident it was an experience and well worthwhile to tweak the noses of the CO and some of the wise guys so smoothly.'

On this April afternoon, two months after the court martial, His Majesty's enemies were to provide the target for Wardrop's anger and guile. The crew in the turret of the tank – the wireless operator, gunner and commander – had been listening to the radio, trying to make sense of what was going on around them. There had been air attacks, explosions, British army vehicles barrelling past and contradictory orders. Having backed their vehicles into fighting positions, Wardrop and the other driver had got out of their cabs, climbing on top of the A13s to spot any far-off foe.

Some time after four o'clock the commander of their brigade came on the radio, telling his battalions he was about to issue orders. Major Winship leapt out of his tank and into a small armoured car to travel the short distance to battalion headquarters where he joined Lieutenant-Colonel Drew and the other squadron commanders sitting by the wireless, preparing to take down the brigadier's orders. But by the time he started to speak, C Squadron could already see the tell-tale dust clouds of approaching armour, the sand kicked up by tank tracks hanging in the air, backlit by the low sun. Tank commanders reported these sightings edgily. They wondered when their boss would be back. Meanwhile, as the brigadier tried to deliver his orders people were cutting in on his frequency, giving the latest sightings of the enemy. When two or more stations transmitted at the same time on a wireless network they simply jammed each other out. The brigade commander grew steadily more irate as he backtracked, resuming the orders he was laboriously trying to deliver. Then others would chip in – they did not recognise some of the code words he was using. All the time, the enemy was rumbling closer and nobody had an idea what the plan was.

For C Squadron, watching the tanks taking shape in the desert in front of them, the imperative was clear – in moments they would be in action. One of the drivers could make out the men atop the enemy vehicles: 'The crews were sat on top of their tanks and seemed to be unaware of what was waiting for them.' At last Major Winship came roaring back in his scout car and jumped into his tank. More than an hour had been lost but he was barely any the wiser about the big picture. Instead he received the breathless reports of his men about how close the enemy were getting. As the squadron readied for action its drivers jumped down from their turret-top vantage points, back into the cabs of their A13s. Owing to the latest crop of mechanical failures, the squadron consisted of nine such tanks rather than the fourteen that had made it through the desert. In front of them they reported fifty enemy tanks, as well as trucks and field guns. It was an entire battle group.

The main part of the enemy manoeuvred into an arrowhead formation. They were a couple of thousand yards away and closing. Over the radio Major Winship told his squadron 'stand by to open fire at eight hundred yards'. He didn't want them to reveal their firing positions until the enemy were close enough for the A13's two-pounders to have a marked effect. But then a message suddenly came in from Lieutenant-Colonel Drew: make sure the vehicles to the front are not 6th Tanks. He was fretting that C Squadron might be about to open up on Crickmay and others in their captured Italian vehicles.

Moments later, C Squadron's commanders saw the first flashes from the muzzles of the approaching armour. Winship ordered the reply. Very soon the enemy was returning their shots with interest and the sky was rent with the barking of tank gunnery. Almost immediately, the British tanks began to take hits. They were not the Italians that the first reports had identified; this was the Afrika Korps and C Squadron was being subjected to the first big set-piece attack of its Libyan campaign.

The force that manoeuvred in front of them was a battalion of seventy Panzers backed up by some self-propelled anti-tank guns and infantry from a machine-gun unit. They greatly outnumbered C Squadron and did not waste time on any elaborate manoeuvres. They simply cruised forward in a frontal attack, firing as they went.

For Gerry Solomon his first taste of action, a few days before, had been 'hair raising'. It had happened at night, and he watched the tracers in the armour-piercing shot 'flying backwards and forwards, wondering if one was going to hit you'. Wardrop was not encumbered by such fears, calling C Squadron's fight 'the quickest, deadliest duffy I've ever seen'. The Germans had been probing British defences since 20 February, but the sightings of unusual vehicles were discounted by senior British officers who did not think that the newly arriving expeditionary force was ready for action. The view coming down the British chain of command was that these fleeting glimpses must be of Italians, and never mind that the 5th Tanks or King's Dragoon Guards had been calling in reports of German vehicles. By 2 April headquarters' confidence in the identity of this enemy had disappeared, and plans for dealing with such an offensive quickly crumbled.

One by one C Squadron's machines were being hit by German shot. Sometimes there would be a shower of sparks and the shell would fly up in the air at some crazy angle, a ricochet visible by its burning tracer; at other times there was a crump or clang as it struck home, penetrating. 'There seemed to be nothing in front but tanks coming on,' said Wardrop, 'but we kept firing and they slowed down, and finally halted and shot it out stationary.' The Germans had opened up at anything up to fifteen hundred yards, stopping at about nine hundred yards from the British. Once they had identified the enemy position, the Germans sent a force of armour around to turn its southern flank.

It did not take long for some of the squadron's tanks to be knocked out. When the German flanking company appeared to the south it was able to fire on the sides of the British tanks, negating their hull-down positions. The order came from Drew to pull out. A couple of tanks were burning, the second-in-command's disappeared and another had pulled back because an enemy hit had jammed its turret. Later, the word among the crews was that the second-in-command and a couple of officers had attempted to launch some kind of counter-attack – a futile gesture. There were shouts over the radio as commanders reported their shot striking home, but in many cases the two-pounder projectiles bounced off and the weight of numbers meant that the enemy came on inexorably. The remaining five British tanks fought on, but if they didn't move out they would be surrounded.

Just as the surviving tanks started to pull back, the squadron commander's was hit. An armour-piercing shot would penetrate its target and then, often lacking the energy to exit through the other side, ricochet about inside the turret, ripping people and equipment apart. Crewmen looked anxiously towards the OC's tank. Just one man jumped out, the wireless operator. Smoke began to pour from the hatches; the major's tank was brewing up, burning with him and two other crewmen inside. The tank gunners, looking into their aiming telescopes, had registered several flashes as their shot struck the panzers. There were claims of eight, but how many had been disabled? The Germans reported losses of three tanks, two Mk IIIs and one of the new, more heavily armoured Mk IVs. There were just four C Squadron vehicles still working, including the one Wardrop was driving, but they intended to fight another day. Darkness was encroaching as they headed off east, leaving behind several blazing vehicles.

Nobody could have argued with Wardrop's characterisation of it as a 'deadly duffy'. The squadron had lost twenty-three men, including five officers, in five tanks during this brief engagement. Some had died but most were captured.

Vehicles were streaming east as night fell on 2 April 1941. Just as the Italians had faced a dilemma when coming the other way late in 1940, so the British had the choice of travelling directly across the desert to Tobruk or following the coast road up through Benghazi and Derna, going north of the Jebel Akhdar. Initially, the remnants of 3rd Armoured Brigade, of which 5th Tanks was part, travelled east to a place called Msus, a desert trading post where supply dumps had been left. Here they were able to refuel and rearm, while the officers and vehicle commanders tried to piece together what was happening, before taking the inland route to Tobruk. The previous day they had almost engaged the 6th RTR by mistake, confused at seeing them in their captured Italian vehicles. By going into the desert the brigade had effectively uncovered British forces in Benghazi and other points along the coast, exposing them to the risk of being cut off. In fact, in an atmosphere of panic these units were also trying to extricate themselves as quickly as possible, with the Germans reaching Benghazi on 4 April. Rommel pushed forward relentlessly, determined to take advantage of this chaos, and captured the commander of the British 2nd Armoured Division and his staff.

When the 5th Tanks stopped for the night the few remaining A13s and the trucks formed what was known as a leaguer. The vehicles were parked, usually in an oblong shape with the armour on the outsides of the box and the soft-skin vehicles in the middle. When the battalion was at full strength, A Squadron would form the front face, B and C the sides. But A and B squadrons hardly existed by that point; it was more of a matter of needs must as the Germans harried the surviving elements eastwards. Luftwaffe aircraft were frequently sighted and armoured cars were reported to be making their way around isolated pockets of British soldiers, pushing eastwards all the time. Rommel issued an order that revealed his driving ambition: 'So that every man understands, the objective is the Suez Canal.'

The fearsome machine that had fallen upon the 5th Tanks on the afternoon of 2 April was a German armoured battle group. At this point Rommel's force had not entirely disembarked in North Africa, having just 165 tanks ashore by late February. He had sent forward several battalions of reconnaissance, machine gunners, artillery and infantry, and a single tank regiment. Within weeks, though, the force filled out to the shape that it would take for the next couple of years. The Afrika Korps was a compact organisation, consisting of two armoured divisions (the 15th and 21st), one motorised one (the 90th Light) and some independent units, backed up by an aggressive air component. Although the resources available to Rommel were limited, in the context of April 1941 they were, when added to the substantial Italian army that remained in Libya, quite sufficient to tip the scales of the conflict against the British. In any case, the decisive advantages they deployed against the 2nd Armoured Division that April were not numerical but material and intellectual.

In the vanguard of Rommel's advance, by one of those curious coincidences of war, was his own 5th Tank Regiment. It was their 2nd Battalion that attacked C Squadron on 2 April. The Germans had made a leap in understanding that Lieutenant-Colonel Drew and many others had not: a tank regiment might be the best method for binding men together in a peacetime garrison, training them on gunnery ranges or even shipping them overseas, but it was not the best way to send them into battle. The Germans had already become adept at forming Kampf-gruppen – battle groups – combining armour, artillery, infantry and the supporting arms needed to engage in combat. As they fanned out to exploit their success at Ajdabiya, the Germans dispatched several different battle groups named after the majors or lieutenant-colonels who commanded them. One headed for Benghazi, another raced for Msus, hot on the heels of the 5th Tanks. A couple were formed from tank-battalion HQs, others from the reconnaissance battalion, machine-gun battalion and so on, and each Kampfgruppe traded subunits with others to create a balance of capabilities within it.

The example of one of these groups, Kampfgruppe Ponath, formed on 3 April and dispatched on a breakneck drive towards Derna, shows the method. Ponath was the commander of 8th Machine Gun Battalion, which provided a single over-strength machine-gun company for the battle group. To this was added an anti-tank-gun company, a combat engineer platoon and a couple of field guns from an artillery company. The wheeled vehicles from the two machine-gun companies left out of this arrangement were also requisitioned to provide the battle group with its own reinforced transport echelon for this dash across hundreds of miles of desert.

It was not that the British failed to understand the concept of what they called 'all arms combat', it was rather that they were less good at making it work. At that time, few British officers with the rank of major or lieutenant-colonel had the necessary grounding in what the other elements of a team placed under their command could do. Too much pre-war training had focused on drills with their own troops – be that for the tanks, infantry or artillery. They were largely incapable of forming and leading such ad hoc combat groups with the same confidence as their enemy. Such expertise was available at brigade level, combining armour, infantry, artillery and supporting elements, but these were formations of thousands of troops and around 150 tanks. At the lower levels of command they were less used to operating together, and less happy about it. Years of rivalry between corps and regiments had made them suspicious of each other, and there was frequently bad blood between individual officers.

The Germans, through their experience in Poland or France (where their 5th Tank Regiment had served), had learned the value of flexibility in grouping their forces and applying them. The armour might form the spear tip, but the infantry and anti-tank guns were available as a defensive shield. If the tide turned against them the shield was deployed. If the enemy attack spent itself and it was time to resume the advance or counter-attack, the panzers came to the fore again and the spear was thrust forward.

The material superiority of the Germans could be seen in the strength and reliability of their tanks. The most common type was the Panzerkampfwagen III, which the British termed a Mk III or

Panzer III. It weighed more than the A13 (twenty-two tons, compared to fourteen), a consequence of being more heavily armoured, and the crew occupied a roomier, better-designed fighting compartment. On paper the British tank was faster and more manoeuvrable, matching a more powerful engine with a lighter vehicle, but the Mk III had the sovereign advantage of reliability, as well as support from a skilled tank-repair service. When a problem was encountered – many German Mk IIIs broke down due to sand ingestion on the same inland route to Tobruk that overcame many of the 5th's A13s – a solution was quickly developed and deployed to overcome it. As for trading blows, the German tank initially had a 50mm gun with a performance comparable to the two-pounder, but it was later upgraded to a high-velocity version that was decidedly superior. The Mk III had thicker frontal armour than the British tanks, and this proved to be an important advantage in these early engagements in 1941. At the ranges where the Mk IIIs had initially opened fire at Ajdabiya, the two-pounder shot often bounced off.

In their attempts to step up tank production at the outset of war, the Germans had found that they were able to produce more anti-tank guns than tanks, and by mounting some of these on captured Czech tank hulls or early model German ones that were becoming obsolete, they were able to add panzer jaeger or tank-hunter battalions to their army. To a layman these might look like tanks, being armoured tracked vehicles with a gun, albeit one that was fixed rather than being mounted in a rotating turret. In the battle of 2 April the German tanks had been reinforced by obsolete Mk I tanks converted to tank hunters with 47mm guns. This solution allowed the Germans to field many more vehicles, and for them to pack a heavier punch, gun-wise, than was possible with the turreted designs. The British army did not adopt similar solutions for a couple of years.

*

By 7 April 1941 the remnants of 5th RTR found themselves struggling up a steep mountain road into Derna. After striking hundreds of miles across the desert they had turned north-east, to the western extremity of the mountains, where their commanders thought they might be able to make some sort of stand before Tobruk, little realising that the Germans were racing them to the same spot. 'The tanks, we had six by this time', wrote Trooper Wardrop who was driving one of the A13s, 'were in a shocking state and could do only ten miles an hour.' Of those last six working vehicles, two gave up the ghost on a hill outside the town, coughing and spluttering to a halt. News reached the 5th Tanks that the Germans had gone around behind the town, positioning themselves on an aerodrome east of Derna, along the road that led to Tobruk. This was Kampfgruppe Ponath, the all-arms group that had dashed to the Libyan town in an attempt to cut off the retreat. A British officer appeared at this point to announce that these remaining tanks and one hundred infantry of the Rifle Brigade would have to assault the Germans on the airfield. The tanks crews had stopped for a brew, and looked at one another as this news sank in. They didn't know the German strength or whether they could make it up the next hill, which had to be conquered on the way up to the airfield, but as Wardrop concluded, 'If we want to see our mothers again we'll have to make a fight of it.'

The tanks ground up to the top of the steep incline, and moved into line abreast. The Germans had spotted the impending attack, opening up with machine guns from their vehicles. C Squadron managed to hit several armoured cars with two-pounder shots and gave the German infantry a liberal dousing with machine-gun fire. Bit by bit the British infantry pushed through the defences and the road ahead was clear.

The following day, the remnants of 5th Tanks arrived at the defensive lines that marked the perimeter of Tobruk. It had already become a key strategic spot because of its ample harbour, and was being defended by a force of Australians. As the regiment's last two working tanks entered their lines, the Australians gave a great cheer. Jake Wardrop's tank had given out just fifty miles short of safety. The dynamo could no longer charge the batteries, which had become so flat that they could not even work the ignition any more.

Most of the 5th RTR's men managed to make it to Tobruk, even if the two surviving tanks' crews only amounted to eight soldiers in total. The rest had been swept up along the way, piling into trucks or onto any other wheeled transport that was available. Some of the lorries ended up carrying as many as eighty men, standing packed together on the back. Trooper Solomon and Sergeant Hall had ridden into the port on trucks, as had Lieutenant Crickmay of 6th Tanks.

Very soon Tobruk was surrounded, and its defence became a matter of urgency. The 5th Tanks were formed into two companies of infantry, ready to man the lines if the enemy attempted an assault. There was much despondency as they fell in with rifles and Bren guns, muttering that this was not what they had joined for.

Lieutenant-Colonel Drew, meanwhile, shocked at seeing his regiment driven to pieces for a second time, collected reports from men who had fought on 2 April to draw up a detailed account of exactly what had happened. He penned self-justificatory notes about the poor state of the tanks' engines and the collapse of command and control by the brigade during the battle. In accounting for what had befallen them, he compiled the hard facts: of fifty-three tanks, just two were left. Only nine had been knocked out by the enemy. This meant that the remaining forty-two had been lost due to mechanical failure. At times the crews had deliberately demolished or burned the broken-down A13s; at others, under orders from higher head-quarters, they had stripped off what they could and left them.

Crickmay, who had experienced triumph as well as tragedy in the desert, reflected bitterly on what had happened. The first few days of April had been 'among some of the most exasperating and unpleasant I can remember ... there was a colossal flap on and no one knew what the hell was happening'. His battalion had lost all of its tanks and the unloved Italian machines were also abandoned, so it was also sent to the defences: 'We reckoned trenches and rifles were definitely not up our street.'

The mistakes made in this first encounter were not all on the British side. By driving his men forward so relentlessly, Rommel caused his own attack to lose momentum. His attempts to take Tobruk quickly failed, costing him hundreds of casualties. Dozens of tanks had broken down because they had not been modified for desert conditions. The order urging them forward to the Suez Canal may have been stirring, but it was eminently impractical.

It might be hard to credit, given the fate of so many of his squadron, but Wardrop was one of the few who were not disheartened. He was a fighter by spirit, of course, but he also took pride in C Squadron's stand, calling it 'the only serious attempt made to halt them before Tobruk'. To Jake, the outcome was less important than the spirit they had shown.

With Tobruk surrounded, the survival of that place was to become a matter of strategic importance to the British. German dive-bombers came to visit most days, pounding the defenders and sinking ships in the harbour. Headquarters understood that trained tank crews were far harder to replace than the vehicles they had lost, so ordered men from the regiments dismounted in the late fighting to be brought back to Alexandria by boat.

A fortnight after they had entered the place, some of the 5th Tanks men were sailing out, taking their chances with the dive-bombers. Jake Wardrop went out with one of the later parties, at five o'clock on the morning of 20 May. The obvious dangers of the trip and nature of the debacle that had destroyed 3rd Armoured Brigade troubled him little.

'We went flat out all the way,' he wrote. 'I fell asleep on the deck and put the finishing touches to an already pretty good tan. We landed in Alexandria and by seven that night Stan and myself had borrowed a pound and were sampling the beer in Mustapha Barracks canteen.'

Whatever disasters might have befallen the 5th Tanks, whatever the quality of its tanks compared to the Germans' or the failings of British tactics compared to theirs, these were not matters that Trooper Wardrop wished to dwell upon. It was precisely this indomitable spirit that would prove to be the battalion's most precious asset in the trials that lay ahead.

5

EGYPTIAN SUMMER

The 5th Royal Tank Regiment's exit from Tobruk coincided with the end of spring. Having arrived just after Christmas, the bulk of the soldiers had not experienced the roasting heat of an Egyptian summer. In the Delta, the rising temperatures of April and May brought out some of the water that had soaked in during the winter rains, creating heavy, humid airs that were particularly stultifying when it was still. In the desert, the hotter days of late spring burnt up the flowers that bloomed in the wadis, and turned brown the clumps of grass that dotted the coastal uplands. Once the khamseen, the hot wind from the desert interior, started to blow it could easily raise the temperature by ten degrees. Old desert hands reckoned that during these winds it was more comfortable to keep the folding windscreens of their trucks raised than lowered; otherwise, the experience of travelling fast into the heat was like being blow-torched. Only in the Jebel Akhdar, the Cyrenaican uplands, did the lush vegetation withstand the strength of the summer sun.

During the first weeks after their extraction from Tobruk, the 5th regrouped at Sidi Bishir or 'Sidi Bish', a camp on the coast east of Alexandria. Later that summer they were sent inland to Beni Yusef, not far from the pyramids, the same place from which they had left for the front several months earlier.

The atmosphere at Sidi Bish was helped by the granting of five days' local leave. Not far from the military camp were beachside traders with all manner of delights. There was sea bathing, sport, and the beer flowed freely. Jake Wardrop, his boxing mate Stan Skeels and 'Little George' Stimpson took themselves to Golden Bar in Alex at nine o'clock one morning, and drank for eighteen hours solid. It was a raucous, noisy dive, full of gangs of men coming and going: 'I suppose the whole of the MEF passed through the place – Aussies, Springboks, Kiwis, soldiers and sailors but we sat them all out.' Wardrop and the others survived that visit to the Golden Bar without a scrap, but they had their run-ins with the military police, and had already started a per-sonal snakes and ladders game of promotion to lance corporal or even corporal, followed by busting back to trooper. A fellow member of C Squadron said of Jake and his friends, 'They were this drinking community and you either drank or you didn't.' Preferring to steer clear of trouble, that trooper and many others used their free time to quaff a soft drink in one of the many sol-diers' clubs, take in the sights or see a picture.

Even Jake and Stan took in a film, *The Thin Man*, at the Royal Cinema in Alexandria. Others watched James Cagney in *The Bride Came C.O.D.* at the Rialto, or another time caught Clark Gable in *Gone with the Wind*. In both Alex and Cairo there were literally dozens of cinemas, some even showing the latest Hollywood productions. The routine for men getting back from the blue was to draw pay in Egyptian piastres, find out what was on at the pictures and head into town.

For some of the soldiers, freed from parental or uxorial supervision, leave offered a chance to sample the fleshpots of the cities. The army had plenty of experience of Egypt's brothels, for it had garrisoned the country off and on for nearly sixty years. At times it had regulated the business, sending medical officers to certify the prostitutes free of VD as well as providing condoms for visiting soldiers. Back in the early 1930s one battalion commander in Alexandria, a certain Lieutenant-Colonel Bernard Montgomery, had insisted on inspections of this kind in the face of prudishness from more senior officers because his men required 'horizontal refreshment'. In the 1940s Sisters Street was Alexandria's destination for men seeking not just sex, but erotic entertainment that included everything up to and including 'women performing unnatural acts with animals'. The suede desert boots that many men had acquired in preference to leather ones were soon named 'brothel creepers'. Wardrop, Stan and his friends visited Sisters Street, but Little George claimed it was mainly for 'entertainment', since even in France 'I realised that I was cut out to be a drunkard and that it was quite easy for me to say no to a whore'.

The ways in which the men spent their precious leave were to prove as varied as the accents or cap badges in the Golden Bar. Lieutenant Brian Stone, that lover of music and theatre, was catered for just as well as those seeking pleasures of the flesh. He attended performances by the Egyptian Symphony Orchestra in Cairo and found an entrée to Alexandria's cultural life through friends he made in that city, staying with them whenever he visited. Stone would soak up whatever was on offer performance-wise, for although he loved Beethoven above all other composers, and he became contemptuous of the Italians as fighters, he delighted in attending a performance of Italian opera.

Sportier officers like Lieutenant Crickmay gravitated towards such places as the Gezira Sporting Club for tennis and squash, and regular games of cricket were held there too. Many cavalry officers managed to play polo, stabling their ponies at Cairo clubs. Crickmay's leave life was sufficiently well organised that he had secreted a trunk of civilian clothes – including a dinner jacket – at the Carlton Hotel in Cairo, and his Chrysler roadster was parked out the back. Reaching Alexandria after the evacuation from Tobruk, he hit the town with his best friend, Ted Delson. Ted had joined Crickmay on his trip to Egypt and Libya back in 1937, when both of them were architecture students, and with the outbreak of war managed to get himself posted into 6th Tanks in Egypt. The two were inseparable. After their leave in Alex, Crickmay wrote to his mother, 'You can't imagine what it means to see a few fresh faces and live a normal existence. We had a terrific time and fairly beat the place up ... we never went to bed before three and never got up before 12.'

The balmy days at Sidi Bish were to prove short-lived, for GHQ had dreamt up a plan to throw 5th Tanks back into the fight. For most of May and June they trained on Matilda tanks. These heavier 'infantry' tanks required a change of vehicle and role from the 'cruisers' they had previously crewed, but theirs was not to reason why. The Matilda was far better protected against enemy fire, and that at least could give them some comfort after their experiences in April.

Weeks passed, with crews learning the Matilda's driving and maintenance peculiarities, or taking the vehicles out as squadrons to practise manoeuvring with them. New people had to be fitted in too. The battalion had lost around a hundred men during the late fighting, taking into account dead, wounded and captured. Replacements appeared, officers were promoted, more courses were required. There were still some down times for bathing or drinking, but they pushed on.

On 16 June, the 5th RTR started back up the blue, putting its Matildas on trains and packing up trucks full of supplies. Officers and men steeled themselves to go back into combat.

One week later, camped in the desert a couple of hundred miles to the west, all plans were changed. They received orders to hand over the battalion's Matildas to the 44th RTR, a Territorial unit that was heading into battle. Drew's regiment was to find its way back to Beni Yusef; their superiors had selected them for a new task.

Back in London, April's collapse of the 2nd Armoured Division and the accompanying loss of eastern Libya were regarded as a scandal. The Prime Minister had ordered an inquiry into the matter. Evidence had been gathered by the military, seeking to justify the debacle; there was discussion about the worn-out state of the tanks, and of difficulties of communication. Underlying this were tensions between Winston Churchill and his generals about the direction of the war and the correct use of armoured forces. The army blamed him, in part, for sending thousands of troops to Greece shortly before Rommel launched his attack on North Africa.

Churchill sought to protect himself from the charge of getting distracted by Greece, blaming instead the generals who, he claimed, had not made it sufficiently clear that they would withdraw from Libya if hard pressed. The troops themselves, his report on these events notes with characteristic panache, had acquitted themselves well 'in the midst of so much order, counter order, and disorder'. Distilling the lessons of April's setback, the Prime Minister urged: closer cooperation with the RAF to provide air support; the building up of armoured divisions to consist of at least two brigades (the 2nd Division had deployed only one, the 3rd Armoured Brigade); the provision of more field artillery units to the armoured brigades; and the retention of armoured divisions for offensive rather than defensive purposes. 'The tank formation', he wrote, 'is a weapon little concerned with the lines or flanks of its own troops. Its supreme function lies in its impact or progression.'

During the late spring of 1941 the PM had convened 'Tank Parliaments' at Downing Street, bringing together those who masterminded the development, production and use of such vehicles. While the top brass would frequently despair at Churchill's amateur strategising, he had brought valuable insight to the problem. His determination to build up the tank force (if necessary by importing them, since British industry was unequal to the task), to change its composition and to reserve it for tasks of the highest importance were all welcome news to the tank men – or would have been had they been party to the secret missives Churchill fired off across Whitehall. Even so, the changes afoot were felt with remarkable speed by the armoured force in Egypt, and by 5th Tanks in particular.

In its camp west of Cairo the 5th learnt they were to be incorporated in a reformed 4th Armoured Brigade as part of the 7th Armoured Division. They would be joined in this brigade by the 3rd Tanks (who had been in France and Egypt before being sent off on a disastrous mission to Greece, from which they had just returned) and the 8th Hussars. The brigade would also include the 3rd Royal Horse Artillery and a battalion of lorry-borne infantry. The 7th Armoured Division would be completed with a second, similarly organised, armoured brigade (the 7th) and a Support Group containing additional firepower as well as logistic back-up. Thus the British intended to fight more effectively as an all-arms force.

The inclusion of the Royal Horse Artillery was an important change for the tank men. During April's fight, several enemy tanks had been knocked out by their twenty-five-pounder field guns. The gun, which had been in production since 1939, was one of the few unalloyed success stories of the British armaments industry. It fired an 88mm high-explosive shell more than twelve thousand yards. Towed behind a light truck called a Quad, with a limber (a trailer) full of shells, the gun could be brought into action in minutes, allowing the Royal Horse Artillery to emulate the feats of their mounted predecessors in the Napoleonic wars. A well-trained crew could fire off six rounds in a minute.

By giving each armoured brigade a gunner contingent, its armoured elements could each count on the support of at least one battery (eight guns). The 3rd RHA could open up at the longer ranges at which the two-pounder had shown in April that it struggled, and at the types of target that the tank gun, bereft of a high-explosive shell, could not easily tackle. Of the threats that might be 'stonked' with a barrage of twenty-five-pound shells, the most important to the tank soldier were enemy anti-tank guns.

While the brigade was being formed, the fighting had raged out in the blue. After surrounding Tobruk, Rommel had moved forward to the Egyptian border. He occupied the high escarpment, his troops overlooked the port of Sollum and secured the Halfaya Pass. When British commanders launched a plan to re-take this commanding ground, pushing back into Libya, they ran into serious difficulties. The approach that had worked against the Italians six months earlier, foot down and all guns blazing, now proved a costly disaster. In one gruesome encounter on 15 June, C Squadron of 4th RTR lost eleven of its thirteen tanks in a few hours. Their knocked-out vehicles were all Matildas. Many had been destroyed by German 88s, highly accurate flak or anti-aircraft guns that could be used against ground targets. The Matilda lost its reputation as a safe machine that day, pierced at two thousand yards by shells from 88s dug in so well they could hardly be seen. The 6th RTR, which had just taken delivery of

Britain's latest tank – the A15, or Crusader – also suffered badly, having twenty out of fifty brewed up.

Although the British made a spirited defence against some of the Axis counter-attacks, the operation ended in failure. For those hearing snippets of news back in the Delta this setback confirmed or enhanced certain reputations: of Rommel's skill; of the deadly 88mm gun; the difficulty of taking Halfaya – now dubbed Hellfire – Pass; and of the weakness of their own general-ship. Churchill, barely over his anger at what had happened in April, decreed that the commander of British forces in Egypt must go. A pattern of dismissing those who had squandered lives in unsuccessful operations began.

Nobody in 5th Tanks could have been under any illusions as to the seriousness of it all; many had friends in the armoured regi-ments that had been mauled. Some reflected on their own narrow escape in being ordered to give up their Matildas, but for most the requirements of preparing the battalion for action again took priority over philosophising.

On 21 July the 5th received the first of its new tanks, an American-made curiosity called the M3 Stuart. The old hands of the regiment cast a hard eye over this alien contraption. In some ways it was a similar vehicle to the British-made cruisers, weigh-ing just over twelve tons and armed with a 37mm gun. It was, however, taller than the British vehicles, and there were other points that the sceptic could have made against the Stuart.

American industry, just like that of the other major powers, had struggled to scale up tank production. Technologies had been borrowed from all over. The Stuart's suspension was based on a tractor's and gave a much harder ride than that of the British A13 and newer Crusader. Lacking a sufficiently power-ful diesel engine, the American designers had adopted a seven-cylinder aeroplane engine that ran on high-octane petrol. The motor, like those fitted on American fighters at the time, had pistons arranged in a radial fashion. Stuart drivers soon learned that when it stopped running oil collected in the cylinder that pointed downwards. If they didn't crank the engine for ten minutes to circulate the oil it was liable to blow up when started. Drivers shook their heads when they tried to open their hatches in the hull of the tank – they thought it would be a death trap if they had to bail out quickly. The hatches were eventually modified and the crews began to grow used to their new cabs.

By 21 September the 5th Tanks had received their full complement of fifty-two Stuart tanks. The echelon had forty three-ton trucks, and the total strength of the regiment had filled out to thirty-eight officers and 590 other ranks. That month the 8th Army was formed, composed of more than a hundred thousand troops in seven divisions, more than double the size of the Egyptian force of a year earlier. The Desert Air Force, the RAF contingent in Egypt, had also been reinforced following spring's pounding from the Luftwaffe.

In October the regiment headed up to the Libyan border again, driving hundreds of miles in its tanks. This was when the early moaning about the Stuart tank was forgotten; drivers like Gerry Solomon and Jake Wardrop soon learnt that it was a completely different beast from the British tanks they had been given before. The British cruisers had water-cooled engines, and so when they leaked the men had no choice but to sacrifice their meagre water ration to keep them going. The Stuart's aero engine had a sixteen-blade cooling fan behind mesh at the rear of the fighting compartment. When the engine was fired up it sucked air through the vehicle, past its sweating crew. 'It was beautifully cool, absolutely lovely', reported Solomon. Wardrop decreed that 'they were great little tanks, fast and reliable'.

As they motored up to the border this last was to prove the most salient quality. Frank Cheeseman, one of the 5th's previously hard-pressed mechanics, reported, 'We fitters had nothing to do – they just went on.' It brought Cheeseman to the realisation that the British-made A13s that the regiment had fought and died in just a few months before were 'bloody useless ... mechanically speaking ... they were prototypes, bogged down with teething troubles'. Very quickly the crewmen forgot the official designations of M3 and Stuart, adopting a different name for this new wagon: the Honey.

The Americans sent representatives from the companies that had built the M3 out to Egypt. They made sure the tanks ran well, and sent home reports of any faults. The US was granting the British credit to buy weapons under the new Lend-Lease aid programme, but for the American manufacturers this was a commercial transaction like any other: a client paying millions for new vehicles had to be kept happy. The word was that one of the Americans, watching the M3 going through its paces, had turned to his British audience and, in the manner of the best Detroit automobile salesman, said 'Ain't she a Honey?' The nickname stuck.

One of the finishing touches before the regiment left Cairo was the painting of its distinctive markings onto the tanks. By Tank Corps tradition the vehicles were all named and, since 5th Tanks had been designated E Battalion in the Great War, the names all began with an E – Eager, Envoy, Esk and so on. The crews also put their brigade sign on the front of each tank: a red rectangle containing a white circle upon which was sketched the outline of a jerboa or desert rat. The emblem was already associated with the 7th Armoured Division, and the 5th Tanks were now part of a battle-hardened formation in which people from the Prime Minister downwards set great store.

Arriving in the desert, the regiment settled down to the usual 'schemes' – manoeuvres designed to test the revamped 4th Armoured Brigade's ability to work together. Every soldier understood that the fate of the Tobruk garrison was now a matter of the utmost urgency: a largely Australian force had been under siege since April. The 5th's short stay in the desert port had made a lasting impression on many of them. They were struck by the courage and tenacity of the Australians as well as by the ferocity of the air attacks they faced. Churchill, deeply concerned by the fate of Malta, had grander designs for the upcoming push. The island's defenders had taken months of heavy German bombardment but held on, knowing that Malta was the key British naval and aviation outpost in the eastern Mediterranean. Churchill felt that the recapture of several airfields in Cyrenaica, and the denial of them to the Luftwaffe, could save Malta. It was to the Aussies, though, that the tankies' first loyalty lay, and to their sister RTR battalions that were also hemmed in at Tobruk.

Naturally the Germans and their Italian allies had their own plans to break the stalemate along the Libyan border, but British commanders were confident that these would be constrained by some new strategic realities. Hitler's invasion of Russia on 22 June 1941 had suddenly reduced the importance of the North African front. The flow of fuel, spares and new drafts were all reduced accordingly. Airpower was switched to Russia too, meaning the British would never face quite the same inequality in that regard.

The exigencies of war had demanded that the unreliable old British tanks quickly be replaced with Honeys. With the 5th Tanks' personnel, the changeover from pre-war regulars to war service types was proceeding far more slowly. The new men, sometimes dismissed as civvies during their early months, were getting on. Some losses and the transfer of others to new units had already led to promotions. Gerry Solomon, the volunteer from Suffolk, had put up his lance corporal's tape. Brian Stone and Arthur Crickmay, although both still second lieutenants on the books (and in pay terms too, much to their chagrin), were both sporting three pips on each shoulder as acting captains.

As young officers moved up the ranks their paths diverged from those of the men. It meant that while it was quite possible for a member of the Other Ranks to serve the war through in 5th Tanks or another battalion (if he survived that long), the officers had to leave in order to progress. The hierarchy of head-quarters above the battalion – brigade, division, corps and now the 8th Army – all had to be run by somebody. The command-ers had staffs who looked after everything: operations, supply, manning, and equipment. Captain Crickmay had become one of these, an Intelligence Officer for the 7th Armoured Brigade. He was not far from his friend Ted and the 6th RTR, because they served as part of his brigade. He was close to the 5th too, since their brigade, the 4th, was the other principal force in the divi-sion, and there were many familiar faces among the staff officers.

The rapid expansion of the Royal Armoured Corps presented great opportunities for promotion to the brighter crop of the pre-war regular officer cadre, and the same went for NCOs. It also meant that good men who might once have been regarded as mediocre were being given their head. In Charlie Bull's case, the war provided a fresh start. He had made it to lance corporal during his earlier stint in the regulars but had then been busted, so he began the war as a trooper. There had been trouble too during his brief time in civvy street, when he had been sacked from his job as a bus driver. He was also a womaniser who had fallen in and out of numerous relationships, the last one ending when they had set sail for Egypt. The war ignited in Bull the desire for self-improvement. He had applied himself earnestly to his military duties and by this time had been promoted twice, so was serving as a corporal.

In October 1941, as the desert heat abated, all were preparing once more for a great common endeavour. While Crickmay had experienced the rout of the Italians the previous year, the men of the 5th Tanks had not taken part in a significant offensive operation since their arrival in Egypt. The pleasures of the Fleet Club, the bar in Shepheard's Hotel or even of Sisters Street, all seemed a world away. They were living in the sand again, the life of true desert rats.

Corporal Bull missed his cool beer or egg and chips as much as any man. He was one of those soldiers who became quietly obsessed with his comforts in the field. He didn't like to see himself lose weight or sleep. As the preparations for action continued he wrote home to his mother:

> I am sitting inside the tank writing this as it is a bit windy outside, it's cooler now than what it was a few months ago, the only trouble on the desert is that you get those dust storm sometimes, that is when it tries you, the sand gets everywhere no matter where you go, if you wear goggles it still comes through, gets in your food too, so you eat it, drink it, and sleep in it ... it is getting near tea time now ... it will be the usual thing, corned beef stew, still I like it and I'm nearly always hungry on the desert so I don't mind what it is, I saw a dead camel yesterday a few miles from here near a well, so it might be a nice big steak.

With promotion to corporal, life had looked up a little because Bull had passed the eight-year point in his service and was earning two pounds and ten shillings a week. Unable to spend much in the desert, he was already planning what to do with it. 'I don't know what to do when the War is over, whether to get married or buy a car,' he confessed to his mother. Bull, who had always been the apple of his mother's eye, could already see that the war might raise him in status and spending power in the eyes of his wider clan back in Staffordshire.

Bull's extra money came with extra responsibility. He had been given a tank to command, and would lead one of the new Honeys and its crew into battle. Around them, the desert along the Libyan border was filling with armour.

A great mechanised battle was about to start. Through Lend-Lease, and straining every tank-production sinew at home, the British government had given the 8th Army its biggest force of armour yet. It deployed more than 750 tanks, twice the force available to the Germans and Italians. The 7th Armoured Divisions alone had 450. In addition to the 4th and 7th Armoured Brigades, a newly arrived formation, the 22nd Armoured, had been assigned to them. Although outnumbered in tanks, the enemy had a similar number of troops and an advantage in anti-tank guns. Thirty-five of the dreaded 88s were deployed with forward troops, as well as ninety-six high-velocity 50mm anti-tank guns. The posture of the two armies was geared to the roles they would play in the coming battle, offensive and defensive respectively.

The plan for what was to be called Operation Crusader involved a great armoured left hook, enveloping the Axis forces along the frontier, bypassing the Halfaya defences and bringing the 7th Armoured Division up close to the Tobruk garrison, which would break out to meet them. As the advance developed, an infantry corps would push up the coastal route into Libya. An enormous amount would rest on the initiative and drive of those leading the armour – even men like Charlie Bull. On the eve of battle one of the 7th Armoured Division's brigade commanders issued an order of the day to his men. It concluded: 'This will be a tank commander's battle. No tank commander will go far wrong if he places his gun within killing range of an enemy.'

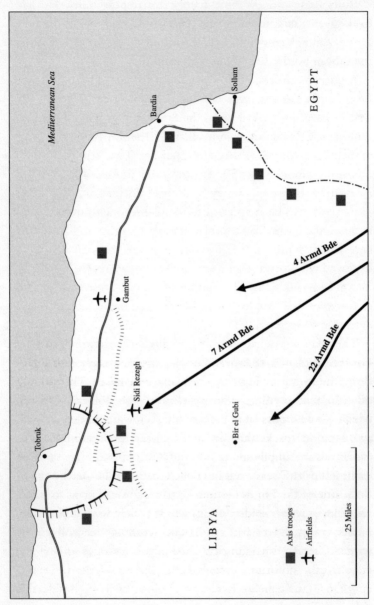

OPERATION CRUSADER, 18–20 NOVEMBER 1941

Mediterranean Sea

EGYPT

Sollum

Bardia

4 Armd Bde

7 Armd Bde

22 Armd Bde

Gambut

Sidi Rezegh

Bir el Gubi

Tobruk

LIBYA

Axis troops

Airfields

25 Miles

6

CRUSADER

For the 5th Tanks, 18 November 1941 marked as pleasant a day's desert motoring as any of them could remember. They moved off at six that morning, crossed the 'wire' – the Egyptian–Libyan border – two hours later and not long after that pulled up with the echelon trucks that had gone ahead with supplies. The Honey could happily motor along at 40mph, but its aero engine made it a thirsty beast. A fill of petrol could get burned up in less than fifty miles. Throwing cans of gas into the hot tanks was a risky business: the soldier detailed for the task wore a greatcoat, long trousers, gloves and a balaclava, while his mates stood by with fire extinguishers in case some of the spilt fuel ignited and engulfed the unfortunate crewman in flames. Under other circumstances the echelon lorries would have been at considerable risk, travelling ahead of the regiment. But on this first morning of the operation to relieve Tobruk the 7th Armoured Division was travelling fifty miles inland, well south of the Axis defence of the Halfaya Pass, and executing the generals' left hook without difficulty.

B Squadron, in which Corporal Bull was serving, had been made up to a strength of sixteen Honeys: four troops of three tanks, with another four in squadron headquarters. Most squadrons had between five and seven officers; the major commanding, second-in-command (a captain), three or four troop leaders (lieutenants) and sometimes a second captain, who dealt with admin matters. Within each troop the tanks were often referred to by the letters of the radio alphabet the crews used at the time: Able, Baker and Charlie. Bull, appropriately enough, was in the Charlie tank. His new responsibilities were many, and never mind the stresses of the coming fight. He became the father to the crew, even if a man were older than him, resolving their disputes, allocating tasks and measuring their exhaustion.

He had to command the tank in battle, keeping formation with the others, telling the driver when to speed up or slow down, while all the time scanning the horizon for danger. The 5th, in common with other experienced regiments, had already learned that the man in charge had to keep his head up out of the commander's hatch much of the time, exposing himself to the risk of being hit. The best way to pinpoint an enemy firing at you was to spot the flash of the gun as it went off – often kicking up a tell-tale cloud of dust around the muzzle. It was usually followed one to two seconds later by a noise as the shell streaked by. The high-velocity 50mm and 88mm guns made a sound like ripping paper as they passed. Once combat was joined in earnest, the tankies had learned to watch out for yellow and green tracer streaking across their path or over their shoulders: these marked enemy fire, whereas the British ammunition factories used a phosphorous in the tail of their shells that burnt red. Registering these fleeting sights and sounds – muzzle flashes, passing shells and tracer – often meant the difference between life and death. In action, everything would depend on locating the enemy swiftly and killing him before he could do the same to you.

Stopping at their replenishment point, the vehicle commanders jumped down from their turrets, giving Corporal Bull a chance to confer with his troop sergeant and commander (in the Baker and Able tanks respectively). Positions would be checked on the map. Every commander needed to keep abreast of exactly where they were, and to which point they were headed, because if his machine broke down and the rest of the squadron disappeared over the horizon he would have to be able to deal with any resulting dramas on his own. On this march, however, the Honeys, unlike the British tanks they had used before, drove on sweetly with barely a hint of trouble.

They motored for the rest of the day, covering a total of eighty miles. The Germans had outposts from a reconnaissance battalion in this part of the desert, each made up of a few men with an armoured car. These were sent packing by a few 37mm shots from the Honeys. The following day, the 5th drove another seventy miles, turning northwards towards the coast late in the day. When the 7th Armoured Division swung around, its armoured brigades were splayed like the points of a trident, each around twenty miles apart: the 22nd brigade was furthest to the west, the 4th (which included the 5th RTR) held the easternmost position – the one closest to the Egyptian frontier they had crossed the day before – and the 7th Armoured Brigade was in the centre, ahead of the others.

During the afternoon of 19 November 7th Armoured Brigade pushed on towards Sidi Rezegh airfield, a key Axis base several miles south-east of the Tobruk perimeter. They had achieved near complete surprise as the brigade commander, a cavalry brigadier named George Davy, reported:

... as we came in sight of the airfield, some three miles short of it, three aircraft started taxiing to take off and became airborne. The 6th Tanks opened up the throttles. I said on the wireless 'Gallop', the going was perfect, and downhill and in a few minutes, at 40 knots, we were on the aerodrome, and rounding up the astonished prisoners, with 19 operational Italian aircraft dispersed on the ground.

Captain Arthur Crickmay was acting as a crewman on Brigadier Davy's tank, witnessing the same 'memorable scene', as he and the divisional commander came to a halt among the surrendering Italian airmen.

If there was a moment when the vision of dashing armoured forces set out by tank advocates during the inter-war years came to fruition, this was it. In two days they had bypassed the enemy front line, advancing 150 miles into his rear and appearing at the aerodrome with complete surprise. The Desert Rats had struck a blow that caused even a commander of Erwin Rommel's skill to stagger, disorientated. Early brushes with the 4th Armoured Brigade had led the German general to believe that the main British thrust was well to the east of Sidi Rezegh. In addition, Rommel had not long returned from leave in Italy, and had been focused on his own plans to finish off the Tobruk garrison, remaining convinced that the British were not ready to strike. Operation Crusader was two days old before he had a full enough sense of what was going on to order a counter-attack. The 7th Armoured Division's thrust threatened his panzer divisions with being cut off. More urgently, Axis supply lines were also interrupted.

During the two weeks of intense fighting that followed, the usual hierarchy of command often broke down on both sides, for the battle pitted several different groups of mobile forces against one another in an arena about a hundred miles by sixty, where the concept of front lines often became meaningless. So, for example, late on 19 November the 7th Armoured Division might face counter-attack from Axis forces to the west of them (where the Italian Ariete Armoured Division was poised in reserve), to the east (where Rommel's German divisions had been bottled up), or from the north, where a narrow corridor remained between Sidi Rezegh airfield and the Tobruk defences. Those Axis divisions, similarly, came to realise there were British to their east (the infantry divisions pinning them to the border defences), west (the 7th Armoured and a couple of infantry divisions that were soon reinforcing it), or the south, from the route the British had used to bypass their defences in the first place. In this situation, where radio communications were at best temperamental, reports confused and threats lay to every point of the compass, the skill of tank commanders of even junior rank was paramount.

In the 22nd Armoured Brigade, a formation of callow Yeomanry (i.e. cavalry reservist) regiments thrown into action, these abilities were sadly lacking. They had attacked the Ariete division on 19 November, coming badly unstuck. Having started the operation with 163 brand-new Crusader tanks, they had lost more than half by the evening of the second day, leaving thirty behind due to breakdowns and losing more than fifty to the Italians. One 22nd Brigade officer reflected bitterly, 'We had no experience of battle ... we were "green" and without infantry support to take prisoners.'

The 3rd and 5th Tanks, and 8th Hussars of the 4th Armoured Brigade, were veterans, old regular army regiments that had already seen plenty of hard service. Their Operation Crusader started easily but gradually grew more trying.

While the 22nd Brigade had been coming to grief to the west, A Squadron of 5th Tanks got into a scrap with the Germans as it reconnoitred German positions. Lance Corporal Gerry

Solomon was driving his Honey when word came through that the troop leader's tank had been hit. The vehicle quickly brewed up. Men jumped from their nearby Honeys to help the three crewmen who were seen to bail out. Solomon rushed to help the gunner, Trooper Reg Bone, quickly seeing that 'he had absolutely nothing on at all and his skin was rolled up everywhere'. Blast and heat had stripped the trooper of all clothing and great stretches of his skin. He was smeared with burn ointment and they called for an ambulance. The wireless operator and Lieutenant Moss, the troop leader, were also burned, but not as badly. During the wait for the ambulance the casualties screamed out in pain. Eventually it arrived, but Gerry and the others realised that, being so far from the former front line, it would take days to get Trooper Bone to a proper hospital. 'You imagine being tossed about in an ambulance and they were not very well sprung,' Solomon reflected. 'Believe me, they were dreadful things for anybody with no skin on their back.'

With the casualties sent on their way, it was unsafe to hang about with so much German armour on the move. Solomon's commander suggested they should find out what had happened to Lieutenant Moss's driver. They all understood that he had not come out of the stricken Honey that stood smouldering, the violent inferno of fuel and ammunition having abated. They peered into the driver's compartment, where Trooper Charlie Stokes had been sitting. 'All that remained of him was a blackened, shrunken, skeleton,' reported Solomon. 'The metal rims of his army issue glasses were still sitting on his head.' Word later reached the squadron that Trooper Bone had died of his wounds. That night, Solomon reflected on the shocking things he had seen, and began to tell himself that his decision to volunteer for the tanks would be the last time he put himself forward for anything in the army.

The following day A Squadron was involved in a much larger action. Rommel had realised the danger he was in, but not yet the extent of the British advance. Responding to the incursion that he knew about, following the 4th Armoured Brigade's skirmishes of 18 and 19 November, he ordered his troops to strike south. Kampfgruppe Stephan, an all-arms battle group under the commander of the 21st Panzer Division's tank regiment, advanced into action. Early on the morning of 20 November C Squadron spotted dozens of enemy tanks moving towards them. The tank strength of Kampfgruppe Stephan and the 4th Armoured Brigade was similar, at around 150 to 160 vehicles, but the Germans had more anti-tank guns and their Mk IIIs were better protected and better armed than the Honeys they faced.

For the British, getting to the right range for a 37mm shot (or a two-pounder one for the Crusader tanks used by other regiments) required them to approach within a thousand yards of their enemy – ideally to about eight hundred yards. Yet the Germans' armour-piercing shot from 50mm guns was effective at fifteen hundred yards. Colonel Stephan's battle group also had a few 88mm flak guns attached that could engage at a range greater than 2500 yards. As battle was joined on 20 November, the 5th's Honeys started firing away, but were achieving little. They were sufficiently well practised in their drills that they were able to fall back and call on artillery support with few losses.

Captain Brian Stone of A Squadron described what happened:

... each tank had fired an average of two hundred and fifty shells ... as well as the tank guns there was a regiment of RHA [twenty-five-pounders of the Royal Horse Artillery] and the German divisional artillery firing. We had been pushed back mile after mile, keeping in one line and countering enemy attempts to outflank us by clever juggling with reserve squadrons on the part of the brigadier, and an overcast night had come just in time to prevent the enemy profiting from our growing disorder.

The 8th Hussars took the brunt of this delaying action, but the 5th RTR had lost five tanks late in the day. Stone described the action in which so many thousands of shells had been fired as 'the most noisy and concentrated battle in my experience'. Second Lieutenant Lester, one of the troop leaders, was killed late in the day. Stone helped bury the twenty-five-year-old sub-altern that night. He filled two petrol cans with stones and left them as a crude headstone above the grave in the sand, promising himself that he would come back to inter Lester properly – a task that would prove impossible since he could never find the grave again.

Within a few days of the operation starting A Squadron would be down to just one officer, Captain Stone having been separated from them during a night supply run. As 20 November finished, his brigade could at least reflect on a job well done in their contest with the German battle group. The Honey commanders had, however, received a salutary lesson in what to expect from their 'pop gun', as many had started calling the 37mm weapon, against the latest-model Mk IIIs.

Having spent the night on Sidi Rezegh airfield, the 7th Armoured Division's commanders realised that they needed to decide matters while they still had the power to do so. They feared that Rommel's troops would escape through the narrow corridor between themselves and Tobruk. In addition, they knew that the British garrison would be trying to push out to them. It was therefore decided to send the 6th Tanks north towards a place called El Duda in order to seize it and link hands with the Tobruk garrison. Between the airfield and the defences was a low rock escarpment which provided the vital ground for the battle. Mindful of its importance, holding open his line of communications westwards and dominating the airfield, Rommel had placed the 90th Light Division of the Afrika Korps astride the escarpment, and thickened the defences with four 88mm guns.

On the morning of 21 November Brigadier Davy, Captain Crickmay's boss commanding the 7th Armoured Brigade, was faced with the fateful decision of whether to push north. Reports indicated large German armoured formations moving towards him from the south-west. The long-awaited counter stroke from Rommel was beginning. At the same time he had already issued orders for the capture of El Duda, and feared that if he cancelled the operation he would let down the Tobruk garrison trying to break out. So the push northwards by 6th Tanks, supported by infantry and artillery, went ahead.

The Crusaders of 6th Tanks set off early, aiming to reach their objective by half past eight that morning. Crickmay found a vantage point on a hillside as they roared off, the Liberty engines of their tanks powering the machines forward. The Crusaders were accompanied by infantry in trucks and the brigade's twenty-five-pounders were soon barking in support, but it was not long before the 88s started striking home, stopping each Crusader with a shudder and the crump of metal on metal. Then, after a moment, smoke would billow from the hatches and the tank would start to burn. Observing them through his binoculars, Crickmay began to have the sickening feeling that he was watching disaster unfold just as the Earl of Lucan had at the Charge of the Light Brigade nearly a century earlier.

Within a couple of hours the attack was smashed, and not a single one of the British tanks taking part was still in working order. The commanding officers of 6th Tanks and the infantry battalion were both captured and many others were dead. Among those who perished was Crickmay's best friend, Ted Delson. Apart from half a dozen Crusaders that had been held back at Sidi Rezegh, 6th Tanks had been entirely destroyed. The futility of it was underlined when Brigadier Davy heard that the Tobruk garrison had been four hours late in attempting their push south and so the whole thing could have been cancelled. Captain Crickmay would endure many bitter reflections about the loss of so many dear friends, but as 21 November wore on he did not have the luxury of indulging them.

German attacks on the airfield built up through the day; artillery, tank and machine-gun fire was poured onto the defenders. Their position was becoming untenable. To make matters worse, they had just sacrificed a regiment of tanks and hundreds of infantry to no purpose. It was in the maelstrom of flying metal that Brigadier Jock Campbell won a Victoria Cross for organising the defenders. One eyewitness told of 'the wounded Jock Campbell rushing around in an open car amidst a shower of bullets inspiring all with acts of great gallantry and with exhortations in the brusque language of the polo ground'. But the Germans kept creeping forward, silencing British strongpoints. Brigadier Davy decided that the handful of tanks used by brigade headquarters needed to join the fray. 'Arthur, put away your maps,' he told Crickmay, 'and get on the gun.' Their Crusader pitched into the firefight.

It had not taken long for the tables to be turned on the 7th Armoured Division. From catching the Axis troops completely off guard on 19 November they were, just two days later, fighting for survival. The 22nd Armoured Brigade had been reduced to a battalion-sized force (about thirty tanks), and the 7th had lost almost every bit of armour it had. Hopes now rested on the 4th Armoured Brigade which, so far, remained largely intact. In the afternoon of 21 November it moved to a position a few miles south-east of the airfield.

Just as Arthur Crickmay had lost his innocence at Sidi Rezegh, so it claimed a bit of Charlie Bull. As they got underway helping those on the airfield, it was cold and the crews wrapped themselves up as best they could. Corporal Bull still shuddered, and started to wonder whether it was fear. He realised that he had been eight years in the army, and had come through France and the Libyan battles of April without ever seeing a dead man. Back then his tank, like so many others, had packed up rather than being knocked out. What he had witnessed was chaos and retreat, but not yet carnage. There was an element of bluff among many of the old regular army men; they could talk a good game but had not actually seen a full-scale tank battle before. That was soon to change.

It was past three o'clock when the 4th Armoured Brigade started to close the last few miles to the airfield, moving north-west from a point at which it had spent the previous day largely unengaged. The commander put 3rd and 5th Tanks up front, with the 8th Hussars moving up in reserve. By this time renewed German attacks had overrun the eastern part of the landing strip (the right-hand side, as the 5th looked down on it), while Brigadier Campbell's support group hung on at the western end. The scene that presented itself to the Honey commanders who crested the last ridge before Sidi Rezegh was one of confusion and destruction.

'My God, what a shock,' wrote one of them. 'There were hundreds of vehicles, tanks, guns and burned-out aircraft spread out in utter confusion amongst the smoke of shell bursts and gunfire . . . I found it impossible to determine who was friend or foe. It was the most terrifying spectacle I have ever seen.' Indeed, the confusion was such that as the 3rd Tanks moved down onto the airfield the frightened yeomanry of 22nd Brigade took them for enemy and engaged them.

The 5th RTR, on the right of the brigade's advance into this scene of chaos, was hit by enemy panzers and anti-tank guns and several machines from A Squadron, leading the battalion's advance, were struck. Soon the whole battalion was in action as the German tanks pushed forwards. 'To see them sometimes reminded me of battleships,' Charlie Bull would later write home, 'they just used to keep coming and we would be pumping shells at them as fast as we could, then our artillery behind us would open up and it was a grand sight and a relief too.' Ammunition boxes, blown-off bits of vehicles and bodies were strewn across the airfield. One Honey commander saw two men who had fallen across one another, lying dead in the shape of a cross. For the tank drivers, going forward into this maelstrom often involved driving over bodies; if a man was obviously wounded they tried to steer around him but sometimes, if the vehicle was coming under fire, they had no choice but to close their eyes and press on.

Once on the pan of the airfield itself the crews felt horribly exposed. German anti-tank gunners squinting into their sights lined up on any working vehicle they could spot. A shower of solid shot would then pelt the hapless British crews, sometimes striking the vehicle harmlessly, sometimes knocking off vital components or entering the crew compartment. 'My tank was hit and the driver killed instantly,' recorded an officer of the 3rd Tanks. 'Further shots hit us, severing the tracks, setting alight the bedding stowed on the running boards, smashing the glass vision blocks, and jamming the machine gun. At last the tank was reduced to such a shambles that I ordered "Bail Out".'

Several times the Honeys rushed forward, firing into the enemy until they ran low on ammunition. Another squadron would then take over, while the first went back to replenish their supply of shells. Moving up, Jake Wardrop and other members of C Squadron were led forward by Brigadier Jock Campbell in person, who was driving about in his open tourer: 'We went storming up to these tanks, firing as we went.' German artillery shells started to crash down among the Honeys as they traded blows with the Mk IIIs. Wardrop's tank rocked as a Mk III scored a direct hit, breaking a track and scattering the contents of their ration bin, including the commander's precious bottle of whisky, across the sand. Sitting immobile in the midst of so much enemy fire, Jake reflected that 'it wasn't a very healthy position to be in, but it could have been worse; it wasn't raining'. A passing tank from the 3rd RTR gave them a tow and Wardrop managed to fix the track during a lull in firing. With the sinking sun just visible through the pall of smoke hanging over the airfield, Lieutenant-Colonel Drew withdrew his battalion, arguing that the fight on the runway had become so confused that they could achieve little. In fact one of the tank officers, having seen how 3rd and 5th RTR became mixed up in the swirling dust, announced as he left the aborted attack, 'You've never seen such a balls-up.' At this point the 5th Tanks had twenty-four of its Honeys still working, having started the day with forty. Bull, Wardrop and the others pulled a couple of miles south, driving into leaguer as an inky darkness fell.

One tank from A Squadron never received the order to pull back. As the armour-piercing shot flashed back and forth, the tank under the command of Corporal Harry Finlayson had its radio antenna shot off. Finding the Germans surging on both flanks he drove forward, around some of the leading panzers, so that he could engage them from behind with the 37mm gun. He slapped a fresh round into the gun and the gunner fired, not much more than fifty yards from the back of a German tank. Before the crew could repeat the feat the Honey slewed around violently, as if kicked by some giant. An 88mm round had gone through the rear of the vehicle, blasting much of the engine out of the back and onto the sand. Finlayson and his crew survived the hit and bailed out, but all four of them were quickly captured and became German prisoners of war.

The rest of the battalion, little knowing what had happened, got back to its evening leaguer and a practised routine. After refuelling, rearming and gulping down some food and hot tea, the men would usually bed down for a few hours' sleep. But that night it was not to be. Radio messages told of a desperate fight not far away; the Germans had captured the 4th Brigade echelon and the nearby brigade headquarters had been surrounded and was about to fall.

Fighting at night was a risky business, with a high chance of killing friends rather than foes. Tank gunners simply had to look through their telescopes at the target their commanders directed them to and hope for the best. That night, the evening of 22 November, was particularly bad since there was no moonlight. Somehow, though, the 5th found the brigade echelon 'closed in and gave them the charge'. After some frantic close-range fighting in which tracers criss-crossed the sky in a shifting lattice of fire, the enemy was driven away. But the Germans had exacted a heavy price, claiming that they had 250 prisoners from 4th Armoured Brigade and had smashed it as a fighting force. They were overstating their success, as indeed British unit reports did repeatedly, adding further to the confusion that engulfed the generals on both sides.

Extricating the 5th RTR proved a difficult matter, and by the time they had done so the battalion was down to sixteen Honeys. What had happened to the others? A couple had gone up in showers of sparks, lighting up the gloom. But what about the remainder?

Sergeant Emmin Hall of C Squadron was in command of one of the missing vehicles. When his unit had pulled back Hall withdrew, but soon realised something was wrong. His sense of direction told him the tanks were not heading back to the leaguer they had left a few hours earlier. He looked about, straining his eyes in the darkness, trying to make out the signs on the Honeys in front of him that would tell him which squadron and regiment they belonged to.

Hall had commanded one of the last remaining tanks from France, nursing it up to Cherbourg. Some of the men called him

Henry Hall, after the famous English bandleader of that name. He was highly rated among the crews as an unflappable professional, who looked after them like a father. At twenty-eight, Hall was only a few years older than many of the other men, but this made a world of difference. Unlike most of them he was married, and had a daughter called Margaret, born in 1939. With an alcoholic miner for a father, a stepmother who he didn't get on with and two brothers who had died in childhood, Emmin Hall had tasted much that was bitter about working-class life. He had grown up in a two up two down in Nuneaton, and memories of being close to starvation, for example during the General Strike, were etched in his memory. While serving on the North West Frontier several years earlier he had seen many a British soldier whose throat had been cut by Pathan tribesmen. This background had made Hall an exceptionally tough man, but it had also instilled in him a great sense of compassion and responsibility towards his young crewmen.

As the column negotiated the dark desert in November 1941 the sergeant was determined to get them all through. When they stopped for a moment Sergeant Hall jumped down and raced up to one of the machines in front of him, discovering that it belonged to the 3rd Tanks.

That night Hall's Honey and four others from the 5th leaguered up with the 3rd, or what remained of it. Hall picked his way through the leaguer so that he could report to the major in command. He found a small man called Wilson, who was clearly close to the end of his tether; Sergeant Hall was sent away with a flea in his ear and told to come back the next morning. Trudging back towards his own tank, the sergeant thought he recognised the voices he heard inside a vehicle, so he banged on its side. It belonged to Warner, the 5th Tanks padre, who, much in the style of Brigadier Campbell, had spent the day weaving about the tanks, through shot and shell, in a civilian shooting brake. Warner had given himself the task of recovering crews from knocked-out tanks and carrying them to safety.

Under the hammer blows of Axis counter-attacks, the 7th Armoured Division was being smashed to pieces. Troops of survivors were scattered here and there, and the control of senior officers was breaking down. When morning came, Major Wilson told Hall to form a troop of the 5th Tanks Honeys under his own command. They sallied out, got involved in a scrap with a column of German tanks and withdrew hastily.

By eleven o'clock on 23 November, Hall's tank, along with six others from the 3rd and 5th, had been placed in some scrub in a wadi. In order to save themselves after the last engagement they had driven the best part of twenty miles away from friendly lines. Most of the tanks had almost no fuel or ammunition left, so the crews did not attempt to man them as enemy gunners spotted the vehicles later that day and took long-range pot shots. Instead, the men lay on the ground and hoped nobody would take them prisoner. At times Hall could not work out where the major had gone, which struck him as another failure of command.

As night fell 3rd RTR somehow managed to get a couple of echelon lorries through the enemy to the stranded group in order to top them up with fuel and ammunition. After dark they set off, trying to cover the twenty miles back to British lines as quickly as possible. They were barrelling along when they realised they had sailed right into the middle of a night leaguer belonging to an armoured unit. They stopped, and Hall explained what happened next:

At this moment I was just getting out of the tank and my driver was also getting out and he looked up and said 'Germans'. I nodded and said 'yeah'. So he got back in, I got down and said to him 'start up and go like hell'. He said 'but they're walking in front of the tank'. I said 'just run over them and keep going'. So he started up and there were a few screams as we made good progress through them and got away from there.

How many men they had killed in order to avoid capture, they would never know. But Hall reckoned that they could only have survived being in the middle of the enemy leaguer because the Germans must have taken them for Italians.

Hall and the other remaining Honey crews made it back to 3rd RTR that night. Like Captain Crickmay, the sergeant had lost his best friend at Sidi Rezegh. Hall, who the C Squadron crewman looked up to as a rock of courage and sanity, told friends that there had only been two occasions during the war that he had cried. The first was on 23 November, when he emerged from that confused and terrifying ordeal to realise that his oldest friend in the regiment hadn't made it.

During the week that followed the first heavy fight on Sidi Rezegh the fortunes of the combatants ebbed and flowed. The British were driven from the airfield but maintained their salient deep behind Axis lines. The Afrika Korps had thrashed about like a caged beast, striking south during the first days of Crusader then west to Sidi Rezegh. They went back east towards the Egyptian frontier and then finally, in the last days of November, westwards yet again. Each one of these moves was accompanied by death and destruction, the attrition of infantry, artillery and of course tanks.

For the 5th Tanks each day brought fresh combat. On the 24th they hit an enemy infantry column, taking forty prisoners and destroying many trucks; the following day they had beaten a heavy German attack. On another occasion B Squadron hit an Italian tank column, knocking out several vehicles. In each of these engagements Honeys would be struck by armour-piercing shot, sometimes many times over without going out of action, and sometimes pulling back for repair. Maintaining supply lines through the southern desert in the face of German counter-attacks was a nightmarish proposition. Early on, the nightly supply run by the 5th Tanks echelon had been captured. Although many of the men subsequently escaped from their captors, several of the unit's mechanics did not, which increased pressure on the survivors. The fitters worked around the clock and their efforts, combined with a couple of vehicle deliveries that made it through, topped the 5th back up to twenty-six working tanks by 30 November.

As vehicles were knocked out or officers switched from damaged Honeys to working ones, there was constant chopping and changing within the squadrons. Wardrop hopped between vehicles so often that he had pared his kit down to 'my toothbrush, my money, revolver and my blue pullover'. He also made sure to keep his small blue notebook – the one in which he was recording a diary of his experiences for his mother's benefit – in the pocket of his shorts. Each day, the men got up after a few hours' sleep at most and pressed on. Captain Stone in A Squadron described his morning battle routine: 'Up at four o'clock ... dragged on my boots, had a mouthful of whisky, wiped my face with eau de cologne, tied my bedroll on to the tank, and climbed in and began fumbling with the headphones over a face which had not been shaved for days. I felt as if I had been doing the same thing every day of my life.' Stone also kept one small volume about his person: *The Elizabethan Plays*, an anthology of love, betrayal and melodrama in which he buried himself when he needed to escape the grim reality of the desert.

In this action, which went on for weeks, the social divisions that had regulated so much of life before the war became meaningless. 'Orders were never necessary,' wrote one RTR officer about the relationships within his own vehicle, 'not that the use of naked authority was ever the best way to control a tank crew. Nowhere else did such a small body of men with such diverse backgrounds, interests, and education live so much together in such close contact with the enemy. In such conditions no man could hide his fear or weaknesses for long.'

Operation Crusader had, by the end of November 1941, reached its own dramatic crisis. The British command had realised that possession of Sidi Rezegh and the escarpment to the north of it (that 6th Tanks had been sent to take on the 21st) constituted the key to bottling up Rommel's troops. After the breaking up of the 7th Armoured Division there, infantry had been sent to secure the place. On 1 December the 4th Armoured Brigade was told that the Kiwis were under tank attack and needed to be given support 'at all costs'.

Advancing across the airfield for the second time, to where the New Zealanders were dug in just north of it, the Honey commanders surveyed the scene of devastation once again. Corporal Charlie Bull and his Honey had somehow come through the battles of the previous fortnight unscathed, but on this morning he was not to be so fortunate. He could see an Italian tank up ahead and ordered his gunner to engage it. They knocked it out and pushed on. But nearby, having spotted the advancing armour, enemy anti-tank guns opened up.

With a flash and bang the turret of Bull's Honey was pierced by solid shot. It slammed into a rack of ammo boxes for the tank's Browning machine guns. In the open air a box of machine-gun bullets going off can seem no more threatening than firecrackers, but enclosed in a metal turret the effect of these multiple explosions can be devastating. Seeing the gunner and wireless operator covered with blood Bull helped them to bail out of the tank. Out on the sand, he 'flapped a bit at first as I put my hand to my face and there was blood all over me and I could taste it in my mouth'. Bull checked his own wounds. It was not as bad as he feared – the shock of the enemy round hitting the tank had given him a black eye, and there were several cuts on his face where bits of metal from the exploding bullets had pierced his skin.

Making his way on foot, Corporal Bull and his crew saw the cost of the battle up close and in vivid detail. They passed a New Zealand casualty station that had been overrun by the Germans: 'There were some very grim sights and I hope I never see them again.' They also found the crew of the Italian tank they'd put out of action not long before. It was not often that a crew came face to face with their own handiwork, the seriously wounded soldiers lying by their vehicle, moaning, 'praying, calling on all his saints'. The German wounded that Charlie saw bore their burden in sullen silence.

Having assisted the New Zealanders in what became a withdrawal from their position near the airfield, the 5th Tanks were moved back once again and spent the following days in continued engagements with the enemy. Whatever the differences that one-time professional soldiers like Wardrop or Bull might have felt from the men who had joined the battalion since war began, searing experiences like those of Sidi Rezegh were uniting them in common adversity. For Lance Corporal Gerry Solomon, driving one of A Squadron's Honeys, the final actions of Crusader provided a particularly close shave.

A few days after the Sidi Rezegh action of 1 December, Solomon was driving forward when a 50mm solid shot came through the front armour of the tank hull, inches away from him. With earphones on, engine and battle noise all around, Solomon didn't even hear the strike or see a flash. He told the sergeant commanding his tank what had happened, but received a sceptical reply. Solomon 'went to pick this thing up and of course it was hot'. After waiting until it had cooled down, he then passed the 50mm shot over his shoulder to the sergeant in the turret behind him, saying, 'There you are, this just come in the front door.' When the crew stopped they all inspected the hole in the front, dealing with the closeness of the escape with deadpan humour. One of the men stuffed some rags into the hole, Solomon telling him, 'Well, at least that will keep the draught out.' Privately, though, the Honey driver reflected that you could be lucky once or twice with a hit like that, but how long would your luck hold?

On 7 December, having manoeuvred his forces for the best part of three weeks, Rommel finally gave up the game. He ordered German forces to make a general withdrawal to the west, a step that would uncover Benghazi and allow the British to race forward to much the same positions that they had occupied in April 1941. At first the Italians refused to accept this order, since it meant once again surrendering a substantial part of Libya to the British. Although nominally in charge, they were learning that the Germans put their own interests first, and they had no choice but to follow.

Wags in the 8th Army had grown used to employing horse-racing terms like 'gallop', 'sweepstake' and 'derby' when describing the various panicked moves to save themselves during the previous weeks. This time, though, it was a canter, and much more to their liking. 'This was the period at which the steeple-chase really began,' noted Wardrop. 'We ran round them, over them and underneath them.'

On 19 December 5th Tanks received orders to return to Alexandria, having travelled most of the way back to El Agheila. Although many divisions remained in the field after the gruelling fight, the armoured brigades needed to refit.

So what of the outcome of Operation Crusader? Rommel extracted his key forces ruthlessly. He preserved his two armoured divisions and the 90th Light, while sacrificing Italians and indeed some German units that had been fighting hard down at the eastern end of his deployment on the Egyptian frontier. For this reason, when the final reckoning was done, there were 29,000 Axis missing (most of them captured, including 13,800 Germans) versus 7500 British. The 8th Army had more killed, though: 2900 compared to 2300 Axis fatalities. The Allies sacrificed more tanks too. But Tobruk had been relieved, and several Cyrenaican airfields made available to the RAF. At the end of it all, the two armies had, in the view of one newspaper correspondent, fought 'very near the point where one side or the other must collapse through sheer exhaustion. Some five or six hundred tanks had fought one another to destruction or impotency.' Michael Carver, an RTR officer who observed these events in one of the headquarters directing the battle, later wrote that the British army emerged from Crusader with a sense of failure because 'the enemy had consistently appeared to have the better of the tactical battle'.

Certainly the fight ended untidily for the British in that the Germans were able to save most of their troops from the intended British encirclement. For many Tommies, it was one more episode in the Rommel legend. Quite a few German officers saw it differently. They knew that Rommel's drive and personal bravery were second to none, but they also felt that his tendency to fly about the battlefield, taking personal control over units in violation of the chain of command, had only increased the confusion. 'In the end', the Chief of Staff of the 15th Panzer Division noted, 'divisions took matters in their own hands simply by acting on their own initiative without reference to orders.' The German ability to act without clear guidance from above was central to the tactical success that Carver described. The British commanders, by contrast, were often slow to react to unexpected events and quick to fall into recrimination if things went wrong.

For the tankies, a sense of having lost was more to do with

grim personal reflections. Weeks of combat in which they had watched units, sometimes hundreds of tanks strong, manoeuvring, fighting and perishing in the desert made many conclude that their previous experiences had been a pantomime by comparison. One of the 6th RTR troopers, a veteran of the early desert fighting, described Sidi Rezegh as 'the first real battle of the war'. An RTR officer who had also come through it all knew that a deep tie had been established with his surviving comrades, remarking that 'I felt a close bond in which none of the more recent arrivals could be admitted.'

As for the 5th Tanks, Sergeant Hall had lost his closest regimental friend; Lance Corporal Solomon had been able to do little to help Trooper Bone after he had been horrifically burned; Captain Stone had buried one of his mess mates in the sand; and Corporal Charlie Bull had his innocence about death blown away.

'I cannot think how the Delsons will be able to bear the news, being so extraordinarily devoted a family', wrote Captain Crickmay soon after the battle, pondering the loss of Ted, 'and I feel very depressed about it now I am back in Cairo where we had so many good times together.' In time, Crickmay digested the huge struggle that he had just taken part in, declaring it a 'pyrrhic victory'. The human cost, coming after the humiliations of France and April's rout at the hands of Rommel, simply increased the desire in many for vengeance.

During the month of the Crusader battles the 5th Royal Tank Regiment lost twenty-seven men, with a great many more wounded or captured. Compared to some units, including the 6th Tanks, this was not an especially heavy price. But it was enough to have shocked the battalion deeply. Returning from the front the men lost themselves in the bars and brothels of Alexandria – but there would be a reckoning, and it started before 1941 was out.

7

NEW YEAR, NEW BROOM

Within a few days of receiving their order to return to Cairo, 5th Tanks had signed their surviving Honeys over to other regiments, along with the echelon lorries. The men were trucked back over the Egyptian frontier, and then boarded trains for Cairo. Leave followed, and for a few days the men found their own private oblivion. Wardrop and his drinking pals headed into Alex, and didn't even make it to the Golden Bar. 'We went into a rather small street corner bar', Stimpson later recalled, 'and we stayed there for three days, we had our hair cut there, were shaved daily, meals were obtainable, the bar never closed so beer with brandy and dry ginger chasers was always on the table, we were discreetly informed that should we desire them, females were on hand.' Meanwhile Charlie Bull, alarmed at how thin he'd become during Crusader, was eating plates of steak and chips, and Stone was listening to Beethoven and travelling to see Biblical sites in Palestine.

For those running the battalion, a different kind of catharsis was imminent: the sort that results from an organisation that has lost itself in blame and recrimination. The 4th Armoured Brigade, in which they had fought, shed plenty of blood during the fighting, but it emerged from the late operations looking quite healthy in comparison to the other elements of the desert rats, the 7th Armoured Brigade, 22nd Armoured Brigade and Brigadier Campbell's 7th Support Group. On one level, those running the 4th Brigade ought to have felt proud of having more survivors, but many of the men who had come through Crusader were afflicted by doubts, memories and guilt.

The 7th Armoured Brigade had largely been wiped out during the bitter battles around Sidi Rezegh airfield. The generals decided that it needed to be rebuilt and sent away from the scene of its recent nightmare. On returning to Cairo, its surviving members took delivery of new Honeys painted in jungle green: they were going to Burma. Captain Crickmay, as a staff officer with the brigade, would be going with them. That was just as well for him, since everywhere he went in Cairo he saw reminders of his dead friend Ted, and the others killed in the destruction of his old battalion. 'It's very gloomy here without the chaps and I miss them a lot,' he wrote during the final days of 1941. 'One really feels quite ashamed to find oneself survived.'

There had been times during the fighting when the 4th Armoured Brigade had not come to the aid of others as quickly as the division's commanders had been expecting. Early on, for example, on the day 6th Tanks had been destroyed, the 4th Armoured Brigade had spent the entire day unaccountably stationary, about ten miles south-east of Sidi Rezegh. That wasn't the only time this had happened. Now, with so many men grieving for lost comrades, charges of sitting back were bound to take on an emotive character.

Some blamed the brigade's commander, Brigadier Alec Gatehouse, for not doing more. For his part, Brigadier Gatehouse seemed to nurse much the same grudge against Lieutenant-Colonel Dinham Drew of the 5th RTR. Drew, defending himself on paper over the conduct of an engagement during the recent operation, claimed Gatehouse had ignored the 5th Tank's achievements, adding, 'I feel perhaps the fact that we suffered no casualties was regarded as a matter of censure rather than praise.'

One face-saving excuse deployed by Drew with Gatehouse – and by the brigadier with his own bosses – was that of poor communications. Both men claimed that their failure to seek out the enemy at certain times had been due to contact being lost. While it was true that command and control had at times broken down completely, Brigadier Gatehouse was unlikely to accept from a subordinate commander an excuse that he himself was deploying so energetically with his superiors. Heads were rolling and Drew, who had been wounded during the latter part of Operation Crusader, was removed from command.

If at times during the late operation Drew had deliberately dragged his heels in order to save the lives of his soldiers, it had worked, for most had come out of the battles unhurt and the 5th was hardening into a veteran formation. However, this tactic also meant that many blamed him for what had happened. Haunted by the memory of so many of their tanks burning, Lance Corporal Solomon and his mates nicknamed the old man 'Colonel Brew'. For many officers in the battalion, it was precisely Lieutenant-Colonel Drew's age that was the problem: he had appeared exhausted and bewildered during the late operations. It was time for both him and a couple of the squadron commanders to be replaced by men who could take the strain of such fighting.

Drew was succeeded by Robbie Uniacke who, at thirty-six, was a decade younger. Uniacke had joined the Tank Corps during the inter-war years, was in charge of training recruits in 1939 and had been a staff officer in 3rd Armoured Brigade (5th RTR's parent formation at the time) in April 1941, when Rommel routed it. During Operation Crusader he had led the echelon ahead of the regiment into Libya, and frequently took command of the 5th Tanks at times when Drew had been unable to. Respected by the men as a less harsh figure than the disciplinarian 'Detention' Drew, Uniacke's looks made the ladies at the Gezira Sporting Club flutter – he had been described by photographer Cecil Beaton as 'the handsomest man outside films'.

New men were also installed in A and C Squadrons – both officers had shown considerable heroism during Crusader as captains forced to take over in moments of crisis. They too were younger, tougher and more driven than the generation they replaced. The displacement of the old, regular army ex-Tank Corps officers was gathering pace. In France and their first battles in North Africa, the CO and a couple of his majors had even been Great War veterans. By early 1942, those holding regular commissions at the outset of war were becoming a minority within armoured battalions in Egypt. Called-up reservists like Crickmay and Stone had taken many jobs, war volunteers were arriving through the system as nineteen- or twenty-year-old troop commanders, and some relatively young holders of pre-war commissions, like the new commander of A Squadron, were being advanced at a dizzying speed.

For someone like Hitler, or Joseph Stalin, the losses the British suffered in regaining eastern Libya, as well as capturing so many enemy soldiers, would have been perfectly acceptable in exchange for the strategic advantage achieved. But the Crusader battles had marked a collective loss of innocence, both for the men of a battalion like the 5th RTR and for the old regular army officer corps as a whole. In the Royal Armoured Corps the mauling of the Yeomanry regiments of 22nd Brigade, or the destruction of 6th Tanks, led to an angry rejection of 'Balaklava charges' – rushing headlong to their destruction like the Light Brigade in the Crimean War. The deployment of this tactic seemed to combine the worst traits of the Tank Corps diehards, who insisted their beloved machines could do it all on their own, with those of the cavalry generals who wanted to do everything at the gallop.

Summing up the lessons of Operation Crusader, the official 7th Armoured Division report noted that the enemy simply wasn't playing by rules that would have allowed Balaklava charges to succeed: 'The German will not commit himself to tank v tank battle as such. In every phase of the battle he coordinates the action of his anti-tank guns, field artillery, and infantry with his tanks and he will not be drawn from that policy.' While the British matching-up of artillery and armour had improved greatly, the armoured division still lacked enough infantry. Reflecting on the pounding received at Sidi Rezegh, the 7th Armoured Division's staff concluded: 'Suitable defence troops must be readily available ... these defence troops must rapidly prepare a defensive area capable of withstanding the most powerful counter-stroke which the enemy can possibly deliver. In this defensive system the correct role for the tanks is mobile reserve well outside the defence perimeter.'

The result of this soul-searching was that the British adopted an essentially German model for their armoured divisions. The 7th Armoured Division was to be reorganised, with one armoured brigade and one of motorised (i.e. lorry-borne) infantry. It would consist of three battalions of tanks, four battalions of infantry (three in the motorised brigade and one in the armoured brigade), as well as artillery, reconnaissance and other support. And just as ideas marched forward into 1942, so did technology.

As the new year began, the 5th were to get a new broom to sweep the enemy from the battlefield. On 27 January, ten new tanks arrived: the M3, or General Grant. Other new machines followed, until B and C Squadrons each had thirteen Grants. A Squadron kept Honeys – and its role as a reconnaissance force – for the time being.

The arrival of the Grants was greeted by enthusiasm bordering rapture in many quarters. The commanding officer of 3rd Tanks said the change was of such a magnitude it was 'like going from wood to steel at sea'. Driving the Grant up and down on the training area, Jake Wardrop opined, 'They were super, the finest things we had ever seen.'

Grants were big machines, and at twenty-six tons almost twice the weight of a Honey. They were better protected, with 50mm frontal armour, and heavily armed. In the turret they mounted the same 37mm 'pop gun' as the Honey, but there was a 75mm canon in the hull. This arrangement, of having a smaller gun designed to pierce enemy tanks up top and a bigger weapon for general purpose use down below, created a very tall vehicle, and one in which the hull gun, unable to rotate, had to be fired in the direction you were pointed. The new machine's arrival necessitated reorganisation within the squadrons since the old Honey was crewed by four and the Grant needed six or seven men. The commander and 37mm gunner were in the turret, with the driver, 75mm gunner, wireless operator and 75mm loader in the large fighting compartment in the hull. However muddleheaded, this approach had also been adopted by some other French and British designers.

The 75mm gun was not primarily designed for tank killing – its projectile left the barrel travelling at 2050 feet per second, compared to the 2700 of the British two-pounder. It could, however, lob a sizeable shell filled with high explosive accurately over a long distance. Both the two-pounder and the 37mm gun the battalion had hitherto used fired only armour-piercing slugs: solid metal, without explosive inside. The 5th RTR's Grant crews would soon decide the 37mm gun was largely redundant, preferring to engage enemy tanks with the 75mm since its performance against them was quite adequate, and excellent against soft targets. With the Grant, a German Mk III could be knocked out at a thousand yards and, more importantly given recent experience, a German anti-tank gun could be engaged at anything up to twice that distance. The shrapnel from a high-explosive shell could cut the enemy gun crews to pieces. The Royal Horse Artillery were good, but bringing their twenty-five-pounder field guns from their limbered state, pulled behind a lorry, into action could take precious minutes, whereas the Grant's 75mm gun allowed the tank crew a near-instant response.

Of course, the Germans were not standing still either. The Mk IV tank, with a short 75mm gun, had been in service for some months, but in March a few arrived in Libya with a long-barrelled, high-velocity 75mm weapon that packed a much heavier punch. Mk IIIs, meanwhile, were being refitted with the high-velocity 50mm gun that had already been used to great effect on a wheeled carriage as an anti-tank weapon. But the effect of these advances was for the moment limited. The 'Mk IV specials' had arrived without ammunition, and just nineteen Mk IIIs had been up-gunned. The Grant had therefore given the British a distinct edge, if only for a short time.

Being so large, the Grant's propulsion presented its designers with a particular problem: US manufacturers were still in the process of developing big diesel engines capable of pushing such a heavy vehicle forward. The Grant's makers produced one version with twin aero engines, and another with six linked bus engines. While slaving multiple motors together like this might have seemed like a recipe for breakdowns, the Grant proved reliable enough. Once again, American engineering had come up with the goods.

Most of the tanks made for the British were produced just

outside Detroit, at the Chrysler Tank Arsenal. There the production-line techniques pioneered by Henry Ford were being applied to armaments with extraordinary results. Although the first tank only came off the line in April 1941, Chrysler made 750 in the following September. Two months later, the plant went to twenty-four-hour production six days a week as it powered towards a target of four thousand tanks a month – a figure greater than Britain had managed during the entire first year of the war. One of the British liaison officers at the Chrysler Tank Arsenal noted that 'the Americans were infinitely more jealous of their industrial reputation' than manufacturers at home, quickly modifying their vehicles in the light of reports from the field. Hundreds of the new Grants were shipped direct to North Africa, where the 5th Tanks were among the first to get them.

On 16 March 1942 the battalion began entraining to head up the blue once more. They had a new organisation, new kit and new leaders. There followed a period of weeks in which the crews got to know these new realities while exercising on the desert near Tobruk.

Jake Wardrop found he was driving his new squadron leader, Major Paddy Doyle. During Operation Crusader Doyle, a commissioned ex-ranker, had run B Squadron, bringing it through numerous scrapes and earning himself the Military Cross. Having survived a couple of brew-ups, Doyle was the sort of character whose apparent indifference to danger sat well with the men.

Captain Stone and Lance Corporal Solomon also found themselves under new management, a major called Richard Ward. Like Doyle, he had emerged to take command during Crusader, survived numerous scrapes and was awarded the MC. Tall and bespectacled, Ward smoked a pipe and radiated an intense energy.

Watching the new boss in action, Stone recorded his mannerisms:

After nightfall, as we were fully rested and not under battle conditions, we gathered round Richard's staff car through force of habit ... as he sucked at his pipe and snorted into his whiskey. He always snorted when he felt strongly about anything, for his determination was so great that it simply bubbled out of him. Whether he was issuing battle orders or giving one of us a ticking off there was always a confirmatory snort at the end to convince those around him that he meant what he said.

Ward was a regular army officer who had been commissioned in 1937. The war offered him the chance to rise very fast or die trying. Having been wounded twice during the Crusader battles, escaping one Honey in which his driver was killed, he can have been under few illusions as to the risks. But the war also allowed him to take command of A Squadron at the age of twenty-four, something that would have been unthinkable in peacetime. He was determined to make his squadron the best, and was quite ready to apply the kind of energy and determination that many had felt the older generation of majors were lacking.

Among the rank and file, Ward's standards could prove irksome. Gerry Solomon, who was promoted to corporal early in 1942, felt that his new commander 'hadn't got time for civvies in the army'. Another member of A Squadron, a driver who recently had joined, said Major Ward was 'very strict, a hard man. He was not very popular, a hundred per cent would agree with me.'

For all his scepticism about amateurs in the army, Ward soon placed Corporal Solomon in command of a tank. War meant a fast track for the capable soldier too, giving Solomon in eighteen months' soldiering the coveted post it had taken Charlie Bull more than eight years to achieve, and which Wardrop had yet to attain. But Solomon's promotion was soon in jeopardy.

During one of the early manoeuvres soon after they had gone to the desert, Ward spotted that Solomon's crew had lit a fire to make tea just before dawn. This ran counter to squadron standing orders, that said no flames should be kindled in the leaguer prior to first light. The major sent one of his crewmen over, who told Solomon, 'Dickie saw your fire. You're on charge, I'm afraid.' This meant that Solomon would face military discipline, including a fine and the possible loss of his rank. Solomon replied that he couldn't care less.

By the time he was interviewed by Ward, in the cool air of a desert morning, the young major's anger had abated a little. The corporal saw no point in evasion, telling his major, 'It was one of my people, I take full responsibility for it ... [he] lit the fire too early.' Ward replied, 'I am not going to punish you, because if I punish you, you will lose your stripes, so you are admonished.' Solomon considered the entire episode petty and unnecessary given the dangers they were running. But he nonetheless learnt a lesson about being responsible for his new crew's actions.

From top to bottom, the army was changing leaders. Corps and divisional commanders were being sacked, so why not the Commanding Officer of the 5th Tanks, one of its squadron leaders or a mere corporal in charge of a Honey? Those who believed in summary action generally argued that it was necessary to raise the army's professionalism to the level of the Germans.

Problems had been evident since early February, when the general commanding the British front line had been sacked. Rommel had struck forward at the end of January, advancing from the Agheila position that he had fallen back to in late December and forcing the British to abandon Benghazi for the second time. This setback, early in 1942, created new anxieties in London and Cairo, since the British government had been pouring resources into the Middle East, expecting to consolidate the gains of late 1941 not see them whittled away.

The 8th Army had at least prepared a defence in depth, seeking to do something about the fact that there was no really defensible geographic feature between the Agheila bottleneck and the Egyptian border hundreds of miles to the east. They fell back to the Gazala Line, a belt of defences about thirty-five miles to the west of Tobruk. These defences – minefields, barbed wire and tank traps – snaked from the Mediterranean southwards about forty miles to Bir Hacheim, a desert fort in the Beau Geste style where, aptly enough, the Foreign Legion served as part of a Free French brigade. Along the line, and for some distance behind it, a series of infantry brigade positions or 'boxes' had been prepared. These crowned key features, dominating certain routes, and were prepared for all-round defence. If the enemy bypassed them, the defenders would be able to emerge from the box in order to raid his lines of communication.

Occupying the Gazala Line gave the British particular advantages, and it certainly simplified their logistics, for they had

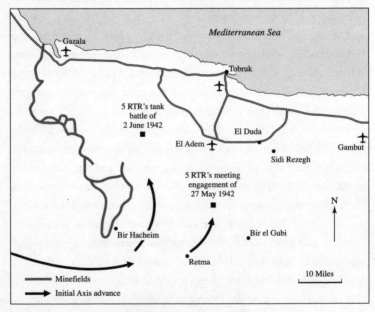

THE GAZALA BATTLES

the excellent harbour of Tobruk close to their front, and the railway from Egypt was slowly being extended into Libya. However, falling back to these defences carried risks too. The Gazala Line did not extend all the way to the impassable sands of the Saharan interior; you could still get around Bir Hacheim at its southern end. Those who led the 8th Army could not afford to adopt a defensive mentality either; particularly not when they were toe to toe with someone of Rommel's ability.

At GHQ in Cairo, under pressure from Churchill in London, the staff was planning a new offensive to regain Benghazi and drive on further to the west. British generals had started to think in practical terms about how they might fight all the way to Tripoli, eliminating Axis forces from Libya. They felt the right preparation was essential and had set 1 June as the date for returning to the offensive. Alas Rommel had also been thinking of a decisive drive forward, preparing a full-scale assault codenamed Operation Venezia.

On the afternoon of 26 May 1942 Axis artillery started pounding Allied lines close to the Mediterranean. They had started an attack on the main British defences, while sending their armoured divisions south for a great enveloping manoeuvre. Rommel recorded:

At 20:30 hours I ordered Operation Venezia, and the 10,000 vehicles of the striking force began to move. My staff and I, in our place in the Afrika Korps column, drove through the moonlight towards the great armoured battle. Occasional flares lit up the sky far in the distance – probably the Luftwaffe trying to locate Bir Hacheim.

The Germans had sent their picked forces around the south of the Gazala Line. Little did the slumbering men of 5th Tanks know, but their brigade lay squarely in the path of this hammer blow.

8

DISASTER IN THE CAULDRON

Dawn on 27 May 1942 brought an air of tense expectation to the 5th Tanks. The crews were all sitting in their machines, engines running. They had been stood to in the early hours, when reports of enemy armour moving to the south began to circulate. Many of the men had, however, simply carried on snoozing inside their vehicles. As the sun peered over the horizon some took the chance of a crafty brew. Using a cut-down fuel can, the crewman would put some petrol on the sand in its base, then toss a match onto it. Placing another can on top of this impromptu stove, the tea leaves, sugar and condensed milk were poured into water as it came to the boil, making a delicious *jildi* or desert brew.

At half past seven the order came through to move to battle positions. Five minutes later the Grants and Honeys lurched forward, the crewmen feeling that kick of whatever metal they were resting on as the driver engaged first gear, opening the throttle. Picking up speed, each tank made a gentle nod forward, emphasised by the movement of the radio antennae flying their squadron pennants, each time the driver changed up a gear. The echelon men remained in the leaguer for the moment, packing up at the more leisurely pace their duty allowed.

Throughout the small hours, reports had been flying between divisional and corps headquarters and that of 8th Army, detailing the movements of large amounts of armour to the south. Some commanders had taken action, others had remained largely passive. A debate had been going on for some weeks about whether Rommel, if he struck first, would do so in the centre of the Gazala Line or to the south of it, bypassing the Free French at Bir Hacheim. With the weight of reports now suggesting that something very sizeable was going on to the south, the way in which the information was interpreted owed much to the position each general had previously taken as to where the attack might kick off, with a critical few still refusing to believe what was happening.

The 4th Armoured Brigade's tanks were ordered to a pre-arranged position, expecting a march of many miles to the south from their night leaguers. However, just a couple of miles after they had set off the 5th Tanks ran into the 21st Panzer Division. The radios came alive as the first sightings revealed the awful truth: there were a hundred enemy armoured vehicles to the west (i.e. between the 5th Tanks and the British defensive mine-fields, which Rommel's men had avoided by coming around Bir Hacheim) and seventy more German tanks to the south. The regiment immediately swung into battle formation so that the Grants of B and C Squadron could engage them.

Back at the leaguer, where the echelon was enjoying its morning tea, the sounds of battle being joined quite so near to them caused panic. Jumping into the cabs of their lorries the drivers heard shouts of 'Drive towards the sun!' and 'Go hell-for-leather for the sun!' Their best hope of survival was to head east as fast as possible. The trucks roared off, devil take the hindmost, as well-aimed German shells exploded among them.

The advancing enemy caught some of the other units in the brigade before they had left their night leaguers. The 8th Hussars were particularly hard hit.

Meanwhile, the Commanding Officer of 3rd Tanks reported that 'the leading enemy tanks had halted about 1300 yards away. All our tanks were firing, there was no scarcity of targets . . . good show.'

The 5th Tanks opened up with the Grants' 75mm guns, claiming many hits. The twenty-five-pounder artillery joined in the action. Rommel had not expected the 4th Armoured Brigade to be there, or to run up against Grants so quickly, noting 'there was a British surprise waiting for us there, one which was not to our advantage, the new Grant tank used for the first time on African soil'.

After two hours of pounding the brigade issued an order to withdraw, so its units fell back (northwards). While its engagement with 21st Panzer had not gone badly (with 5th Tanks least harmed, having no tanks knocked out, and the 8th Hussars worst affected), the wider picture was one of surprise, consternation and paralysis in the British command.

To add to the problems facing 4th Armoured Brigade, their immediate superior, Major-General Frank Messervy, commanding 7th Armoured Division, had gone off the air at a quarter past nine that morning. Moving with his tactical headquarters, the whole lot had run into a German reconnaissance unit and were captured. Across the southern part of the 8th Army area, enemy units were surprising supply echelons, seizing their dumps and attacking British leaguers.

Moving to Gambut airfield, the 5th found their echelon that

evening. When their trucks had driven towards the sun earlier in the day, this is where most had ended up, along with survivors from other transport squadrons. Lieutenant-Colonel Uniacke discovered that several lorries from his echelon had been destroyed by artillery fire as they tried to flee. He also learned that the 8th Hussars had only a few Grant tanks left, having lost the best part of two squadrons' worth that morning. To a great extent, the 5th Tanks were now the only effective strike force left in 7th Armoured Division.

During 28 May each side tried to recover its balance and discover the full extent of its problems. Rommel's position was quite similar to that which the British had faced after they outflanked Axis lines in November 1941. His daring manoeuvre had succeeded, but enough British forces survived to put his mobile corps (of three German and two Italian divisions) in danger. Meanwhile, the Axis supply situation was very tricky. On the second day of fighting, the 15th Panzer Division had halted due to lack of fuel. Rommel initially tried to push north to the sea, in order to cut off the British defensive boxes of the Gazala Line that lay between him and the rest of the Axis force to the west. Later he resolved to smash a path through the line, in order to open a channel of communication to his supply dumps. While the British in November had been able to keep the supply line of their 'left hook' or enveloping force open through the southern desert, Rommel found he was in great difficulties doing the same around the Bir Hacheim position at the south of the British line. The French forces holding the defensive box there caused heavy casualties to the Italians and 90th Light Division when they attempted to storm the place. British attempts to support the French, meanwhile, meant that Rommel's units around Bir Hacheim were themselves coming under attack.

On 30 May 5th Tanks mustered what effective force it could from A Squadron in order to send them south on a raid against the enemy supply lines. Seven Honeys set off in the afternoon, accompanied by two petrol lorries and an ammunition lorry from their squadron echelon. The Honeys were so thirsty that the lorries with extra fuel were essential to the plan. Major Ward took command of the operation. He may have been ambitious, but the dangers in what they were about to attempt were so obvious that he confessed his 'feelings on getting my orders were mixed'. They made their way down past Bir Hacheim, where the beleaguered French shelled them, assuming they were German, and spent the night on their own on the southern part of the battlefield. One tank was sent back with mechanical problems, leaving six to complete the mission.

The following day Ward's group negotiated its way to a position on the western side of the Gazala Line, finding its way around British minefield to a point on the edge of a plateau where it was felt enemy supply columns might pass. Having concealed their tanks, they sat and waited in the broiling sun, hoping they were well enough hidden to allow the head of the convoy to pass most of them before action was joined. The westernmost Honey would deal with the tail. Hopes of a successful outcome must have been fading when, at three o'clock, a large Italian army convoy appeared not far to their front. It was escorted by three armoured cars, which Ward ordered his crews to take out first when the ambush was sprung. 'As the head drew level with me I opened fire,' he wrote. 'Pandemonium broke loose. The convoy tried to scatter, but finding us on all sides, stopped. The leading armoured car stopped dead when hit and the crew got out.' The Honey on the western end of Ward's line shot at the other two armoured cars, brewing one up with its third 37mm shell. By this time the other had escaped, and the major knew they would have to work fast.

More than two hundred Italians, along with dozens of trucks, had fallen into their hands. Ward knew the escaped armoured car would raise help, so time was short. The British intended to disarm the Italian prisoners and get the convoy moving back towards safety. Then, to Ward's consternation, 'every man without exception leapt from his vehicle with his suitcase, stripped off all his clothes, and changed his underclothes!' If they were going to be prisoners, they might at least have clean drawers.

Ward and his A Squadron crews managed to shepherd the Italian convoy, complete with its supplies, back to their own lines. They sped back around the Bir Hacheim box, whose defenders shelled the passing tankies again, and up to the 5th Tanks' leaguer with their prize. The bespectacled young major was so delighted with his haul that he suggested the naval tradition of awarding prize money might be appropriate. At Headquarters 4th Armoured Brigade they had charted Ward's mission by his radio broadcasts, noting in their log – a little archly – that the ambitious major 'reported that they had captured 200 enemy MET [motorised enemy transport] at the exit of the southern gap in the minefield. This figure dwindled to 50 and later to somewhat less, the previous figure having been the result of wishful thinking and dust.' Any sense of triumph on the part of the returning Honey crews was further diminished by the news that the regiment's leaguer had been hit by a heavy air attack shortly after they had left the previous night. Some seventeen members of the 5th RTR and its supporting artillery battery had been killed, and forty wounded.

The wider battle had now tilted, with the capture on 31 May of the 150th Brigade's defensive box, after fierce fighting. The loss of this key ground, near the centre of the Gazala Line, allowed Rommel to open a supply route west, preventing the strangulation of his own armoured corps. For the British, the already vexed question of 'what next?' was complicated by the blowing in of a khamseen wind that restricted visibility across much of the battlefield.

British generals still nurtured hopes of hemming in the Germans and destroying them in the Cauldron, an area east of the 150th Brigade box and around fifteen miles south of the Libyan township of Acroma, and a few miles south of the road junction that the British called Knightsbridge. There, they believed, a natural depression in the upland escarpment might give them the chance to focus their fire on the Germans by shooting down on them. By launching a series of armoured attacks into the Cauldron, however, they soon squandered their advantage in tank numbers, with the fate that befell Lieutenant-Colonel Uniacke's battalion repeated several times.

Late on the afternoon of 2 June, the 5th Tanks set off to investigate reports that German tanks had been sighted to the south. The khamseen was still blowing, forcing the tanks to stay close together in order to maintain visual contact. Major Ward's A Squadron was in front, acting as the regiment's eyes, with B and C Squadrons in their Grants following in line astern. The sand was blowing so badly that Uniacke decided to halt them. There they waited for three hours while the wind whistled through their wagons and sand came in through any open hatch.

Suddenly, through the murk, someone sighted German tanks to their right. A Squadron had sailed past them before halting in the sandstorm. Over the radio net, Sergeant Hall of C Squadron heard Uniacke order all tanks to turn right and form battle line. The sergeant told his driver, who slewed the machine around through ninety degrees. The two Grant squadrons had manoeuvred quickly from a line astern into a line abreast, so they would be able to deliver the fire of both Grant squadrons.

Sergeant Hall issued orders to his crew:

We began firing; my troop officer was the first to be hit and set on fire. It was a case of firing into the enemy tanks as fast as you could and there wasn't much chance of jinking forward or back because the tanks all along our line were beginning to burn. To claim any tanks would be quite wrong, because all the tanks could do was to fire at the enemy as quickly as possible from one to the other as they were doing to us.

Down in the hull of the tanks, the 75mm gun belched fumes each time the breach dropped so that the loader could throw in another shell. Some of the tanks were calling out 'Target!' over the radio net, signalling they had got a hit. But something was not right. The 5th's Grants were being picked off. Emmin Hall noted ominously, 'As I looked along the line I could only see burning tanks.' One working Grant raced behind them and Sergeant Hall saw that Major Doyle, his squadron commander, was riding on the back of it with his crew, having escaped their own tank, which had brewed up. In among the cacophony he spotted the padre's station wagon weaving around the burning hulks. There were men packed inside as well as standing on the back, lying on the bonnet and hanging off doors. The sergeant reckoned there must have been more than twenty crewmen being carried off by the padre.

Trooper Stimpson had graduated from driving to being the wireless operator in one Grant that was hit by two shells, just moments apart. The driver was dead and so was the 75mm gunner near him in the hull. The loader for the big gun was not responding to their shouts. 'Our commander gave the order to bail out just as the tank was hit again,' he wrote in his post-war memoir. 'When I landed on the engine covers and had a look around, the scene was unbelievable, tanks "brewing up" all along the line, men running in all directions, the air was full of shot and shell, all now coming our way.' Stimpson's commander, Sergeant Fry, jumped up onto the back of another tank, but moments later a shell landed, blowing him to pieces. The gunner made a run for it, but was shot through by an armour-piercing shell that had missed one of the Grants. In moments, four of Stimpson's crew of six had been killed, leaving him and a passed-out man still inside their Grant (who would be taken prisoner) as the only survivors.

For the crews, it was a point of honour not to leave their comrades behind. But with so much shot and shell flying it was also extremely dangerous. One tank picked up four survivors and sped off towards the rear. When it arrived at a place where it thought safe to unload them, the commander looked behind the turret to discover there was only one man there. A shell had landed on the rear of the tank, leaving a grim residue of blood and tissue. The sole surviving crewman had one arm blown off and was close to death, but they managed to save him.

With the skies darkening, there were no clear orders coming across the radio, only curses, claims of hits and reports of their own vehicles brewed. Hall looked across to Sergeant Ned Hartley, commanding the other surviving tank in his troop. Their troop commander was out of action; Sergeant Hall gave a hand signal to his comrade to pull back. Slowly the two Grants began to reverse, leaving behind so many burning vehicles.

Stepping back for half a mile, Hall decided it was finally time to turn around and drive away from the fight. Just then he noticed that one of his tank tracks had been broken by an enemy shot. So, under fire, he and the crew had to repair the track. By the time night fell, Hall and Hartley had pulled back six or seven miles, finding themselves leaguered with the remnants of 3rd Tanks, just as he had during the Sidi Rezegh battle. Surveying the exterior of his vehicle properly for the first time, Hall counted the scars from fourteen enemy rounds.

Brian Taylor, a trooper in A Squadron who had joined the regiment just a few weeks before, found his Honey stopped dead and burning. He bailed out. 'I ran and ran as fast as my legs could carry me,' he said, 'and then I realised I was running in the wrong direction, right into the German tanks.' Judgement overcoming panic at last, he turned around and pelted back through the burning hulks that littered the desert, with firing still going on all around him. Taylor ran onwards, past a Honey with its turret lying beside it, blown off by the force of an internal explosion. He was close to despair that his regiment had already pulled back, but then spotted a Honey slewing to a halt. Its crew were taking a big risk in stopping at all, and they pulled away while Taylor was climbing over the side, his foot on one of the tracks. For a moment he thought he would lose it, but managed to hurl himself onto the rear decks as the tank sped off. 'They had picked me up and they weren't even from my battalion – I think they were from 3rd Tanks.'

A few miles away, Lieutenant-Colonel Uniacke was moving back in a stricken tank. Seeing wounded men lying in their path, and knowing that his vehicle could not steer properly to avoid them, Uniacke dismounted, hoping to move the casualties out of the way. But a spate of heavy firing ensued, killing the colonel.

That night a mood of despair permeated the 5th Tanks leaguer. Some fifty-one officers and men of the tank crews were dead or missing. They had started the day with fourteen Grants, but nine had been knocked out, two damaged (but recovered) and two – those of Hall and Hartley – ended up with 3rd Tanks; only one had made it back to their leaguer, along with just eight Honeys. The surviving officers decided to fortify their men by a time-honoured method: a large rum ration was broken out.

How had they failed, given the superiority of the Grants to the panzers they had been up against? Among the crews, it was generally held that the German tanks had tempted them to give battle, but that 88mm guns had then done much of the damage. However, the fact that Hall's Grant and some others had survived so many hits suggests that smaller-calibre weapons had been used against them – one or two 88mm hits would have been sufficient to brew them up. Despite this, the crews blamed the big German flak guns for their setback. One recently joined member of B Squadron noted 'this set back in the Regt seemed to have a demoralising effect on the men and I in particular began to doubt the effectiveness of our tanks. Admittedly I had only been in action just over a week, but the word "88" coming over the intercom made all the tank crews panic.'

The battalion's failure was put down by some to its vehicles being too spread out. There was some muttering from the Grant crews that the light tanks of A Squadron had peeled off very swiftly to leave them to their fate – and certainly a much larger proportion of the Honeys had survived. Visibility had been poor as they advanced towards the Germans, and this had both masked the enemy and created confusion as they began to take casualties from well-sited anti-tank guns. A tighter formation might have allowed the 5th RTR to reinforce faster those who ran into the ambush, so overwhelming the Germans.

Jake Wardrop was not there on 2 June, but he knew all about the effects of 88s on tanks and men's minds. A couple of days before, he had been driving forward in the twilight:

> I was closed down but looking through the periscope I saw the greeny-white tracer of one coming straight at us. I thought to myself 'that's ours' and there was a thump on the front, then another, and bump again on the front ... I looked back into the turret and there was nobody there.

Half of Wardrop's crew had bailed out. Since doing this without ensuring your crewmates had managed to do the same was as grave a sin as a tankie knew, the Glaswegian driver's anger flared. Wardrop later found the young officer who had been in the turret, who asked his driver, 'Did you not hear me give the order to bail out?' Having got the tank back to the leaguer successfully with the other couple of crewmen who had stayed in, Wardrop knew that the vehicle had not failed them; rather, it was the young officer's nerve. 'I just spat on the ground at his feet and walked away,' recorded Wardrop. 'If there had been nobody there I would have punched his nose.'

The Scotsman had missed the disaster of 2 June as he was part of a group that had gone to Tobruk in order collect new tanks to replace earlier losses, returning soon after with twelve fresh Grants. During these bloody fights of early June, the system of supplying replacement vehicles and crews worked well enough. The battalion managed to fight on with one squadron of Honeys under Major Ward and a composite squadron of Grants commanded by Doyle.

Many new men were coming into the squadrons, and it was down to the old sweats to measure whether they were up to the job, since being in action almost every day meant that there was no margin for error. This led to some difficult judgements, particularly about young officers. Those who had survived the battles of France, the early fights in North Africa or Operation Crusader retained the respect of the men. Officers such as Dick Ward and Paddy Doyle blended experience, drive and common sense. Some of those who now arrived, often subalterns in their late teens or early twenties, were more suspect. During the bitter battles of June 1942 the experienced non-commissioned officers in the 5th acted to limit the damage that these greenhorns could do.

Sergeant Hall had already placed his troop leader in a supporting role, as one soldier noted: 'Henry Hall ran that troop.' When a new officer appeared, Second Lieutenant Grey, 11 Troop formed their own view of the man. Jake Wardrop, who was driving one of the tanks, thought him 'a good lad but he worried too much. It was his first time and he wanted to make a good impression.' Wardrop's friend Stan Skeels, who was the wireless operator on the same tank, surreptitiously removed a valve from the radio set 'and told him the set was duff'. The young officer did not feel he could stay on the tank if he was unable to speak to his squadron leader. Once Grey moved on to another vehicle Skeels replaced the valve and the crew carried on. A fellow member of 11 Troop argued that 'nobody in their right mind wanted to be in a new troop leader's tank, they just hadn't got the experience. And experience ... kept you going and won the day really. You couldn't afford to go around losing tanks all the time.'

The battle-worn tank soldiers who survived these dark days often felt that the new troop leaders were not being given the right training before they arrived. They had been equipped with skills that the soldiers had discovered were useless, such as sig-nalling in Morse code, and were still being told that firing on the move was the best tactic. If the veterans of the 5th had learned one thing, it was that their first shot had to be on target, since the flash and dust it produced were likely to give their position away. Firing on the move made a miss with that first shot more likely; it was part and parcel with the approach that had led to Balaklava charges. Instead they preferred to get into a good position, choosing their firing moment and target carefully before unleash-ing their first shot stationary.

Fighting through June the 5th Tanks and the rest of 4th Armoured Brigade were slowly whittled down by continuous combat. Major-General Frank Messervy, the commander of 7th Armoured Division captured at the start of Rommel's Operation Venezia, had escaped and was (briefly) back in command. 'In my opinion [4th Armoured Brigade] was by now not really an effective fighting force,' he later wrote. 'Its units were a con-glomeration of tank crews from various regiments, its tanks were nearly all reinforcement tanks, many of which were not fit for battle.' Much the same was happening in other parts of the 8th Army.

On 10 June, after a fortnight's heroic resistance, the French in Bir Hacheim were overwhelmed. Three days later the Guards were forced to abandon the Knightsbridge box, causing the effective collapse of the Gazala Line. The British had to leave not only their defensive position but the massive stores they had built up for their planned offensive and, pretty soon, the whole of eastern Libya.

'Most of us were suffering from chronic exhaustion', wrote Captain Stone of A Squadron, 'and my memory of those days is a weird phantasmagoria in which the only reality was the divine bond between us all which forced feats and bravery and kindness from our worn out spirits. On and on and on went the endless clamour and weariness.'

Stone had always been a little too refined for some on the squadron, humming his Beethoven and toting that book of Elizabethan plays. Consequently, his squadron leaders had banked his intellect, generally using him to organise things or for administrative tasks, for instance bringing up the nightly supply run. But in the wake of the 2 June losses, Stone wrote, 'at last I got a troop of tanks'.

On 21 June, Major Ward gave Captain Stone orders to take a small column north, raiding German transport as well as assisting any British vehicles they found moving eastwards. The column of Honeys, infantry and artillery moved off at half past three in the morning, but two hours later, and about twenty miles south-east of Tobruk, began a game of cat and mouse with some German anti-tank guns 'firing a few shots at us, running away, to reappear somewhere else'. The enemy was becoming adept at knowing how long a twenty-five-pounder might take to come into action – often just a few minutes – and scooting out of the way before they could be hit.

With each move forward Stone scanned the horizon, desperate to spot some tell-tale sign of one of the guns, but finding their small size and a strange, thick mist hanging in the desert hollows were making it impossible. Of the engagement, he wrote: 'I was in contact with these fly-by-night anti-tank guns for six hours. During the first two hours I laughed at the whistle of solid shot, during the third and fourth I was tense and apprehensive, and during the last two I was very weary and uneasy.'

This game of manoeuvres ended without a decisive result, and though one Honey took a 50mm round through its engine all crew members survived. In the middle of the day, they were pulled back, the squadron leaguered up and the crews promptly set to work getting a brew of tea and cooked breakfast on. Not long after this cherished activity had begun Major Ward walked over to tell Stone that Tobruk had fallen. He realised at once that the thick mist he had seen was in fact smoke that had blown across from burning supply dumps. Rommel's troops had attacked straight into the port city, capturing thirty thousand men and thousands of tons of stores in the process. For Stone, 'it was the unhappiest day of battle I ever had'.

A general withdrawal had begun, with a plan to fall back well inside Egypt to a new line of defence that was being prepared. In many places, the 8th Army insisted, it was heading back in accordance with this plan. In others, the move east turned into the usual kind of 'flap' that the army had become all too familiar with during 1941.

Just a few weeks earlier the generals had been stockpiling supplies for a great push forward, but were now in a headlong retreat. The 8th Army had more and better tanks than its enemy, and the troops were in high spirits. How on earth had the tables been turned? Many British soldiers answered with one word: Rommel.

The fall of Tobruk was, in the view of that German

commander, 'for every one of my "Africans" . . . the high point of the African war'. He promptly issued an order of the day congratulating his men for what they had achieved since 26 May, ending, 'Now for the complete destruction of the enemy. We will not rest until we have shattered the last remnants of the British 8th Army.'

It was wrong to explain it all in terms of one man, but Rommel personified a type of leadership that the British were evidently lacking. 'One of the first lessons of motorised warfare', Rommel wrote, 'was that speed of manoeuvre and quick reaction in command are decisive.' Time and again, he noted, the British had been strangely passive, or failed to concentrate their forces properly. It was the absence of hesitation on Rommel's part that had of course allowed him to launch his Venezia offensive in late May, before the British were ready to order their own attack.

The deductions from the bitter disappointments of the Gazala battles were much the same from the ranks of the 5th Tanks to Winston Churchill's office. The Prime Minister was visiting the White House when he received the news of Tobruk, 'a staggering blow' in the words of one of his party. Commanders from brigade to division (such as Frank Messervy) and indeed the 8th Army itself were sacked.

Captain Stone wrote that 'behind us lay two years of appalling wastage of life'. One of the men who had joined the 5th RTR during those hectic battles felt that 'we have been out-gunned, out-manoeuvred, out-generaled; in other words, led up the garden path'. From now on it was a matter of survival and all the army were in full retreat, but the army commanders called it a strategic withdrawal. Wardrop agreed that their generals had been deficient, but drew hope at least from the fact that 'we were never licked; we knew that we had chased them once and we could do it again'. The Commanding Officer of 3rd Tanks insisted that Gazala had not been an unmitigated disaster because in its starting engagement, that of 27 May, they had at least brewed 'more German tanks than they knocked out of ours'.

In the 4th Armoured Brigade they compared their grim experience of the previous weeks. Sergeant Hall's tank might have survived fourteen hits and Wardrop's fifteen, but there was one Grant in 3rd Tanks that had been struck twenty-five times and was still running. Some of the surviving crewmen had bailed out of five or six tanks during those weeks. From the German attack through June and July, the 5th Tanks had forty-six men killed with a similar number missing.

In the Egyptian port of Mersa Matruh, the 5th Tanks halted, reassembling its squadrons, echelon and HQ. They slept the sleep of the dead, and A Squadron feasted on a deer shot by Major Ward. In Alexandria there was a run on the banks and panic as rumours of the Axis forces' approach swept the city. At the front, however, the 8th Army – and 5th Tanks in particular – were already planning ways in which they could gain their revenge.

9

THE PRICE OF FAILURE

By early July 1942 the 5th Tanks had returned to Cairo, reformed themselves and headed back up the blue. Such was the air of crisis that there was no time for the lengthy rest or retraining that had marked their previous returns to the Delta. The 8th Army occupied a new front line at El Alamein, just a hundred miles west of its Egyptian bases. There the two armies eyed one another while the strategic preparations for fresh offensives were made.

During the two years since the start of the desert war, the armies had raced back and forth along the North African littoral as the balance of advantage between them had tipped. The Allies, although they had twice taken the Libyan city of Benghazi, had not managed to get past the Agheila–Brega choke point, where the Germans had fallen on 5th RTR and others in late March

1941. For their part, the Axis troops had not reached the Delta, though in their advances of 1940 and 1941 they had got a good distance into Egypt. With the shattering of the Gazala Line and fall of Tobruk, Britain's enemies entered Egypt for the third time in the summer of 1942. Their strategic momentum, however, was ebbing away. Huge resources had been switched to the Russian campaign and, in part as a result of this, the Axis ability to give air cover to its forces in the Mediterranean had declined. The Royal Navy and RAF were hence exploiting this greater freedom of action, interdicting enemy shipping or air traffic across that sea. This made Rommel's logistical headache bigger, and eased that of the 8th Army. For as British troops fell back to the Alamein position, with the low hills that made it one of those rare defensible points along the desert coast, fresh supplies and men continued to pour into the ports to their rear.

A Squadron of the 5th was occupying the outposts in front of the battalion, which was one of their usual roles as the reconnaissance squadron. It was eight o'clock in the morning, and Captain Brian Stone was eyeing the southern part of the ridge running north to south that they were sitting on. He was trying to spot a German anti-tank gun that opened fire on them whenever they crept close to the top of the ridge. With him was an observer for the Royal Artillery, who was ready to whistle up a twenty-five-pounder barrage on the enemy gun crew, if only they could be spotted.

Stone's spirits had lifted since the fall of Tobruk, and the 8th Army more generally understood that the Alamein position was where their retreat would stop and the Germans be invited to try their chances again. The captain knew that his two tanks would be relieved at nine by those of another officer, Lieutenant Geoffrey Rawlins, one of the A Squadron troop commanders. Both men by this time looked up to Major Richard Ward, their pipe-smoking squadron commander, as a real authority figure –

a status he had gained by courage and judgement rather than age.

Before his relief arrived, Stone decided to take his tank and the other on outpost duty with him. They motored a little way south before creeping up the gently sloping ridge in front of them, using for cover a shallow valley or re-entrant that ran up towards the crest of the ridge at right angles. As they neared their objective, expecting the crack of an enemy shot at any moment, the tanks slowed to a crawl to keep their noise and dust down. Then, suddenly, 'not two hundred yards away was a 50mm anti-tank gun pointing straight at me, and fifteen yards away from it were the crew, frolicking over their breakfast in their slit trenches'. Stone looked to the left of this little party of Germans, spotting a couple of machine-gun nests. Then, turning to the right of the gun, further along the ridge, he saw something else – perhaps some piece of artillery equipment.

Stone was amazed that he had made it so close without being detected. These anti-tank guns had driven him mad at times during the preceding weeks, but now he had the opportunity for revenge. He ordered his gunner to open up on the breakfasting Germans with the machine gun mounted next to the main gun of their Honey. With bullets chopping up the dust around them, the Germans dived onto the ground or into trenches to save themselves.

The captain and his two tanks then motored back to the Royal Artillery observation post 'in a state of high jubilation'. When Lieutenant Rawlins arrived the two A Squadron officers hatched a plan. They would go back to the German position with their four tanks, attack it and capture the anti-tank gun. They radioed Major Ward to ask his permission for the raid and he agreed, 'and told me not to come until he came, as he wanted to see the fun'.

So, a little later that morning the four Honeys set off with

Major Ward and the artillery people following not far behind. The twenty-five-pounder battery standing one mile away had been warned off, and the gunners stood cradling shells, ready to start pouring fire onto the enemy as soon as it was called for.

The tanks made their way up the re-entrant to where they had seen the German gun, racing up the last two hundred yards. Ward decided to call for an artillery fire mission in support. As the first couple of Honeys reached the ridge crest, they opened up with machine guns at the German gun crew, who were running for it. Stone 'arrived at the gun first by fifty yards and there, not twenty yards ahead of me, was a wall of bursting 25 pounder shells'. Captain Stone was bellowing orders in the turret, watching his gunner reload the machine gun when there was a thump. 'We were hit and both my legs went numb.' An anti-tank round had penetrated the turret.

Stone heaved himself onto the turret roof, flopped down onto the engine decks to its rear and, with another winding fall, crashed down onto the sand behind the tank. It was then that he could survey the extent of his injuries: 'I saw that one of my legs was shot off below the knee, and the other had three largish holes, one of them on the shinbone and another on the side of the knee.' Most probably, the solid shot fired by the enemy gun had taken one leg off and the 'spall' or bits of metal it sent flying off the inside of the turret had badly damaged the other. Geoff Rawlins was soon on the scene; he gripped Stone under the armpits and started dragging him away from his knocked-out tank. There was an awful ripping noise, another shot went flying over their heads and Rawlins's tank was knocked out too. To make matters worse, their own twenty-five-pounder shots were falling dangerously close.

Both officers took cover amid the deafening sound of falling shells, catching glimpses as they did of German soldiers crawling towards them.

◄ Charlie Bull snapped in an Egyptian studio as a corporal.

Arthur Crickmay, another Egyptian study, complete with voluminous khaki drill shorts. ►

◄ Jake Wardrop, pictured in Italy in late 1943.

Brian Stone, at a picnic with friends in England before setting out for war. ►

◄ Gerry Solomon, who volunteered for the armoured corps on the outbreak of war.

Emmin Hall pictured after the war. ►

Emmin Hall (*far right*) with men from his crew during the Gazala battles. Their exhaustion and determination is equally apparent.

Lieutenant-Colonel Robbie Uniacke (*right*) pictured during Operation Crusader late in 1941, in front of HQ Troop Honeys.

An A13 scales the pass leading to Derna airfield during 5th Tanks' retreat of April 1941. By this point only six of the battalion's tanks were still working.

An A13 tank awaits Rommel, soon after the battalion deployed into Libya in March 1941.

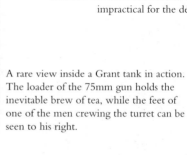

An A10, as used by A Squadron, speeds through the desert. The crewman taking a picture wears the type of RTR black coveralls that were soon found to be impractical for the desert.

A rare view inside a Grant tank in action. The loader of the 75mm gun holds the inevitable brew of tea, while the feet of one of the men crewing the turret can be seen to his right.

Major Richard Ward (*centre*) confers with Lieutenant-Colonel Jim Hutton (*right*) atop his Crusader.

Winston Churchill shakes hands with Brigadier Pip Roberts during his visit to the Alam Halfa position. Jim Hutton, CO of 5th Tanks, stands between them, his back to the camera.

Lieutenant-Colonel Dinham Drew, sitting on his Honey, confers with his attached Royal Artillery liaison officer during the Sidi Rezegh battles, displaying the closer coordination with the guns that typified Operation Crusader.

Lieutenant-Colonel Hutton briefs Montgomery soon after he assumed command of the 8th Army. The general had not yet taken to wearing the RTR beret.

5 RTR's commanders: Lieutenant-Colonel Jim Hutton driving the jeep, with Major Richard Ward (A Squadron commander) beside him, while Major Paddy Doyle (C Squadron) uses the roof of a lorry to give him a better view over the flat desert landscape.

An 88mm flak gun examined by its British captors after the breakthrough at Alamein. The mere mention of one on the radio net could cause crews to panic.

A 5th Tanks Grant destroyed during the Gazala battles, the blown-off turret and buckled hull plates bearing witness to the force of the internal explosions that destroyed it.

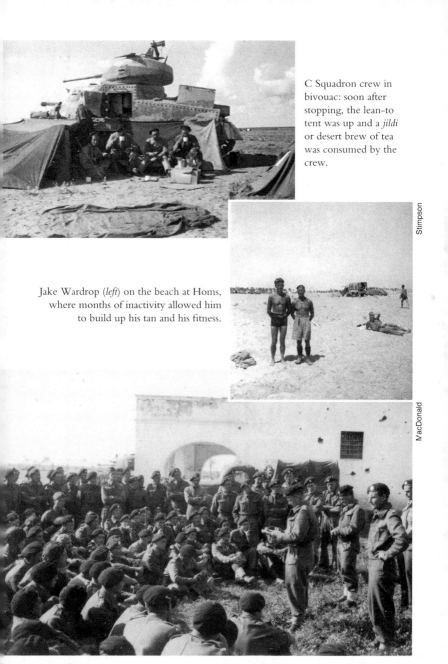

C Squadron crew in bivouac: soon after stopping, the lean-to tent was up and a *jildi* or desert brew of tea was consumed by the crew.

Stimpson

Jake Wardrop (*left*) on the beach at Homs, where months of inactivity allowed him to build up his tan and his fitness.

MacDonald

A Griff talk in Tunisia, not long before the end of the war. Keeping the members of every quadron informed about a forthcoming operation became standard procedure from the ummer of 1942 onwards.

Lieutenant–Colonel Hutton's Crusader rumbles forwards in early 1943, its flag bearing the scars of months of intense fighting.

'This is a fucking lark isn't it?' Stone called out to his friend.

'Yes, it wasn't Richard's fault was it?' Rawlins replied.

'No, he couldn't do anything about it,' shouted Stone, who crawled into the abandoned German gun pit for cover.

Very quickly the other two tanks they had brought with them had also fallen victim to the unseen enemy theat. There followed a nerve-racking time as German attempts to capture the stricken crews were met with fresh barrages of British artillery fire. Rawlins rescued a couple of his crewmen and then, alone, chose to try to fight in this desperate situation, firing a sub-machine gun at the enemy until one of them killed him.

With Rawlins dead, the Germans again tried to effect a rescue and capture mission. At one point, farcically, an officer called out to the wounded British captain, 'It is not fair. We are trying to get up our Red Cross armoured car to help you and your artillery is shelling it.' Stone laughed, calling back 'You're telling me it's not fair.'

Several times parties made their way forward, once carrying a Red Cross flag, but on each occasion the Germans were beaten back by British artillery fire. Stone tried to whistle Beethoven's 9th to keep his spirits up but realised no sound emerged from his cracked lips. He was lying propped up against the anti-tank gun that was their original target, in the blistering heat of a July sun. Three or four hours had passed since his leg had been blown off and he had not yet bled out, but 'I was getting weaker, and my thoughts more remote from reality, soaring higher and higher into a phantasmagorical musical blissfulness where I could catch the melody and mood of any music I knew.'

Stone was drifting in and out of consciousness, and close to death, when he was finally rescued by a German stretcher party in the late afternoon. He was aware of an RAF Hurricane swooping low to strafe the position where he was being treated, before drifting into the oblivion of morphine.

A Squadron's 'little party' of 6 July had ended in disaster. The German gun they had set out to capture was one of three, the apex of a triangle formation. When the British had reached it the two other artillery pieces deployed in depth had dealt with them. Four tanks had been knocked out, Major Ward scooping up two dead and three wounded before setting off in his surviving vehicle. Stone and seven Other Ranks were listed as missing. Some Grants had been brought up during the engagement and one of these, commanded by Sergeant Emmin Hall, dropped a high-explosive shell onto the anti-tank gun as the engagement died down. Hall, knowing the heavy price that had been paid for Stone's jaunt, reported in his strong Midlands accent over the radio network: 'Gun blown to buggery.' His Commanding Officer replied, 'Well done, but don't like your language.'

That night the survivors of A Squadron's little officers' mess would sit down to a morose supper minus two of their number. Stone, who had loved nothing more than the banter of his fellow officers as night fell in the desert, found himself wrenched away from them, crippled, captive. It was a fate that had already consumed scores of men from the 5th Tanks. The prisoner's family often had to wait many months to learn his fate, while comrades still serving in the battalion sometimes never heard what had become of the crewman who, until the day before, had shared their every trial and tribulation. Captain Stone was flown by light aircraft to Mersa Matruh, where he was handed over to the Italians. From there he was moved by ambulance up through Sollum and Halfaya, and all the way back to Tobruk. Racked with pain from his wounds, Stone endured operations to clean up his stump and stop him losing the other leg. The seriously wounded British in this hospital were looked after by captured South African medical orderlies, wasted by hunger as the rations the Italians spared them were so meagre.

In late July, three weeks after his capture, the young captain was put on a hospital ship bound for Naples, on which quite a few bunks were taken up by Germans. Stone had been deeply struck by the bravery of the men who had rescued him but, only half-conscious at the time, had not had the chance to speak to them. On board the hospital ship he struck up conversation with an Austrian officer, an Afrika Korps interpreter who told him that things would have been different on the Russian front. 'German soldiers always preferred to go to Africa,' he explained, 'because there it was war as they understood it, with brave men on both sides and a leavening of sport and chivalry.' Stone found the German's confidence that a job running one of the occupied countries was awaiting him at the end of the war a little unnerving. Once they reached Naples the wounded captain found himself in an Italian convent hospital, whereas the able-bodied prisoners were taken to camps.

Many other British captives also felt gratitude towards the Germans for the way they had been treated. When Tobruk fell, simply feeding the thirty-three thousand 8th Army captives would have posed serious problems for any army. 'I received water from them – it was very scarce at the time, and a cigarette,' wrote one man taken in the Libyan port, adding, 'in the German army, as with other armies, we learnt that the frontline chap was OK but it was those that came after who were less than desirable'.

The rear-echelon troops that most 8th Army captives encountered were generally Italian. One prisoner noted that, soon after being taken by the Italians, 'we were subjected to systematic thieving and looting'. As they journeyed through its prisoner system the captured 8th Army men discovered much about the inefficiencies of the Italian state – whether that was in the provision of supplies, delays to shipping or the woeful organisation of its army. In this sense they shared anger and frustration at things that were already only too well known to the Germans or indeed the rank and file of the Italian army.

Corporal Harry Finlayson, like Captain Stone one of A Squadron, 5th Tanks, had been taken at Sidi Rezegh the previous November and endured the fate that many prisoners dreaded when being conveyed across the Mediterranean in Italian transports. His ship was torpedoed by the Royal Navy, leaving him washed up on a beach half dead. 'We were kicked and slapped and beaten with rifle butts by the Italian guards who found us,' he recalled. After being taken to a camp near Brindisi in southern Italy, Finlayson endured 'terrible hunger and thirst'.

Finlayson and his comrades from their knocked-out Honey initially stayed together, working as forced labour building shore defences for the Italians. At rest in their camp, 'very often you would sit down and reminisce and you'd think, If only my radio aerial hadn't been blown off, I would have got back. But then if I'd carried on fighting I probably would have been killed.' Many of the prisoners developed a hearty contempt for the Italians. The little respect entertained for them on the battlefield was further eroded by poor administration, slender rations and beatings once in captivity. Corporal Finlayson's wife was initially told he was missing, then on Christmas Day 1941 received a telegram informing her that her husband had been killed in action. It was well into 1942 before she finally learned that he was a prisoner of war, by which time she had been in receipt of a war widow's pension for several months.

Many other prisoners were given nothing to do in Italy, so simply sat around in badly run, unsanitary camps. 'We were not looked after well,' a captured trooper in 5th Tanks related. 'We weren't allowed to exercise or keep clean so soon we were covered with bugs, fleas and lice – we would borrow a cigarette so that we could burn the lice out of our clothing.' For this soldier, like Corporal Finlayson, it took months for his family to find out that he was still alive. His fate was only confirmed when they received a pro forma postcard given to prisoners of war by the

Vatican as part of its humanitarian work and returned to Britain via the Red Cross.

Many men succumbed to what was referred to as 'Prisoneritis', which Brian Stone described:

> During the first days everyone sat or walked in groups, exchanging stories of their capture and discussing the battle just ended. Those discussions were endless, and yet they got us nowhere. Everyone was very bitter and sad about the defeat, casting about for explanations of it ... [Prisoneritis] lasts about three weeks at its highest pitch then gradually relaxes its hold on the victim until it is no more than a dormant sore that can be rubbed into painful activity by fresh contacts with things like newly taken prisoners, meetings with old friends, or fresh bad news.

Underlying these feelings was a sense of guilt. For Stone, there were endless replays of the events of 6 July: the loss of his friend Rawlins, of his esteemed driver – and father of four – Trooper Ryder, and of others under his command. It had taken long enough for the regular soldiers in his battalion to trust Stone with the command of a troop, and what had he done with it? Some shared his feeling of responsibility for costing men their lives, others that they had failed their comrades in the battalion or might have done more. Many knew only too well that they were no longer able to play their part in the great cause of defeating their enemy. As the summer wore on they were able to pick up some news from Italian papers that were brought into the camp. Sometimes Allied communiqués were printed, and it was from these that the prisoners learned that the desert battle was reaching its climax in Egypt.

10

THE TIDE TURNS

In the days after Gazala, the 5th Royal Tank Regiment, and the 8th Army more generally, once again started to pick up the pieces. This time, however, things were fated to be different. It started with leadership.

The 5th Tanks were, in August 1942, getting used to their new commanding officer, Lieutenant-Colonel Walter Hutton. Like many an officer of his generation, Hutton went by a nickname rather than the name his parents had given him. The soldiers, taking another bandleader, Jim Hutton, as their inspiration, called the new boss Gentleman Jim or Fearless Jim. By this stage of the war, the men of the battalion had sufficient experience of tank warfare to make them a difficult lot to impress. The most significant factors proved to be courage, energy and a bond of common experience as to what worked on the battlefield and what did not.

Gazala had shown once again the gruelling nature of modern warfare. It was a young man's game, and Hutton had succeeded to command the regiment at thirty. His predecessors had been significantly older: Robbie Uniacke was thirty-six when he was killed, and Dinham Drew had relinquished command at forty-six. Tall and wiry, Hutton wore the typical British officers' moustache and the right spirit of determination for rebuilding his battalion.

When it came to courage, Hutton had won the Military Cross in Palestine during the 1936 revolt and the Bar during Gazala while leading a squadron of the 3rd Tanks. The nickname Fearless Jim made reference to the RTR motto, 'Fearnaught', but Hutton's courage had little to do with rashness. He had learnt all the tactical lessons the 5th's NCO tank commanders like Sergeants Hall and Bull or Corporal Solomon knew only too well.

While Hutton embodied traditional military virtues, his methods of command owed much to modernity. With soldiers isolated in their tanks, many hardly knew anyone outside their troop, let alone the squadron. Their connection to the wider world of the battalion was through the radio. All members of the crew usually wore headsets, because it was through these that they heard their vehicle commander give instructions. This also made them party to what was being said over the radio net, although few young crewmen would have had the courage to press the 'send' button and actually speak on it.

In this sense, the 5th Tanks was different from most regiments in the Royal Armoured Corps (in this context the terms 'regiment' or 'battalion' meant the same in British usage, a group of squadrons commanded by a lieutenant colonel), which operated a system in which each squadron kept to its own frequency or net, and the couple of officers who ran it had two radios in their tanks, one tuned to the squadron net and the other to the regimental frequency where the different commanders could speak to their overall boss. The 5th Tanks had everyone on the regimental net, a method they had used since the early days of the North African campaign. Its disadvantage was that with around sixty stations tuned to the same frequency – the tanks of three squadrons as well as the supporting infantry company commander, artillery battery commander, the echelon commanding officer and so on – in a fast-moving battle, any lack of discipline might see the system descend into chaos. For if one tank piped up, perhaps panicked because it had just been hit, its commander might jam out the Commanding Officer in the middle of important orders, stopping everyone else from hearing those instructions. The great advantage of the regimental net system was that it kept everyone in the know. If, for example, one squadron was reporting that it had sighted the enemy, the rest of the regiment would be aware of it and, knowing the formation they were in, would understand from which direction danger emanated, and which of their comrades might soon be in need of support.

With wireless communication it was often a matter of less is more. Hutton understood this perfectly. 'We all had great faith in him, he knew what he was doing, he never shouted, he always asked for advice as to what happening,' said once NCO in C Squadron. 'We knew he'd got his finger on the button, it was apparent that he knew what he was doing. He had a great respect for us and we had a great respect for him.'

After months in which the army had driven hither and yon in the desert, often confused and disorientated, Hutton used the radio net to project calm control, 'in a nice pleasant voice, just like an announcer reading the news'. He was the antithesis of the over-excited cavalry CO bellowing 'Charge!' into his microphone. Wardrop wrote of Hutton, 'The lads would have done anything for him and gone anywhere with him – if he had said we were going to make a frontal attack on the gates of hell, they would have been off like a shot.'

This type of leadership fitted very well into the wider prescription of what the 8th Army needed. Early in August, Churchill had appeared in Egypt to dismiss both the commander of the 8th Army and his boss, General Sir Claude Auchinleck, Commander-in-Chief of British forces in the Middle East. After the first choice to command the 8th Army was killed in a plane crash, Lieutenant-General Bernard Montgomery was hurriedly summoned out to the Middle East to do the job, which he took over on 13 August 1942.

Montgomery had many qualities: he was famed as a trainer of soldiers, was decisive, self-confident to the point of arrogance and had shown a good eye for separating the winners in the British army officer corps from its dross. His faults were to become as legendary as his qualities, but at this point he was one of the few officers of proven ability who could have led the 8th Army without being intimidated either by Rommel's reputation or the tasks ahead.

Taking over the army, Montgomery was shocked to find preparations underway for a defence of the Delta, and a general withdrawal should Rommel beat them on the Alamein position. The senior officers appeared confused and intimidated by their German opponent, and indeed mention of Rommel's name had at one point been banned by Auchinleck. Addressing the staff of 8th Army on the evening of his arrival, Montgomery told them,

I do not like the atmosphere I find here. It is an atmosphere of doubt, of looking back to select the next place to which to withdraw ... all that must now cease ... here we will stand and fight; there will be no further withdrawal. I have ordered that all plans and instructions dealing with withdrawal are to be burnt ... if anyone thinks it can't be done, let him go at once; I don't want any doubters in this party . . . I understand Rommel is expected to attack at any moment. Excellent. Let him attack.

Having described graphically the change of atmosphere that he wanted to bring about, the general told his audience, 'You must see that atmosphere permeates right down through the 8th Army to the most junior private soldier. All the soldiers must know what is wanted.'

The spreading of the commander's plan through the entire army became a hallmark of Montgomery's command – and many would have argued that it had already been achieved by the Germans, who wanted any NCO to be able to take over the task of his officer if he fell in battle. It was in this very aspect that Hutton, through his manner and use of the regimental net, was perfectly in tune with Montgomery's new atmosphere. Even the most junior trooper in 5th Tanks already knew what was wanted, if they were listening through their headphones.

Lieutenant-Colonel Hutton's standing in the 5th Tanks grew not just because of his adoption of these command methods, but because he was so candid with the men about the dilemmas facing him as a commander. In the 'up or out' culture that had spread through the British officer corps after the war's early set-backs, commanding officers were under intense pressure from their superiors to achieve results. The more ambitious ones might even seek missions that they knew would involve sacrificing their men. One 5th Tanks NCO recalled hearing a talk from Hutton when he told his men that he had managed to steer them clear of disaster. 'I keep getting away with it,' Hutton said, 'but there may be a time when I can't get away with it.' The corporal who heard these words reflected, 'he was almost apologising for us having to be there . . . a lovely man'. Here was evidence of some-thing recognised more widely among the younger generation of officers: Hutton's brand of honesty paid great dividends with citizen soldiers.

In the chain of command that stretched upwards from squadron to battalion to brigade, division, corps and then 8th Army, those at the top and bottom were now in tune both in the prescription of 'no more retreats' and in the methods being used to communicate it. But what about the levels in between? So often during the Crusader battles of the previous November, or those of the Gazala Line just a few months before, the 5th Tanks had either sat idle or been thrown into costly, ill-thought-out missions. Their generals at these higher levels of command had been painfully slow to react to events, indecisive, and had frequently played out personal rivalries at the army's expense. As far as the ordinary tankie was concerned, many had also not grasped the futility of Balaklava charges, throwing tanks forward, often to costly failure. Skilful commanders were at a premium, but here too change had arrived at last.

The 5th Tanks had by this time been switched to a different brigade, the 22nd Armoured. This formation had made a disastrous desert debut in November 1941 with the charge of its yeomanry regiments against the Italians. By the summer of 1942 it was so battered that it had to be remade. The remnants of one regiment, the 2nd Royal Gloucestershire Hussars, were folded into 5th Tanks, while the 4th County of London Yeomanry absorbed a sister regiment and the 1st RTR was brought in. The motorised infantry battalion was the 1st Rifle Brigade, and there was a regiment of Royal Horse Artillery too. Holding most of the army's surviving Grants as it did, the 22nd Armoured was called, in some quarters, Egypt's Last Hope.

The brigade commander also exemplified the 'younger and fitter' model. 'Pip' Roberts, whom Hutton knew very well as a former Commanding Officer of 3rd Tanks, had been made the brigadier at the age of thirty-five. Small, snub-nosed and fair-haired, Roberts cut a contrasting physical presence to the taller Hutton, but the two men were in tune tactically. Roberts was the brighter intellect, a gifted staff officer whom the exigencies of war had elevated to lead his brigade of several thousand soldiers after just eight months in command of 3rd RTR. Roberts represented a different generation from men such as Alec Gatehouse, the Great War veteran who had commanded the 5th RTR's brigade during Operation Crusader, being quicker to appreciate a situation and react accordingly.

The 22nd Armoured Brigade had been placed in a key sector of the army's Alamein defence, called Alam Halfa. It was widely expected that Rommel would execute an enveloping movement from the south, as he had three months earlier at Gazala, before pushing north to isolate the forward lines. The low hills at the Alamein position did not present the kind of formidable obstacle to movement that could be found further west at Halfaya, but they did provide natural strongpoints around which minefields and other defences could be organised more effectively than they had been at the Gazala Line. The Alam Halfa ridge, running roughly east–west, formed a roadblock in the path of the expected Axis movement from the interior to the sea. In a desert that was generally monotonously flat, by occupying the distinct scarp present at Alam Halfa its defenders would be able to look down on an advancing enemy forced to drive across miles of open desert, while keeping 22nd Brigade's tanks hidden from view. Within days of taking command, Roberts was visited by Lieutenant-General Montgomery, whom he did not at first recognise, since the new commander was not yet a public figure nor had he been serving with the desert army. They toured Roberts's positions and the new 8th Army commander was pleased by what he found. For his part, the brigadier absorbed the message of his new master, circulating a secret memo to

Lieutenant-Colonel Hutton and his other commanding officers on 24 August, which told them that an attack by Rommel was expected within days, and reminded them of the brigade's mission and that 'it is essential that all ranks should know these plans and, most important of all, that they should know that no withdrawal from our present position is even contemplated'.

Under the Montgomery regime a style of command that was often remote, mysterious and ill-explained ended. In its place came something better suited to smart, motivated soldiers in a citizen army. 'Griff talks' would be given regularly, in which the commanders' views of the bigger picture and the role of their soldiers within it would be explained. Brigadier Roberts insisted that 'inspiration comes from the officers and officers must assemble their men and talk to them . . . the plan is sound and will not be altered and if this is realised by all ranks it cannot fail'. Under the new order, the commander of the 8th Army might address his commanders at battalion level directly, bypassing the corps and divisional generals, or let his thoughts trickle down the normal chain of command via a series of Griff talks. Getting ideas across was deemed more important than observance of hierarchy. As they stood ready to meet the expected onslaught, Roberts's brigade was visited by the Prime Minister, the Chief of the Imperial General Staff, and once more by Montgomery. Lieutenant-Colonel Hutton met Churchill, and was observed speaking to him for some time by the men. As they prepared to meet the expected German onslaught it could hardly have been clearer how much was at stake and that the eyes of their country were upon them.

During the early hours of 31 August 1942, forward elements of 22nd Brigade sighted the Germans moving north. British intelligence, mainly from intercepted signals, had pinpointed the time and place of this thrust with considerable precision. The Germans, having negotiated British minefields and got out into what they assumed was clear desert, were heading for an ambush, being shadowed all the time by reconnaissance squadrons in front of the Alam Halfa ridge.

Brigadier Roberts was prepared to meet them. His armoured regiments were arrayed along raised ground from his left to right: 5th Tanks, 4th County of London Yeomanry, 1st Tanks. Bulldozers had scraped out firing positions that would allow the Grants to engage with their 75mm guns while protecting the lower part of the tank from return fire. In some broken ground to the front of 1st Tanks, the anti-tank guns of the Rifle Brigade and Royal Horse Artillery had been cleverly hidden. They had six-pounder (or 57mm) weapons, excellent high-velocity cannons that had proven themselves during the Gazala battles and were now appearing in increasing numbers. At the other end of the brigade's position, at the rear of the 5th Tanks and shielded by the curve of the ground, was a battery of twenty-five-pounders belonging to the 1st Royal Horse Artillery. Behind all of that, in reserve, were the Scots Greys, another armoured regiment that had been loaned to Roberts for the battle. They had all moved into their positions in darkness and were on radio silence to avoid detection. Roberts's commanders called in to him by field telephones, with lines laid back to brigade HQ.

At Point 102, atop the ridge, Roberts watched the forward German elements heading towards his position: 'Now I can see the enemy myself through my glasses. They are coming straight up the line of telegraph posts which lead in front of our position.' The spearhead or leading element of 15th Panzer Division was making directly for them. His own people were lying low, with orders not to open fire until the enemy was within a thousand yards. And then the Germans stopped, evidently scrutinising the rocky ridge in front of them. The head of the column then started to turn to its right, or eastwards. Had they spotted something, or were they just adjusting position to keep to the centre line of their

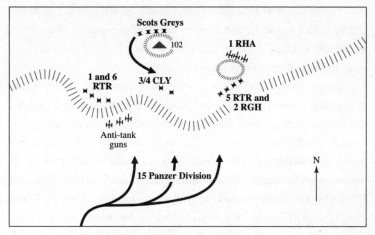

THE BATTLE OF ALAM HALFA

advance? It was already nearly six o'clock in the evening and a tense day's waiting in position was coming to its crisis. Roberts did not know what to do, because he feared they might move eastwards past his well-prepared defence, parallel to the ridge and into the area of another brigade. He orders some Grants to move out of their prepared scrapes to attract the Germans' attention.

Without knowing whether they had been seen, he toyed with the idea of sending the Grants down to attack the German flank when the column stopped again, this time turning directly towards his position and only twelve hundred yards away. Roberts spotted that the spearhead of the advance was made up of Mk IV Specials, tanks armed with the latest long-barrelled, high-velocity 75mm gun, and would have been aware that these tanks, and the Mk III Specials, could make short work of Grants. But it was too late, the leading German tanks were now just a thousand yards away. The Yeomanry reported they could count eighty-seven enemy tanks; the 5th RTR commanders counted seventy. And then the crump of high-velocity gunfire began, the enemy firing first.

'Before we start firing we lose a tank,' recorded a Grant troop commander from the County of London Yeomanry. 'Heydey 1 is on fire and he is bailing out. He has a dead man in his tank and one or two wounded.'

'Now everyone opened up,' wrote one 5th Tanks Grant crewman, 'the 75 mm of the tanks, the anti-tank 6-pounders, and the RHA with their 25-pounders over open sights. As a wireless operator all I could do was sit beside the driver and watch through his visor, while I listened to reports from other tanks which were reporting hits or of being hit.'

Under fire from the Mk IVs, the yeomanry's Grant squadron was losing its battle. Their tanks began to burn, all twelve of them knocked out in a matter of minutes. But the Germans were also losing armour. Some of their tanks were knocked out by six-pounders just a few hundred yards in front of them. The action was reminiscent of that fought by the 5th Tanks on 2 June, for while the Germans focused on enemy tanks, trying to close the distance for a better shot, they missed the concealed British anti-tank guns right in front of them.

The 15th Panzer continued coming forward, but slowly, and stopped close to the foot of the ridge. Some of the six-pounders had been overrun by that time, but others were firing away heroically at ranges of just a few hundred yards. The German commander had lost enough Mk IVs to know he was in trouble. He ordered a couple of companies to explore around to his right, where 5th Tanks held their positions. In response, Roberts countered by sending the Scots Greys to move down the slope, filling the gaps between the burning yeomanry tanks and feeding the battle.

'Here they come, Five, hold your fire a bit longer,' ordered Fearless Jim over the radio. 'Now! Let them have it!' The 5th's Grants opened up with better results than the yeomanry, brewing several panzers. But still the Germans tried to push on in the failing light, some of their reconnaissance vehicles making it through around the left of the 5th and towards the RHA's gun line. Half a dozen German tanks had reached a line barely a thousand yards from Point 102 and the brigadier's command post when, in the dusk, A Squadron caught up with them. The intruders were knocked out. In the centre of the brigade, the Scots Greys had stabilised the situation.

Burning German tanks were arrayed in front of the Alam Halfa position, with tracer zipping back and forth between the two sides. As it became completely dark the Germans pulled back a few hundred yards. Their first attack had failed. The darkness under which they had hoped to recover their damaged armour and regroup was short-lived as RAF planes dropped powerful flares, illuminating their targets for bombing strikes.

Rommel was dealing with fearsome logistical problems. His armour was running low on fuel, his artillery was rationed in the number of rounds it could fire and the RAF was making serious inroads on his supply convoys. Just as the Italian advance of two years earlier had lengthened its own supply lines and shortened those of the British, so too at this moment the advantages enjoyed by Rommel's enemy began to stack up, not least in cutting the flying time for many RAF squadrons based in the Delta.

On 1 September the 15th Panzer Division made further attacks on the 5th Tanks sector of the Alam Halfa position. In one or two places vehicles pushed onto the ridge, but the British were not in serious danger. A second attack had faltered.

'Next morning,' wrote Rommel, 'between ten and twelve o'clock we were bombed no less than six times by British air-craft ... swarms of low-flying fighter bombers were coming back to the attack again and again and my troops suffered tremendous casualties. Vast numbers of vehicles stood burning in the desert.' The 4th Armoured Brigade, sweeping along in its

Honeys, raided German supply lines to the south of the Alam Halfa position, destroying scores of trucks. The German field marshal broke off the attack, inveighing against the Italian failure to get enough supplies through to him and the Luftwaffe's inability to protect him. If Lieutenant-Colonel Hutton's men had been able to talk to their mates who had already fallen into captivity, they could have told them from their own bitter experience that Rommel was not simply making excuses when he blamed the Italians upon whom he relied for much of his logistic support.

In the 5th Tanks the men knew that Alam Halfa marked a sea change. They had knocked out plenty of German tanks before, but with little difference made to the bigger picture. 'We had heard of a change in command,' wrote one trooper of B Squadron, 5th Tanks, 'but as this had happened in the past with little or no effect, we took very little notice. Over the ten days or so that we were involved in the battle there was little time to think about new commanders. But now it was different.' In the days after Alam Halfa preparations intensified, with Montgomery mandating physical training every morning for his army. As they readied themselves for the next round of fighting, 'the colonel came to each squadron and told us personally what the General required, and also that he would in future from time to time be giving us talks on the situation and what would be expected of us in any future attack'.

'It is impossible to exaggerate the difference to morale which this policy made,' said another conscripted tank trooper who ended up in the 5th RTR, 'for the rank and file intentions became "ours" and not "theirs". There was no particular adulation of Montgomery but here was a man who knew what to do and took the trouble to explain this to the people who would carry it out.'

Digesting the lessons of the battle, Brigadier Roberts

circulated two papers to his commanding officers, outlining his views. He reflected on the power of the Mk IV Special in out-ranging the Grants, and how it might be countered by use of the six-pounder anti-tank gun. He also sought to prepare his battal-ions for the moment when they would assume the offensive. Referring to the bitter experiences of the previous year, Roberts acknowledged that 'in the minds of many, as far as armour is con-cerned, this immediately implies a series of Balaklava charges, albeit supported by artillery. These tactics ... will only be resorted to in extremis.' Instead, the pattern for the type of offen-sive he envisaged was something that might have been familiar to Wellington, as the brigadier explained: 'We intend to move from one position to another and make the enemy attack us in ground of our own choosing.'

After Rommel pulled back, Montgomery and his staff knew well enough that the Axis forces would not simply give up the game. Mussolini and Hitler expected the British to be finished off in Egypt, even if they were unable to provide the resources to achieve this aim with ease. For his part, the new British com-mander had ambitious plans to form a third command within the 8th Army, the so-called *corps de chasse*. His intention was to com-bine two armoured divisions recently deployed in the Middle East (the 8th and 10th) with an infantry one. He intended to hold Rommel on the Alamein line, retaining the new corps as a mobile reserve, and then, once he had exhausted his enemy, throw it forward as the spearhead of a new British offensive. This was how superior Allied numbers would be used to clinch and then exploit victory.

Would the men who had just won Alam Halfa be part of this? Headquarters 8th Army knew they were exhausted and had just lost dozens of tanks in the late battle. The normal procedure would have been to pull them back to the Delta for refitting. Calling the battalion together, Hutton told the men who squinted at him in the sunlight that everyone who wanted to stay in the desert and continue the fight should take one pace forward; those who couldn't face it should stay put. At the given moment, the entire 5th RTR stepped up. 'Only those who have experienced a similar decision being resolutely taken by such a large body of men', wrote one member of C Squadron, 'will understand the emotional pride felt by everyone concerned.'

Notwithstanding this grim determination to see it through, the 7th Armoured Division – the Desert Rats – which Roberts's brigade (including the 5th Tanks) joined once more, was not due to play a big part in the battle Montgomery was planning. They were not, for example, the division chosen to receive the three hundred new Sherman tanks that had been shipped from America. Instead they were to take their place near the southern end of the Alamein line, acting as a reserve and moving forward through British minefields when the time for a general offensive came. Much of late September and early October 1942 was therefore spent training for this breakthrough battle, as well as absorbing new men and equipment to bring them up to strength again.

Time and again the battalion, brigade and division rehearsed aspects of the fight that lay ahead. Lieutenant-Colonel Hutton had constructed a sand table or model of the terrain that would lie to their front, briefing his squadron commanders, officers and eventually all tank commanders on what to do.

Montgomery expected the Axis forces to exhaust themselves attacking the Alamein line of defences. He then intended to use fresh divisions to take the offensive. The main blows would be struck in the north, close to the sea, by other divisions. The Desert Rats' role would be to help pin the enemy to the south, breaching minefields to their front when the time was right in order to attack.

In the plan they rehearsed, the 7th Armoured Division would

move forward five miles before fighting through two minefields. The first, codenamed January, would be tackled by 22nd Armoured Brigade, led by sappers and supported by the rest of the combined arms team. Four lanes would be cleared, one of which would be 5th RTR's responsibility. Once this had been achieved, the division's motor brigade (i.e. infantry heavy) would pass through the breaches in January, moving a couple of miles westwards to tackle the second minefield, 'February'.

Briefings also detailed the enemy forces they could expect to meet in the southern part of the front. The Italian Folgore Parachute Division sat on the Desert Rats' main objectives, fielding 3440 men and twenty-four anti-tank guns. It was a well-regarded force, as were the mobile reserves available to come to its help, the German 21st Panzer and Italian Ariete divisions.

At nine o'clock on the morning of 23 October Lieutenant-Colonel Hutton briefed his regiment on the operation they were about to perform, outlining in standard army form relevant information, their intention and their method, before moving on to administrative matters. When he got to 'intention' he stated baldly, 'The German Afrika Korps and the Italian Libyan Army will be destroyed.' His listeners knew better than anyone that there was a world of difference between stating such a thing and achieving it, but their confidence in Fearless Jim ran high. The 5th would take twenty-four Grants (twelve each in B and C Squadrons) and eighteen Crusader tanks (A Squadron) into action. Several of the Crusaders had been equipped with the same six-pounder anti-tank gun that had been used to such good effect at Alam Halfa – compensation to some extent for the loss of the reliable Honeys that they had grown so fond of.

By the early hours of 24 October, halfway through the mine-field breach, they were learning just how tough it could be. The British offensive had been launched with a huge artillery barrage and the men could hardly sleep with the excitement of what lay

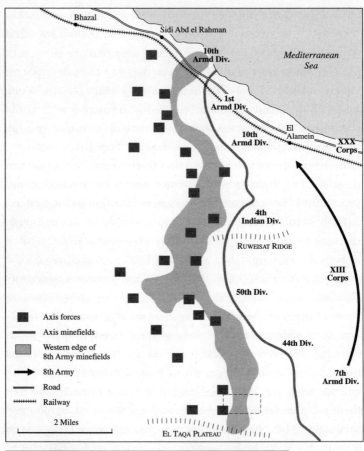

Bhazal
Sidi Abd el Rahman
10th Armd Div.
Mediterranean Sea
1st Armd Div.
El Alamein
10th Armd Div.
XXX Corps
4th Indian Div.
RUWEISAT RIDGE
XIII Corps
50th Div.
44th Div.
7th Armd Div.

◼ Axis forces
— Axis minefields
▨ Western edge of 8th Army minefields
➤ 8th Army
— Road
++++++ Railway

2 Miles

EL TAQA PLATEAU

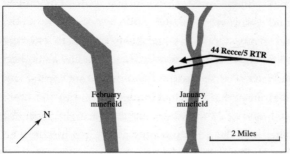

44 Recce/5 RTR

February minefield
January minefield

N

2 Miles

ALAMEIN

ahead. But they had soon learned that enough of the Italian parachutists survived the shell fire to crew their 47mm anti-tank guns to good effect.

As B Squadron came through into the gap between the two enemy minefields, 'the "Baker" tank of our troop was just taking up position to our left when there was a loud explosion, and smoke and flames poured from it'. They had been knocked out by one of the Italian guns. With daylight appearing, machine-gun fire and high explosive was poured onto the Italians in their trenches. For their part, the enemy guns were zeroed on this ground and from ten past five 'very heavy shelling had started' on 22nd Armoured Brigade, 'and it continued all day'. For many of the tankies this meant staying closed up for many hours, their sensations of the fight ranging around them coming through the thick glass of their vision blocks or the sweaty headphones clamped to their ears.

For some, including Major Paddy Doyle, the commander of C Squadron, this partial view was not good enough. He kept his head and shoulders out of his tank, taking in the battlefield all the time, and eschewing a helmet as the battalion had since France. Perhaps inevitably, it was not long before he collapsed down into the turret, his head pierced by shrapnel from an enemy airburst shell. Jake Wardrop, who was driving the major, and Stan Skeels tried to patch up Doyle's wounds as best they could. They called on the radio for the Medical Officer, but he was stuck on the other side of the minefield. Having tried initially to bandage Major Doyle on the ground beside the Grant, Jake and the others soon thought better of it, as shrapnel and bullets whizzed about their ears. They heaved their commander back into the tank, setting off back through the January minefield gap against the oncoming traffic in order to save his life. They got him into an ambulance, later helping themselves to the major's whisky and cigarettes for their trouble: 'I didn't think Paddy would be doing

much smoking or drinking for a while.' Then the wireless operator took command of the tank, and it headed back into the
fight.

The Italian parachutists were in a hopeless position, and by half
past eleven many had experienced enough pounding. White
flags began to appear. In places there were reports of desperate
enemy commanders trying to machine-gun those who were
giving up, but the 5th Tanks and its Rifle Brigade infantry had
soon gathered two hundred Italian prisoners and seven anti-tank
guns. The January minefield had been successfully crossed and it
was time for the next phase of the operation to begin.

Fighting through the February minefield proved an even
tougher proposition but, fortunately for the 5th, it was not their
job. The division's infantry brigade had to do it, supported by the
4th County of London Yeomanry. Facing enemy armoured
counter-attacks, the yeomanry took another hiding, losing many
of its tanks. By 26 October the initial phase of Montgomery's
Alamein offensive was over and a day of rest decreed for the
22nd Armoured Brigade.

Elsewhere, things had proven stickier than the 8th Army
expected. To the north, in the area close to the sea where their
main effort had gone in, the Highland Division had taken heavy
casualties in the breakthrough battle, and some of the newly
fielded armoured battalions had also suffered considerably.
Montgomery knew that it would be hard for tanks alone to
break through the dense belts of minefields, trenches and anti-
tank guns, so he deployed the northern armoured divisions in
support of infantry tasked with 'crumbling' Axis positions.
Inching forward, often under heavy fire, was a terrifying and
bloody business. After a few days of it, the infantry generals were
grumbling that their armour was not delivering the goods,
despite suffering heavy tank casualties. Having initially sidelined
the veteran 7th Armoured Division (because it was considered by

many to be battle-weary) Montgomery called upon them to come north in order to help.

On 4 November the 7th Armoured Division pushed forward, driving through the smoking remnants of newly arrived armoured regiments, the dead of Highland battalions and the panzers knocked out in Axis counter-attacks. The enemy had been ground down so effectively that only a much-battered Ariete armoured division, which had also moved north during the preceding days, was left to oppose Pip Roberts's brigade. The Italian M13 tanks were, he wrote, 'no match for our Grants and hardly equal to the Crusaders or Stuarts'. They laced the Italians with tank and artillery fire. The brigade called up its new Crusaders, armed with six-pounders, so they could get some gunnery practice. It was beginning to look like a slaughter, with Roberts noting that 'the Italians must have felt all hell had been let loose. We outgunned them so we stood back and picked them off. There was no object in closing in and getting casualties.'

In many places the Germans were now withdrawing their surviving forces, taking all available transport and thus stranding their Italian allies. Hitler attempted to countermand Rommel's order to withdraw, but it was too late. The Axis forces had lost five hundred tanks at Alamein, the British and Allies around the same number, but whereas this left the Germans with just twelve panzers by 4 November, the British still had more than six hundred. Rommel knew they could not turn to face their enemies until they had reached a defensible point. He understood also that they could not rally in time to take up the El Agheila defensive position that they had occupied twice before, and considered giving up Libya altogether, but resolved eventually to halt his forces at Wadi Zemzem, to the east of Tripoli.

A great drive forward was beginning for the British, one of those turnings of the tables that veterans of the desert war had already experienced, which seemed to place the Axis forces in an impossible position. Large numbers of prisoners were taken as the British caught up with stranded columns or broken-down transport. During the period from 23 October to late November (i.e. Alamein and the subsequent retreat past El Agheila), the Axis forces lost more than thirty-five thousand troops: 2300 killed, 5500 wounded and 27,900 prisoners. This last number emphasised how disastrous the withdrawal was for Rommel and his Italian allies. Angry recriminations raged within the Axis headquarters, for twenty thousand of the prisoners were Italians, many from infantry divisions with no motorised transport at all, and so had been quite unable to save themselves.

The 8th Army now hurled itself forward as the November rains came, and the logisticians strained every sinew to fuel the advance. The small losses of armour sustained by the 5th during the Alamein battle were quickly made up, and new people arrived too. Some were from the Royal Gloucestershire Hussars, others from the fresh divisions that had wrecked themselves during the late battle. In some cases their constituent regiments were already being broken up. The value of armoured units with desert experience had been proven once again. Arriving at the 5th Tanks from 47th RTR, a territorial unit that had come to grief in a minefield, one soldier commented: 'The 5th were a regular battalion who by this time had had to take in many non-regulars to replace casualties. Their attitude was that of professionals, with a very different atmosphere from the 47th.'

There had been attempts to raise the standard of the newly arrived battalions, not least by attaching veteran soldiers to them. Sergeant Charlie Bull had experienced Alamein with the Wiltshire Yeomanry, who had lost most of their tanks during the first few days of the operation. By mid-November he was back at Sidi Bishir, re-equipping with the yeomanry and wondering where his mates from the 5th Tanks had got to. The mood of the army had already changed, buoyed by victory. Men were already beginning to think about a way home. Charlie, being the sort of man he was, hoped to tuck into a Christmas dinner far superior to the one he'd had the previous year.

'What do you think of the 8th army now, doing well aren't they?' Sergeant Bull wrote back to Staffordshire. 'I should think they will be in Benghazi soon . . . and the farther we go up that way the nearer we get to England, it would be nice to sail from Tripoli.'

Field Marshal Rommel fumed that he had not been given the tools to finish off the 8th Army; the Axis forces had been beaten by material superiority. But at Gazala a few months earlier the British had also deployed more tanks and field guns than the Germans and Italians. The difference then was that those who led the British had squandered this advantage with ill-coordinated, piecemeal manoeuvres that simply allowed Rommel to beat them in detail. Now that different people were in charge at nearly all levels, the 8th Army's advantages were being used to full effect. They were advancing quickly, and Lieutenant-Colonel 'Fearless Jim' Hutton drove his people as hard as any to reap the rewards of the late victory.

11

THE DRIVE TO TRIPOLI

Driving forward, Jake Wardrop spent long hours peering through the armoured hatch in the front of his Grant. Each day after Alamein brought new surprises: scenes of chaos among the retreating enemy; driving rain that suddenly arrived, turning the desert to mud; a German railway engine driver who saw the British tanks coming, unhitched his wagons and sped off west. It was a time of high spirits among the 5th Tanks, and it was also a time for paying the Boche back for some of the things that had happened during the past year.

'The bugle had blown and we couldn't stop!' the Scottish tank driver wrote in his diary. 'There were thousands and thousands of prisoners. If we happened to stop beside any, we nipped out, pinched their watches, binoculars or anything they had and carried on.'

Reaching the airfield at El Adem, about fifteen miles south of Tobruk, they surprised the Luftwaffe. The Grants opened up with 75mm high-explosive shells before the enemy gave up, Wardrop noting: 'There were not many of them to put their hands up really, because that 75 is a deadly weapon and in any case, the lads were fighting mad and, who knows, some of them may have dropped a bomb on the Clyde.'

Being survivors of so many fights, there were men who wanted revenge and others who would not take any chances. In one incident during the long advance, a group of a few dozen Italians had been so desperate to surrender that one had jumped on a Grant tank from B Squadron. The commander had shot him, and the gunner, fearing an attempt to storm the tank, had then machine-gunned the rest. Such incidents were unusual, but the attitude of many in the 5th Tanks to taking prisoners was businesslike, to say the least

The battalion pushed on, along with the 7th Armoured Division, to the scenes of its previous battles along the desert road south of the Jebel Akhdar and on to Agheila. Montgomery knew that issues of logistics prevented a headlong rush after the Axis forces, for there had been times in the days since Alamein when his advance had run out of fuel. Work progressed swiftly to restore the railway to Tobruk, and to reopen Tobruk's port and that of Benghazi to supply ships.

Exhaustion showed itself in the 8th Army's long-serving formations. By the end of November the 5th Tanks had just eight working Grants and three Crusaders. These machines had already been showing signs of wear when the regiment fought at Alam Halfa three months earlier, and since then they had motored hundreds of miles. The battalion was pulled back to a camp near Tobruk to refit. There followed some weeks in which the precise shape and equipment that the 5th RTR would take on changed several times. At one point they were to convert to the new

Sherman tank; at another, they were to be rebuilt to a strength of thirty Grants and twenty-two Crusaders.

The war in Africa had entered a new phase. The Allies had started landing (mainly American) troops in Algeria on 10 November. This spelt doom for the seventy thousand survivors of Rommel's Alamein army because they now had an enemy to their back (or west) as well as the 8th Army to their front (east). Having rationed Rommel's war materiel for so long, Hitler decided to open the taps at the eleventh hour, despatching new German and Italian divisions to Tunisia: forces that, had they been sent earlier, might easily have clinched victory for Rommel. Among the new armoured forces shipped over were small numbers of the new Tiger tank, a fifty-seven-ton monster armed with the dreaded 88. Multiple rocket launcher units were deployed with the *Nebelwerfer*, a trailer-mounted weapon originally designed to lay smoke screens but which could also lob high explosive projectiles with an awful, morale-sapping noise that caused the British to christen them Moaning Minnies. Effectively, though, this late reinforcement could barely compensate for the losses suffered at Alamein and the change in the balance of forces following the landings in Algeria. On 8 December Rommel had written to his fourteen-year-old son, 'If it goes on like this, we shall be crushed by the enemy's immense superiority.'

For the 5th RTR the new phase of the campaign meant several things. They would not be going back to Cairo or Alexandria. Many of them had been in the desert since March, and little imagined then that they had already enjoyed their last leave back in the Delta. Home somehow seemed to be getting closer too, that was their constant thought, and the road there lay ahead of them, not behind in Egypt.

As far as Wardrop's interests were concerned, the fact that he would not be returning to the Golden Bar and other drinking haunts was a good thing. He had been fighting continuously for many months, which kept him happy and also steered him clear of leave-time trouble. Jake had managed to hold on to his corporal's stripes and to the job of driving the squadron commander, a coveted post for the major's crew were always among the best men in the squadron. Now, promotion to tank commander was in the offing for Wardrop.

Christmas was celebrated with a special shipment of turkey, pork, vegetables and beer. Many men took their chance to get hopelessly drunk. Although Jake had not been able to hold on to his guitar during the desert campaigns, he and the others rarely missed the chance for a song. Modifying the lyrics of popular songs had become something of a pastime for the 5th Tanks. Many an hour sitting stood to in the tank or grinding their way along some stony track was spent by the tank crews lost in thought about how the words might be adapted to their own situation.

Some of these lyrics were barely modified references to sweethearts and homes far away, others were more explicit and some simply attempted to raise a few smiles at the mention of shared experiences. The tune to 'Home on the Range', familiar to the soldiers from westerns and concert parties, was given these new words:

O give me a home where no Jerry tanks roam
Where no Mark IVs or armoured cars stray
Where flap is a word that seldom is heard
And no Stukas and Messerschmitts play

O give me a land where there's no blinking sand
To get into your ears and your stew
Where no B echelon with another flap on
Goes screaming out into the blue

For I'd rather exchange the thirty yards' range
And a couple of cities quite near
And instead of this war we would watch Arsenal score
And replenish ourselves with more beer.

The army's Christmas present to 5th RTR took the form of Sherman tanks, which started arriving on 16 December. The Chrysler Tank Arsenal was pumping them out by the thousand each month, and the battalion was soon familiarising itself with the new machine. One RTR officer described the arrival of the Shermans as 'a tremendous boost to our morale'. The Sherman shared many parts in common with the Grant, from its suspension assemblies to the 75mm gun. At twenty-eight tons the Sherman weighed a little more than its predecessor but the level of armoured protection was similar. The real advantage was in the layout of the new tank's fighting compartment – the place where the tankies fought their battles.

Shifting to the Sherman meant reducing the crew from six men to five. The new tank mounted its 75mm gun in the turret, which was a much better arrangement. It allowed the commander to show much less of the tank to the enemy when he took up a hull-down firing position, and enabled the crew to turn the weapon quickly through 360 degrees. Wireless operators much preferred the Sherman because they were moved up next to the commander from a position in the Grant's hull where they could see little (and had to squeeze themselves up into the turret in order to retune the wireless set). The wireless operator on the Sherman loaded the main gun, and also had his own turret hatch next to the commander's. This last change proved very important to the matter of self-preservation: not only could he get out faster, but the wireless operator could add his own eyes to those of the commander in scanning the horizon for the tell-tale flash of an anti-tank gun firing or some other danger up ahead.

The crews gave the Sherman a positive reception for all these reasons. Alas for them, the army's initial shipment of the new vehicles was not followed by any further Shermans until months later, so B and C Squadrons prepared to go into action in 1943 with a mixture of Grants and Shermans. During the early part of January preparations for the next phase of the battle were continuous. Lieutenant-Colonel Hutton followed the same methods he had before Alamein, briefing first the squadron leaders, then all vehicle commanders and finally giving Griff talks to the battalion as a whole. Each set-piece operation to breach an Axis defence line contained an appraisal of the risks ahead. The Germans had already shown their skill with rearguard actions. In many places a well-sited anti-tank gun or mines had brought the British to a halt. Now they were preparing to assault a more formal defence of lines a few dozen miles to the east of Tripoli.

On 14 January 1943 they moved off at last to breach the Tripoli defences. The 7th Armoured Division led the advance, and Monty's 'Tac HQ' – the small headquarters that he used near the front line – went with them. The tankies were under the eye of their master, and indeed by this point Montgomery had started wearing an RTR beret with his general's badge fixed beside the tank regiment one. He had already shown a taste for unconventional headgear and for collecting the badges of his regiments, but the tank beret would prove to be a lasting indicator of his respect for the regiment.

By 16 January the division had passed through a dummy minefield and the craggy defile of Wadi Zemzem. It was an ideal place to mount a defence, and indeed the Axis forces had at one point intended to do so, but the 8th Army found little resistance there. While they had been training for far worse during the preceding weeks, there were places where rearguards with anti-tank guns, machine-gun nests and artillery in support did put up a fight. So while the armoured division pushed forward, some battalions had a harder time of it.

The 5th Seaforths in the Highland Division, for example, found themselves in a hard-fought night action on 21–22 January. They were pinned down for hours by three machine-gun nests and a sniper. When, shortly after dawn, the Germans bailed out of their positions fearing they were about to be out-flanked, the Scottish battalion counted the cost: six officers and seventy-five men killed or wounded. It was a sobering lesson in what a few determined defenders – perhaps just one dozen Germans in this instance – could do.

A few hours after this action, the 5th Tanks took the lead of the 7th Armoured Division, pushing to the Tripoli ring road. Just short of it, the familiar flash and ripping sound of an anti-tank round greeted them. The tanks moved into defensive positions and some Shermans from B Squadron began what was called a 'snipe shoot', trying to pick off the enemy gun positions with high-explosive shells. When the enemy fire slackened the tanks pushed on again and by half past four on the morning of the 23rd they were at the city gates. Lieutenant-Colonel Hutton and some officers went ahead to recce. They had taken the capital of Libya three months to the day after the opening of the Alamein offensive, having advanced 1400 miles.

It took a few days to secure the city, then rumours abounded that there would be a parade to mark the 8th Army's success. There were jokes that the first supply ship into Tripoli would be carrying boot polish and Blanco so the battle-weary soldiers might smarten themselves up. For the 5th Tanks, an officer, sixty men and a handful of tanks were detailed to join the parade. The men wore battledress (khaki serge jackets and trousers), black berets and whitened belts, holsters and puttees. The whole party was duly assembled on 3 February in the city's majestic colonial square.

'The drill and turnout by the 5th R.T.R. was perfect despite the months since any drill,' remarked one recently joined member of B Squadron who took part. 'If there had to be a ceremonial occasion the 5th would ensure it was done properly. This was pride in the unit.'

Churchill appeared in an RAF uniform on the saluting dais. With him were Montgomery (wearing his RTR beret), General Harold Alexander (the overall Commander-in-Chief Middle East), General Sir Alan Brooke (Chief of the Imperial General Staff, i.e. head of the army), and Lieutenant-General Bernard Freyberg (an indomitable New Zealander, representing the wider Empire effort).

The Highland Division took pride of place, marching behind their massed pipes, as the 8th Army celebrated its success. The effect on every spectator was undoubtedly electric, but for the men taking the salute it stirred deep emotions: at last, after the disasters of Dunkirk, the fall of Singapore to the Japanese and the Gazala battles of six months earlier, there was something to cheer about.

'I felt a large lump rise in my throat and a tear run down my face,' wrote General Brooke of the Highlanders marching past. 'I looked around at Winston and saw several tears on his face, from which I knew that he was being stirred inwardly by the same feelings that were causing such upheaval in me ... I was beginning to live through those first successes that were now rendering ultimate victory possible.'

Churchill gave an address to the soldiers, the text of which was then printed and circulated to the many who were not there. He congratulated them on their feats of arms, and shared with them some of the planning for the final defeat of the Axis powers in North Africa. He thanked them on behalf of the country before ending:

After the war, when a man is asked what he did it will be quite sufficient for him to say, 'I marched and fought with the Desert Army.' And when history is written and all the facts are known our feats will gleam and glow and will be a source of song and story long after we who are gathered here have passed away.

Quite a few of those who heard Churchill's words regarded them as political hokum, commenting that the old man would have his cigar and brandy and would go home the next day, whereas many fights still awaited them. But the message that they had made a great contribution to the war effort did sink in, as did the Prime Minister's insistence that each night they pitched their tents they did so nearer home.

By the time Churchill's party flew on to Algeria to meet senior American commanders, the advance was already resuming. The 7th Armoured Division needed a few more days to repair its vehicles and get ready for the trials ahead. The soldiers managed to visit the souks, buy souvenirs and take in a film. Jake Wardrop rooted out supplies of alcohol, befriended some Italian colonists and promised to meet up with them after the war. Within weeks Wardrop would finally go to the 'top deck', taking over command of a tank: 'I was pleased because I'd changed gear long enough.' He had joined Sergeant Henry Hall and the others in that select club of battle-hardened commanders who played the key role in driving the 5th RTR forward.

The army that launched itself towards Tunisia was a veteran force that had been buoyed in its confidence by months of continued advance. The spirit of friendly rivalry was intensifying between its squadrons and regiments; each competed to cross the finishing line that now seemed to appear like a mirage ahead of them.

12

THE FINISHING LINE

As the British forces pushed on towards Tunisia, the atmosphere was charged. In place of the blame or suspicion that had often permeated relations between its officers when trying to explain bad news during the previous year's fighting, a new spirit of competition – attempting to take the credit for each new advance – had become evident.

Unit rivalries, once marked by muttering about who had been too slow to come to the aid of a fellow battalion in a tight spot, now gave way among the Other Ranks to speculation about who might win the laurels of entering certain towns first. The 8th was racing the 1st Army, approaching from the west, to reach Tunis first. Generals commanding divisions played out their rivalries, and so did brigadiers or commanding officers. Within the 5th Tanks' brigade, the 22nd Armoured, Lieutenant-Colonel

'Fearless' Jim Hutton's competitive instincts were sharpened by the knowledge that the 1st Tanks had been taken over by Michael Carver. Having gained command of fifty tanks and more than six hundred men at the age of twenty-six, Carver arrived with a reputation for fearsome intelligence as well as long service in the desert. Pushing forward during the early months of 1943, he kept up a steady stream of reports to his brigadier, describing in detail 1st Tanks' feats of arms. So 'Fearless' had to be on his mettle too.

Like many others within the armoured corps who had swallowed the bitter medicine of defeat during the early war years, Hutton revelled in the atmosphere of a victorious advance. The swift advance since Alamein brought countless opportunities to take prisoners, destroy equipment or see new evidence of the Axis collapse. In short, the 5th RTR, like other seasoned desert formations, enjoyed paying Rommel's boys back in full. While many of the men remembered their boss's avuncular concern or calm in battle, there was a hard side to Fearless Jim too. Writing up one of his subalterns for the Military Cross, Hutton declared, 'His aim at all times has been to kill Germans, an admirable intention which he has fully achieved.'

In this last respect, as in so many others, Hutton was in tune with the old sweats who provided the backbone of the battalion. While some characterised the desert as a 'gentleman's war', there were too many sergeants and corporals in units like 5 RTR who nursed deep grievances about comrades lost or Axis cruelties they had witnessed. Sergeant Emmin Hall, like many of the men, had been taking photos throughout their North African campaign, getting them processed in the Delta when on leave. In the album of desert pictures that he assembled, there is a shot of a makeshift German graveyard, complete with wooden crosses. Underneath this image Hall had written, 'good Germans'.

Within the 5th Tanks there was competition among squadron

leaders, but Major Ward, that brooding, bespectacled, brainy boss of A Squadron, had more or less seen off the competition. He was selected to train other captains and majors at a special Royal Armoured Corps school in Palestine. One of his students recalled, 'He didn't suffer fools. Any praise from him was high praise indeed because he had the reputation as one of the best squadron commanders in the desert.' By February 1943 Ward was at the head of A Squadron again, acting as the regiment's reconnaissance screen. His task was vital: probing enemy defences, getting them to open up and revealing their position while at the same time ensuring that he did not lose too many men or tanks.

The squadron was equipped with Crusader tanks armed with the very effective 57mm or six-pounder anti-tank gun. Ward did not like the Crusader when it first appeared, because it was mechanically less reliable than the Honey they had used before. Eventually, though, he had given in to the army way of doing things, accepting that the British-made tank did have some advantages when armed with this powerful new weapon; it was faster than the Shermans and Grants that equipped the other two squadrons, and more squat than them (being two feet lower than the Sherman and nearly three than the Grant). Driving into the Tunisian hill country of well-watered farmland, the issue of concealment became more important again, with the Crusader better able to take up observation positions.

Ward's squadron had been generously equipped with vehicles for its reconnaissance role. It had four tanks in each of its troops (instead of the three in B and C Squadrons), giving anything up to twenty-two Crusaders when squadron HQ was included too. It also had several small two-man scout cars called Dingoes that could move around inconspicuously, making little more noise or dust than a car. Using four tanks per troop, Ward was able to work his tanks in pairs when losses or stealth required.

As the regiment moved on, Gerry Solomon found himself in command of one of the Crusaders. Solomon had celebrated his twenty-seventh birthday in Tripoli, and had just put up his third, or sergeant's, stripe. His sense of humour had survived the disasters and loss of the preceding three years, but the enthusiasm that caused him to volunteer for the tanks and leave Ipswich in the first place had been replaced by a gritty determination to see the war through. His tank worked in a pair with that of a more senior sergeant named Broadbent.

By 20 February they were moving towards the Mareth Line, the main Axis defence in the eastern part of Tunisia, going around a town called Medenine. The western arm of the Allied offensive in Tunisia, the 1st Army and other forces advancing from the Algerian beachheads, had run into trouble, so General Montgomery wanted to assist them by creating a risk towards the enemy's eastern defences. At times that morning Sergeant Solomon found himself the leading tank of the leading squadron, in the leading regiment within the leading brigade of the 7th Armoured, Monty's leading division. The pressure to keep pushing on was intense.

The 5th Tanks and the rest of its brigade were moving forward quickly, but with the knowledge that enemy ambushes might be set on any hilltop or defile. The vegetation and season gave the place a more lush appearance than the wilderness they had spent much of the previous couple of years fighting over. The topography was different too, with a hilly countryside, deeply incised wadis and a better developed system of roads. In many Tunisian villages, the advancing Desert Rats met with a warm welcome from the French colonists whose hard graft had helped to create this flourishing landscape.

Twenty Second Armoured Brigade pushed to the right around Medenine, hoping to avoid any traps in the built-up area and to enable them to intercept any lagging enemy as they left the place.

Fifth RTR were performing the mission of 'Protection Front' – acting as spearhead – for the 22nd Armoured Brigade, with A Squadron spread out in line abreast and the other two squadrons following behind, ready to come into action. From around ten in the morning shells started to drop among their vehicles. Someone in the hills ahead and to their left was on the lookout, spotting for artillery batteries.

Tanks fanned out, and some were driven into wadis to present less of a target. The shells still dropped among the Crusaders of A Squadron, which pushed on ahead of the regiment. Its vehicles were now miles ahead of the rest of 8th Army. When the squadron stopped to observe, changing the order of march once it moved off again, experienced sergeants like Broadbent and Solomon knew the opportunity to settle back and let someone else take the lead was not to be squandered. However an officer, a twenty-five-year-old lieutenant called Douglas Low, volunteered to push even further in his Dingo.

Having spotted enemy vehicles leaving Medenine on a road running to the north-west, Lieutenant-Colonel Hutton ordered some Shermans from B Squadron to take up a position overlooking this route. The tanks moved into hull-down positions and crawled up behind a ridge, with their gunners looking down their sights so they could call 'stop' to the drivers when they were in position to shoot with as little of the tank showing as possible.

Moments later they opened up with their 75mm guns, lobbing high explosive into Germans trucks. They knocked out several vehicles including a half-track towing an 88mm gun. It was a job well done for the road was two thousand yards away, and the engagement at a range that would have been unthinkable with the A13s or Honeys. Neither of these earlier tanks had been issued with high-explosive shells either.

Lieutenant Low's Dingo scout car had pushed on, appearing near the road a couple of miles ahead to watch the enemy trucks driving to and fro, as if the British weren't there. Low had not been with the regiment long but had already notched up a reputation for foolhardy bravery: Solomon called him a 'crazy bugger'. Watching the Germans sailing up and down the road, Low's driver, Trooper Brian Taylor, was astounded to see his lieutenant open up with the Bren gun mounted on their Dingo for self-defence. 'The traffic carried on, bullets pinging around them, just ignoring him,' said Taylor. Not satisfied, Low radioed Major Ward that he was in a position to take prisoners, sauntered into the road and started flagging down vehicles.

It was not too long before the officer had detained five vehicles and a total of twenty-three Germans, including three officers. Major Ward, meanwhile, had ordered two Crusaders to close the gap between his squadron and the Dingo. Trooper Taylor was becoming increasingly nervous about their ability to hold on to such a large number of prisoners. Sure enough, the Germans soon enough realised that just two men stood between them and liberty. They jumped their captors, disarming them and stripping the two tankies in order to stop them escaping.

To the south-west, the two Crusaders pushing forwards with all due speed had run into trouble. One of the tanks had been brewed up by an unseen anti-tank gun. The other tank was soon knocked out.

That evening, after dark, Low suggested to Taylor that they escape. Their captors proved negligent and the two British prisoners seized their chance to run into the night. The lieutenant suggested they split up to improve the odds. Trooper Taylor was soon recaptured, but Lieutenant Low made it back to the battalion, where he was recommended for an immediate Military Cross for his bravery and initiative. The cost of this decoration, however, was that Trooper Taylor had fallen into captivity and two Crusaders had been knocked out, with three men killed and one seriously wounded. Sergeants Solomon and Broadbent counted their luck that it hadn't been their Crusaders that were hit.

Having pushed on to take Medinine at such speed, the battalion went into positions nearby. The 8th Army was catching up, fortifying the surrounding hills because it needed to bring up supplies: there was intelligence that the Germans would soon mount a counter-attack. In keeping with the new tactical orthodoxies that had been embraced by British generals, the armour would be kept back while the infantry with their anti-tank guns and artillery support took the shock of the onslaught. The armour could then be used to counter-attack or resume the drive forward once this threat had been dealt with.

It was on 6 March 1943 that the attack finally came to fruition. At six o'clock in the morning German artillery began to fire at the British positions, lobbing shells and rockets. After their bombardment German mechanised columns started to move down the slopes of the hills to the north and east of Medinine. Elements of three panzer divisions were attacking. Awaiting them were thousands of troops from the Highland and 2nd New Zealand divisions as well as a Guards Brigade and the Queen's Brigade, which formed the motorised infantry part of the 7th Armoured Division. 'They just let the tanks come on, and we just watched it as spectators,' said Sergeant Solomon.

When the range was right the crews of dozens of six-pounder anti-tank guns raced to their weapons and began to engage the enemy tanks. One after another the Mk IIIs and IVs ground to a halt, flames licking around the turret hatches followed by black smoke. One squadron of Shermans from 1st Tanks moved forward to join the shoot. By the time the Germans broke off the attack at five in the evening, the British were reporting to have knocked out fifty-two tanks (the Germans admitted to forty) without a single loss on their own side. The 1st RTR claimed eleven of those kills, but the majority were thought to have been caused by well-hidden six-pounder anti-tank guns.

'A great gloom settled over us all', wrote Rommel, reviewing the day's action. They had just used their last powerful armoured reserve – and lost much of it – trying to forestall the Allied advance on Tunis. The German field marshal knew that the war in North Africa was effectively lost. He cursed the fact that the 8th Army had had time to reinforce its Medenine position and that Montgomery had outwitted him. On 6 March at Medenine the Germans had repeated the kind of mistakes that the British made before El Alamein, driving into a well-planned anti-tank ambush and suffering greatly disproportionate casualties as a result. The operations of the 8th Army's armoured divisions reflected a careful digestion of two years' hard-won operational experience. Rommel summarised the change in British tank tactics:

With the light tanks sent out in advance, the heavier, gun-carrying tanks remained more and more to the rear. The task of the light tanks was to draw the fire of our anti-tank guns and armour. As soon as our tanks had given away their positions, the heavier British tanks opened a destructive fire on all the targets they had located, from a range of 2700 yards and, if possible, from the rear slope of a hill ... the British shot up our tanks, machine-gun nests and anti-aircraft and anti-tank gun positions at a range at which our own guns were completely incapable of penetrating their heavier tanks.

British tankies might have quibbled with a few aspects of Rommel's song of sorrow, but he had identified the essential elements of the armoured tactics being used against him. In the drive from Tripoli to Tunis it was the German army at Medenine that mounted the closest thing to a Balaklava charge. The British had moved forward as 5th Tanks had in taking that Tunisian town, using A Squadron in the van, flushing out the enemy, bringing their Shermans into play from hull-down positions and exploiting the range of their guns. It was a type of attack that they would mount repeatedly as the 8th Army resumed its advance towards the Mareth Line.

Like the defences of Tripoli, the Mareth Line was to prove more of a trial for the infantry than for the Desert Rats of 7th Armoured Division, who were kept back from the initial break-through operation. Even the foot soldiers, however, were able to breach the Mareth defences – originally laid out by the French to defend them from the Italian army in Libya – without suffering high casualties.

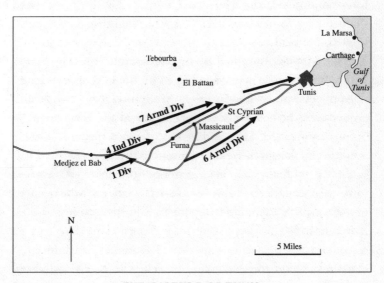

THE CAPTURE OF TUNIS

Increasingly, the Axis forces in North Africa – a quarter of a million of them – were being herded into a small pocket on Tunisia's coastal plain. They fought for weeks to defend the mountain defiles above the coast, switching forces back and forth to oppose the two Allied armies converging on them. With defeat staring them in the face, Field Marshal Rommel succumbed to exhaustion, handing command to Colonel-General Hans-Jürgen von Arnim.

During these months, the contest often assumed a desperate nature. The Axis forces knew they were fighting with the sea to their backs. Some in 5th Tanks said that the gentlemanly conventions the Germans had observed, such as not machine-gunning bailed-out tank crews, disappeared from Alamein onwards. It was rumoured that Field Marshal Herman Goering, head of the Luftwaffe, had ardently advocated reinforcing the Afrika Korps rather than withdrawing it, in the belief that they should fight to the last extreme. A mechanised formation of air force volunteers, the Herman Goering Division, had been shipped over to defend Tunis. 'We were told that they were all single men, ready to fight to the end,' said Sergeant Solomon. The Goering Division had been given some of the Tiger tanks with which the Germans now hoped to mount their last stand.

At the end of April, after weeks of advancing, the two British armies were in contact with each other as the final drive on Tunis was planned. HQ Middle East decided that the advance into the city should be mounted from the west, along an axis that was in the 1st Army area. Veteran troops from the 8th Army were to be used to undertake this task, so arrangements were made to transfer the 7th Armoured and 4th Indian divisions into the 1st Army sector. The tanks were loaded onto transporters to be driven via the Kasserine Pass, where Rommel had inflicted a sharp reverse on the Americans in February, to a point about twenty miles from the Tunisian capital. It was there on 5 May that Lieutenant-Colonel Hutton issued his orders to the 5th for the final push.

The advance into Tunis required the British to move northeast up a valley that undulated with small hills. Many of these eminences had been fortified by the Germans with machine-gun nests and anti-tank guns. Tanks were hidden in some of the copses. The attack launched on 6 May carried the 7th Armoured forward on the heels of the 4th Indian Division. The latter, a seasoned desert formation that had been in action since the start of the war, mixed battalions of Gurkhas or the Punjab Regiment with some British ones. In the 5th Tanks it was firmly believed that the Indian division would show little mercy: 'If they happen to run out of ammo, that doesn't bother them in the slightest: out come the knives and there are no prisoners.' Moving past the outer lines of German defences taken that morning, one Sherman commander noted, 'They had taken guns of all sorts in their stride – there were 88s, and 105s and stiffs all over the place.'

Now the 7th Armoured Division led the advance, moving with two armoured regiments up: the 5th Tanks on the left and 1st Tanks on the right. Each used its A Squadron Crusaders to feel the way forward, and they often took fire. As dusk came in the brigade had covered more than half of the distance between its starting positions and the outskirts of Tunis. Elements of A Squadron 5th Tanks moved into observation positions.

Parking up their tanks, Sergeant Broadbent suggested to Solomon that he inspect a nearby farmhouse. Solomon took a tommy gun from the tank, telling his crew to train the Crusader's turret on the windows as he approached the house. Moving gingerly around to the back of the building, he called out in schoolboy German for anyone inside to come out with their hands up. No response. He moved around the house, through a gate and into its courtyard, sub-machine gun levelled in front of him. As he stood in the courtyard alone, wondering what to do next, two German soldiers walked out of the house. 'They were big lads, over six foot, and they belonged to the Herman Goering Division.' They eyed Sergeant Solomon for a moment and then put their hands up. He moved forward slowly and relieved each man of a side arm. He realised 'they were more scared than I was'. The sergeant marched his captives out of the courtyard and back into view of his crew. They were the first German prisoners he had ever seen close up. Some tankies commented on the fact that their captives were always clean shaven, smelling of German army-issue soap, others that they were surly and uncommunicative. The thing that really struck Solomon was how afraid they were, something he put down to the effect of the 4th Indian Division and the rumours about its behaviour that must have been flying about the German lines.

It was the following day, 7 May, that the Afrika Korps really showed its teeth for the last time. Their morning started with a strafing run by half a dozen Messerschmitts, sending people diving for cover. It marked a change from being hit by Allied planes, something that had happened several times in the last days of the advance. Moving forward with the 1st Tanks on their right again, the 5th soon bumped into a powerful defensive anti-tank-gun screen of at least six and possibly as many as ten 88mm guns arrayed on the top of a hill to their front. Several lorries were also spotted disgorging infantry into trenches near by. In the open desert an 88 battery of this size could have made short work of an armoured battalion, but the British used the folds in the ground and vegetation to conceal their advance as far as possible.

Across to the right, 1st Tanks had encountered another formidable obstacle: 'a Tiger tank appeared on top of a ridge ... from which position it completely commanded the plain to the west and north-west of it'. With an almighty crack, the first shots rang out. Moments later, the major commanding A Squadron of 1st Tanks felt his Crusader being spun around. The Tiger had hit its engine, bringing the vehicle to a dead halt. The crew bailed out, all fortunately having survived the hit. What to do? Neither the six-pounders on his surviving Crusaders nor the regiment's Shermans could harm the Tiger at the range they found themselves. Instead, the 1st Tanks whistled up a heavy twenty-five-pounder stonk, and this dealt with the enemy tank. While both the 1st Army and the 8th Armoured Brigade, part of Monty's force, had already encountered Tigers, this engagement was the first time for 7th Armoured Division.

The 5th Tanks, meanwhile, brought several Shermans from B Squadron to a position where they could engage the 88s to their front. Opening up with 75mm high-explosive shells, they soon spotted flashes and secondary explosions as their rounds struck home. Two of the German guns were knocked out and two others abandoned by their crews. Further along the ridge another 88 had been hitched up to its halftrack and was being towed off the ridge when it was engaged and destroyed by 1st RTR. A defence that might once have terrified them had been neutralised without British losses.

At half past two that afternoon Hutton ordered Dickie Ward to take A Squadron into Tunis. He attached a platoon of infantry from the RBs (the 1st Battalion, the Rifle Brigade) and a troop of Shermans in case they met with serious opposition. The sights and sounds that met the tank commanders as they moved through the suburbs were overwhelming: shots were fired at them here and there, and were met with a response of a 75mm or six-pounder shell through the suspected window; parties of Germans were darting about, many trying to surrender; local people, French colonists in the main, were cheering the Allies from the windows, and in places offered them champagne.

Sergeant Solomon, moving his Crusader into a residential street, was struck by how European it all looked. The houses were built in the French style, there was plenty of greenery and a drizzling rain. In this particular street, everybody initially stayed indoors. Seeing one front door cracked slightly open, Solomon dismounted and greeted the face in the opening. The man inside asked in French whether they were from the 1st Army or 8th Army. When he replied the 8th the door closed for a moment and then the family emerged, to be followed by people from dwellings all the way down the street. They were smiling, slapping the soldiers on the back, thanking them. To Solomon, 'it was all very moving'.

The rest of the battalion, seeing no effective resistance being offered to A Squadron, had moved down in their wake. The Axis army had gone to pieces, and more than two hundred thousand soldiers would soon be in the bag. For the Desert Rats, taking this number of surrenders proved to be problematic. In places columns of Germans under an officer seeking to surrender were simply sent on their way towards some other friendly unit. At one point a French woman appeared toting a revolver and the national flag, marching a column of seventy-five Germans she had taken into the custody of the RBs.

When the German consul and his staff were captured they affected a haughty disdain for the soldiers, at one point insisting that the British shift their luggage. The wags in the Rifle Brigade, many of whom were cockneys, started to jeer the consul, calling out 'Carry yer bag, mate?' like urchins looking for a tip at a railway station.

Each day, the battalions would send a 'bag rep', or report on what they had seized, to brigade headquarters. The 5th Tanks one noted down by the 22nd Armoured Brigade staff on 8 May is extraordinary: 'We have taken today approx 5000 [prisoners of war] of which 80 per cent are German, also 100 planes on the ground … have taken about 20 guns, assorted including 3 naval coastal defence guns … also a quantity of [anti-aircraft equipment] and 2 hospitals one of which has in it about 700 Italians, and the other 3–400.'

As 5th Tanks started to drive north of the city, for many of the men the opportunities for drink and loot were too good to miss. Sergeant Wardrop 'developed a fault' on his tank, stopping it so that he could sample the fun, with the result that 'we had quite a lot to drink and the floor of the turret was covered with bottle of rum, brandy and wine'. A luckless Italian soldier waiting in vain for evacuation at the quayside was relieved of his guitar, and Wardrop had everything he needed for a proper sing-song.

With so many prisoners to be frisked, 'we missed a lot of loot [but] I got a couple of pistols, a camera, a watch, and some binoculars', one of the Wardrop's C Squadron colleagues wrote home. Then, perhaps sensing that his parents might disapprove of it, the trooper added, 'they are all confiscated by the MPs [Military Police] so why shouldn't the fighting troops get them?'

The 7th Armoured Division pushed beyond Tunis for a few days of mopping-up operations, but essentially the war in North Africa was over. The failings of the Axis high command meant that the Afrika Korps was starved of resources for much of the two years that it had fought, but was then sent them in abundance when the situation was hopeless. In addition to hundreds of thousands of prisoners, the Allies seized aircraft, ships, storehouses and all manner of warlike impedimenta.

One reason why Hitler and Goering had suddenly resolved to support the North African campaign was that, distracted by the huge battles on the eastern front, they had not been able to see the strategic consequences of the rapid retreat that began at Alamein. In a matter of months they had gone from seeing their troops about to overrun British Egypt to losing Libya and almost their entire army. This, in turn, was a mortal blow for the Mussolini regime. Il Duce had invested his prestige and huge resources in the Libyan colony, and with Allied forces victorious they would soon be poised to invade Italy itself.

In the convent hospital near Naples where he and other seriously wounded prisoners were confined, Captain Brian Stone had been carefully reading between the lines of the Italian communiqués printed by the pro-fascist newspapers that lay about the wards. Fragmentary news of Alamein began to come through. 'Over and over again I was with the boys in battle,' wrote Stone. 'I was out in front of the regiment doing my old job of reconnaissance, sending back reports to Richard [Ward].' Air raids on Italian targets had been stepped up throughout the autumn and winter, leading to a marked change in atmosphere among their Italian warders. In December their hospital had been visited by a Red Cross repatriation committee. Despite the 'total war' ideology, there had already been swaps of men too badly wounded to fight again. In February, Stone and others had been told 'You go home'. Hundreds of wounded men were concentrated in the Tuscan town of Lucca in March before being put on a train for Lisbon, in neutral Portugal, in April. Stone was heading back to England. When the boat carrying the men docked in Southampton on an overcast morning, there was no band or welcoming committee. The men were taken by hospital train to Basingstoke where nurses formed lines to cheer them as they arrived. The wounded officer went to sleep looking forward to 'ordinary days in sweet England, leaning to walk with an artificial leg'. His nine months of captivity, and his war, were over.

For the rest of 5th Tanks, there had also been hopes that the end of the campaign might mark the start of that journey. Hadn't Churchill himself told them in Tripoli that each night they pitched their tents closer to home, and that it would be enough for any man to have said that he had served in the desert army? They had done their bit, no doubt about it. Spirits, though, had fallen not long after the liberation of Tunis when they were ordered to retrace their march seven hundred miles eastwards to Homs, a coastal town in Libya. There they were left in a desolate spot far from the easygoing cafés and grateful *mademoiselles* of Tunis. Camped out in two-man tents among the coastal dunes, with sandstorms and on the old desert diet of bully and biscuits, health problems soon multiplied in the battalion.

The officers set about digesting the lessons of the last months, be they of better coordinating airpower, defeating Tiger tanks or conducting reconnaissance in the close country of southern Europe. Major Ward's A Squadron remained a model formation, winning a couple of brigade gunnery competitions, which featured the tanks firing into targets among the dunes. Ambitious commanders had no intention of letting up on training, for the competition that had flourished among them in the drive for Tunis was now focussing on the next big 'show'.

'Fearless' Jim Hutton and Major Ward had both won the Distinguished Service Order for their part in the late events. The DSO was the army's decoration for superior leadership in battle, so it was prized by those hungry for promotion and higher command. Ward's DSO citation began, 'Yet again this officer has shown outstanding personal courage, initiative, and leadership while commanding the light squadron of this battalion.' Lieutenant-Colonel Hutton's citation talked about the taking of Tunis, when 'the performance of this regiment during the operation must be considered a tribute to its high state of readiness and splendid spirit'. Below the official typewritten part of the citation, the commander of the 7th Armoured Division had written on the paperwork as it made its way upwards, 'His determination to drive on at top speed imbued his regiment with the greatest dash at a most important time when any delay would have been fatal.'

Although the 8th Army cared little for sartorial elegance, the ribbons for these decorations (DSO and Military Cross for officers, Distinguished Conduct Medal and Military Medal for Other Ranks) were sewn onto the battledress blousons that they wore daily. A young subaltern addressed by a superior with the DSO and MC ribbons knew it was 'very big stuff'. When multiple awards or bars had been given – for example, Hutton had twice been awarded the MC – the effect was even greater.

Parading one morning with the rest of his squadron at Homs, Sergeant Solomon noticed that Major Ward had sewn the DSO ribbon onto his battledress. Telling the men to gather round after formal part was over, he drew their attention to the ribbon. 'It doesn't really belong to me,' the sergeant reported that Ward told them, 'it belongs to you but as I am the squadron leader I have the privilege of wearing it.' Solomon still had an uneasy feeling about Ward, sensing that he never quite accepted the civilians in uniform in the same way that he did the old regulars. He also considered his major to be so ambitious that the idea that Ward might feel the DSO really belonged to the whole of A Squadron just made him laugh.

Ward was posted away from the battalion soon after that parade, for the army wanted to ensure that its regular officers still served in the staff jobs and did the training courses required for promotion. Given the fashion for bringing on dynamic younger officers, this meant propelling them through jobs in quick time: Ward could consider himself lucky that he had been allowed to stay in command of A Squadron for more than one year, a posting that might in peacetime have gone on for two or three.

There was little time to dwell on his departure, for the 5th once more began serious war-like preparations as the summer temperatures reached their height. The battalion had been entirely converted to the Sherman tank – more than fifty of them – and was busy repainting them in a brown and green colour scheme.

On 11 July 1943 members of the 22nd Armoured Brigade trooped into the Roman amphitheatre at Leptis Magna, an ancient site close to their beach camp at Homs. There they were given a lecture by the corps commander about the forthcoming invasion of Italy. Just the day before they had heard news that the first phase, landings in Sicily, had taken place. The 8th Army had been committed to the battle on the Italian mainland. Going home would have to wait.

After this news, and in view of the lowering of spirits among some of the men, Lieutenant-Colonel Hutton decided to give the soldiers three days off. They were free to bathe in the sea, sleep or do whatever else took their fancy. It was rumoured in the battalion that Hutton, who was highly sensitive to his soldiers' mood, had tried to use the amount of sickness in the unit as a pretext to remove it from the forthcoming operation. This may have antagonised his superiors, for on the last day of 5th RTR's unilateral holiday the brigade commander, Brigadier 'Looney' Hinde, arrived unannounced in the camp. Declaring the state of the battalion to be an outrage, he unceremoniously sacked Hutton. The warm words of Hinde's own boss, the divisional commander, on Hutton's DSO citation and all the other praise he had drawn from Monty downwards were not enough the save the Commanding Officer. As so often in these wartime clashes of ambition and personality, those higher up simply backed the chain of command, and Hinde was Fearless Jim's boss.

This was deeply shocking to the 5th Tanks. Hutton had managed to achieve a unique balance between his own tactical aggression and the orders of the high ups on one side, and the common sense of his veteran tank commanders, who had seen too many vain sacrifices, on the other. While some officers shrugged off the sacking, feeling it was a regrettable part of dirigiste wartime methods, the Other Ranks in the 5th RTR took it very badly.

When Hutton left the Homs camp on 15 July the entire battalion paraded, lining the route. More than 420 men signed a souvenir poem that was presented to him. He drove in an open jeep past the men he had led for the previous thirteen months, one noting that 'as he passed I could see that he was crying, Fearless Jim who would have taken on all the Boches in Germany on his own'. Another tankie felt 'it was a terrible day for the battalion and everyone was upset and depressed'.

The poem composed for Hutton was suitably heroic, ending:

The Fighting Fifth is ready, morning, noon, and dead of
   night,
And if Jerry wants his ground back, by the gods he'll have
   to fight.
So off now we'll go to leaguer for a short but hard earned
   rest,
And the Hun will still remember that our guns are
   pointing.

In the 5th's bivouac the battalion's songsmiths composed some verses that summed up in a more direct form the feelings within it. It could not have been put on the Commanding Officer's wall, where senior officers might have seen it, but doubtless Fearless Jim was all too aware of the emotions it contained. The ballad they called 'Famous Battalion' told of their campaigns fighting across North Africa:

So for miles in the desert they travelled
With fair Tunis their goal in the end
In their mind's eye a picture of Blighty
And a sack full of credit to spend

For miles in the desert they wandered
This famous battalion pushed on
Until at last they captured Tunis
The North African War was won

All the promises they made were forgotten
All the plans they had made all fell through
For no sooner had they taken Tunis
Then they whipped them way back in the Blue

Faced with a landing in Italy within weeks, the upset of Lieutenant-Colonel Hutton's departure and the disappointment that they were not going home had to be checked. A new commanding officer had been appointed from the 6th RTR. There was an understanding within the army that an incoming CO could bring in one or two of his own people. The new man chose Captain Arthur Crickmay, whose long circular journey from the 5th at the outset of the war via Egypt and the 6th Tanks to 7th Armoured Brigade and Burma had finally brought him back. What was more, in a battalion still smarting from the departure of Fearless Jim, the new boss gave Crickmay what he felt was the best job in the 5th Tanks.

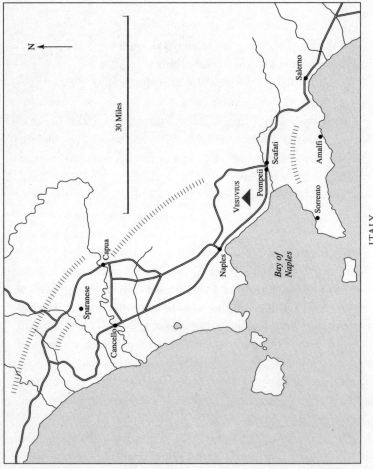

ITALY

13

INTO ITALY

Captain Crickmay's first days back with 5th Tanks should have been easy, but instead produced an unexpected trauma. He had driven across from southern Iraq, through Beersheba to Cairo in the record time of three days. From there he had gone forward by ship to Libya, arriving in the beachside camp at Homs by early August. It was roasting hot, and although the task of preparing for Italy was stepping up there was still plenty of sea bathing and regimental sport going on.

The dominant impression that Crickmay formed was of a unit 'a bit pleased with itself' after its triumphal advance from Alamein. Since that victory, the army had relaxed some of its usual restrictions on press reporting in order to boost morale at home. The 7th Armoured Division, having soldiered in the desert in relative obscurity since 1940, had been the subject of newspaper reports. A few months before his return, Crickmay had noted in a letter home that the division was 'at last getting a little publicity after three years continually on the job'. Reaching the 5th RTR, he could see that this small quotient of glory had already caused the men to stand a little taller.

Crickmay was twenty-seven by this time, and had been soldiering for four long years. He had impressed his superiors sufficiently that they were thinking of him for the sort of plum jobs that army officers with regular commissions had hitherto jealously guarded. The captain had been given command of the 5th RTR's reconnaissance section, which was further divided into two troops, each under an officer, one of them being Lieutenant Low. Since his attempt to take twenty-three German prisoners several months earlier, Low had managed to twice be recommended for the Military Cross.

Some had remarked that Low would win the Victoria Cross or be dead before the war was out. The soldiers who had seen him in action were less awed by the young officer, believing his antics to be rash and extremely dangerous.

Among the pastimes that Low and others had adopted to dissipate the boredom at Homs was fishing with high-explosive charges. One afternoon soon after Crickmay arrived, Low decided to demonstrate his technique. As it happened, Sergeant Gerry Solomon was also watching. Low took a half-pound explosive charge, pressed a detonator on a thirty-five-second fuse into it and ignited the bomb. Walking into the surf, he held the device 'like a shot-putter'. Twenty-five seconds passed; Crickmay and some of the others started shouting 'Throw it, for God's sake!', but Low remained impassive. Then there was an explosion, and the others rushed into sea. Low's headless body was dragged from the water, in Solomon's words, 'like a great white fish'.

Crickmay threw a towel over the lieutenant's corpse and

dismissed the others on the beach. Had Low's action been bravado, a display of nerve, or suicide? Crickmay tended toward the latter, but 'Why did he do it? No one had a clue. [It was] a disagreeable start to my time with the Recce.' The line between the type of man who could drive towards a line of 88s in a cramped metal box with every chance of being incinerated and one who had lost all sense of danger was perhaps finer than many of them would have cared to admit.

The command that Crickmay had taken over was naturally meant to embody some of the battalion's more daring types. It had come about due to a reorganisation of regiments under which A Squadron had been equipped with Sherman tanks, losing in the process its coveted status as the light or reconnaissance squadron. The generals, learning from costly battles in North Africa and anticipating campaigns in Italy and northern Europe, had decreed that armoured units be strengthened to fifty-plus Shermans, and a new reconnaissance troop created in their headquarters company. While A Squadron continued to think of itself as something special, the baton of pathfinders that it had performed so effectively in the late Tunisian campaign had been passed to the new Recce Troop.

During the summer of 1943 the brighter minds of the Royal Armoured Corps in North Africa had given much thought to the type of fighting they would face in Italy, and how it would differ from the late contest against Rommel. In charting a way from their expected landing site towards the north, up the Italian 'boot', they were expecting to negotiate a narrow coastal strip that was heavily cultivated and frequently cut by rivers running from the inland hills to the sea. This meant movement would inevitably be channelled into a small number of routes that a determined enemy could easily defend. Engagements would take place at very close range. Tall crops such as corn, hedges and orchards could all be used as cover by enemy soldiers lying in wait. The hills rising steeply from the coastal shelf created many tight bends on the roads, where someone might be waiting around the next corner. In short, both the patterns of cultivation and the landscape would make engagements at very close range far more likely.

If the aim of the Recce Troop was to find the enemy before it had a chance to knock out the leading British tanks, stealth would be more important in their business than armoured protection or firepower. Crickmay's new command was therefore formed with very small, lightly armoured vehicles: Dingo scout cars and Bren carriers, which were diminutive tracked vehicles originally designed to haul heavy weapons for the infantry. In 5th Tanks each Bren carrier mounted an American 50-calibre heavy machine gun and a crew of three or four men. The troop was divided into two sections with a mixture of nine of these vehicles each, which, when added to two more in troop HQ, gave Crickmay a total of twenty machines under his command. It wasn't quite the squadron role he had hoped for, but the prestige of this new venture made up for it.

The challenge of taking this selected team forward into battle was just what Crickmay needed. He had not commanded soldiers since leaving 6th RTR two years earlier. Instead, he had served as a staff officer in 7th Armoured Brigade, initially succumbing to the allure of a change of routine and the desire to travel. During the months that followed he had managed the most extraordinary voyages, to Burma, India, Iraq, Palestine, Lebanon and Syria. While Crickmay was a natural explorer who loved to sketch the scenes he took in, these journeys had ultimately proven unsatisfying, for during the early days of the desert war he had felt the searing realities of combat and longed to get back to them, writing home, 'One can bear the thought of inaction for a while, but inaction coupled with a future in which there appears to be no hope of any further action except back to India (God Forbid) is too much.' Watching tanks manoeuvring in the desert of southern Iraq one evening, he had written, 'Whenever I see a squadron roaring across the desert with the mast head pennants fluttering in the breeze I have a great urge to get back.' So bored with staff duties did Crickmay become that he had even applied – unsuccessfully – to become a pilot in Bomber Command.

Summoned in July 1943 to return to an active unit at last, he had packed his bags with alacrity. Crickmay knew that by leaving 6th Tanks he had allowed others to get ahead of him in the race to command a squadron. He also knew that the exigencies of war had changed the composition of the RTR officer corps. In many cases, the young men sent out to lead troops simply could not gain the respect of their soldiers. One solution to this, and to a shortage of suitable applicants more generally, was to commission more men from the ranks. Crickmay confided to his mother, 'I am not even sure that I want to go to 6th RTR as a matter of fact, they are what you might call a rum lot these days, mostly ex-sergeants from the [Officer Cadet Training Unit], excellent fellows no doubt, but a bit trying en masse.' Crickmay was no snob – indeed his soldiers would regard him as unusually close in his relationship with them – but he did think too many promoted NCOs could make for boring conversation in the officers' mess. In 5th Tanks there were also men who had been elevated from the ranks, but whatever reservations he might have had fell by the wayside at the thought of returning to active soldiering.

The downside to Crickmay's posting to 5th Tanks, apart from the obvious risks in commanding the Recce Troop, was that he rode in on the coat-tails of the new Commanding Officer, Lieutenant-Colonel R. N. Wilson, generally known among RTR officers as 'Dicker' Wilson (though the men were to give him many other nicknames). Wilson's qualifications for command were similar on paper to Hutton's, for he had led a squadron of 3rd Tanks during the Sidi Rezegh battles of 1941 before ending up as second-in-command of 6th Tanks. However, Dicker proved a negative opposite to the beloved Commanding Officer he replaced: small and shrill compared to Hutton's tall and languid; interfering instead of laissez-faire. Rather than dashing about in an open Ford like the bronzed Hutton, the soldiers soon noticed that the new man kept the hood up on his staff car and was a 'pale-skin type', unwilling to expose himself to the elements, let alone the Germans. By the time the 5th Tanks embarked at the port of Tripoli for Italy on 10 September, negative impressions of Wilson were already filtering through the battalion. Indeed the taint of 'yellow belly' had already been spreading in C Squadron, where Sergeant Emmin Hall remembered Wilson as the barely functioning officer to whose squadron he had briefly been attached when separated from 5th Tanks during Operation Crusader in November 1941. There were, no doubt, a few officers who would like to have seen Crickmay, as the new man brought in by Wilson, fail. It all added to the pressure on the captain as they set out across the Mediterranean, heading for the beachheads at Salerno.

Chugging along in their landing ships through the dusk the tankies knew they were close to their destination as the noises of war increased. They heard the drone of bombers going in to pound the Germans and frequent thumps and crumps of artillery supporting those ashore. A few miles off the beachhead they watched the battleship HMS *Warspite* turn and deliver a broadside of shells from its fifteen-inch guns. It was an awesome spectacle, sending a sheet of flame from the naval guns and the most shattering noise that many of the men had ever heard. In the early evening of 15 September the landing ships beached, and the armoured vehicles fired up their engines, clanking down the dropped ramps of their vessels. In most places the arrival of 7th Armoured Division was uneventful. However, Lieutenant-Colonel Carver, commanding 1st Tanks, had arrested the captain of his landing ship at gunpoint and locked him in his cabin. The naval officer had, for petty reasons, refused to let them disembark and Carver had taken control.

The scene that greeted the tank soldiers as they came ashore that evening was one of congestion and confusion. A British corps placed under the command of the US 5th Army had started landing six days earlier. Some of those in the first wave had been foolish enough to expect little resistance. Mussolini had been deposed in July, following the landings in Sicily, and the Italian government that followed had concluded a secret armistice with the British that was made public the day before the Salerno landings. The Germans, rather than give up the game, had simply elbowed the Italians aside in order to resist landings on the Italian mainland. At Salerno a nearby panzer division had quickly organised several battle groups that counter-attacked the lightly armed landing forces. There had been some hard fighting, with significant casualties and leading commanders to consider whether they would have to re-embark their troops. There had also been some moments when some British troops that had fought in North Africa had actually refused to obey orders, believing the army had broken a promise to send them home.

Following on as the second wave of the assault, the Desert Rats soon discovered the tensions that simmered in the beach-head. The imperative was for breakout, and enormous naval gunfire and air support was being applied to pummel the enemy as they sought to contain the Salerno landings. The 7th Armoured Division was meant to get things moving again, but the difficulties of mounting mechanised operations in southern Italy were immediately apparent. Obstacles – man-made and natural – confined them to a small number of routes. If the enemy dominated those routes with fire or denied them by demolitions and mines, progress was going to be agonisingly slow. Even a small ditch a few feet deep could block the path of a lorry or tank if the culvert crossing it was blown, so this was exactly what the Germans were doing in hundreds of places: the low-lying land was littered with drainage channels as well as streams.

For days the 5th Tanks waited while a British infantry division fought to secure a narrow pass that would allow them to escape the beachhead and advance north, towards Naples. Nearly two weeks had passed since they had come ashore before the word was finally given for the 7th Armoured Division to move up. The 5th RTR was assigned to the division's motorised infantry brigade (the 131st or Queen's Brigade), inching slowly up the road to the recently secured defile.

Moving forward in the half-light of dawn on 28 September, Crickmay, wedged into his little Bren carrier, spearheading the brigade, division, corps and 5th Army, realised that quite a lot now rested on his Recce Troop. He noted:

On a single road with ditches and trees on each side, advance to contact is always an anxious business. The lead vehicle is 90 per cent certain to 'buy it', because the well concealed anti-tank guns will see you sitting in the middle of the road before you see him. In many squadrons it was customary to toss up for who was to be the lead vehicle first.

Having flipped their coin and assigned the order of march, Recce Troop moved off. There were plenty within the regiment who wondered whether carrying out reconnaissance in a small carrier or Dingo would be suicidal compared to the Crusader tanks they had driven into Tunis. Crickmay's vehicles were open-topped, so the crews were more vulnerable to artillery shrapnel, and the armour plate itself would only stop small arms. One of Crickmay's soldiers recorded that 'we had to use our ingenuity to improve the situation. We covered the machine with sections of spare track, gash bogey wheels and as many sand bags as the suspension would bear.' Rolling forward, the carrier crews suspected these measures provided little more than a morale boost.

A couple of hours later they reached a small town called Scafati, where the capture of a single bridge over the River Sarno was central to the Allied advance. Seeing the Germans setting it for demolition, Shermans from the 5th Tanks' B Squadron dashed to capture the crossing before it was reduced to rubble. They succeeded, but were soon under fire from anti-tank guns and snipers. In North Africa, commanders had learned that survival meant keeping your head out of the vehicle in order to spot the flash and tracer of enemy fire, but in the Italian villages buildings offered all kinds of vantage points to hidden German gunmen.

Scafati turned into a nerve-racking, day-long fight. The tanks had been placed under the command of a battalion of the Queen's Regiment, forming part of a well-balanced all-arms force. The infantry shinned up onto roofs to clear the Germans and soon an artillery forward observer had lodged himself in the bell tower of the town church, calling in twenty-five-pounder fire against German targets. Even so, radio reports kept up a toll of losses. Armoured vehicles had come up to a blind corner on the road, where it skirted the flank of a steep hillside. Rounding this bend, the Recce Section had a Bren carrier knocked out by a German tank, and its crew wounded. There followed a sustained German counter-attack that lasted well into the night, during which a couple of C Squadron Shermans were also knocked out. The overall outcome was not in doubt but, as many battalions had already learned in Italy, fighting through successive enemy defence lines would require a daily sacrifice of men and vehicles, which would be chipped away in German rearguard actions.

The following day, 29 September, the 5th Tanks lost another couple of Shermans and an experienced commander from C Squadron. On the 30th, one of the sergeant commanders in B Squadron was killed. They continued to move forward, but with a growing sense of frustration at the short range of the engagements. There could be no question of standing back 1500 to 2500 yards from the enemy and lobbing high-explosive shells from the Sherman as they had done in Tunisia. The Italian vegetation and topography meant it was all happening at much closer range.

'All the tanks which have been lost through anti-tank guns have been due to very well sited and camouflaged [self-propelled guns] which have opened up between 80 and 120 yards,' reported Dicker Wilson soon after the engagement. 'They were quite impossible to see.' In its advance at Scafati, the 5th Tanks had sent one of its squadrons to each of the Queen's Brigade's battalions, leaving no role for Dicker Wilson. He freely confessed that 'we all hate like poison' this parcelling-out of armoured units. It was something that, under British doctrine, the commanders of 'Infantry tank' brigades had long got used to, for moving along slowly with the footsloggers was the role of their Matilda, Valentine, or now Churchill armour. But special formations like the 7th Armoured Division were meant to be kept back, ready to act as a whole to exploit breakthroughs or counter enemy ones.

By the time 1st RTR took over the lead on 2 October, the 5th Tanks had already learned some difficult lessons in the nature of campaigning in mainland Europe. They now understood that fighting through vineyards, orchards and wheat fields, where movement was channelled down a small number of roads, put the infantry and its commanders in the driving seat. The long drives of the days advancing from Alamein to Tunis, as well as the open spaces of the desert, were gone for good.

Moving back to the rear of the division after a few days in action, the 5th Tanks had more opportunities to enjoy the fruits of liberation. For the Italian population, which was being treated with increasing violence by the Germans, did indeed regard the advancing British as liberators. Unlike others in the battalion, Captain Crickmay had not experienced the joyous hospitality of the French colonists in Tunisia. 'The greeting by ecstatic, jubilant, Italians was overwhelming,' he wrote, 'flowers, fruit, and kisses.' While most men in the battalion thoroughly enjoyed this, some could not set aside their prejudices acquired during years of fighting the Italians in Africa, or from a Little Englander's sense of his own superiority. 'The local inhabitants are just ghastly,' wrote Dicker Wilson, 'dirty, and generally on a par with the Wog.'

After years of bully beef and hard tack biscuits, these really were days of abundance. Armfuls of American rations had been scooped up at Salerno. When an overnight stop permitted it, a breakfast of bacon, tomato and eggs would be fried up on makeshift stoves beside the vehicles. Throughout the day snacks in the form of bunches of grapes, peaches, apples or fresh bread were found along the way. At night in the Italian villages, wine, grappa and brandy flowed.

Sergeant Charlie Bull, commanding one of B Squadron's Shermans, was always on the lookout for a good meal, and so made the most of this culinary plenty. He even took the necessary steps to ensure his breakfast-egg supply.

'We've got a tame hen on the tank,' he wrote home. 'We had two but one went in the pot and we decided to keep the other. She climbs on the tank to roost now, I don't know how long she will reign, we might get hungry one day . . .'

The impressions the soldiers formed of hospitable locals and of a wonderfully improved diet were tempered, naturally enough, by the sudden death and the arbitrary nature of the destruction they saw all around them. As the army moved north, passing Naples, visitors reported that much of the city had been flattened by Allied bombing. Soon after setting off, Crickmay had seen the joyous expression of an Italian farmer who, observing the British approaching his village, had whipped on his horse and cart in order to greet them. Moments later man and beast were blown apart, victims of an anti-tank mine left by the retreating Germans. In many villages the locals told of war crimes too. 'I could tell you lots of things the Germans have done to the Italian people, things you would hardly believe,' Sergeant Bull told his mother.

In deliberate, painful steps the 5th Army continued north-wards, crossing the Volturno, another major German defensive line about fifteen miles to the north of Naples, on 13 October. Progress then slowed again, as the infantry divisions worked their way through fields until on 22nd the 5th Tanks found themselves pushing into the town of Sparanese. They were operating as a whole battalion again, to the colonel's delight, with the attached infantry and guns under his command rather than the other way around. Their progress was checked, though, by the fire of an 88. As the leading tanks stopped and Recce Troop vehicles pushed forward to explore there was the hurried clatter of Spandau fire: there were German machine-gun nests on a couple of the hill-tops beside the town. Further progress was now dependent on the Recce Troop finding a chink in the enemy defence.

Each way they tried they found obstacles, blown crossings or booby traps. As Crickmay tried to crack this conundrum, a large explosion announced that a Dingo had set off an anti-tank mine, seriously wounding two of its crew. The commander of A Squadron was wounded and evacuated back to a casualty clearing station trying to find a way through too. Night fell with the battalion pinned down in the fields around Sparanese.

The following day Crickmay decided there was nothing for it but to go forward on foot, setting off at first light with a corporal from his troop. They had armed themselves with Thompson sub-machine guns and hand grenades. Picking their way through the crops, their progress was interrupted several times by the zipping sound of machine-gun bullets passing just over them. The pair would go to ground, wait until the enemy's attention waned and then move on. Bit by bit they managed to find a way around the fields until they were just a few dozen yards from one of the machine-gun positions.

At a given signal, Crickmay and his corporal closed the distance in seconds, opening up with their weapons at point-blank range. One of the Germans in the weapons pit was cut down, but five surrendered. Realising what was happening, the machine-gunners from another of the German positions started pouring fire onto the position that Crickmay had just taken. But they were too late: the two tankies were already on their way down, taking the first Spandau and five prisoners with them.

Returning to British lines, the prisoners were handed over for interrogation and Crickmay made his report on the lay of the enemy defence that he had unlocked. By the afternoon tanks were in motion, heading for positions where they could fire at the remaining German machine-gun nests. The following day, the operation to capture Sparanese was completed and the advance resumed. Crickmay was written up forthwith for the Military Cross by Dicker Wilson.

By November, 5th Tanks had been pulled back to the Sorrento peninsula. The word was that they would soon be handing over their vehicles and heading home. During this period, the soldiers were allowed several trips into Naples, where many searched out fabric or stockings for the women they had not seen in years. Others found food or drink, Corporal George Stimpson packing a box of fresh oranges in his kitbag. The great hope, rarely voiced but yearned for across the battalion, was that they might be home for Christmas. Others used the waiting time to visit the ruins of Pompeii or walk the slopes of Mount Vesuvius.

The army they had left, meanwhile, was fighting and suffering at the Germans' new defensive line of Monte Cassino. The Desert Rats were glad to be taken out of the line for other reasons too: the balmy late-summer weather they had experienced after Salerno had given way to winter cold, rain and mud, adding to the misery of the grim slugging match developing around Cassino.

The Italian interlude had been a strange period for the 5th Tanks. It had underlined how different fighting in Europe would be, particularly if the terrain was difficult. Dicker Wilson was one of several commanding officers who tried to analyse the recent fighting so that changes might be made prior to any fighting in northern Europe. All knew that the long-discussed 'second front' would mean a landing in France, even if many of them hoped it would be someone else's turn to do that fighting.

Wilson felt that the way movement was channelled onto a few highly congested routes in Italy spelt trouble: 'Road congestion is dreadful at times', he noted. The German defence of rivers or villages made all-arms cooperation more vital than ever – but their ability to deny roads to the Allied forces made it impossibly hard to achieve. If your troops were constantly getting stuck in traffic jams, who did you want at the head of the bottleneck? Tanks, infantry, artillery, engineers or a combination of all of them? In some places, this difficulty could be solved by leaving the road and driving over fields, but this was a problem because even the armoured divisions had far more wheeled vehicles than tracked ones, which could easily sink into soft ground. In Italy self-propelled artillery had appeared, with twenty-five-pounders mounted on a tracked, armoured hull derived from the Sherman, but what about the motor battalion, the infantry who belonged to an armoured brigade and were meant to operate closely with the tanks? 'They are', wrote Wilson, 'too thin on the ground and cluttered up with a lot of unnecessary transport which takes up too much road space.' He favoured the type of partnership that had been used by his division at Scafati, getting the Queen's Brigade out of its lorries and on their feet around the tanks. Other officers, however, were also reflecting that in more mobile operations what was really needed was infantry in armoured, tracked carriers, or at the very least half-tracks like those the Germans had used since the start of the war.

Wilson also considered the problems of command and communication, feeling that little information was coming down from his masters at brigade headquarters. The heroes of the Italian hour, he thought, were Recce Troop, which was 'more important than ever we thought ... the only information a CO can get is from his own Recce Troop. It means the standard has to be very high indeed.'

The CO's delight with the way Arthur Crickmay had commanded Recce Troop meant not just an MC, but transfer to the post of adjutant. The return to what he called the 'bumph war', which came with being Dicker Wilson's administrative assistant, might have irked Crickmay, given how delighted he was to have escaped his staff job with 7th Armoured Brigade, but he knew that taking on this task meant every chance of promotion within the family of the 5th Tanks and, of course, less of getting killed. For years Crickmay had struggled against the high-handed attitude of pre-war regular officers, and since they tended to regard the post of adjutant as being reserved for one of their own he relished the chance to take it on. Working at the boss's right hand was generally felt to be a good for future Commanding Officers and tank squadron commanders. Crickmay therefore seized his chance, which marked a fitting end to what had been an excellent little Italian war for him.

As far as Dicker Wilson was concerned, the campaign had not been such a pleasant one, for in their months since landing at Salerno his new battalion had taken resolutely against him. His officers despised his shrill, unforgiving manner, while among the men the whiff of a man who was reluctant to share their dangers had settled about him. The tanks of his headquarters had landed late at Salerno – through no fault of his – and his attempts to hold back, trying to remain in radio contact with his brigade headquarters, had aroused contempt among the seasoned tankies, as did his taste for comfortable night-time lodgings while the squadrons lay out in the autumn downpours.

The regimental net, that tool that had been so important to 'Fearless' Jim Hutton's laconic style of command, had proven to be Wilson's undoing. After the Volturno crossing he had one day complained over the radio that he could not hear his forward troops. Major Paddy Doyle, C Squadron commander, had then been heard remarking on air that the CO ought to 'come up to within the ten-mile range of the set'. This aside – which had apparently been meant for the consumption of Doyle's own crew, but had 'accidentally' been sent out over the regimental net – summed up the way the battalion's veterans felt about their new Commanding Officer, and further undermined his authority. Other wags claimed that Wilson's tank had been fitted with an especially large radio aerial, so that he might remain well to the rear. Some of the soldiers freely admitted that, given the circumstances of Hutton's departure, any new commander would have found him a hard act to follow. But nothing could have undermined Wilson's authority quite so comprehensively than the perception that, far from being 'fearless', he was the complete opposite. The CO had seen the lack of regard in which the battalion held him when, shortly before the fight in Sparanese, he had ordered commanders and operators to wear steel helmets when looking out of their turrets. Since they had lost several commanders in Italy this might have seemed like a sensible precaution, but it was in fact one that was very unlikely to stop a sniper's bullet. More importantly, it infringed the code adopted by the unit's hard men since it had been bellowed out by the late Major Winship during the 1940 campaign in France: if they were going to die, they would do so wearing their RTR berets. Lieutenant-Colonel Wilson's order was therefore ignored, except by the hapless fellows who crewed the two tanks under his nose in battalion headquarters.

One of Crickmay's friends had warned him of Wilson's 'excessive cheeriness' and, given this, along with his commitment to preparing the battalion for its next trial, Wilson does not seem to have worried too much about the personal criticism. Rather, he began to form the impression that 5th Tanks was an organisation that needed firm management lest its more wayward spirits come to dominate it. He planned to use his authority to achieve his goals, with Crickmay as one of his executives.

At four o'clock on the afternoon of 20 December, the 5th Tanks set sail from Naples. The likes of Gerry Solomon, Henry Hall, Charlie Bull and Jake Wardrop (all of them now sergeants since the latter's promotion) had not been home for three years. For Arthur Crickmay, who had initially been posted out to 6 RTR in Egypt, it was even longer. They had endured countless battles, lost too many friends and all five had escaped tanks hit by enemy fire. In the process they had become the 'Famous Battalion' of their song, part of the Famous Division that was the 7th Armoured or Desert Rats.

During their summits with Allied chiefs, Britain's war leaders had promised that veteran troops would be committed to the second front, or invasion of France. This included the Desert Rats, 50th and 51st Divisions (both infantry formations) and a couple of other armoured brigades. The status of the 7th Armoured as an outfit known by the British public to have been victorious from Alamein onwards meant they fitted squarely into the 'veteran' category. Given the sensitivity of preparations for the invasion of France, their redeployment to Britain was therefore meant to be a matter of great secrecy. They had removed the Desert Rat patches from the sleeves of their battledress and were not supposed to tell anyone in their letters home that they would soon be on their way. Their exact destination was also a closely guarded secret. The Germans, however, had learned what was afoot. Before they had even sailed, Lord Haw-Haw, the Nazis' tame British radio announcer in Berlin, warned the 7th Armoured to watch out for torpedoes on the way home.

14

HOMECOMING

The passage up the Clyde on the morning of 6 January 1944 was a moment they had all been longing for. It was bitterly cold and a mist or smog hung low over the inky waters as their ship cleaved its path forwards. Men crowded along the handrails, each lost in a private reverie of home. They had bypassed the German U-boats and although a layover in Algeria denied them the pleasure of being home by Christmas, this was near enough.

During the last days of their voyage the officers had gathered together in a state room to be briefed about the plans for putting the battalion on trains to take it south to England. It was just the people they needed to move, since all of their tanks had been handed over to the Canadian army prior to leaving Italy. The officers had not actually been told where 5th Tanks was going. It was all a matter of great secrecy.

When they got to their destination the soldiers would be entitled to disembarkation leave. Men like sergeants Bull, Solomon, Hall and Wardrop, who had been away for between two and four years, would be entitled to twenty-one days. Captain Crickmay and a few others who had been serving abroad for more than four years, were entitled to twenty-eight, although Crickmay was sceptical, given his role as adjutant, that he would be able to take the full entitlement. Crickmay also wondered how he would recover the three trunks of clothing and kit – including his dinner jacket and golf clubs – that he had left at the Carlton Hotel in Cairo.

Watching the shore as they glided into Glasgow, the soldiers spotted people going to work and the shipyards busy with activity. The great steel hulks of new destroyers and merchantmen were taking shape on the slipways. The dockyard workers saw the soldiers too, gliding by, and despite all the supposed secrecy they knew it was the 7th Armoured Division returning home. A great din began to rise above the shipyards, following the ship down the Clyde as it went, the noise of metal on metal. 'They were banging with spanners and crowbars, banging on tins making a hell of a noise,' recalled Sergeant Solomon. 'It was quite a welcome.'

Back on terra firma, they were herded onto trains. During the years of their absence rationing had come in, great swathes of urban Britain had been flattened by bombing and families divided by war had grown estranged. Clattering along through the smoke-stained grime of Glasgow and then out into the Borders they noticed that all the station names had been taken down – a measure intended to confuse German saboteurs or downed aircrew, but which confounded millions of British rail travellers instead.

At a station in the north of England one of the tankies, whose father was a railwayman, had managed to chat to the lads in a signal box and discover that their destination was in East Anglia. The battalion was to travel south to its new base, and only then could the business of getting them off on leave begin. Each soldier had been issued with the chits and bumf necessary for their time at home, noted in orders as 'food ration card for appropriate number of days; soap coupons; cigarette and sweets card for NAAFI; railway warrant and leave pass; AB64. Officers will also get clothing coupon.'

For a few weeks the battalion remained at a holding camp while the soldiers took off for leave. Jake Wardrop, retracing the route back to Glasgow, faced a long journey, Gerry Solomon a short one to his village near Ipswich. There were married men who faced a loving and longed-for reunion with their wives, and others who dreaded it. Rumours abounded about women who had given birth to other men's babies while their husbands were away. Some, like Charlie Bull, set off home with a determination to marry.

Sergeant Bull had only been back in his native Staffordshire for a few days when he took Peggy Fessey, an eighteen-year-old local girl whom he had met at a dance hall, to marry. They tied the knot on 24 February 1944 at the Register Office in Burton upon Trent. Bull's family was shocked at the sudden choice Charlie, who was twenty-nine by this time, had made. There had always been a bit of swagger about him, but the war had boosted his self-belief and desire to live for the moment.

With Deryck MacDonald, a lofty young captain who had served much of the war with A Squadron, nuptials followed a more romantic pattern. He soon got in touch with Brenda Pitt, whom he had met back in Thursley Wood in the summer of 1940, in order to make his intentions clear. This couple also married during disembarkation leave in February, their ceremony taking place two days after Sgt Bull's. They returned to Thursley for a church wedding, with MacDonald in uniform.

Brian Stone, MacDonald's old friend from the squadron who had returned from captivity in Italy a few months earlier, was his best man. In photographs of the day Stone wears a suit with a buttonhole and looks confident enough with the artificial leg he was learning to master. After the vows, they retired for their reception to the same house at the top of the hill where the young subalterns from 5th Tanks had gone for their Saturday night dances.

For the likes of Wardrop and Solomon the significant woman in their life was still their mother. In letters back from Italy the men had been able to say they were coming home, but security restrictions had prevented them from specifying when. Once back, some enterprising types had been able to make telephone calls home from railway stations or their camp. But when Solomon took the train back to Ipswich he was surprised to find his father waiting for him at the station; he had apparently been working on supposition and rumour.

Solomon's homecoming was not easy. During his years away his parents had once been cabled by the War Office to say that he was missing in action, and twice (erroneously) to tell them that he had been wounded. His mother had prayed nightly for his safe return. Standing at last in the hallway there were tears, but the family barely touched on his experiences in the desert. Like many returning 8th Army men, Solomon chose to avoid discussion of battles and loss, in part at least because he knew that the war was far from over. Three of Mrs Solomon's five sons were in the army, and one in the Royal Navy. Her husband was in the Home Guard to boot. Somehow they had all survived so far. The war, reflected Sergeant Solomon, was proving 'quite an ordeal for her'. While he was home, the sergeant's father picked up a minor wound during an air raid, and it was the cause of laughter around the dinner table that of the family's five warriors it was the one serving at home that got hurt first.

*

The emotions of soldiers returning to camp after their twenty-one days' leave were not good. For most it was a terrible wrench to leave behind the pubs, pals and parents that meant home. Almost immediately they began asking when they might go on leave again: after all, soldiers serving at home while they had been away had got home leave every few months. One 5th Tanks man calculated that if they all took the leave owing to them from three years overseas they would be gone until May or June. They were, however, soon swept up in intensive training for the dangers that lay ahead, and about which there differing attitudes.

The Gerry Solomon who had sailed from Britain thirsting for adventure had been left behind somewhere in the desert. Instead he had resolved never to volunteer for anything else in the army ever again, 'not even a Christmas club'. Nonetheless, he accepted that it was part of the bargain he had made back in September 1939 that if the army sent him into action, he must go and do his best.

For Jake Wardrop, lost in thought as he travelled south from Scotland, there was 'a smashing attack of the blues, and an almost overwhelming desire to get on the Great North Road and thumb a lift straight back again'. But Jake also harboured a longing to get back into action. That he enjoyed the fight was clear enough to anyone who knew him, but he also felt a sense of wanting to settle scores. He had lost too many mates already to shirk what lay ahead. His particular friend Stan Skeels, his boxing buddy and partner in many a street fight in Alex and Cairo, had been killed in an accident aboard the tank landing ship just before Salerno. After he died, Wardrop pledged revenge, reflecting, 'it will take a lot of square heads to settle up for Stan'.

Even before going home on leave Wardrop had resolved to fight on as a tank commander. He knew that there would be options to go off and train other men – which might even involve promotion – or to take a job further from the front line in the battalion's rear echelon. He rejected them, and perhaps to insulate himself from any family pressure when he was back in Glasgow had written his mother a remarkable letter before he got there. As a candid insight into the mindset of those hardened men who would lead the 5th RTR's crews on the last and most dangerous leg of the war, it is worth quoting at length:

I want to make sure . . . that you know how I feel about it, so that if anything happens you will not upset yourself too much. There are a crowd of us who have been in tanks all the time since we came here and at different times we could all have had easy jobs on transport but not one has ever taken it. I know why I have not and I suppose the others think the same. It is because of John and Stanley and all the others who have gone, it is a trust we have left and if I stopped now and skulked around until the end I would never hold my head up again and I have a feeling you [would] be ashamed of me a bit too. It seems a long time to keep going but we must otherwise we shall be letting them all down and they will have died for nothing . . . I am a tank commander, I've told you before I think, I've been one for a while and I shall continue to be one until the end. What the end will be I don't know, and who am I to say, but if it should be the wrong one don't worry. I've played the game as it seemed to me the right way to play it. I have respected the women and given my rations to the little children because they were hungry and I've shot the Germans down and laughed because of John and Stanley and in any case they started it.

Not all of the battalion's long-serving soldiers had the same view. Some had resolved, if they had any control over their destiny in this wartime army, to avoid going back into action. The odds of achieving this were better for officers and non-commissioned officers than for the rank and file because the forces needed these men in training establishments, headquarters and other places far from the rumble of guns. One officer in the battalion who had twice been wounded in action in North Africa and caught malaria in Italy noted, 'Some of us ... who were considered "war weary" were given the chance of a soft posting.' In his case, this meant running a unit of Royal Armoured Corps replacement crews for the coming invasion.

It didn't take long after returning from leave for Lieutenant-Colonel Mike Carver, commanding the 1st RTR, a sister battalion in the same brigade as the 5th that had been serving for even longer in the Middle East, to notice that quite a few had put in for transfers. Carver remarked:

> Several non-commissioned officers who had splendid records of gallantry and devotion to duty as tank commanders, applied to transfer to units less likely to be in the front line again. They were undoubtedly influenced by their wives, from whom they had been separated for several years and who resented their husbands going into the heat of battle again, when so many others had been in Britain all that time and not risked their lives in action.

Neither the 1st nor the 5th Tanks could afford to let many of these men go, so the NCOs were often told they would have to soldier on. Having tried to get out, maybe even promised a wife or mother that they would do so, some of these soldiers had crossed a psychological line that would make it more difficult for them to carry on. This was to prove just one of a whole collection of discontents that started to multiply as soon as the units had reassembled.

Moving on 11 February to Shakers Wood in Norfolk, the 5th Tanks was shocked by the poor standard of its new accommodation. The men were billeted in freezing, leaky Nissen huts in the middle of a pine forest, far from civilisation. Any notion that they could catch up on some of the pleasures they had missed while in the desert was undermined further by the posting of lists of soldiers who were to be sent for training on the new types of tanks with which they were to be equipped. This meant sitting in stuffy classrooms under the charge of officious instructors, many of whom had sat the war out safely at home but expected deference from their pupils. As Desert Rats, their ability to put up with training academy bullshit was all but spent.

As for their new machines, this also proved a major bone of contention. Most of the armoured units scheduled to take part in the landings in France were to continue with Shermans. The 7th Armoured Division has been chosen to receive the latest version of the British designed and built cruiser tank, the A27 Cromwell. In 5th RTR they had become unashamedly Americanophile in tank matters, so they cast a jaundiced eye upon the new vehicles. Soon there were loud complaints about the poor reliability and fighting qualities of the Cromwell. 'Our first impression of it was that someone had dug up an A13 from the museum and was having a very bad joke,' said Sergeant Wardrop. The difficulty of escape from the driver's compartment when the turret was at certain angles led to mutterings about a 'death trap', and the slab-sided turret (as opposed to one with angled sides and thus a better chance of deflecting an enemy shot) compounded the sense that the Cromwell had been conceived by base barnacles rather than front-line tank soldiers. The cramped crew stations enhanced a feeling of vulnerability for those inside, whereas the roomy interior of the Grant and Sherman had been good for morale.

There were some who could see more positive qualities to the

Cromwell. The restricted interior resulted in part from the fact that it sat a couple of feet lower than the Sherman (making a smaller target), was much faster and its Meteor engine was derived from the tried and tested Merlin aircraft motor. Reliability had indeed been designated the principal quality required of the Cromwell – ahead of firepower or armoured protection – by the Whitehall and army committees overseeing tank production, following the angry reports in 1941–2 about the hopeless performance of the A13 and Crusader. In time, the tankies would learn that this work had paid dividends.

While the discussion of the new tank among the old sweats in the Shakers Wood Naafi became increasingly expletive-filled, in the early spring of 1944 few in the Royal Armoured Corps had appreciated the real Achilles heel of the Cromwell, and indeed the Sherman. This lay with the inadequacy of the 75mm gun fitted to both tanks. Early reports from Tunisia and Italy, where new German tanks had been encountered, indicated that they were fearsome opponents. The Mk VI or Tiger had already demonstrated its near-invulnerability to Allied tank guns, while the Mk V or Panther proved superior to the Sherman in almost every aspect and, critically, in its firepower.

By 1944 Britain, in common with all of the other tank-producing belligerents, had realised that the challenges of firepower, protection and mobility forced certain engineering compromises. To these could be added the problems of manufacturing reliable vehicles.

The requirements of a tank gun to knock out enemy armour did not necessarily fit with those needed to provide support to the infantry or knock out enemy anti-tank guns. Solid shot armour-piercing rounds had to be sent on their way as fast as possible, with as big a bang as the gun breech could stand. High-velocity rounds flew in a low trajectory and were designed to kill tanks relatively close to the firer. The high–explosive (HE) projectiles that destroyed other targets by means of the shrapnel spread by a charge inside the shell were best fired at slower speeds on a more arching trajectory. The lack of an HE round for the British two-pounder tank gun had been bitterly felt during the early desert battles. Tank crews had reacted with unbridled relief when they got the American Grant with its 75mm main gun, for it gave them adequate anti-tank effectiveness against types such as the Mk III and Mk IV with its armour-piercing shot and good performance against other targets with its HE. As the war progressed, the British had fielded new anti-tank guns on wheeled carriages – the six-pounder and seventeen-pounder. Both were very good at knocking out enemy tanks but had poor HE capability. The War Office had therefore decided, fatefully, in late 1942 to stick with the 75mm gun (the same type on the Grant, Sherman and Cromwell) as a compromise or multi-role solution. This provoked heated controversy within the Royal Armoured Corps.

Faced with new enemy threats, the brass had issued bizarre tactical directives about how the British tank soldier might tackle his enemy with a 75mm gun that could not defeat the Tiger's frontal armour. While still encamped at Homs in Libya, the 5th Tanks had practised a technique of setting the fuse on an HE shell with a one-and-a-half-second delay and aiming it at a point a couple of hundred yards in front of the target. The idea was that the shell would bounce off the ground, activating its fuse, and then fly over the Tiger, exploding above its turret to injure the crew (assuming they had left the hatches open). Other tactics relied on these new enemy super tanks being available in small numbers so that one group of Shermans would attract the enemy's attention frontally while another tried to manoeuvre to the sides or rear where their shells could do more damage.

Many officers had realised that the seventeen-pounder (a 76mm weapon which fired its shell at high velocity; the shell left its barrel at 2900 feet per second, compared to 2050 for the standard 75mm tank gun) that had come into service during the last months of the North African campaign provided their one real answer against the Tiger and Panther. Shortly after his battalion's encounter with a Tiger on the outskirts of Tunis in May 1943, Lieutenant-Colonel Carver had written presciently to the commander of 22nd Armoured Brigade: 'If they are to be effectively and quickly dealt with we must have some tanks equipped with a 17-pounder or gun of equivalent performance. The ideal would be to have one tank per troop in the heavy squadrons equipped with 17-pounders.'

By the time the brigade was in Shakers Wood, nearly a year later, this was precisely the solution that the British army was, in great secrecy, about to deploy. The Cromwell turret could not accommodate the seventeen-pounder gun, but a modified Sherman could. The new hybrid of British gun and American tank was called a Sherman VC or Firefly. One was to be allocated to each troop of 5th Tanks, making it one Firefly and three Cromwells in each. The advent of the new vehicle was both a boon (the US Army had nothing similar) and a problem. What tactics would they employ if only one in four tanks was capable of meeting the latest panzers head on, and that sole tank was slower and higher than the others? Plans to build a version of the Cromwell with a turret big enough to accommodate the seventeen-pounder encountered all sorts of difficulties, although a couple of hundred Challengers, as they were called, did roll off the production line. The Royal Artillery, having employed the wheeled version of the gun with excellent results, also mounted it in a tracked, turreted vehicle, the Achilles tank destroyer. These various projects – Firefly, Challenger and Achilles – continued in great secrecy during 1944 but were ultimately limited by the number of these excellent guns that could be produced. Also, the development of an HE shell for the gun lagged behind, so there would be no choice but to field these vehicles in mixed formations with Cromwells, Shermans and Churchills (the main heavy tank for infantry support).

If these solutions sounded like a nightmarish compromise between military need, new technology and industrial capacity, it should be understood that the other belligerents faced similar dilemmas. By late 1943 Germany's tank production had fallen behind that of Britain. When the huge manufacturing lines of the USA and Soviet Union were included, the Germans were only managing a small fraction of their enemies' output. Aerial bombing played its role in stunting the industry, but the high-craft cottage-industry methods of German tank assembly probably did more. Faced with a dramatically worsening balance of armoured forces, the Germans had stepped up the mounting of powerful artillery pieces on tanks that were no longer fit for the line of battle. So a Mk II tank with a turreted 20mm gun, comparable in vintage to the British A9 and useful during 1939–41, was converted into the Marder, a tank-hunter mounting the powerful 75mm anti-tank gun. Rather than compromising HE performance by developing special shells for these weapons, field artillery pieces were mounted on some chassis, for example turning the same obsolete Mk II panzer chassis into a Wespe 105mm self-propelled gun. The Mk III panzer provided the basis for the Sturmgeschütz (StuG), which appeared both in an anti-tank version, with a 75mm high-velocity gun, and as an assault gun, for supporting infantry attacks, with a 105mm one.

With each of these designs, moving away from a turreted weapon mounting allowed a heavier gun to be installed and an effective vehicle either returned to the battlefield after conversion, or manufactured from stockpiles of existing parts. There were disadvantages too, not least that conversions like the StuG were best used in camouflaged, defensive positions because, lacking a rotating turret, it was hard for them to respond quickly to multiple threats from an unexpected direction. But as the German high command prepared for the opening of a second front in France, and watched their armies being beaten inexorably back on the Eastern Front, a defensive style of war was precisely what they were practising. As Lieutenant-Colonel Dicker Wilson and the rest of 5th Tanks had discovered in Italy, a well-placed StuG could remain undetected by Recce, lying in wait until it was able to destroy a tank at close range.

Even the Red Army, guided by an obsession with offensive tactics, followed a similar philosophy with its armoured vehicle weaponry, but the prodigies of production made possible by Stalin's command economy meant the emphasis was less on conversion and more on new production. So by 1944 Soviet factories were churning out thousands of the excellent T-34 tank, with its turreted general-purpose gun, as well as SU-85 tank destroyers and SU-122 assault guns. British, German and Red Army designs all prompted tactics that made use of a mixed fleet of tracked vehicles with different types of guns mounted with varying degrees of flexibility. Although British tank crews expressed disbelief at the choices made by their leaders in producing something like the Cromwell, all armies were struggling with inelegant compromise. Only the US army was truly hamstrung, since its emphasis on mass production and preference for the 75mm medium-velocity gun would see them heading for France pretty much bereft of an answer to the Panther and Tiger. The British, at least, had the Firefly.

In 5th RTR and other battalions there had been lively debate among the old hands about how best to use that secret tank, which none of them had actually seen. Some believed it would be better to group fourteen or fifteen together in a single squadron rather than parcelling them out at one per troop. Then, this Firefly unit could remain in reserve unless it was needed to fight the Germans' best tanks. But the armoured corps dictated the policy of allocating one of the seventeen-pounder vehicles per troop, giving a total of four Fireflies per squadron, and twelve in the battalion as a whole. Early in March 1944 the men on Cromwell crews headed north to Kirkcudbright in Scotland in order to practise firing the guns on their new tanks. Those picked for duty on the Firefly, meanwhile, were heading back to school, at the Royal Armoured Corps Depot in Bovington.

The battalion had decided that the job of commanding a Firefly be given to highly experienced men who could best make use of it to kill enemy tanks. To be chosen to use this secret weapon was therefore a mark of confidence in a unit where there were a great many seasoned men. The job would be given to a sergeant or corporal, but the troop sergeant as well as the subalterns who commanded each element of four machines (i.e. three Cromwells and one Firefly) were exempted from consideration. This meant that Emmin Hall and Charlie Bull, both skilled troop sergeants, would remain on Cromwells. Various reasons were given for this policy, but it was generally understood in the battalion that the officer or troop sergeant would be in the lead when moving towards the enemy, and the front tank often bought it, so it was better to keep the precious Firefly at the back of the troop, under the command of someone else.

Gerry Solomon and Jake Wardrop were among those chosen to command Fireflies. They picked up their rail vouchers and headed off to Dorset to learn about this strange new weapon. Much of the early training was on the automotive side, since working examples fitted with the seventeen-pounder were only just starting to be produced. The Sherman was, of course, quite familiar to them, since 5th Tanks had been using them since early 1943, but various changes had been made to the VC model. The bigger shells fired by the new gun required the removal of the lap gunner, who sat next to the driver in the hull. In his place was a rack for seventeen-pounder shells. Because of the length of the gun, and the extent to which its breech travelled backwards into the turret when it was fired, the back of the tank's turret had to be cut off and a new armoured box welded onto it. This allowed the 19 Set, the tank's radio, to be further back, preventing it from being smashed by the recoiling gun. Solomon, Wardrop and the others soon heard, from those who had seen the seventeen-pounder fire, about some of the other consequences of its enormous power.

By mounting the gun in an enclosed turret instead of having the breech in the fresh air, as on its original towed carriage, the consumption of the explosive charge that sent the shell on its way had been slowed very slightly. When the gun recoiled and the breech opened the propellant was still burning, which led to reports of singed hair and sometimes even light burns among the men in the turret. As this happened at the gun's rear, a great sheet of flame shot from its muzzle. By channelling some of the force of this explosion backwards as the weapon fired (using a device called a muzzle break on the end of the gun tube) the great recoil was partially dissipated. But the drawback was that this increased the amount of dust thrown up by the blast as it vented from the mouth of the gun. In short, given the amount of fire and blast produced by firing the seventeen-pounder, the Firefly crews would be telegraphing their presence to the Boche. A first-shot kill would be essential.

As spring went on, the 5th Tanks' vehicle fleet multiplied. Many of the Cromwells were picked up from flat cars at Brandon station, near to the Shakers Wood camp. In the Recce Troop the Bren carriers used in Italy were supplanted by a new version of the Honey light tank, the M5. Dingo scout cars, grouped in what was called Intercom Troop, were replaced with Humbers. Even in April 1944, though, the Fireflies had not yet been delivered – it would be early May before parties of trained crews were sent to pick them up from the factory. They were building towards a strength of sixty-one heavier tanks (each of the three squadrons having nineteen Cromwells and Fireflies, and battalion headquarters four Cromwells), as well as eleven Honeys and nine Humbers. This larger organisation meant that when the echelon, other supporting elements and Left Out of Battle (or reserve) crews were taken into account the 5th RTR would land in France with about eight hundred men. This required a great influx of new soldiers; around one third of the men had joined the battalion after its return from Italy. The new lads were quickly integrated into crews and into their troops, each of which occupied a Nissen hut in Shakers Wood.

One trooper, who had originally been posted to the 5th Inniskilling Royal Dragoon Guards but found himself diverted after a couple of months to B Squadron of 5th RTR, noted the differences eloquently:

> None of the men in the 'Skins' had seen action since the fall of France in 1940; there was a lot of emphasis with them on 'bull', Blancoed equipment and inspections ... but the greatest difference was the unbridgeable gap between officers and men. 5th Tanks, on the other hand, were a hard bitten active service unit who knew the value of good men, whether officer or trooper; 'bull' was at a minimum ... they did not pride themselves on their Blancoed equipment but did pride themselves on their professionalism as tank fighting men.

Greenhorn troopers soon found themselves being regaled with tales of the desert. This 'gripping', as the old sweats called it, was meant to impress upon the newcomer what was expected of him, as well as helping to pass the time during many a boring evening. If one veteran heard another laying on the war stories a bit thick, it became the custom for him to remove his beret and put it on his head upside down, indicating 'You're overdoing the gripping.' It was not an easy business, integrating old men with new, particularly in a camp as inhospitable as Shakers Wood rather than in the field, where a newcomer was soon swept up in the daily duties of being on a tank. One young officer believed it led to 'a lot of ill will and even open friction'.

One thing that immediately struck the newcomers was the amount of Arabic the old hands had incorporated into their slang. Second Lieutenant Roy Dixon, who had been inspired to join by the newsreels of the desert war that he had seen in the cinemas of his native Dover, arrived in February 1944. The soldiers had by this point sewn the ribbon of the Africa Star medal onto their battledress and Dixon, still a teenager when he turned up at Shakers Wood, was the only man in the battalion not to wear one.

In order to escape the tensions of their forest camp, men were sometimes allowed to take lorries into nearby towns such as Brandon, King's Lynn and Wisbech for a drink. Freed from the supervision of their superiors, these trips often produced brawls. Some men took a particular pleasure in fighting Americans, who they resented for wooing British women. When an American GI was found drowned in King's Lynn the town was put out of bounds to them, and Wisbech to the British, in order to cut down the number of punch-ups.

The disciplinary problems, new arrivals, training courses and requests for leave or transfers put great pressure on the adjutant, Captain Arthur Crickmay, and the others running the battalion. Day after day men were marched into Lieutenant-Colonel Wilson's office for CO's Orders or summary punishment – often for being absent without leave. This took most of the afternoon, which left Crickmay to finish his normal paperwork in the evening: 'I was almost always in my office until 22.00 hrs, seven days a week, thrashing through all the bumph ... fairly awful.'

There was so much to do before the invasion of France that Dicker Wilson drove everyone hard; there was no time for slacking.

It had been clear, even when General Montgomery had visited 22nd Armoured Brigade back in February, that a great many men were unhappy. The general quickly urged the soldiers drawn up in front of him to break ranks and gather around him. He had told them that a hard fight lay ahead, but that they would be given great support from the air and sea. He disparaged the quality of the German troops holding the coastal defences. This 'party' was not going to be too bad, he assured them, at which one soldier was heard to mutter, 'Not too bad for those who are going to be dead.' When three cheers were called for, one of the newly arrived B Squadron men said, 'the only cheers came from the officers'.

These tensions built through the spring as leave was refused, men charged and training intensified. By May 1944 open revolt was brewing in the 5th Tanks.

15

THE REVOLT

By April 1944 feelings in the Shakers Wood camp had reached an intense pitch. Everyone knew that they were to be thrown back into action within weeks. Many wanted to go home one more time, but knew that the chance for any further leave was disappearing. Their Commanding Officer, Lieutenant-Colonel 'Dicker' Wilson, had resolved meanwhile to drive the men hard, stamping out moaning and punishing those who were caught slipping out to pubs or absenting themselves in other ways without permission. As the days went on, the view of Wilson among most officers and nearly all of the NCOs grew steadily more antagonistic. In the sergeants' mess a caustic running commentary greeted each new order from the CO's office. Sergeant Emmin Hall was particularly contemptuous of the man he and many others called 'Screaming Willy'.

Hall had by then assumed something of a legendary character within the battalion. The NCO returned from North Africa with the Military Medal and a Mention in Dispatches. 'He had repeatedly proven himself to be an outstandingly gallant and capable tank commander,' Lieutenant-Colonel 'Fearless Jim' Hutton had written on Hall's MM citation. Hutton had also praised the sergeant's leadership skills, noting that 'on several occasions he efficiently commanded a troop in the absence of an officer'. During both the Sidi Rezegh fight of November 1941 and following the battalion's disaster of 2 June 1942, Hall had led to safety tanks separated from the main body of the unit. It was during the first of these episodes that he had first encountered Wilson and taken an instant dislike to him.

Viewed from the Other Ranks' tier of the army hierarchy, Hall's status was even greater. It was generally reckoned that he was in charge of 11 Troop, whether an officer was present or not. The way in which the sergeant had gently but firmly forced fresh-faced subalterns into a completely subsidiary role was greatly admired by many within C Squadron, and was even celebrated in one of the songs its soldiers had composed. One of the things newcomers to 11 Troop arriving in Shakers Wood had been told by the veterans was that their sergeant was exceptionally careful with his crews' lives, and that he had led them through many of the most difficult periods of the desert war without loss. Few in the unit knew about his unhappy upbringing, but Hall's family would later conclude that his intense protectiveness towards the young crewmen put under his charge was a consequence of it. His long period at the rank of sergeant made him unusually experienced but, despite this, his superiors evidently did not consider him suitable for promotion to sergeant-major or even officer rank. His reading and writing were poor, he could keep up with the battalion's best drinkers and he was also a known womaniser.

Hall, who by this point was thirty-one years old and had been serving in the army for eleven years, was one of the cadre of regular sergeants and sergeant-majors who were vital to the battalion's plans for France, particularly given that hundreds of new men had joined since the return to Britain. These long-serving commanders were the backbone of the 5th Tanks, and Fearless Jim had acknowledged it. 'The spirit of the battalion was second to none,' he wrote, adding, 'It was the superb quality of the senior NCOs which gave a very special strength.' By April 1944 only a minority of the soldiers in the 5th Tanks shared with Sergeants Hall, Wardrop and Bull the distinction of having fought in so many major battles since the French campaign of four years earlier. Every squadron had its stalwarts, who were known and deferred to by the newly arrived nineteen- or twenty-year-olds: among them Arthur Cornish and 'Jumbo' Hill in A; 'Knocker' Knight and 'Pluto' Ellis in B; and 'Snowy' Harris and Jake Wardrop in C.

Naturally it was the veterans who felt most keenly the injustice of their lack of leave and the fact that 7th Armoured Division, after fighting so many battles, would be part of the first wave on D-Day. In the spring of 1944 this unhappiness had reached open defiance – some men had scrawled placards with the slogan 'No Leave, No Second Front' and posted them in the Nissen huts. This act, along with the growing surliness of some soldiers and a good many cases of men disappearing without permission to the pub, formed a direct challenge to Wilson and his system of discipline. The grumbling was all the greater because Wilson had installed himself comfortably with his nearest and dearest at a nearby country house belonging to his wife's family. Unhappiness had broken out in several other battalions, including the 1st and 3rd Tanks, but the 5th was known to be 'bolshie'. That said, the RTR's *esprit de corps* still counted for a lot; there were other units where things were far worse. The 50th or Tyne Tees Infantry

Division, another formation brought back from the Mediterranean for D-Day, was so unhappy with its lot that it was at one stage reported to have more than a thousand soldiers Absent Without Leave, with some said to be hiding out in the New Forest.

As the 5th Tanks stood working on the tank park one day, a recently joined member of B Squadron asked a few questions about their Commanding Officer. 'Some of the old desert men suggested [Wilson] might meet with an accident if he remained with us much longer,' recorded the new trooper. 'I . . . was told to remember how easily a turret-top machine gun can go off; they are always left loaded, are they not, and safety catches are not used.' While talk of murder may have been hyperbole, it was nonetheless a mark of how detested Wilson was.

In the 1st Tanks, under a dynamic and respected leader such as Lieutenant-Colonel Carver, the officers remained solidly behind their boss despite the bleak conditions afflicting them, but in the 5th RTR this support was ebbing. In most cases the old sweats had remained on the non-commissioned side of the rank structure, but a handful had taken the exams and gone to OCTU (the Officer Cadet Training Unit), returning as subalterns. Jackie Garnett, a pipe-smoking, Durham-born miner's son who had been given command of 1 Troop in A Squadron (often referred by the Arabic word for one, *Wahed* Troop), was one. As the mutterings grew in Shakers Wood, Garnett provided a link between the officers' and sergeants' messes. There were plenty of officers who had already concluded, in the words of one, that 'Dicker Wilson simply wasn't up to the job'. His decision, as the battalion marched past after church parade one Sunday, to take the salute with Mrs Wilson and his children beside him confirmed in many of their minds the impression of a jumped-up martinet. The second-in-command and adjutant, the officers who worked most closely with the CO, had both been appointed from outside the 5th Tanks and found themselves largely isolated in their loyalty to him as he tried to re-impose a tight discipline on the battalion.

Lieutenant-Colonel Wilson was aware of the grumbling and decided to stamp it out by asking the men to sign a 'loyalty chit', a piece of paper that committed them to serving in the coming campaign without further ado. It was a gamble, pushing men who had risked their lives so many times while serving under charismatic COs like Hutton and Uniacke to sign such a paper and, sure enough, its circulation in the camp soon inflamed feelings. It was regarded as 'a slur on all we had done so far'. In many cases, the sergeants and corporals shuffled into the huts that housed their squadron offices muttering unhappily, but did sign it. Sergeant Emmin Hall, however, refused. When the major commanding C Squadron remonstrated with him he stood firm. In fact, Hall's discussion with his boss may have raised the stakes of the confrontation because Hall told his OC that he had no desire to shirk the invasion of France and would gladly go into battle with 11 Troop, but that he would not serve under Lieutenant-Colonel Wilson. Hall explained his motives by saying that they had been in action together before (during Operation Crusader in November 1941) and that he believed his Commanding Officer was likely to lead the men to disaster.

This clear revolt against the system of military subordination caused tremors as word spread through the camp. For Lieutenant-Colonel Wilson and the others principally concerned with maintaining military discipline (the adjutant, Captain Crickmay, and the regimental sergeant major), there could be no question of looking the other way. The sergeant was marched into the colonel's office under escort and cross-examined about his refusal to sign. Hall stood his ground, with the result that Dicker Wilson swiftly issued the order to place the man under close arrest. And so Sergeant Emmin Hall, MM, MID, was locked up in one of the huts that served as a battalion jail, and a court martial fixed for 15 April.

Around Shakers Wood, reports were soon flying. There was disbelief among some that matters had gone as far as the arrest of such a stalwart NCO, and discussions in the sergeants' mess about staging some sort of demonstration. In standing up against Wilson, the admiration many of the NCOs felt for Hall was redoubled. The sergeant, meanwhile, rebuffed all entreaties to change his mind.

For Captain Arthur Crickmay, the requirements of duty and gratitude meant supporting his CO. The adjutant had worked all hours while trying to stamp out signs of ill discipline within the battalion. It was Wilson, after all, who had rescued him from the misery of staff work, given him the Recce Troop in Italy and recommended him for the MC. Others in the officers' mess felt more torn. 'Many, probably most, were unhappy about the morale of the regiment,' wrote one B Squadron subaltern. 'Nevertheless, they were under an absolute obligation to support their Commanding Officer and could, therefore, show no sympathy for the discontents of their men.' If a popular commander like 'Fearless' Jim Hutton could be sacked for upsetting his brigadier, what chance did a sergeant have of challenging the hierarchy?

With Sergeant Hall's court martial drawing closer by the day, tensions were rising and it was clear to some that the situation could not be resolved justly (i.e. in Emmin Hall's favour) if the chain of command was to be respected. Dicker Wilson had, after all, been put in place by his boss in 22nd Armoured, Brigadier 'Looney' Hinde, in part to get a grip of the 5th Tanks. It would take representations – unofficial ones – to somebody outside the battalion and brigade. At this point, Lieutenant Jackie Garnett 'got things moving', making contact with some former 5th Tanks officers outside the brigade.

On 13 April Brigadier Dinham Drew, erstwhile CO during the 5th's campaigns of 1940–1, appeared at Shakers Wood. That in itself did not come as a bolt from the blue for Dicker Wilson, since a number of senior officers were visiting units of the 7th Armoured Division as preparations for the invasion of France were completed. After his time in 5th RTR Drew had brief spells in command of armoured brigades in the desert before being sent to Iraq, where he had known Dicker Wilson. Returning to England to run a training establishment, Drew had effectively been sidelined as he was too old for further operational command (he was approaching fifty by this time). As Drew surveyed the Shakers Wood camp with his hawk-like bearing he asked after Sergeant Hall, with whom he had served in India during the 1930s as well as in the 5th. He was taken to see the sergeant in detention, where the two men talked about what had happened. The brigadier also visited the sergeants' mess, where he was able to discuss the battalion's morale with others he trusted.

Leaving the battalion, Drew understood that he had no formal authority to involve himself in the 5th's problems, but did have a deep-seated emotional need to resolve the situation before it returned to combat. So he engaged the commander of the army's eastern district and the two men returned to Shakers Wood the following day. Drew negotiated a deal with Hall whereby all charges against him would be dropped if he agreed to sign the chit. This was not a climb-down because the sergeant was also promised, in terms that only the three men in the room would ever know, that his grievance – Dicker Wilson's command – was being addressed.

A few days passed, for by now preparations for D-Day had reached such an intense pitch that the commanders of the battalion, 22nd Armoured Brigade and the 7th Armoured Division were rarely in the same place.

On 4 May the thunderbolt finally fell on Shakers Wood. Lieutenant-Colonel Wilson and his second-in-command were dismissed. They packed their things and left without ceremony. The trial of wills between a sergeant and a lieutenant-colonel had been won by Emmin Hall. In the sergeants' mess and across the tank park there was jubilation; Screaming Willy had been vanquished. Of the team Wilson had gathered around him, only Captain Crickmay and the regimental sergeant major remained. Crickmay had quickly become such a respected figure in the 5th Tanks for his bravery and common sense that he was not tainted by his association with the departed CO. But his own feelings were expressed candidly in a letter to his mother. In the battle over discipline he sided clearly with Wilson, telling her, 'You will be sorry to hear my colonel and 2 i/c have both got the sack. They were a little too frank in what they said to the powers I fear. It was a great pity just as we were getting things organised.'

For the army the immediate question was who to take over, given that D-Day was just one month away. It was clear that it would have to be someone who was party to all the operational planning and training that had been taking place in East Anglia. The man chosen was Charles Holliman, known throughout the RTR as Gus Holliman, who was serving as second-in-command to Lieutenant-Colonel Carver at 1st RTR and thus billeted in the next camp in Shakers Wood. In asking themselves the question about what kind of man could impose his will on a battalion where the sergeants might easily have concluded that they were now in charge, senior commanders had chosen someone of almost unsettling personal bravery and physical presence.

Holliman was just twenty-six when he took over 5th RTR. Tall and powerfully built, he conformed to the sportsman ideal of the tank officer, excelling at rugby and happily belting out centuries at cricket. Although commissioned into the Tank Corps in 1937, he had soon gravitated towards special forces and commanded probably the hardest men in the 8th Army, the Rhodesian Section of the Long Range Desert Group. Returning to 1st Tanks as commander of A Squadron, it had been Holliman's Crusader that was knocked out by a Tiger on the outskirts of Tunis in May 1943; he had simply taken over another tank and carried on. He had twice been awarded the MC in the Middle East.

With Holliman's appointment the trend of sending younger and younger men to lead these tank battalions reached its zenith, for the new Commanding Officer was a full twenty years younger than Drew had been when he stood down. Mike Carver, a great friend of Holliman, had also been twenty-six when he took over 1st RTR.

During the days between the departure of Wilson and the arrival of Lieutenant-Colonel Holliman, the regiment moved to its marshalling area at a school near Ipswich, codenamed Camp R5. There they were to collect their vehicles and men, moving down to docks on the River Orwell where they would be loaded aboard tank landing ships. Even at this late stage much was still happening. Gus Holliman turned up at R5 on 17 May, taking as his second-in-command Major Rob Maunsell, a decorated former Royal Gloucestershire Hussars officer who had been with 5th Tanks since Alamein and had very much entered its fabric. The following day, Holliman gave the battalion a Griff talk about the hard fight that lay ahead.

As the battalion waited behind the screens that had been erected to hide the final preparations from prying eyes, Sergeant Gerry Solomon and a dozen others raced up to Nottingham to pick up the last six Fireflies needed to complete the regiment. They drove their 'secret weapons' down the public highway, all the way to Suffolk, stopping in Cambridge to fill up with petrol and drop in on Solomon's cousin for tea.

By 21 May the battalion was giving men day passes for a final trip to London. It was a last chance for those who were about to enter action to catch a picture, get drunk or lose their virginity. Four days later the leave passes stopped and the men were confined to camp. The last days of waterproofing their vehicles (for when they dropped off the ramps of their landing ships) were completed and the battalion moved down to the quayside to load up.

The commanders gathered at the head of each squadron column to check their timings and chat about the reception the Germans might have in store for them, but one man was absent. Sergeant Emmin Hall had followed Lieutenant-Colonel Wilson into exile the day before their battalion left for Camp R5. In one of his first acts as Commanding Officer, Holliman had decided he must get rid of this rebellious NCO, lest the rest of the sergeants' mess conclude that they could now pick and choose their superiors. Hall's war was not over: he had been posted to the Staffordshire Yeomanry who were also about to embark for France. For the sergeant this was a crushing blow, to be sent away from the battalion he had come to regard as his family and had been in action with so many times. Hall told friends that he had cried twice in the war, the first time when he lost his best mate in the Sidi Rezegh battles of November 1941. Now, as he left 5 RTR's camp, he had cried again.

As for Wilson, few would miss him. One evening Sergeant Wardrop scratched his own personal epitaph for the departing CO, using a pencil in a tan-coloured notebook he had picked up on his travels. It was damning: 'Fat, rather short, frightened, blusterer, bad language, no manners, or rather those of a pig. Almost ruined the unit but we managed on account of good majors and good chaps.' The best of those chaps, Emmin Hall, had left the camp too.

The operation the 5th Tanks' soldiers had embarked upon had been the subject of millions of man hours of staff work and other preparations. As they pulled up on the road the tank commanders noticed signs with numbers on them, each of which matched a serial chalked on the side of their vehicle. The tanks were embarking in Suffolk, but the 5th Tanks' echelon, dozens of trucks, had been earmarked to go through the Port of London. Along hundreds of miles of coastline in harbours from the West Country to East Anglia, similar scenes were playing out as the greatest invasion in military history got under way. Every conceivable arm of the military was represented, from barrage balloon operators to chefs, mine clearers to gunners. Millions of tons of stores were readied for loading onto thousands of landing craft, for the initial landing would have to be sustained lest it falter. And in among this huge tableau of human activity, at a quarter past eight on the morning of 5 June, the landing ships carrying 5th RTR pulled away from the quayside and set off for France.

16

INTO THE HEDGEROWS

It was the middle of the day on 7 June when 5th Royal Tank Regiment's vehicles advanced towards the ramps of their landing craft. The vehicles had been waterproofed before leaving Suffolk – or at least sufficiently protected to drop off the front of the vessel and into four feet of water without being swamped. For each of the drivers, opening the throttle gingerly, edging his vehicle close to the edge of the ramp and then feeling the front tip over, it was a moment of anxiety. Some found themselves driving off into just a few inches of water, most that the front of their tracks touched the sand before the back end of the vehicle dropped off the ramp. In two cases, though, they drove off the front only to disappear under the waves, the crewmen having to swim for their lives from their drowned machines. These dramas, while terrifying for the few involved in them, formed just a small part of the vast scene that unfolded as vehicles chugged ashore on Gold Beach.

During the previous day 130,000 Allied troops had been landed successfully in Normandy. Although it had originally been planned to put 7th Armoured Division ashore on that first day, with the idea that they might assist a dash inland, everything had gone a little slower than expected. Any delay in the disembarkation of one unit had a knock-on effect on the wave of landing craft due to follow on behind. For the tankies coming ashore on the 7th, it was a relief to be on terra firma. Their crossing required the landing ships to skirt around the Kent coast and then sail hundreds of miles westwards. The Allies had used a complex deception plan to convince the enemy that the landing would come in the Calais area, where the sea crossing was shortest, rather than in Normandy. That this ruse worked so well, and that the landings on the 6th met with isolated opposition, came as little comfort to the men sailing from East Anglia, since their route took them right under the super-heavy guns of the German coastal defences in the Pas-de-Calais. After spending the night off the Isle of Wight, the group dashed across the Channel, 'the little ships of our squadron plunging along in a lumpy green sea, their ensigns streaming white against a lowering sky'.

When they arrived, they were relieved not to have been blown out of the water or strafed by the Luftwaffe. Vehicles gathered on the sands, surrounded by thousands of men manoeuvring vehicles and stores. Major Deryck MacDonald took out his camera and snapped some pictures of his A Squadron before they moved inland to the battalion assembly point. Captain Crickmay, who as adjutant came ashore on board the Commanding Officer's tank, recorded, 'So much for D+1. What an anti-climax, and how dull and grubby after Salerno.' They were ashore in any case, and the long-promised second front to help the Soviet Union by putting pressure on Hitler's forces in the west had at last materialised. The

Germans were wrong-footed by the location of the landings, but soon began a concerted response. On 6 June they had five divisions in the Normandy area, mostly the type of second-line troops that Monty had promised they would be when giving his Griff talks. The sole panzer division, the 21st, was one rebuilt from scratch after its original namesake, and the Desert Rats' frequent opponent, had been captured in Tunisia. However, the mobile reserves originally deployed to meet a possible landing in the Pas-de-Calais were soon on their way, including an entire corps of SS panzer divisions. Hitler, meanwhile, ordered his men to contest every mile in the hope they could contain the Allied landings, before mounting powerful counter-attacks to push them back into the sea.

The day after they came ashore A Squadron were sent off a few miles to the west, in order to support an infantry brigade that was fighting to get around Bayeux but had met with opposition at the Château de Sully. The 5th Tanks had practised this type of infantry support mission during their exercises in East Anglia, and were quite familiar with parcelling out squadrons from Italy. However, as they drove towards the château they noticed that the countryside presented ideal defensive territory. While there were open fields in places, where bewildered dairy cows watched the tanks rumble past, many of the villages were surrounded with small enclosures, orchards and walls. In Sully, as elsewhere, some of the roads had high earth embankments topped by tall hedges, which made it difficult even for someone commanding a tank to see over into the field.

Coming up a gentle rise into the village of Sully, they pushed towards the château, a place where an eighteenth-century house had been added to surviving medieval towers which were being defended by the Germans. As tanks from 1 Troop under Lieutenant Garnett pushed up one of the lanes, he and his wireless operator had their hatches open. They had already heard the

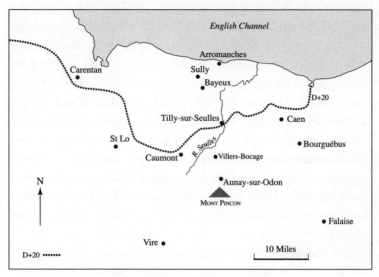

THE BATTLE OF NORMANDY

distinctive sound of snipers' bullets cracking near by, so no one was keen to have his head out of the turret. Instead they were sitting, trying to make out the lie of the enemy defences through their periscopes. Suddenly a grenade dropped into the operator's lap, which he swiftly lobbed out of the turret before it could explode. Drawing his Webley revolver, while Garnett grabbed a Sten sub-machine gun, the two men emerged from their turret to see German soldiers standing on the back of their tank. Their eyes met for a moment, before Garnett emptied a magazine into them. Just behind, another Cromwell had been boarded, its crew similarly dispatching their attackers with pistols. How had it happened that the enemy had got so close without being seen?

Reaching the château, the 5 RTR tanks started to pump 75mm high-explosive rounds into its buildings and towers. A

German self-propelled gun managed to feel its way around the flank of the attacking force, opening up on a Sherman Firefly, which it destroyed. After a few hours of combat the British managed to drive the Germans from the château, and A Squadron returned to their night leaguer on the north-east side of Bayeux. Three men from the 5th RTR had been killed and several wounded; they had all received some unpleasant lessons in Normandy fighting. The hedged enclosures that were a feature of the country the French called the *bocage* could allow an enemy to get very close undetected. If engagements took place at a hundred yards or even less, a weapon like the Firefly could hardly be used to good effect. Sergeant Gerry Solomon, commanding one of the squadron's Fireflies, was actually unable to fire any rounds during the Sully engagement because he could not get a decent sight of the enemy. Furthermore, the tanks would be vulnerable not just to self-propelled guns but to all manner of anti-tank weapons including the Panzerfaust, a hand-held rocket-powered grenade that could allow even the humble foot soldier to knock out a tank from a distance of sixty yards.

It was the middle of the night before the squadron was back in its leaguer, the tanks refuelled and rearmed and the experiences of the day were digested. Moving through the darkness Corporal William Bridge, another of the A Squadron Firefly commanders, approached Lieutenant Dixon, his troop leader. Bridge, a tall, fair-haired Welshman, had been through many of the desert battles and his veteran status qualified him for command of the Firefly. As a green officer, the diminutive Dixon literally and figuratively looked up to Bridge. The corporal, however, told his officer that he couldn't go on. His hands were shaking, his nerve had gone, he told Dixon: 'I've had it in a big way.' It was a dilemma for the young troop leader. Bridge was twenty-four, and had married while on leave in his native Cardiff a few months before. Was he one of those ones who had tasted home life and simply couldn't bear to face combat again? The troop officer did not want to risk having in his troop a commander who was incapable of performing. Dixon told the corporal that they had only a few hours to sleep, adding, 'There is no way I can replace you when we're going to be moving off again at three o'clock in the morning, so you'll have to just do another day and then I'll do my best to get you relieved tomorrow.' Corporal Bridge replied, 'Fair enough,' and the two men kicked off their boots and retired to their bedding rolls.

Two days later the 5th Tanks returned to action, moving a few miles south of Bayeux, which had by then been secured within the British bridgehead, to support the infantry once more. Within a couple of days of the Allied landings the Germans had begun to feed in their panzer and other reinforcement divisions. By 10 June they were attempting a large-scale counter-attack which had as its objective Bayeux. The sector into which 5th RTR was moving that morning was being contested by the Panzer Lehr Division, a picked unit armed with Mk IV and Mk V or Panther tanks and supported by the usual artillery and self-propelled guns as well as panzer grenadiers or mechanised infantry. With both sides trying to advance in the close Norman countryside, units became interpenetrated, offering vulnerable flanks and increasing the chances of getting cut off. This also increased the scope for confusion, sometimes with deadly results. During close-range fighting C Squadron had lost two tanks on the 10th – knocked out by British tanks from the neighbouring 8th Armoured Brigade that mistook the camouflaged 5th RTR Cromwells for enemy Mk IVs.

The following day, advancing towards the village of Tilly-sur-Seulles, the 5th Tanks found themselves crossing some relatively open ground as they fixed the likely enemy positions in the woods ahead of them. Lieutenant Dixon's 3 Troop was leading the way. The thump of a firing tank gun quickly halted them. They scanned for enemy firing positions but soon concluded that anyone who had shot at them had moved off. Dixon realised that his Firefly was not responding to radio messages and, impatient to get on, leapt out of his vehicle. The tank did not appear to be damaged as he climbed up, seeing Corporal Bridge in his commander's hatch. Dixon would soon make the terrible discovery that the German shot has pierced the Firefly's commander's cupola at chest level, cutting his head and shoulders from the rest of his body:

> I ... looked down into the turret and there of course, [there] was this horrendous sight of the headless body and blood in all directions and the rest, and the couple of the crew on the floor of the turret covered in his blood and oh God, you know. And I thought, This is a fine way to start the war!

Corporal Bridge had been killed instantly. As Dixon surveyed the grisly scene Garnett jumped up onto the Firefly. 'Oh my God, what do we do now?' the young subaltern asked. 'Go on. Shove off and get back to your tank and carry on,' replied Garnett. As Dixon trudged back to his Cromwell he replayed the conversation he had with the corporal a few nights before. Had Bridge had a premonition of his own mortality? Could he, as the troop commander, have got the corporal removed from duty more quickly? He could not dwell on it. Across the battlefield the sounds of combat continued. The 5th Tanks had lost two Cromwells as well as Bridge's Firefly. Their accompanying infantry from the 1st Battalion of Rifle Brigade had briefly managed to infiltrate the woods ahead, but were beaten back by the Germans who sent two Mk IV tanks converted into flamethrowers or 'Flammpanzers' to support their own foot sloggers.

It would take more infantry to clear the woods and villages that lay ahead of them, but this was available in the form of the 56th Infantry Brigade, which grouped one of its battalions with each of those in the 22nd Armoured Brigade. For 5th Tanks, this meant forming a plan of attack with the 2nd Battalion of the Essex Regiment. The tankies had sized up the Essex men, very few of whom had been in action before, and concluded, in the words of one sergeant, 'They did not seem to have a great deal of idea what it was all about, these chaps.' Studying the objective he had been ordered to take, the Commanding Officer of the 2nd Essex resolved on an assault forthwith.

The 5th Tanks, who occupied positions on the edge of a village called Bernières, watched the Essex men filing forward into their forming-up point just after two in the afternoon on 11 June. One of the NCOs in B Squadron described what happened next:

> They appeared to be very new, and too spick and span for the work in hand, but knowing what had happened in the previous attack on the wood, we were surprised and shocked to see them lined up as if on the square, and as we began the cover fire they started to walk slowly forward, upright, towards the wood with their rifles 'at the port'. In a few minutes the line was massacred; those who had not been hit fell back against us.

After this disaster, the Essex men returned to the attack again, this time crawling on their bellies through the cornfields. They penetrated the woods, where they found dug-in Germans supported by Flammpanzers. These were knocked out, with the infantry, who carried an anti-tank grenade launcher called the PIAT, and the 5th Tanks both claiming the credit. The success was to prove short-lived, for it stimulated another German counter-attack. It proved horribly costly, with the Essex battalion taking two hundred casualties. While the tankies marvelled at the ineptitude of the green infantry officers who could have ordered such a thing, the Essex men accused the 5th Tanks of holding back and preserving themselves rather than providing close support as the foot soldiers fought and died in the woods at Bernières. Despite the taunts of the Essex men, the day had hardly been cost-free for the 5th, which had lost five tanks: Corporal Bridge's Firefly, two Cromwells and two reconnaissance-troop Honeys.

Under orders from their superiors, the 22nd Armoured Brigade was pulled back into its battalion leaguers that night. There was another operation in the offing. During the encounters of the previous two days south of Bayeux, the two sides had essentially cancelled each other out. The Germans had failed in their attempt to retake the medieval cathedral city at the centre of the British bridgehead, and the British to expand it southwards in the way General Montgomery had hoped. The Desert Rats had encountered Panthers in this fighting (indeed it was probably such a tank from the Panzer Lehr Division that killed Bridge) and had found it a depressing experience. The Panther was armed with a high-velocity 75mm gun that had no problem brewing any British tank. At forty-four tons, the Panther was fully twenty tons heavier than the Cromwell, roomier inside and with thicker armour. The thing that struck many of the British crewmen was the cleverness of the German design, which raked the frontal hull armour (known as the glacis) steeply, and angled the hull as well as the turret sides. 'It was some tank and no mistake,' reflected Sergeant Jake Wardrop after examining a knocked-out Panther near Bernières. 'I took a good look and decided that I would examine no more of them as it was bad for my morale to see that thick sloping front and the length of the barrel of the gun.'

By the end of the first week of fighting, the sort of battle they faced in Normandy was becoming clearer. The early predictions of rapid advances had soon been shown up, and by 12 June the Allied bridgehead was around fifty miles across, but extended just twelve miles inland at its deepest. Despite these shortcomings, the forces landed on the 6 June on separate beaches had linked up to form a continuous area, and they had rebuffed the initial German counter-attacks, causing them heavy losses. During the first twelve days of the campaign, for example, the Panzer Lehr Panther battalion had gone from having eighty-six combat-ready tanks to just twenty-three.

The narrow front of the Normandy bridgehead was becoming congested as fresh Allies landed and Germans converged from different directions. The fight would eventually suck in six British or Allied armoured divisions and eight independent armoured brigades in their sector, versus six panzer divisions and three independent heavy battalions equipped with Tigers. In this crowded arena, where geography usually favoured the defender, it was the infantry whose numbers were more important. The potential effect of a small number of men had been demonstrated in its most extreme form at Omaha Beach on 6 June, when a pair of Germans armed with a single Spandau machine gun were reckoned to have mown down something approaching two thousand American attackers, killing several hundred of them. Where hedgerows and folds in the ground reduced engagement ranges to a hundred yards or less, a foot soldier with a mine or Panzerfaust could easily negate the tank's advantages. But Montgomery's army was constantly short of infantry. The Mediterranean and Far Eastern campaigns relied heavily on foot soldiers, so when it came to north-west Europe Montgomery had been obliged to give artillery and armour a major role in the 2nd Army, the formation that formed the British centrepiece of his 21st Army Group. Infantry formed just 16 per cent of its strength, artillery 17 per cent and armour 7 per cent, with the remainder being support troops.

As the engagement on 12 June had demonstrated all too clearly with the heavy losses suffered by the Essex regiment, it was the foot soldiers who would have the toughest job in the battle that lay ahead, accounting for 16 per cent of the 2nd Army's strength but 71 per cent of its casualties in Normandy. Monty wanted armour to act most often in close support of the infantry in a way that the Royal Armoured Corps had originally envisaged for its heavy 'I' or infantry support tanks. Just three of the corps' brigades in Normandy were, however, equipped with the heavily armoured Churchill tank, the remainder having the Sherman or Cromwell that tank commanders considered too lightly protected for such roles. The scene was set for many arguments between infantry and armour about who was letting whom down. Inevitably, given the lives lost and time frittered away, these disputes became highly emotive. In the 22nd Armoured Brigade War Diary, the terrain had been described on 8 June as 'unsuitable' for armour and, two days later, 'the need for more infantry was felt time and again'.

Montgomery did not want excuses; he wanted to break out of the bridgehead, and quickly. By 12 June an opportunity had presented itself. In thrusting towards Bayeux, the Panzer Lehr had left its western or left flank hanging. A push by US units in the opposite direction, meanwhile, had made good progress. Allied commanders detected a gap in German lines that with a rapid advance would allow an attacker to manoeuvre around to the rear of the villages that the 22nd Armoured Brigade had just been engaged in, perhaps cutting off a substantial enemy force. While the Desert Rats might have thought the jobs they had been given during the first few days were not really suitable for an armoured division with speedy, but lightly armoured cruisers, the opportunity had now arisen for them to show what they could do.

17

VILLERS-BOCAGE

The morning of 13 June presented an unexpected surprise for SS Hauptsturmführer Michael Wittman. He had pulled up his tanks beside the road, hiding them in some woods because of the risk of Allied air attacks. His men had only just entered the Normandy battle zone. One of the seven vehicles under his command was not running properly and the crews were working on it when they became aware of tracked vehicles moving along the road just a couple of hundred yards to their front. Wittman had taken post near the road because it offered a lofty vantage point. Bayeux lay about twelve miles to the north and the British front line, where the Essex had taken their heavy losses, about seven miles in the same direction. From near his hide, Wittman could also gaze north-east down the Odon Valley, an area where tens of thousands of German troops were fighting, towards the city of Caen. About one mile in the other direction (i.e. south-west), he could look down on the township of Villers-Bocage. Wittman's company had been committed to the fight the previous day, amid rumours that British armour was moving in this sector.

Looking onto the road, at about nine o'clock, the SS officer was able to see Cromwells and Fireflies parked almost nose to tail. Their crews had jumped out and were having a smoke or getting a brew on. They had reached an objective, Point 210, and were awaiting further orders. The men came from A Squadron of the 4th County of London Yeomanry (4th CLY) and they formed the vanguard of the 7th Armoured Division. The 4th CLY, along with 1st RTR, 5th RTR, the 1st Rifle Brigade and supporting artillery, formed 'Looney' Hinde's 22nd Armoured Brigade, who in turn were part of the 7th Armoured Division, numbering around fifteen thousand men in total. The division had been given the mission of executing a bold thrust through a gap in the German defences, and on 12 June had motored south without opposition. Early the next day they had moved off again, to execute the 'hook' part of their manoeuvre to take the Panzer Lehr Division in the rear. They had turned eastwards, with the 4th CLY in the lead.

Hearing that A Squadron had taken the high ground beyond Villers, the CO had stopped in the middle of the village itself with his HQ tanks and accompanying infantry, while his other two tank squadrons lined the road behind him to the west. Curious villagers had emerged to greet the Brtish soldiers, and the atmosphere among the yeomanry crews was cheerful.

Ordering his men to mount up, Wittman set off. A Squadron, parked in blissful ignorance just yards away, had presented him with an opportunity that he could not possibly miss. The thirty-four-year-old officer was a decorated tank ace, with 117 kills to his credit, mostly on the eastern front. His tank, a Tiger, was part

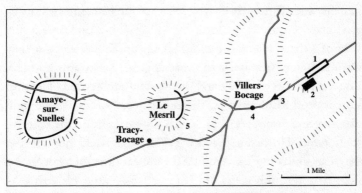

1. Furthest advance of A Sqn, 4th CLY
2. Initial position of Wittman's Tiger Company
3. Route into village taken by Wittman's Tiger

4. Place where Wittman's Tiger was knocked out
5. Position of C Sqn, 5 RTR during afternoon battle of 13 June
6. 7th Armd Div 'box' defended on 14 June

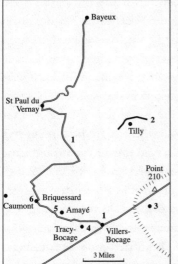

1. Route taken by 22nd Armd Bde on 12/13 June
2. Forward units of Panzer Lehr Division
3. Starting point of Wittman's Tiger Company
4. Position of C Sqn, 5 RTR, during fighting of 13 June
5. Position of 5 RTR during German attacks of 14 June
6. Position of 1 RTR during German attacks of 14 June

VILLERS–BOCAGE

of the 101st SS Heavy Tank Battalion, the first unit equipped with these formidable machines to enter the Norman fray.

The 5th Tanks were second in the 22nd Brigade's order of march. With C Squadron at their head, the battalion had occupied positions in Tracy-Bocage, a village about one mile to the west of Villers. Much of the 5th could not see Villers, for they were stretched out along the road that led westwards but sank into a dip between Tracy and the next village beyond. Those in C Squadron fanned out on the eastern edge of Tracy, affording them a good view of Villers, which was well within the range of their guns. However, the 5th RTR men could not see the mayhem unfolding near Point 210, out on the other side of the village, as Wittman's Tiger began its attack on the 4th CLY.

Wittman started by knocking out two tanks at the rear of A Squadron, to prevent them falling back to the rest of 4th CLY. He then set off on the main road down the hill into Villers, where he began a rampage along the main street, sowing death and destruction on his way. A couple of close-range shots from Cromwells bounced off the fifty-seven-ton leviathan as it made its way along the street brewing up British tanks. With each bark of the 88mm gun those watching and listening from their vantage point in Tracy could imagine the magnitude of the disaster unfolding in the village below. Many in the CLY chose to bail out before the inevitable, others served their weapons until the bitter end. 'Major Carr, the 2 i/c, fired at it with his 75mm', recorded a CLY Cromwell commander of one of the engagements at no more than fifty yards, 'but heart-breaking and frightening, the shots failed to penetrate the [Tiger's] side armour even at this ridiculous range.' They fired at Wittman's rear armour after he had passed them, only to watch mesmerised as the Tiger's turret slowly turned around to face them and the inevitable destructive blast of its 88 ensued. At about half past ten the 4th CLY's CO was heard over the radio ordering, 'Burn your tanks and get out!' He was captured soon after giving this message. Wittman carried on a little longer, before turning to leave the village. He had come under fire from a Firefly and needed to replenish his Tiger with shells. As he came close to the eastern end of the village his tank was disabled, probably by a six-pounder anti-tank gun, so Wittman and his crew bailed out.

In the hours that followed, the commander of the 7th Armoured Division fed reinforcements into the village. Some companies of infantry from the 1/7 Queen's (a battalion of the Queen's Regiment, part of the division's motor brigade, the 131st or Queen's Brigade) went into the village, combining with surviving tanks from B Squadron of the 4th CLY to lay an ambush. When a couple of Tigers and a Mk IV returned to the fray that afternoon, the British were at least waiting for them.

Just as they sent more troops into the fight, so did the Germans. Another company from the 101st SS Heavy Tank Battalion, under Hauptsturmführer Möbius, this one with up to ten Tigers, was manoeuvring round Villers towards Tracy. Some German infantry was also being thrown into the eastern side of the village, ready to tackle the Queen's and bundle away the prisoners who had already been taken. To the north-east, mean-while, a small Kampfgruppe from the Panzer Lehr, with fifteen Mk IVs and some infantry, pushed out to the northern fringes of Villers, trying to secure the division's flank.

The afternoon fight saw some notable British successes. A couple of surviving Yeomanry Fireflies and infantry crewing six-pounders successfully knocked out Tigers belonging to Möbius's company. Whatever panic and misfortune the Yeomanry might have endured that morning, one of the Tiger crewmen described the afternoon battle, where they were up against determined resistance in the village streets, as a 'nightmare'.

Late that day, though, the advance of German tanks around the village brought them under the guns of C Squadron, 5th

RTR, from their posting on the forward slope of the hill near Tracy. Sergeant Jake Wardrop, commanding his Firefly, was on the qui vive. After what had happened that morning, many of the 5th's crews waited in abject fear.

It was Wardrop's loader who spotted the Tiger first, moving a few hundred yards ahead of them and to the right. Moments later the little valley echoed to the sound of its 88 going off. The radio was alive with panicked reports. Snowy Harris, the troop sergeant of the group to their right, came running through the undergrowth towards Wardrop's tank. He shouted up that his Cromwell had just been knocked out, and two of his crew killed. It was not long after that Wardrop spotted a vehicle 'as big as two Glasgow corporation tramcars side by side' in the trees 250 yards to their front. Wardrop dipped his head into the turret and told the gunner to traverse the big seventeen-pounder gun to the right. The gunner could not see, but Wardrop told him to fire anyway. With an almighty bang it went off and the spent brass casing clanged onto the turret floor. Wardrop ordered the gunner to pan a little to the left and fire again, into the trees: 'They had the wind up on the Tiger now and it was reversing as fast as it could go and we followed it down with another two shots.' Despite firing four rounds, the Firefly had not disabled the German tank, possibly because the gunner was so afraid that he missed. Sergeant Wardrop was disappointed not to get the kill, but delighted to have sent this mighty enemy packing. He was a man who had studied the effect of fear on himself and others during his four years of war and now, his body still flooded with adrenalin, Wardrop registered its symptoms: 'I discovered then that I was having some difficulty in swallowing and in keeping a muscle in my knee from twitching. The lads told me too that I had been sitting on top of the tank shouting "Come on you square-headed bastards!" such is the red rage of battle.'

To the sergeant's right, a second Tiger had contacted 10

Troop, also from C Squadron. The troop leader had fled his tank with the crew. To the other side, one of the Cromwells had been hit and its turret jammed. The men had bailed out, extracting one seriously wounded comrade, but the crew of the vehicle behind, belonging to the troop sergeant, had also fled their vehicle, claiming that the damaged Cromwell was blocking their field of fire. During the fight of that afternoon six Cromwells had been lost by members of C Squadron. One, Sergeant Harris's tank, had been knocked out by a Tiger and another seriously damaged by enemy fire. Wardrop reflected, 'I'm afraid there was a bit of flapping all round and sad to say one or two even bailed out without being fired on or firing a shot themselves.' In fact, four Cromwells had been abandoned undamaged, with Wardrop reserving particular scorn for Lieutenant Allen and Sergeant Weng, who had bailed out with their crews. Another commander, Lance Corporal Stainton (himself standing in as commander for a sergeant wounded the previous day) had jumped out of a Cromwell, leaving three crewmen behind him. They were taken prisoner a little later, after abandoning their tank because they couldn't get it started.

That evening the 7th Armoured Division pulled back one mile to the west, to a more defensible feature, the crown of a hill where another village, Amayé-sur-Seulles, provided a natural rallying point. The Desert Rats had put themselves five or six miles ahead of the nearest Allied forces and they now feared being surrounded. The division was therefore deployed into a state of all-around defence atop the hill while the remnants of the 4th CLY, 1/7 Queen's and the 5th Tanks pulled back to this 'box' on the evening of 13 June. A combined force made up of 1st RTR and a battalion of the Queen's were holed up in a village a little to the west, where they were securing a bridge necessary for the division's withdrawal to friendly lines. At half past nine their higher headquarters agreed to a request for large-scale air raids on

Villers, and as the night wore on the 7th Armoured Division witnessed the ghastly spectacle of the community being smashed, along with many of its civilian inhabitants.

Crowded into an area little more than 2000 yards in one axis and 1250 in the other, the men and vehicles of the 7th Armoured formed a tempting target for artillery. Soon enough the shells were raining down on them as they recounted the shocking experiences of their day and endured the long night. The check they had received was frightful: the 4th CLY had lost twenty-five tanks (eighteen Cromwells, four Fireflies, and three Honeys); 1st RB had lost fourteen half-tracks, eight Lloyd carriers and eight universal carriers. In the fighting for the village itself, the 1st RB had eighty-three casualties, many of whom had been taken prisoner. What proportion of this impressive total was accounted for by Wittman himself was unclear, but it was undoubtedly significant. The 5th RTR's loss for the day was returned as four Cromwells. Two of those abandoned by their fleeing crews had been driven back into the box position by more stout-hearted crewmen from other C Squadron tanks.

Sergeant George Stimpson, one of Wardrop's oldest friends in the battalion and another of the cadre of NCOs who largely ran C Squadron, had organised the recovery of Lieutenant Allen's tank, for which consideration he helped himself to all the supplies on board. That night in the leaguer at Amayé, the lieutenant approached Stimpson to ask him what had become of these goodies. 'Where did you *leave* the tank, sir?' asked the sergeant. Receiving no reply, Stimpson taunted the young officer: 'Perhaps there are [some] panzer grenadiers enjoying a good strong brew and eating mixed fruit pudding.'

After a night of shelling, sniping and feeling the ground tremble as the Lancaster bombers unloaded on Villers-Bocage, 14 June dawned. The 7th Armoured Division was stranded six miles south of the main British line. There were American troops a little nearer at hand, the 1st Infantry Division having reached Caumont, to the west of them. However, additional German units from the 2nd Panzer Division had been coming into the area since the previous afternoon. This latest German reinforcement had been based in Amiens before D-Day, not far from the expected Allied landing sites, but the policy of air attacks on bridges that might have assisted the drive against the bridgehead had been so successful that the 2nd Panzers had to go all the way south to Paris before returning north again to Normandy. This took them nearly a week, and even when the first elements of the division arrived their tanks were far behind. Undaunted, the panzer grenadier regiment and armoured reconnaissance battalion from 2nd Panzer had gone into action, feeling their way around 7th Armoured Division's night leaguer from the eastern side until the Germans had it covered on three points of the compass (only the route west was open).

For much of the morning, the British atop the hill used their shovels to dig better positions, checked their tanks were fuelled up and broke out fresh rounds for the twenty-five-pounders. German artillery fire had largely abated, allowing this vital work to go on. At the same time, a fierce debate was going on between the two brigadiers (of 22nd Armoured and 131st Infantry), the 7th Armoured Division commander and their corps HQ. While they talked, the Germans were organising ad hoc Kampfgruppen. While the exact composition of these forces is unclear, the panzer grenadiers and armoured cars from the 2nd Panzer Division formed their nucleus, with some Lehr Panzer Mk IVs and possibly Tiger tanks of the 101st SS in support. The attack had to be spearheaded by infantry because of the nature of the terrain, so the Germans began to send troops forward to infiltrate the British position. This caused the defenders to open fire, and reveal their positions.

By the afternoon a full-scale battle was in progress, both

around the Amayé box and at the satellite position to the west in the village of Briquessard, which was held by the 1st RTR group. Moving forward, groups of German infantry began to appear in the orchards and fields to the south of the main position. The Queen's greeted them with Bren-gun and rifle fire, but as the numbers showed no signs of slacking it became clear that a determined German attack was under way. Twenty-five-pounders from the 5th Royal Horse Artillery took aim at Germans just a few hundred yards away, firing over open sights. They fused their shells to airburst just above the attackers, and with each explosion the defenders could see the leaves fluttering down from trees lacerated by shrapnel, imagining the suffering of those who lay beneath. One of the Queen's company cooks – who also happened to be a crack shot – took aim at a German sniper who had climbed a nearby tree and hit him; a great cheer went up as the man fell from its branches. As this went on, Typhoon fighter bombers orbited the box, waiting for vehicles and other targets to appear a little further away from the perimeter then diving down on them with a whoosh of under-wing rocket fire or a crackle of cannon.

At the headquarters of the 5th Tanks, a US artillery liaison officer presented himself to Lieutenant-Colonel Gus Holliman and offered to bring dozens of heavy American guns into play from the Caumont sector. 'Whaddya want? A Serenade or an Obligato?' asked the New Yorker. These were terms for particularly heavy artillery-fire missions. Holliman simply pointed out the area where he believed the attacking panzer grenadiers had concentrated and told his ally to get on with it. Great rippling bombardments of American shells soon plastered the hillsides.

The German assault reached its peak intensity at about seven o'clock that evening. By then Holliman and Crickmay were crewing a couple of Cromwells that belonged to battalion headquarters, tanks equipped with fire-support howitzers.

Anticipating that the Germans could soon be in their position, Holliman ordered 'Be prepared to engage with the 95 [howitzers].' It was soon after this that 5th Tanks brought in an American Serenade fire mission right in front of B Squadron. The tanks crews, meanwhile, were firing their machine guns into the fields to their front, pumping 75mm high-explosive shells at anything that moved and, in one case when the enemy was just feet away, lobbing hand grenades from the turret. Sergeant Wardrop described the action memorably: 'B Squadron tanks had a good party and cut down the Boches as they came, SS men they were, all washed and shaved and singing the Horst Wessel song, there were a lot of them would sing no more after that day.'

A couple of hours before this, Brigadier 'Looney' Hinde had been to see Lieutenant-Colonel Mike Carver in Briquessard to tell him that his combined force of 1st Tanks and the Queen's should hold their positions because the rest of the division would be evacuating through their position that night. Carver was annoyed; he had also beaten off heavy German attacks and felt 'confident that we could hold the position, extended though we were, against all comers'. Hinde told him that the 50th Division, to their north, had made no progress during the day closing the gap, and that the corps commander had therefore ordered 7th Armoured to fall back. It was a difficult moment for the division as a whole because many of them felt that while they had suffered a bloody check the day before, they had wrought their revenge on the Germans on the 14th and could kill as many as chose to attack them. They estimated the enemy casualties at five hundred. German returns, meanwhile, suggested that anything up to fifteen of 101st Heavy Battalion's Tiger tanks had been put out of action during the fighting of 13–16 June, nine destroyed and six seriously damaged. The Lehr group had lost four Mk IV tanks on the 13th and several more the following day.

Remarkably, given the way it was subsequently written up by many, the tanks put out of action on the two sides in these three days of fighting – around thirty on the British side and twenty-five or so German – were not so different. The British though, by virtue of their bombing of Villers-Bocage and withdrawal from the position, were unable to recover vehicles put out of action that might have been repaired (including a few whose crews had fled), something the Germans were able to do with some of the Tigers.

Sitting in the CO's tank at dusk, Captain Arthur Crickmay listened in to the 22nd Armoured Brigade net, waiting for the order to move out of the box. At that moment the German attack seemed to reach a new intensity, as did the defensive fire being called in by the British: 'The noise of the enemy shelling and the devastating weight of our artillery support was deafening.' Then, inexplicably, the artillery on both sides stopped. Brigadier Hinde announced on the radio net, 'Right that's it. Let's go.' The tanks and wheeled vehicles revved up and began to move. Men from the Queen's jumped on the armour, riding out of the box on Cromwells and Fireflies.

'The enemy attack was completely smashed,' recorded Crickmay. 'We moved off in pitch dark and clouds of choking dust, to the steady clanking of tracks and the dull roar of Rolls-Royce engines. It seemed too much to expect of the enemy to let us go unmolested. But they did. They'd had enough.'

Driving through the night, the division headed north, entering its new leaguer positions at about six o'clock in the morning on 15 June. There they fell onto the ground and into sleep. Lieutenant-Colonel Holliman did not leave it long before taking steps to address the poor performance shown by C Squadron. Allen was swiftly removed from command of his troop and several other men who had bailed out or pleaded nerves were dispatched to the Pioneer Corps, a shameful fate for soldiers from a celebrated division like the 7th Armoured. A stray shell that wounded the officer commanding C Squadron spared Holliman the unpleasantness of dismissing him too.

The Villers–Bocage action was over, but a fierce argument about its meaning was just beginning. German propaganda photographers had slipped into the township during the few hours between 4th CLY's debacle and the bombing on the evening of the 13th. Pictures of the smouldering vehicles were shown in the Nazi press, the superhuman qualities of Wittman and his SS crew extolled and the officer recommended for a further decoration.

While it was entirely natural for Hitler's papers to trumpet the humiliation of 7th Armoured Division, something similar broke out in certain quarters of the British army. Accusations of blame about what had happened on 13 June soon resounded about the Normandy bridgehead.

Those who thought the division arrogant after its North African experiences pointed out the key role played by infantry in confronting Wittman's tanks, from hitting them with six-pounders and PIAT launchers to trying to drop petrol-soaked blankets onto the huge machines from upstairs windows as they passed along the Villers streets. As for the fact that some Cromwell crews from both the CLY and 5th Tanks had abandoned their vehicles in 'Tiger fright', this was something the division clearly wanted to suppress.

The counter-argument that emerged from the 7th Armoured ran that the CO of the 4th CLY was guilty of shocking march discipline and, in the words of one 5th RTR officer, 'should have been court-martialled had he not been captured'. Furthermore, having suffered the consequences of this poor leadership, the losses inflicted on the Germans during the fight of the latter part of 13 and 14 June had allowed the British their revenge. Assertive types like Lieutenant–Colonel Mike Carver of 1st RTR argued that the division should never have been withdrawn after handing the Germans such a beating on the 14th, and that it was the failure of the 50th Infantry Division to make any significant advance during the two days of the Villers battle, despite the evident precariousness of the 7th Armoured Division's salient, that meant hard-won gains – an advance of six miles into enemy territory – had to be forsaken.

Senior officers within the 7th Armoured were conferring within hours of reaching safety, and soon circulated a written version of events in order to pre-empt further criticism. Brigadier Hinde summed up the battle: 'The idea of a massed weight of armour punching a hole in blind country in face of [anti-tank] guns and tanks of superior quality is not practical. As was foreseen a year ago we are at a grave disadvantage having to attack Panthers and Tigers with Cromwells and Shermans.' He also urged the speeding-up of a programme to issue the Firefly crews with a more powerful anti-tank round (the armour-piercing discarding sabot projectile), and to field more seventeen-pounder-equipped tanks within the division. At around the same time that Hinde fired off his memo, Brigadier Peter Pyman, an RTR officer serving on the staff of XXX Corps (and desert veteran of the 7th Armoured Division), launched his own salvo in the paper war, claiming that much of the German army consisted of Panthers and Tigers, which British crews had no real answer to.

These defensive memos exaggerated the difficulties facing British tank crews and prompted a backlash against the old desert hands who were the army's real experts in armoured warfare. If, for example, most British tanks could not defeat the Tiger, were the tactics wrong? Or was it the failure of the higher command more generally to exploit the Villers advance, and what did that imply about General Montgomery's leadership? Fearing more bail-outs and political trouble at home, Monty tried to counter any defeatism with a 'public letter' to the War Secretary on 25

June, in which he asserted 'We have nothing to fear from the Panther or Tiger tanks ... provided our tactics are good, we can defeat them without difficulty.' Given what he knew about the poor performance of the 75mm gun on most Cromwells and Shermans this was fanciful at best, and caused anger among the crews. The army group commander had been irritated both by 7th Armoured Division's performance and by the strong advocacy of men like Hinde, Pyman and Carver in justifying their case. Many of the Desert Rats felt that, from this time onwards, Monty was prejudiced against them.

One figure who observed the row at XXX Corps HQ was Brigadier James Hargest, a battle-hardened New Zealand infantryman. He lambasted the 'dismal failure' at Villers-Bocage, but implicitly put the blame on the County of London Yeomanry. In an echo of the British army's 1930s arguments, he felt the mechanisation of the cavalry was connected to the Royal Armoured Corps' shortcomings in Normandy. Hargest wrote, 'A great deal of their failure is due to the retention of the absurd regimental system. Because there is no work for cavalry the cavalry regiments were given tanks. The officers are trained in armour not because they like armour, but because they are cavalry men ... the Royal Corps [i.e. Royal Tank Corps, or more properly RTR] is sound and every unit in armour should belong to the [RTR].'

Brigadier Hargest had watched both the 7th Armoured and the 50th Infantry or Tyne Tees Division – both seasoned formations from North Africa – in action that month. After being with the armoured divison he judged, 'The tank officers complained to me that they were in need of infantry and in this they were right.' He noted that while the 50th had performed its tough mission on D-Day with alacrity, continuous combat was wearing down its ability to fight. From 6 to 20 June the Tyne Tees Division had taken 202 officer casualties and 2730 other ranks, and its foot soldiers were becoming increasingly sluggish unless their officers led the way. Describing the British infantry more generally, Hargest noticed a marked difference from Kiwi or Australian troops. The British soldier 'demands leadership by officers', he believed. 'I notice that as soon as men lose their officers in the thick growth they lose heart.' The only aspect of the operation that Hargest praised with unalloyed superlatives was the Royal Artillery, which could bring in accurate bombardments with amazing speed. These remarks, made in dispatches during June 1944, conformed to the views of many of the RTR officers who had served in the desert but, it should be noted, were made by an observer neutral to the British army's old tribal feuds.

What the New Zealand brigadier and the RTR men knew only too well was that with the Normandy campaign assuming a more and more positional or attritional character, success or failure would rest largely with 2nd Army's infantry – mostly British but also with three Canadian divisions and some other small national contingents. Clearing small fields, orchards and Norman villages required acts of great bravery by men on their feet. Montgomery knew both that he did not have enough of them, and that there was likely to be a public outcry if casualties reached Great War proportions. He had little choice but to keep pushing forwards, employing ever greater firepower from land, air and sea in an attempt to limit infantry casualties. The tanks would have to be part of that, whatever the fear of Tigers, 88s and Panzerfausts that they had learnt in June.

18

PLUTO'S TIGER

The road march of 17 July ended in the usual way, with the tanks pulling into the squadron lines of their leaguer, the wheeled vehicles nestling in the middle and men jumping down from their vehicles in the soft sun of the early evening to inspect their vehicles or get a brew on. Their faces were caked with grime, for the little farm roads of Normandy had been pounded for weeks by so many vehicles that a fine tail of dust was churned up by every tank, giving the German artillery aiming points and the crewmen an unending task of keeping themselves clean.

The 5th Tanks had moved into a brigade concentration area near the River Orne. For weeks the battle had raged around Caen, the city several miles to the south of where they were being held. During the opening phase of D-Day the river had marked the left or eastern boundary of the landing force but a bridgehead across it had been re-established and three armoured divisions were about to be pushed across in a bold attempt to break the Caen deadlock, an operation codenamed Goodwood.

Milling about the leaguer that evening were fifty or sixty old-timers who formed the real cadre of the regiment, embodying the fighting spirit it would need in the days ahead. Lieutenant-Colonel Gus Holliman, their Commanding Officer, was respected, as were a handful of the other officers including Bob Maunsell, the second-in-command, and Arthur Crickmay, the adjutant. Many, however, were regarded by the battalion's long-serving non-commissioned officers as a liability. The sergeants and corporals who had fought their way through the desert and who still chose to remain in tanks as opposed to the easier options of going to the echelon or some training base saw it as their particular duty to uphold the 5th RTR's name as one of the army's original regular battalions. While the old sweats were now a minority in a unit in which more than eight hundred men served, there were still enough of them to command the great majority of its tanks. They strove to prevent further bail-outs and to take revenge for the comrades already lost.

Jake Wardrop had put it in those very terms when writing to his mother several months earlier, and many others felt that way. These men, who had escaped from dozens of knocked-out tanks between them, from Sidi Rezegh to Alamein and Normandy, would provide the backbone needed for the fight that lay ahead. There was Snowy Harris, square-jawed, quiet and heroic, fighting alongside Jake in C Squadron. Sergeant Solomon and the likes of Lieutenant Garnett carried on in A, and Charlie Bull was soldiering on in B Squadron. Alongside Sergeant Bull served another one of the battalion's most formidable old characters, Sergeant Vincent Ellis, known to one and all as Pluto.

Ellis had won the Military Medal in North Africa, singlehand-edly recovering a Grant that had been abandoned by its crew, and been selected to command a Firefly in Normandy. During the Villers-Bocage episode he had been seen standing on the back of his tank while snipers' bullets pinged off the armour, scanning for targets with a pair of captured German binoculars. 'It was a regular thing that he would do, standing on the back,' said one of the younger members of Pluto's troop. 'He was a bit of a nutcase really, perhaps a bit bomb-happy.' The sense of a man who was oblivious to danger due to his long exposure to combat added to the aura of quiet menace that accompanied many of the 5th's NCO commanders. Ellis had been a gamekeeper in civilian life, but few who knew him in uniform would have tried their chances at poaching from his land. 'Short, stocky, with black hair and dark unshaven, impassive face', another trooper in B Squadron noted, Pluto 'said little but got on with the job alright'. The gunner on the sergeant's Firefly described him as 'a sturdy chap like a little bulldog, tough'.

In an attempt to convince their crews that they stood a good chance against Panthers and Tigers, the British army had laid on demonstrations, within the bridgehead, of firing at captured German tanks. In one it had been shown that the Panther's frontal armour could be pierced at seven hundred yards by the seventeen-pounder on the Firefly. Crews had also been instructed that the armour was considerably weaker on the Panther's sides, giving a chance even to the 75mm-gun armed tanks to brew one. As for the Tiger, there were mercifully fewer of them, just three battalions which were by this point somewhat depleted, and all in the British sector. The Cromwell men knew, though, that the best way of dealing with these threats was to call up a Firefly, and the commanders of those modified Shermans (including Wardrop, Solomon and Pluto Ellis) in turn understood that the Germans would attempt to pick them off first. Whatever the recriminations that followed the Villers affair, Lieutenant-General Richard O'Connor, the corps commander for the Goodwood operation, wanted the 7th Armoured Division to know that he still considered them the best. In a message to troops on 17 July O'Connor, who had commanded the division himself early on during the desert war, wrote, 'Please convey to all ranks my great satisfaction that 7th Armoured Division have, after three years, again come under my command. Their record as a fighting division is unsurpassed.'

During the weeks since Villers these armoured formations – the 7th, 11th and Guards divisions – had been largely kept from combat in the hedgerows. Instead infantry units, often backed up by Churchills or Shermans from the independent armoured brigades, had fought the grim struggle for each mile of territory. Casualties had been high, reaching forty thousand by mid-July, and criticism of Montgomery's tactics had mounted.

However, those who lambasted the army group commander often failed to take account of the punishment the German defenders had received. They had lost more men killed and wounded than the Allies, even though their defence force was less than half the size. Their panzer divisions, in part due to Hitler's orders to hold Caen at all costs, had been drawn into a grinding war of attrition in which, despite the excellence of their tank repair services, the vehicles available to each division were being whittled away. The flattened city of Caen had finally been taken and the Germans had replaced several generals, including one who had committed suicide under the pressure of trying to hold the line.

Both the British and US commanders longed to break out of the bridgehead and it was apparent that the open terrain of western France that lay ahead of the Americans offered greater scope. Monty therefore adopted a strategy of trying to draw as many of the German divisions, particularly the armoured ones, into the British sector as possible in order to facilitate an American success. This idea was communicated down through the chain of command, and the 5th Tanks had heard of it in a Griff talk from

Lieutenant-Colonel Holliman. The land to the east of the Orne was open, relatively flat landscape of wheat fields dotted with villages. It was here that Montgomery now called upon his armoured divisions to do their bit. With Caen itself secure, they were about to attempt a breakout.

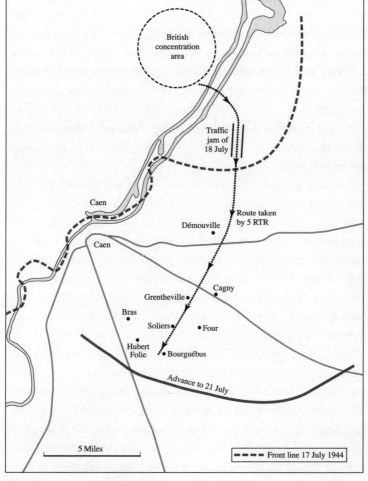

British
concentration
area

Traffic
jam of
18 July

Caen

Démouville

Route taken
by 5 RTR

Caen

Cagny

Grentheville

Bras

Soliers • Four

Hubert
Folie • Bourguébus

Advance to 21 July

5 Miles

- - - - Front line 17 July 1944

OPERATION GOODWOOD

Operation Goodwood was to be launched at eight o'clock on the morning of 18 July by the 11th Armoured Division, under Major-General Pip Roberts. As the brigadier running 22nd Armoured in the desert two years earlier, Roberts had assured his COs that he would not commit them to Balaklava charges against strong enemy defences. Now he would have to urge his troops forward into a perfect killing ground for anti-tank weapons. The plan required the British armour to advance southwards and uphill, across several miles of open plain, to capture the Bourguébus ridge that dominated the countryside to the southeast of Caen. It was not exactly clear what they would do once – or if – they reached this objective successfully, but Roberts expected them to push southwards from the ridge towards Falaise. The area chosen was dotted with villages surrounded by the usual Norman hedgerows, orchards and walls, and were turned into strongpoints.

German generals had placed three divisions in defence of this ground: a static defence (i.e. second-rate) one made up of Luftwaffe personnel; the 21st Panzer Division; and one with more than seventy-eight of the dreaded 88mm flak guns. A couple of battalions of assault guns and the 503rd Heavy Tank Battalion with Tigers and twelve freshly delivered examples of the even more fearsome sixty-eight-ton King Tiger were deployed to stiffen this first line of defence. Behind the Bourguébus ridge were a couple of SS panzer divisions that would act as a mobile reserve. The German divisions in question had already taken many beatings from the Allies: the 21st Panzer Division had around fifty battle-worthy Mk IV tanks, and the 1st SS Panzer Division forty Panthers. These figures, of around one-third effective strength, demonstrated that even though the Allies relied on a tenuous sea bridge for the resupply of armour, they were better able to top up their losses than the Germans who ought to have had the advantages of continuous supply lines back to the Reich, but who were suffering badly from air attacks on those routes and the stretch of two-front warfare. Nonetheless, despite the difficulties they had in keeping up tank numbers, they had still been able to deploy a total of about 325 tanks and self-propelled guns as well as hundreds of anti-tank guns in the Bourguébus area.

Major-General Roberts had made representations about the difficulty of attacking such a formidable objective with his division. He had been promised that a crushing bombardment would precede his advance. When he persisted in raising difficulties, Lieutenant-General O'Connor had silenced him by suggesting that he would get a different division to do it if the 11th Armoured thought it was all too difficult. Thus through appealing to Roberts's personal ambition as well as his sense of duty, O'Connor got his way. Earlier reverses in Normandy, and the command culture fostered by Monty, produced intense pressure on formation commanders, and consequently a good deal a bullying. A few days before Goodwood, for example, the Commanding Officer of 7th RTR had a divisional commander bellow at him, 'Bloody well get a move on or you will be sacked!' when he questioned an order. An entire squadron of tanks was lost when he complied.

That morning, the 11th Armoured Division would lead the way out of the Orne bridgehead, followed by the Guards who would deploy to the south-east (to the rear left of Roberts), and the 7th Armoured who would drive south-west (to the rear right of 11th Armoured, close to the outskirts of Caen).

When 18 July dawned, all hell was let loose on the German defenders of the sector. A thousand-bomber raid was launched by the RAF, dropping sticks of bombs by the hundred across the French countryside, an ear-splitting deluge of high explosive with its rippling shockwaves flattening crops and houses alike. Then the AGRAs (the units of the Army Group Royal Artillery, or heavy reserve guns) joined in, pummelling the corridor seven thousand yards across down which the armour had to advance. Even the Royal Navy let rip from off shore.

In a wood near the village of Cagny, one company of Tigers was caught by the bombing and half lost, with one of the fifty-six-ton behemoths ending up on its roof. Elsewhere, an officer of the 21st Panzers described an assault on the senses so overwhelming that some of his crews lost their minds or even committed suicide in order to escape it. This bombardment had not, however, been aimed in any real sense: although the air reconnaissance analysts would have pleaded that they had found known German concentration areas, the weapons being employed were simply not accurate enough to strike them precisely. So in most cases the bombs or heavy shells fell on fields, churning them up, leaving craters thirty feet deep in places, and making it harder for the advancing British to pass – a problem that was all too familiar to the Western Front Tank Corps pioneers of 1917. Where villages were flattened, most of the defenders survived it in cellars or bunkers, taking up their defensive positions in the rubble as Roberts's tanks set off at eight o'clock.

Most of Roberts's division, including two of three tank battalions in his armoured brigade (the 23rd Hussars and 2nd Fife and Forfar Yeomanry), had not been in action before Normandy. The exception was the 3rd RTR, who ranked along with the 5th and a few other outfits as the true veterans of the Royal Armoured Corps. While some in Montgomery's headquarters thought the old desert hands a little too canny or 'sticky' in advancing at too deliberate a pace, and others believed fresh troops suffered high casualties because they had yet to learn to respect their enemy, the 11th Armoured Division was thought to combine the virtues of both, and Pip Roberts himself was widely respected as a commander. Rumbling across their start line, they initially found everything going to plan.

Peering over the sides of their turrets, Sherman commanders from 3rd Tanks noticed dazed Germans emerging from their foxholes, their hands raised. The tanks kept going, for the prisoners were the business of the accompanying riflemen. Punch-drunk, some of them bleeding from their ears and nose, these concussed defenders staggered away, glad it was all over. Hundreds of prisoners were soon taken, mostly members of the Luftwaffe field division in forward positions. As 3rd RTR pushed on, other units packed in behind it in the Orne bridge-head got the chance to move up. The Fife and Forfar Yeomanry went out to the left, with a brigade of Canadian infantry going across to join up with their own forces near Caen.

It was around half past nine that things started to get tougher for the British. Some of the defenders of Cagny and its outlying hamlets opened up with 75mm and 88mm guns at the Yeomanry barrelling towards them. Within moments twelve Shermans had been hit. Most of them soon took fire. They and 3rd Tanks were firing back with machine guns and 75mm guns, the tankies slackening their pace somewhat as they engaged.

At around this time, 5th Tanks was crossing the Orne bridge several miles behind the leading wave. The Guards were ahead of them, but all of these follow-on battalions of armour, infantry and artillery were struggling to get forward in a small pocket of land that had become a huge green traffic jam. As the hours passed and casualties among the forward troops mounted, there were angry words between Major-General Roberts and Brigadier 'Looney' Hinde of the 7th Armoured Division, who protested that there was not enough space to deploy his units. The more tanks that were packed into the narrow frontage of the breakout, Hinde rea-soned, the easier the job for the enemy 88 gunners.

Whatever passed between the two commanders, the Desert Rats were in action later that afternoon, with the 5th Tanks pushing up towards Démouville. There they discovered another unwelcome aspect of this giant operation. Enemy tanks or guns opened up from places that had already been passed or cleared by the leading troops. They had either been missed or the Germans were sending in reinforcements from the eastern side of the salient created by 11th Armoured Division that morning. Near Démouville one of 5th RTR's Fireflies was hit and lurched to a halt, its commander killed and crew struggling to get out. 'The turret was blazing well,' recalled the gunner of the stricken tank. 'I dragged myself through the hatch which acted as an up-draught for the flames. After rolling about to put out the flames, I ran back to our nearest tank.' Elsewhere, Jackie Garnett's Cromwell was hit too, killing one of the crewmen. The 5th Tanks men were coming under fire from Mk IVs and Panthers. The latter belonged to the SS divisions that were already feeding troops into the battle.

A couple of miles to the south, 11th Armoured Division was still trying to push forward. By the middle of the day the Fife and Forfar Yeomanry were down to twenty working tanks. The advance had stalled short of the village of Bourguébus. In many places the British crews were responding to threats from all points of the compass as German defenders popped up in villages behind them as well as on their flanks and to their front. The battlefield was streaked with smoke from dozens of burning British tanks. Looking through his periscope, one of the yeomanry crewmen saw 'tanks brewing up with flames belching from their turrets. I see men climbing out, on fire like torches, rolling on the ground to try and douse the flames, but we are in ripe corn and the straw takes fire.'

So it continued throughout the afternoon and early evening, with the Guards trying to push out on the left and the 7th Armoured following on behind the 11th. By the end of the day Roberts's division had lost 126 tanks (around two-thirds of the number it had started with). The 23rd Hussars had run into

King Tigers and suffered badly for it, though one of their Fireflies could claim the credit for knocking out the first of these huge tanks in battle. The Yeomanry, ravaged by 88s and other anti-tank fire, had only five or six runners left. Third Tanks, on the other hand, despite being engaged throughout the day, still had nearly half of the sixty tanks it had started with. Was that luck, or the skill of veterans? 'None of us was looking forward to the morning with any enthusiasm,' noted one of the 3rd's squadron leaders. 'The Bourguébus crest with its strongly held villages was an objective that daunted our completely exhausted troops.' The most experienced formation, 7th Armoured, had only been lightly engaged by comparison, but would become more seriously involved the following day.

On the morning of 19 July it fell to 5th RTR to push forward. They had spent the night pulled back behind an embanked railway that offered some protection from the shooting. They were to move south, towards Bourguébus. B Squadron would deploy on the battalion's right, to a fortified village called Soliers. C Squadron deployed, heading for Four, a hamlet several hundred yards to the east of Soliers, or the left as they looked across the fields towards it. The ground dipped slightly to the immediate south of the railway and then rose gently towards the villages that they had set their sights on.

Scanning the horizon, Sergeant Wardop in his Firefly knew both that he would be a priority target and that his wagon could not match the speed of the Cromwells. 'We had gone about a thousand yards and were nicely in the open when I heard a shot from the trees on our left front and the whine of an armour piercing shot passed just behind Snowy [Harris].' There was another crack. The drivers opened their throttles, 'the Cromwells with their Rolls Merlin were much faster than our big lumbering thing and they shot away'. The faster tanks moved in a circular pattern, first to the right, away from the enemy guns, then doubling back into some woods. Wardrop was bellowing at his driver through the intercom 'Give her the boot!' But they could not outpace solid shot.

'There was a loud thud behind, the tank slowed and the turret was full of flames,' wrote Wardrop. 'Woody [the wireless operator] and Jimmy [gunner] were alright and I thought Ted [driver] would be too as he sat almost in front of Woody so I yelled "jump" and bailed for it.' Landing in the field, Wardrop realised Woody was on fire so he and the others rolled him on the ground, patting out the flames with their bare hands. Blisters soon started to come up on the dazed wireless operator's face and hands. The crew began to trudge back through the fields, towards the woods where Sergeant Harris and the other vehicles had taken refuge. As they went, Wardrop turned around to take a last look at his Firefly. It was blazing fiercely, the ammunition inside cooking off with pops and thumps. He had been shot out of plenty of tanks before, but he was sad to lose the latest instalment of the diary he'd been keeping, a blue pullover that had survived numerous bail-outs since Sidi Rezegh in 1941 and Clara, a chicken they had acquired.

The band of survivors got to Snowy Harris's Cromwell, where Woody's burns were treated with some cream from a first aid pack and Wardrop jumped into the troop corporal's seat on a Cromwell. There was a lot of this on Goodwood, just as there had been on Crusader or in the Gazala battles – more senior commanders from knocked-out vehicles temporarily taking control of someone else's tank.

Meanwhile, B Squadron were also in action. As they moved on Soliers they were accompanied by the Bren carriers and half-tracks of two platoons of the 1st Rifle Brigade who were under their command. Sergeant Charlie Bull peered out of his Cromwell, scanning the village of Soliers directly to their south. Pluto Ellis held back a little in his Firefly, as did that of another B Squadron troop with which Pluto was working in partnership.

Getty Images

ergeant 'Snowy' Harris was featured on this popular British magazine cover as the dashing mbodiment of an 8th Army tank commander. His pressed battledress and close shave contrast arkly with the battle-worn appearance of his C Squadron mates in the earlier photograph ken around the same time, during the Gazala battles.

A phalanx of 5th RTR Shermans in Italy, illustrating how mechanised forces got channelled down a few routes in close country, producing traffic jams and frustration among crews used to the open desert.

Landing craft soon after loading by 5th Tanks on the Orwell estuary in Suffolk, prior to setting sail for Normandy.

The flotilla under way a tense time for the crews as they skirted around the German big guns in the Calais region and awaited air attack – note the barrage balloon being towed with them.

A dramatic view of Gold Beach taken by Major Deryck MacDonald, OC of A Squadron, immediately after landing.

h Tanks moves across the River Orne on 18 July 1944, on its way into the oodwood battle.

Infantrymen from 7th Armoured Division atop a Panther knocked out near Soliers on 19 July. The timing and location, on the railway embankment at the outskirts of the village, strongly suggest it was one of the panzers engaged by Pluto Ellis and other B Squadron tanks.

Men from 3 RTR trying to fight a fire on their Sherman during Operation Goodwood; this highly experienced battalion took a leading role in the attack

Cromwells from 7th Armoured Division sheltering in the cover of the embanked mainline railway that cut across the battlefield. It was from this position that 5 RTR started its advance on 19 July.

During the severe winter of 1944–5 tanks were painted white to blend into the snowy landscape. Crews atop the Firefly (*right*) and Cromwell (*left*) wear the 'zoot suit' coveralls that were a hit with the men.

Lieutenant–Colonel Gus Holliman (*left*) and his second-in-command Major Bob Maunsell pictured shortly before Normandy, just after the ouster of their predecessors.

Joyous scenes in Ghent as the liberated citizens mob a 5th Tanks Cromwell crew.

A column from 5 RTR moving into Rethem after bitter fighting to take the town. Refugees can be seen taking their chance to escape.

A column about to move into German woods to clear them. The infantry are riding on the tanks – just as they were when Sergeant Jake Wardrop's column was ambushed under similar circumstances.

The battalion's senior officers at the end of the war. Front row from left: Captain Roy Dixon, the adjutant; Lieutenant-Colonel Rea Leakey, the CO; and Major Deryck MacDonald, commander of A Squadron. Standing to the rear are Major Arthur Crickmay (*far left*), OC C Squadron; and directly behind the CO (and dog), Major Dennis Cockbaine, in charge B Squadron.

In Rethem just after it had been taken, following fierce resistance, members of 5 RTR display a trophy. At one point in the fight surrendering Germans were refused quarter.

C Squadron, with Arthur Crickmay at its head, march to the service of remembrance held at the end of the war.

If the Cromwells drew tank or StuG fire, the Fireflies would then be able to act together in response.

The squadron passed through Soliers amid the crackle of small-arms fire as a few Germans resisted. It did not take long before they decided to call it a day. They pushed on towards Bourguébus, several hundred yards further to the south. The Bourguébus ridge or feature was spoken of by many as if it were some lofty eminence, but for a tank commander approaching from the north no more than a gradual rising was perceptible. The Meteor engines in the Cromwells pulled a little harder that afternoon as the ground rose through Soliers and, emerging on the south side of the village, B Squadron's commanders could see their next target a little above them and to the left of the road that led between the two villages. An industrial railway ran across the landscape to the backside of Bourguébus, but it only became clear to the tank men as they manoeuvred to the right with the intention of avoiding the village centre, choked as it was with rubble, bodies and booby traps. Coming around they could see the railway on an embankment that carried it, eight to ten feet in places, above the fields into the south-east section of the village. It was already after six o'clock in the evening.

Motoring past Bourguébus, a group of B Squadron tanks was brought to a halt when one of the leading Cromwells stopped and began to burn. Within moments they spotted German tanks on the other side of the railway. Both sides opened fire and Pluto's Firefly claimed one of the enemy vehicles. Quickly he ordered his driver to close the distance to the others. But as he drove onto the steep uphill slope of the embankment the front of the Firefly's hull became stuck on a tree trunk. The enemy tanks were soon just a few dozen yards away, on the other side of the railway. They inched forwards and as the great ugly muzzle of the 88 loomed over the rails, B Squadron realised they were up against a Tiger. A little further down the track, a Panther was trying to get into position too. The Germans opened up, 'their shots flying just over the top of the Firefly's turret', according to another member of the troop. But the German commanders had a problem. Their side of the railway was steeply embanked too, and the further up it they went, the harder it became to depress their guns sufficiently to hit the Firefly stranded just in front of them and the more they would expose themselves to all manner of anti-tank fire from the British side of the obstacle.

For a moment it was stalemate. Pluto knew he had to get free of the tree trunk or he would soon die. Asking for assistance over the radio, he got a Cromwell to pull up just behind him, but nobody was keen to leave the protection of their armour to attach the steel towing cables. Finally, Sergeant Ellis himself leapt out, got down behind his tank and directed the rescue. As soon as the Cromwell had towed his tank free he unhooked the cable, manoeuvred onto the bank and put two seventeen-pounder rounds into the Tiger. The Panther was soon claimed too, some giving the credit to Pluto, and others to the other Firefly he was working with.

Pluto leapt from the turret once again, this time running across to his prey, the stricken Tiger, and vaulting up onto it. His crew watched as the sergeant peered about the top of its turret before diving in. He returned to the Firefly a short time later and the crew asked what he had been doing. The two tanks had been so close during their duel that Pluto had noticed the badges of rank on the Tiger's commander. Having disposed of his challenger, according to accounts from members of the squadron the sergeant had gone in search of a prize, assuming that his dead opposite number must have something worth liberating. Finding that the German's arms had been severed by one of the seventeen-pounder's shots, Pluto had searched for them, in the words of one B Squadron man, 'on the assumption that a Tiger tank commander with such splendid epaulettes would surely have a good quality wrist-watch'. Sergeant Ellis did not find it, but returned to regale them with the tale, leaving the squadron torn between admiration and dread of him.

Ellis received a second award of the Military Medal for his actions that day and it was initially, erroneously, reported that he had destroyed three Tigers. Several German tanks were destroyed in the Bourguébus area that day, including Mk IVs, some Panthers and a Tiger or two. While there would be conflicting claims – including from rocket-firing Typhoon aircraft that were supporting the 5th Tanks on 19 July – the close range of the engagement and the fact that he had mounted the vehicle after knocking it out allowed Pluto to say he had bagged his Tiger.

By 20 July Operation Goodwood was petering out. In most places the villages atop the Bourguébus ridge had been taken, and the German defence smashed. However Montgomery faced a tide of criticism, particularly from other Allied commanders. One of the air chiefs remarked that if it had been a thousand tons of bombs to secure an advance of six miles, they would need six hundred thousand to get to Berlin. Even some sympathetic to Monty felt he had over-sold the operation, implying that it would allow a complete breakout from the bridgehead rather than an expansion of it. And what of the cost?

Critics pointed out that more than 450 of the 750-odd tanks available to the three British armoured divisions had been knocked out. Some referred to the losses of 18 July as the 'death ride of the Royal Armoured Corps'. These arguments, however, occasionally served to betray the rhetoric and agendas of those who made them. Critics who wished to flay Monty or the armoured corps ignored key facts: that around 213 of the 'lost' British tanks – fewer than half of the casualties and less than one third of the total – were actually destroyed (with most of the others later repaired); and that an attack across open ground against hundreds of German tanks or self-propelled guns and more than three hundred artillery pieces (including seventy-eight 88mm flaks) would inevitably be costly, regardless of bombardments launched in its support. In the recriminations that followed, Major-General Roberts tried in part to justify the heavy losses in his division by blaming 7th Armoured Division, saying it had seen too much action and was too slow to come to his help on 18 July.

Casualty figures for Goodwood give the lie to Roberts's analysis. The 7th Armoured Division lost somewhat more people than the Guards Armoured, a supposedly keen non-veteran division: 491 killed, wounded and missing, versus 467 in the Guards. The Desert Rats were heavily engaged on 19 July in the central sector of VIII Corps' attack and the wider operation would not have succeeded without their hard fighting. It was the 11th Armoured's losses in vehicles and men – 894 casualties – that were striking, due to the leading role they had played in such a difficult operation, and evidently Roberts sought to justify this.

Many in the 5th Tanks blamed Monty for flinging the armour forward with these grim consequences. Some also remarked that it was the combination of an ambitious commander and so many green troops in 11th Armoured Division, precisely the recipe for a rapid advance that British generals felt they needed, that produced such heavy casualties. One young trooper in B Squadron of 5th Tanks, seeing the burning tanks of the Fife and Forfar Yeomanry, was shocked by the near complete destruction of the battalion and could not help but reflect that when he had passed his basic training he had originally been earmarked to join them. 'Going to the 5th Tanks had probably saved my life,' he reflected. 'The 8th Army boys [i.e. desert veterans] were great and they kept us out of trouble.' It was precisely the reluctance of the Wardrops, Bulls or Ellises to rush on blindly that endeared their men to them. A subaltern from the 1st RBs concurs: 'Perhaps the 11th Armoured were too gung-ho, whereas the 7th Armoured Division were more professional, and moved carefully and slowly.'

Goodwood had also brought home to many the vulnerability

of the Sherman tank, which picked up grim nicknames such as the 'Ronson' (after a well-known make of cigarette lighter), 'Tommy Cooker' and 'Mobile Crematorium'. The fine reputation that the American-made vehicle had enjoyed in the Royal Armoured Corps, such as during the drive to Tunis, had quite literally gone up in smoke. The 11th and Guards Armoured Divisions had used Shermans during the battle of 18–20 July, as did many of the British independent armoured brigades in Normandy. Although many of the 7th Armoured Division men never got over grumbling about the Cromwell they were actually safer in them, and had appreciated the turn of speed that their British-made tanks were capable of during the late fighting.

Sitting back at HQ Captain Crickmay, the veteran of as many battles as any man in that army, saw the high cost of Goodwood not in terms of the divisions involved but the constraints the operation had been under. The Orne bridgehead was too small for three armoured division to deploy rapidly, producing the traffic jam of the 18th, and the frontage over which they had been expected to attack not wide enough. These factors had created the shooting gallery for German anti-tank gunners.

Of course the tendency for blame or regret among the British army came in part from an intimate familiarity with their own difficulties and an ignorance of the enemy's. German divisions had been pummelled, losing around 6500 casualties, and nearly ninety tanks and self-propelled guns. Additionally, the last uncommitted panzer division in northern France had been sucked into the Caen sector, thus easing the US army's imminent breakout operation. One of the officers in the 503rd Heavy Tank Battalion remarked, 'For the first time we had the feeling to have failed.' The German army high command now saw the two-front warfare they were engaged in as unsustainable. On 20 July dissident officers had attempted to kill Hitler. The following day, the army group commander in France summed up the situation with utter pessimism, noting that 'in the face of the enemy's complete command of the air, there is no possibility of finding a strategy which will counter-balance its truly annihilating effect, unless we give up the field of battle'.

On 21 July the 5th Tanks were moved back from the Bourguébus ridge and their echelon established in a factory on the outskirts of Caen. They had come under frequent shelling since they moved into Bourguébus on the 19th, but it did not cease altogether when they relocated.

Travelling back to the echelon, Sergeant Wardop found himself waiting with his crew for a replacement tank. There were quite a few people in the same boat, including Lieutenant Garnett, who had declined evacuation despite suffering burns when he was brewed a few days before. The crowd of crews hanging about at the battalion's main supply base contained an uncomfortable mix-ture of hardened veterans awaiting their new vehicles, green replacements who were keen to get up to the action and men whose nerve had gone. With the latter category, the Medical Officer was hoping that a few days out of the line might calm them down and allow them to go back. Among these men suf-fering from what the army termed 'battle exhaustion' was Captain Daniels, the second-in-command of C Squadron. Daniels had been in the 5th Tanks since late 1942, so had seen plenty of action, but his presence in the echelon irked Wardrop.

'Anybody is liable to crack,' the sergeant accepted, 'but it is not good that a man should be a captain, respected and looked up to because he is a captain one day and the next day he is sliding out of it with some spurious nerves complaint while troopers carry on and on.' Wardrop didn't much like being among the hollow-eyed exhaustion cases, or having to submit to the petty routines that came with being under the Regimental Sergeant Major's eye in the echelon. He was delighted to get away a few days later on his new Firefly.

Others were more sympathetic to those whose nerve was faltering, but almost everyone was feeling the strain. The frequent shelling in front-line positions meant that many men would only leave the tank if nature made it imperative, and pissing into an empty shell case was the most obvious way of dealing with that. One of the senior NCOs had been killed by a sniper when he finally gave in to his guts and left his tank for a crap. The strain of being in constant danger was exacerbated by lack of sleep.

The business of being adjutant meant that Captain Crickmay was doing paperwork until half past two in the morning, before having to get up again at four-thirty. At least his life had improved when, shortly before Goodwood, a large truck with a box body had been purloined to act as his and Lieutenant-Colonel Holliman's mobile office. 'It will be a great luxury for doing ones office work at nights after the days battle, instead of crouching about with a torch inside a tank,' Crickmay wrote home. 'I yell with rage when trying to work in the turret blacked out and closed down.' Reflecting on his years of fighting since 1939, Crickmay told his mother how Normandy had turned out to be very different from his early adventures in Egypt, commenting wearily, 'The war here is a good deal less attractive than in the western desert and infinitely more squalid.'

Crickmay, like Jake Wardrop or Pluto Ellis, had no intention of throwing in the towel and joining Daniels and the others who could no longer face it. If Goodwood was a disappointment it was because such a heavy sacrifice had not had a more obvious effect in shortening the war. But those who soldiered on had become used to fighting, and knew it would have to go on until the Germans were vanquished. Up in 21st Army Group those around Monty insisted that the advance south of Caen had paved the way for the Americans to push south, and for the long night of the Normandy campaign to end. But for the 5th Tanks, the old adage that the darkest hour comes just before dawn would prove to be all too true.

19

THE FIFTH'S DARK HOUR

Dawn on 3 August followed a clear, cool night. A patchy mist had formed in the hollows of the Norman farm country. The 22nd Armoured Brigade had spent the night on a ridge about a dozen miles south of Bayeux. After Goodwood, their division had been pulled back, sent round behind the city once again and fed back down south along a route close to that which they had taken to Villers-Bocage in June. Their nerves had been frayed by weeks of fighting in the close country. They felt they had gone this way then that, often within sight of the spire of Bayeux Cathedral and rarely escaping the smells of death and putrefaction that the war had brought to Normandy. Their generals had been under orders to make progress, and little by little they were achieving it. The British knew their American allies were pushing forward and pressure seeped down Montgomery's chain of command, with orders to 'press on regardless'.

Just as they had on 13 June, that August day 7th Armoured Division was moving to threaten the flank of German divisions near Caen, and the manoeuvre required the Desert Rats to travel south before turning east (or left), hooking around onto ground dominating the Odon Valley. The place chosen that day was the Breuil feature, a ridge giving 230 feet of elevation about four miles south and west of Villers-Bocage.

Operation Cobra, the major US operation to break out of the bridgehead, had started the week before, with very encouraging results. That morning, as the 5th Tanks fired up their Cromwells and prepared to move east, their divisional commander, Major-General Erskine, had be summoned to army headquarters. Little did the 7th Armoured Division know it, but Erskine was being dismissed. He had led them for 18 months, but the whispering after Villers-Bocage and Goodwood had done for him. It was an uneasy divisional headquarters that planned that day's advance, knowing that Montgomery's people were losing faith in them and that the land over which they must advance was overlooked by high ground believed to be in enemy hands.

The 5th Tanks had orders to push downhill, eastwards, just over two miles to a low ridge designated Point 138, which would give them a view over Aunay-sur-Odon, the nearby market town and road hub. A Squadron was designated to lead the way, commanded by Major Deryck MacDonald. Tall, moustachioed, often followed about by his dog, MacDonald had been with the battalion for much of the time since the outbreak of war, and had got married on leave in February. MacDonald sent 3 and 4 Troops ahead, leading the right and left respectively of his force. The 5th's usual partners in the Motor Battalion (i.e. 1st Battalion the Rifle Brigade, the 22nd Armoured Brigade's infantry force who rode in half-tracks and Bren carriers) had already sent some patrols down into the orchard-fringed hamlets of the lower ground where nasty surprises might lurk just a few yards ahead.

Lieutenant Tony Crassweller from I Company, 1 RB, had made his way gingerly to a spot where the road from Breuil passed under a railway bridge at a place called La Lande. He had tiptoed up to the line, which loomed over the road on an embankment. He realised that if he went beyond the bridge he might have to fight with that obstacle to his rear, and if he stayed on the western side of it, he could see very little. Crassweller briefly saw two Cromwells from A Squadron moving down from the high ground. Just as he was walking back to his half-tracks with the handful of riflemen who had accompanied him, he noticed some unusual movement in a house near the railway. He ordered his men to jump in their vehicles and, just as one of them closed the steel door at the rear, there was the zipping sound of a Spandau firing and bullets ricocheted wildly off the back of the vehicle. The infantry had detected the enemy presence in La Lande and radioed back to 1 RB, but there was no quick way to tell the Cromwell crews.

Not long after this incident, and quite ignorant of it, 3 Troop under Lieutenant Roy Dixon pulled up at the same railway bridge, while 4 Troop pushed slowly through Courcelles, a hamlet a few hundred yards to the north. Dixon had been in action with the troop since D–Day. He had passed the test, winning the trust of his troop sergeant Arthur Cornish and the other experienced crewmen by showing a quiet determination to lead his men through whatever Normandy could throw at them. Dixon knew they were all exhausted from weeks in battle and that some were bomb–happy or jittery. Dixon went first, because by this stage of the campaign leadership was paramount and the pressure to push on clear. 'If you wanted to move fast, you really had to lead because you can't go on saying, "You go round the next corner and go and do this and go and do that",' he believed. 'It is easier to go and do it yourself. So very often a troop leader was leading.' Stopping at the railway bridge at La Lande and peering through the tunnel underneath it, Dixon could see the obvious danger that a German ambush might be waiting just on the other side. Going ahead on foot was just part of the drill, and had been since the desert. The implicit understanding was that, if the worst came to the worst, the commander would get killed rather than the whole crew.

Lieutenant Dixon jumped down from his Cromwell, which was about fifty yards back from the bridge, and walked nervously through the tunnel to see what might be hidden by the embankment. There, on his left, about as far away as his tank was from the other side, stood a Mk IV tank, its engine idling. The lieutenant ran back under the bridge but he had been spotted and the German tank started to rumble forward. Jumping back into his Cromwell just in time, Dixon ordered the driver forward. They got through the tunnel first and there was a double flash and bang as both tanks fired at each other – and missed – from a matter of yards. Dixon ordered the Cromwell to reverse fast. The driver went back so suddenly that he threw a track, leaving the machine unable to move. Dixon ran to another of his Cromwells, climbing into the commander's seat, knowing the Mk IV could appear at any moment.

The German tank moved forward slowly, and as the British gunner squinted down his telescope it presented itself under the bridge. 'It was broad side on when we saw it, so it was a perfect target,' reported Dixon, so they opened fire with the 75mm immediately, 'straight into the turret and they immediately jumped out and it caught fire'. As the crew piled out the Cromwell's machine guns opened up on them, so that was one less German tank crew. A battle had begun between the 5th Tanks and their enemies that would rage for the next twenty hours.

While Dixon had been dealing with his emergency, 4 Troop had made its way to Point 138 by eleven o'clock. The early-morning mist had cleared by this time and the crews realised they could easily be observed from a ridge that loomed above them, about one mile to their south. It was across the ridge that a Kampfgruppe from the 10th SS Panzer Division had deployed a few hours earlier, driving north to intercept the British, and whose forward units were now in contact with Dixon and the others. The high ground, meanwhile, offered their observers a view of the hamlets and little enclosures down below that eluded those who now stalked one another in the fields. Fears had been expressed before the 5th Tanks set off that they would be horribly exposed, but their officers had ordered them to go all the same.

Sitting in relatively open ground at Point 138, the Cromwells engaged the German transport that they could see off to their east near Odon. Very quickly, however, the enemy gunners, guided by observers on the high ground, were punishing them for their audacity, dropping shells among 4 Troop's tanks. Realising that a full-scale engagement was under way, Lieutenant-Colonel Holliman fed B Squadron into La Lande to support A Squadron, who were coming under heavy fire. He kept C Squadron in reserve about five hundred yards to the north-west, on the slopes below the village of Saint-Georges.

The position of A Squadron's forward tanks was growing more serious by the hour. Not only had the 10th SS pushed around a dozen Mk IVs into the southern part of La Lande and the next hamlet to its west, La Maison, accompanied by companies of panzer grenadiers, but enemy troops had also been sighted approaching from the north. A scratch formation of infantry with some Jagdpanthers, the formidable tank-destroyer version of the Panther armed with an 88mm gun, were moving down from that direction. To the south, the riflemen of 1 RB became involved in a close-range firefight with the enemy around La Maison.

Dixon's triumph against the first Mk IV proved short-lived, for another one, bypassing the railway embankment, managed to hit his Cromwell. The strike killed one member of his crew and the rest bailed out. Dixon ran to his troop corporal's tank and took charge. The position of the crews on foot was extremely dangerous because SS panzer grenadiers were now moving through the countryside. Soon the bad news reached Dixon that his troop sergeant's Cromwell had also been knocked out, and Sergeant Cornish killed.

At around four o'clock that afternoon the British relinquished Point 138, falling back to the west to concentrate between Courcelles and La Lande. It was known to Holliman that a few tanks had been knocked out by then, and that they had become separated from their infantry. Bereft of help from the riflemen or Queen's Brigade, one of the A Squadron tank drivers, Lance Corporal Shute, had moved on foot with two other men to scout the ground to the rear of those two settlements, seeing if they could find a way back to the remainder of the battalion. They were alarmed to find a company of German infantry taking position in an orchard. Shute and his companions took some prisoners, returned to their tanks and directed their fire into the orchard, as a result of which forty Germans surrendered.

As the evening wore on, columns of smoke rose from the countryside where vehicles were burning. The crews in A and B squadrons were coming to the view that they were surrounded, while Lieutenant-Colonel Holliman, who was back with C Squadron, pulled them a little closer in to Saint-Georges and tried to understand what was happening down below.

In the twilight, Dixon's tank was hit: 'Bloody great flash and everything . . . fire started so we bailed again.' He had started the day with four tanks – three Cromwells and a Challenger (the larger version of the vehicle armed with the same seventeen-pounder that the Firefly had) – but ended it with none. Some of his men were dead, others believed captured. Dixon and the remaining men walked to the nearest friendly tanks they could find in the orchard and made themselves as small as possible. The two squadrons, with around twenty surviving tanks, were now clustered in the enclosures and copses between La Lande and Courcelles. The A Squadron vehicles were in the southern part of this loose deployment and their surviving commanders included Major MacDonald, Lieutenant Garnett and Sergeant Solomon, this last in his Firefly. Nearly all of B Squadron's vehicles were still running.

Once darkness had fallen several men tried exploring on foot to the north and west to see if there was a way out of this trap. It was a fraught business, creeping forward in the darkness, but they had returned without success. The tankies knew that the infantry – both Rifles and Queen's – had been driven back from nearby positions and so they were on their own. Returning from one of these trips, the commander of B Squadron had been accidentally shot in the stomach by one of his nervous sentries. Some of the dismounted A Squadron men decided to make a break for it, heading into the darkness on foot. Others didn't want to take the chance, and Solomon had a couple sitting on the outside of his tank.

The officers had been in touch with Lieutenant-Colonel Holliman by radio, and early that night attempted an escape plan. Artillery fire was brought on suspected enemy positions in part to suppress them, but also to distract from the noise of the tanks starting up. They moved off northwards on a farm track late that night but soon ran into an ambush that claimed the leading tank. One troop from B Squadron got away, but the attempt was scrubbed and the rest of the vehicles moved back into defensive positions. The colonel came up on the radio net and said to the men in the surrounded squadrons, 'I've tried everything I can to get you out; you must form your own defence and I will try again in the morning.' One of the tank gunners who heard the ominous message over his headphones reflected: 'I thought, This is it, and just prayed.'

Realising their opportunity, German soldiers had begun to move through the trees with Panzerfausts, hunting the British tanks. Sergeant Solomon knew their situation was precarious in the extreme. He had been campaigning all the way through the desert and Italy, but he had never found himself in a worse one. He worried about the complete lack of infantry, and he worried about his driver who had been displaying 'signs of the jitters' for days. The last thing he wanted was to discover, when the time came to break out, that the driver had bailed out of the tank in terror. But his ruminations were rudely interrupted for, with a flash and an ear-splitting bang, he knew they had been hit. A Panzerfaust had struck the side of the turret, spraying the inside with molten metal. The sergeant rolled out of the Firefly and onto the ground, wounded. They had to get away from the tank, which had started to burn fiercely. He told the others to run back towards the rest of the squadron before realising that he could not see and would need someone to look after him. His arm was heavy from a wound, he could hardly hear and he had been blinded. Was it the flash or the blood that had run into his eyes from head injuries? He had no idea as he stumbled across the lumpy Norman soil.

While Major MacDonald had been off on foot trying to find another way out, his tank had been hit by a bazooka, with the entire crew killed or captured. They were being picked off in the dark one by one. In another A Squadron tank the driver, Trooper Eric Smith, wondered what was going to happen, and his vehicle commander wasn't any use: 'I'd got a sergeant who'd gone bomb-happy and wouldn't get up off the turret floor.' It was then, in the middle of that long night, when the end seemed imminent for all of them, that the battalion's natural leaders asserted themselves. Sergeant 'Pluto' Ellis had gone jogging into the darkness with a Sten gun, probing German positions once more. Trooper Smith, meanwhile, was approached by Lieutenant Garnett, his troop commander. 'What do you think, Smudger? If we stop here we're either dead or prisoners,' said Garnett with the quiet assurance of a man seemingly discussing nothing more perilous than a trip to the shops. 'Let's have a go to break out. Are you game?' Smith said he was, and Garnett gathered together four tanks behind his.

In the early hours a second barrage of artillery provided their cue. Garnett did not command from the turret; he didn't want to chance any misunderstanding or hesitation on Smith's part. Instead, he sat next to the driver's hatch, outside the armour, steadying himself with a hand on the main gun and ready to shout instructions into Smith's ear. The younger trooper said they 'drove like hell'; another driver, a B Squadron man, said it was 'hell-for-leather'. There were flashes of enemy fire as they went, and more casualties were taken. Some tanks veered off course and the men would be telling stories for years of their impressions of their crazy drive through that Norman night. In one place dozens of German soldiers gripped by fear tried to surrender to them, only to be laced with machine-gun fire as the Cromwells shot past. Another tank crashed through a German road block, and one of the Fireflies was abandoned by its frightened crew, who finally walked back to British lines. Lieutenant Dixon saw little of that drive, crouched as he was on the turret floor of a B Squadron tank, trying not to get in the way of the crew manning the vehicle.

When they got back up to Saint-Georges, Lieutenant-Colonel Holliman was there to greet them. The battalion had emerged from one of the worst twenty-four hours of its entire war: only the desert battle of 2 June 1942 had cost them more dearly.

'We all walked around to see who was there and swap yarns of the previous day,' noted Sergeant Wardrop, whose C Squadron had remained outside the German encirclement during the night. 'A and B had lost between them 18 tanks and a lot of good men, Cornish, Knocker Knight, Cyril Nuttall ... so the unit was in bad shape.' In fact, the battalion officially recognised the loss of eight tanks, although some others were damaged during the night and a couple were recovered on 4 August. The more grievous loss was in men; seven were dead for sure, twenty-three wounded and eight missing. There were fears that some of those who could not be found, from the parties that had tried to make their way back by foot, had been caught by the SS and executed.

As for Lieutenant Dixon, who had fought from three different tanks on the 3rd, he made his way back to the echelon since much of his troop was now out of action. His cool head and leadership had earned him the Military Cross.

Sergeant Solomon and the other seriously wounded had been through a quick triage with the Medical Officer before being dispatched by ambulance back down the line to the casualty clearing station, the army's field surgical hospital. Bouncing around in the back of the poorly sprung vehicle, Solomon had shooting pain from the wounds in his back and shouted at the driver, 'For Christ's sake, slow down!'

At the CCS, a tented camp complete with operating theatre, the new casualties were soon seen by a doctor. Solomon was told that his arm would be operated on soon, and feared for a moment that it would be an amputation. But as he moved back along the casualty evacuation chain there was one good thing at least: he was regaining his sight, although he would never get back the hearing in one of his ears. Coming around after his arm operation, he stared at the tented roof flapping above him. A Scottish nurse peered over and told him, 'You're going home.' After four years of front-line service, it was sweet news. A couple of days later he and other casualties were taken out in a DUKW amphibious lorry to a hospital ship anchored off the coast for the journey home.

He had got through all the flaps in the desert, Sidi Rezegh, Alamein and had been one of those who led the way into Tunis. He'd survived Italy, Villers-Bocage and Goodwood too – but now his war was over. Solomon thought about his surviving mates in A Squadron, and what they were up to, but he was not itching to get back to them. 'I wasn't sorry at all,' he reflected. 'I thought of all I'd done in the war, I'd done my bit anyway.'

The journey he took, across the Channel and then by a specially adapted train to the military hospital in Basingstoke, was one tens of thousands of men had already experienced. The casualty returns for VIII Corps during its Normandy battles of 26 June to 15 August give a detailed picture of the mortality rate. During that period the corps had 2141 men killed and 10,838 wounded, out of an average strength during that period of 68,000 troops. Around 60 per cent of the wounds treated were to the upper body, suggesting infantrymen hit in fire positions or tank crew in the hatches of their vehicles. While the number suffering from burns remained below 3 per cent during the infantry-heavy operations around Caen, during Goodwood, when the three armoured divisions had fought under VIII Corps' command, they rose to 6.5 per cent of the total. Statistics compiled for tank crews across the entire British sector suggested that 50 per cent became casualties while inside their vehicles, 37 per cent outside (most often victims of shelling in leaguers) and 13 per cent while partially outside the tank – usually commanders in their hatches.

Most of those evacuated had a positive experience of the casualty clearing stations and evacuation link back to Britain. One patient in a CCS in July 1944 noted, 'The place seems to be a model of good organisation and kindly treatment.' While many front-line soldiers resented the number of people involved in the support side of the Overlord operation, the quality of this system was at least one of the compensations.

Back at the 5th Tanks, they were trying to deal with other consequences of 3–4 August. A and B Squadrons had to be temporarily amalgamated because of the number of men lost, so the battalion borrowed a squadron from the 8th Hussars. Lieutenant-Colonel Holliman knew that, in addition to replacing these casualties, he had to deal with dozens of soldiers who had become too frightened or traumatised to operate effectively. There had been difficulties with NCOs and some of the officers since Villers-Bocage, including the fact that some of the men who had bailed out of their tanks were still serving. Under the 'rotten apple' theory, they were reckoned to be corrupting the morale of the unit more widely. Several individuals had already been shunted away to other places, but what Holliman needed was more of a large-scale purge. On 17 August forty new soldiers arrived to replace those branded 'unsuitable' for the 5th Tanks during the preceding days. Holliman was helped in this by the appearance of new bosses.

Major-General G. L. Verney had arrived just after the 5th's battle in La Lande to replace Major-General Erskine, the outgoing commander of 7th Armoured Division. A couple of weeks later 'Looney' Hinde, who had 22nd Armoured Brigade since North Africa, was also dispatched, as was the general running the corps. Verney, a driven Guards officer who had successfully commanded a Churchill tank brigade during the early days of the campaign, arrived with a satchel full of the higher command's prejudices against the division – criticisms that had built up from Villers-Bocage to Goodwood and beyond. In many ways, the criticism of the Desert Rats and the unpopularity of Erskine and Hinde with Montgomery seemed to derive from their status as experienced commanders who had defended their troops just a little too energetically against the carping of others in 21st Army Group. Even so, there were genuine problems of exhaustion and of many veterans having lost their willingness to take risks, as Holliman or anyone else commanding a battalion in 7th Armoured would freely have conceded.

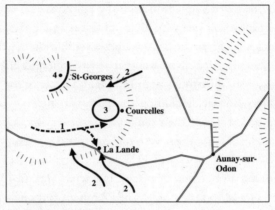

1. Initial advance of A Sqn
2. German counter-attacks
3. Night leaguer of A and B Sqns
4. Night position of C Sqn and RHQ

BATTLE OF 3 AUGUST 1944

'The infantryman can find opportunities for lying low at the critical moment,' observed Verney, 'the tankman can easily find a fault with his engine or with his wireless and this disease spreads rapidly. The commander who finds his men getting canny soon loses confidence and becomes nervy himself.'

Reviewing the elements of his division, Verney considered that 1st and 5th RTR 'were no longer having a go', 1st RB was 'in a bad way' and the motorised infantry of the Queen's Brigade 'was the worst of all'. Verney believed that the arrival of a new commander of 22nd Armoured Brigade and a fresh battalion within it, the 5th Inniskilling Royal Dragoon Guards (which replaced the 4th County of London Yeomanry), would do much to reinvigorate the tracked part of the division, but there were bigger questions over the Queen's. He pointed out that the 1/6th Queen's, the worst-hit infantry battalion, had 118 effective soldiers in its four rifle companies instead of the four-hundred-plus that it should have done.

Many within 5th RTR felt they had been failed by their infantry, particularly the Queen's, at La Lande, where they were left to the mercy of the SS panzer grenadiers. In a private letter Verney gave another example of being let down, shortly after he took command, with a planned night attack with one of the Queen's battalions: 'When the moment came for them to form up the CO found that the majority of the men had melted away, so I had to tell the Corps Commander that he would have to cancel the evening's operation.' This type of failure was wretched for all concerned.

The action of 3 August had exposed not just the exhaustion of the Queen's Brigade – which was bad but a long way from being the worst British infantry formation in Normandy after two months of grinding hedgerow fighting – but the ongoing failure to coordinate tanks and foot soldiers effectively. Since the early days of its Balaklava charges in the desert, the division (and British army more widely) had made great strides in integrating the operations of field artillery, anti-tank guns and air support with those of the tanks. Plenty of German commanders testified to their fear of the British ability to bring heavy firepower so swiftly to bear. However, even once the infantry battalions were topped up with fresh men and aggressive young officers, certain problems still confronted the 7th Armoured after years of war.

Of the four infantry battalions at its disposal, only the 1st RB had armoured half-tracks – a worthwhile solution, but one that still left them half as mobile across country and half as well protected as the tanks. The Canadian infantry was by this time using

Kangaroos in its attacks, Sherman tank hulls that had been converted into infantry carriers. As for the unfortunate Queen's Brigade, they rode in lorries and these could not generally be taken into action because they would be shot to pieces. In an emergency, as during the withdrawal from Villers-Bocage, the Queen's could ride on the tanks, but both sides in the partnership considered this a dangerous expedient.

There were also problems of communication, as events on 3 August had shown. 'Once you were on your feet,' noted Lieutenant Crassweller of 1st RB, 'you had no means of communicating with the tanks, our man-pack radios operated on different frequencies . . . it bugged us all the way through the war.' Eventually, field telephones were installed on the back of the Cromwells' hulls for infantry to use, but you had to be close and it was too dangerous to use it standing up under fire. The 5th Tanks had long ago learnt the value of the regimental net in allowing the whole battalion to share the same picture of an evolving battle, but it remained very hard for dismounted infantry to contribute information (as would have been invaluable to A Squadron at La Lande) or receive it from the tanks.

As a foot soldier who had subsequently experienced command of an armoured brigade, General Verney felt the tanks had been let down by the infantry in the division, and as a result 'suffered far higher casualties than they should have'. This view was shared by an assessment of the 7th Armoured Division from a German corps intelligence staff that noted: 'the infantry soldier is regarded by our own troops as medium. He fights if he has got the support of tanks and artillery; otherwise he takes evasive action.' Overall, though, the German view of the Desert Rats was that 'the fighting value of this division is good'. Verney, like many a new manager keen to make a name for himself, and despite his diagnosis of its immediate faults, recognised the underlying quality of the formation. He thought Montgomery had asked too much of the 7th Armoured, and that the amount of time it had spent in action was blatantly unfair when compared, for example, to the Guards Armoured Division.

If battle exhaustion or desertion were tokens of poor morale, or a division that had seen too much action, the 7th Armoured still compared very favourably with other battle-weary formations. August 1944 was to prove the division's worst month of the war by some margin for courts martial, with twenty-three men convicted of desertion (just nine had been convicted in July). But that total was paltry compared to the 50th or Tyne Tees Division, which had an alarming 134 convictions for desertion in August. The 50th had also been brought from the Mediterranean, but after sterling work on D-Day had been ground down by months of combat in Normandy. The high rate of attrition among foot soldiers, and shortage of suitable replacements, would necessitate the breaking up of one infantry division in October 1944, and the removal of the Tyne Tees from the line of battle by the end of the year. While armoured divisions had been disbanded in North Africa, it did not happen in north-west Europe.

Verney knew that some rest would work wonders for the division. 'Sleep free from anxiety is the essential,' prescribed one of the senior psychiatrists dealing with battle exhaustion in 21st Army Group. But Montgomery and his subordinate commanders knew that with the Normandy battle becoming fluid at last, their most experienced armoured division could not be given time off. There was some maintenance time here and there, and the odd ENSA* show, including one with George Formby. These touring troupes of entertainers transported the soldiers away from the grim realities of Normandy for a few minutes, but it hardly compared to the relief they had been able to gain in

* Entertainments National Service Association

Alexandria or Cairo from the horrors of desert fighting. At this moment, in the late summer of 1944, there could be no leave away from the front because the Desert Rats were essential to the business ahead.

It was hoped by the generals that the newly arrived '5th Skins' would give some cavalry dash to the division too. The newcomers were eyed with suspicion by many of the tankies. Some old sweats had been forced by experience in action to modify the general pre-war RTR prejudice against the cavalry. There was respect for hardened regiments like the 8th Hussars, and the armoured car experts of the 11th Hussars (nicknamed the Cherry Pickers) had won near universal admiration in the desert army. They were 'shit hot', in the words of one 5th Tanks man. But the 5th Skins arrived with little war experience, and their senior NCOs told them to stay away from the 'filthy Fifth' lest they pick up bad habits. This idea, that few of them had experience of combat and might rush on in ways that the veterans had long ago learned were too costly, caused the Inniskilling Dragoon Guards' suspicion to be returned with interest. Around the 5th Tanks leaguer the term 'donkey wallopers' was again used freely, and it was reckoned that if they wanted to rush ahead blindly, let them. The prejudice was much the same with the 1st RTR, one of whom commented caustically in his journal on an advance a couple of weeks after the new mob's arrival in the division, 'Skins in the lead again until they meet opposition! Then it'll be our job.'

The 7th Armoured pushed on and the 5th Tanks, if it had been bloodied and bruised by the action of 3 August, had at least witnessed another demonstration of the extraordinary resilience of its seasoned commanders during the fighting. As for the bigger picture, the American breakout had produced a drive south and then east. A large German force, the remnants of the entire 7th Army, was trapped in the so-called Falaise pocket. They had been fixed in position by the Anglo-Canadian operations of late July and early August, and by the 10th, when Hitler finally realised the dangers of his 'no retreat' directives and authorised a general withdrawal, it was already too late for most of the forces in the Falaise area to escape the Allied encirclement. Instead, they were pounded relentlessly through the middle of the month by aircraft and artillery. As this happened, the 7th Armoured Division was moving eastwards, across the top of the Falaise pocket towards a series of river defence lines prepared by the Germans.

If there were glimmers of optimism at Montgomery's head-quarters they had not yet penetrated the gloom of the front-line tank men. Dreams of home seeped through their exhaustion all right, but it still seemed a long way off. Of the six soldiers mentioned at the start of this account, Lieutenant Brian Stone and Sergeant Gerry Solomon had been too seriously wounded to carry on. Sergeant Emmin Hall had been serving with the Staffordshire Yeomanry but would soon move to a less danger-ous job on a tank-delivery squadron. Sergeants Jake Wardrop and Charlie Bull remained tank commanders in 5th RTR, and Captain Crickmay was about to move from his job as adjutant to take up an important new position. But two out of these three men would not survive the months of fighting that remained.

20

BREAKOUT

The movement of people after A Squadron's heavy loss on 3 August led to Arthur Crickmay being switched to the command of C Squadron and promoted to major. This elevation came almost five years to the day of his abandonment of his career in architecture and farewell to his family in Suffolk to join the army. He had thrown himself heart and soul into tactics and desert navigation, and was one of a handful of veterans in Monty's army who combined service in the 1940 Libyan campaign with Burma, Italy and Normandy. He had escaped death too many times to count. But despite all of his middle-class zeal for mastering the business of soldiering, Crickmay had felt that the regular army men had always regarded him, a war service Johnny-come-lately, as not quite on a par with them. Many were now looking forward to the end of the war, when the army would shrink drastically and only the officers with regular commissions would have a future.

By taking on jobs such as adjutant or squadron leader, which had once been reserved for regular officers, Crickmay had hoped to give himself the option of serving on in the army after the war, but the organisation itself gave little encouragement. It was known that regular officers, some of whom had sat out the war behind desks, were seeking the command of squadrons and battalions. They had been told that the only promotions that would be recognised after the war were those gained in field service. So the command of an RTR squadron, something Crickmay had been longing for since 1942 at least, inevitably came with strings, as he told his mother:

> I've been a major for ten days and am commanding C Squadron. I experienced little satisfaction when the great day dawned ... I've little doubt that some fat pig in the War House [the War Office in London] sensing that the end of hostilities cannot now be long delayed will reckon it's time to get settled into a regiment before peace breaks out so that he will not be out of a job when Whitehall is demobilised. I have already been warned that this is likely to occur.

What Crickmay underestimated, though, was the degree to which the long-standing members of his squadron, and indeed the others in 5th Tanks, would now only accept the leadership of someone whose experience matched their own. Of the ninety to ninety-five men serving on the squadron's fighting vehicles, only a minority were Alamein veterans by this time. There had been many battle losses and dozens of newcomers from Shakers Wood onwards, not least to replace those lately found 'unsuitable' due to battle stress. At the heart of Crickmay's squadron were its sergeants, men who gave it a depth of experience that infantry battalions such as the 1st RB had lost due to casualties. It was also these men who stayed on in tanks by choice, risking their lives daily and shunning less dangerous jobs to the rear. As far as they were concerned, Crickmay passed the test.

Wardrop knew that his new OC 'had been around a bit' and 'had made a name for himself in Italy', an oblique reference to Crickmay's time in Recce and him winning the MC. This was more than enough for the sergeant. Another Alamein veteran, a corporal in C Squadron, soon struck up a vibrant rapport with the major, noting that 'he was not overly familiar, but he had a way of letting the barriers drop. He would join in the sing-songs of the old desert standards, and a lot of officers wouldn't do that.' Whatever else was going on around him, Crickmay retained a wry sense of humour, avidly consuming copies of *Punch* sent out from home, and his dapper dress sense, leading the corporal to remark on the new major's 'immaculate turnout' in the field.

Although Crickmay's initial impression was that running a squadron would be a welcome change from the mind-numbing hours of being adjutant, he was evidently arriving at a difficult time. He was the fifth OC to lead C Squadron in four months. His immediate predecessor, another desert hand, had quit because he had lost his nerve. The second-in-command, a twenty-five-year-old captain named Brian Butler, had also been in battle many times and was struggling to keep his fear under control.

Sergeant Wardrop had noticed the signs of stress in himself, the twitching in his leg or shaking of his hands. He was dosing himself with alcohol, as were many in the squadron. Whisky was coming through from home occasionally, and when they found a Norman village that was not ruined they would visit its café for wine or, better still, calvados, the apple brandy distinctive to the region. Drink, though, could not dilute some of the anger that Wardrop felt as the war ground on. He hated the Germans for prolonging the whole business, and he was increasingly intolerant towards those in positions of authority – not just officers – whom he felt were incapable.

On 9 August, just a couple of days after Crickmay had taken over the squadron, there had been an incident that brought the Scottish sergeant low. His comrade Sergeant Peter Fyfe had been hit by shrapnel as they walked back towards their respective tanks after receiving orders from their troop commander, Lieutenant Hedges. The squadron had been pushing forward across country when German spotters had put in an artillery stonk.

Rushing to the side of Sergeant Fyfe, Wardrop could see the shrapnel had peppered his legs and stomach. He ripped at shell dressings and clamped them to Fyfe's wounds. 'I could not get the bleeding to stop,' Wardrop recalled. 'As fast as one dressing was on it was soaked through. He was getting low and I did all I could but in a minute or two he was dead.'

Wardrop blamed Lieutenant Hedges (a callow youth transferred to them from the 4th County of London Yeomanry when the battalion had been withdrawn from the brigade) because he had insisted on repeating his orders several times. The repetition was pointless, but had allowed the German guns to zero in. Fyfe had died because 'a panic-stricken officer wanted to have someone to talk to'. That night Wardrop found Captain Butler in the squadron leaguer and 'told him straight that Lt Hedges was a no good Englishman, a coward, and that I refused to serve with him in the same troop a minute longer'.

Butler and Crickmay now faced a difficult challenge in running the squadron. If they dispensed with Hedges it would solidify the power of the NCOs to choose their own officers. On the other hand, neither of them was interested in perpetuating a situation where a subaltern got his men killed, and in any case, the second-in-command could have told his new boss, there were already doubts about Hedges. For a short while they tried to deal with the issue by moving Wardrop's tank to another troop, but it soon became clear that the lieutenant had lost the confidence of the sergeants in the squadron as a whole and so he was dispatched back to the echelon, where he could command nothing more dangerous than a couple of lorries.

Short of junior officers, Crickmay gave the command of 11 Troop to Sergeant Sammy Hagan. Its troop leader, Lieutenant Baker, had lasted just a few days: having arrived threatening anyone who held back in action with court martial and firing squad, he had gone sick after his first couple of days' fighting. It was not a new thing for a sergeant to run it, for 11 Troop had after all been Emmin Hall's for months in the desert and Italy. But given the quantities of young officers being produced by OCTU, it did strike Wardrop as an outrageous situation:

> That worm Lt Hedges went to B echelon and skulked for the remainder of the war ... here we had four tanks commanded by a sergeant and a spare officer who had proved himself to be useless, hiding in the echelon, drawing his pay every week while Sammy took on the responsibility of a troop of tanks ... if Lt Hedges was not enough of a man to command a troop, why not make him a trooper and give his two pips and his pay to Sammy who after all was doing the job?

The army medical guidelines for dealing with 'battle exhaustion' – terms like 'bomb-happy' and 'shell shock' were frowned upon – stressed that the unit Medical Officer should examine men in the first instance, and hold them if there was a chance of rapid recovery. For this reason the echelon became the staging post for those who could not fight on in the squadrons. The army psychiatrists instructed that 'unit Medical Officers are reminded that they must deal with milder cases by a judicious mixture of firmness, sympathy and friendly encouragement'.

Some did return to the front line, and others were found easier jobs: Captain Daniels, Butler's predecessor as second-in-command of C Squadron, was sent to a tank-delivery squadron, i.e. one that ferried vehicles from depots to the front line. For the serious cases, however, there was no choice but referral from the 5th Tanks echelon to the battle exhaustion centres established at the various divisional casualty clearing stations in the rear. A couple of the A Squadron men who came out of the La Lande battle on their feet were so traumatised that they were by this time heading homewards down this psychiatric casualty evacuation pipeline.

While the situation – Crickmay dealing with men in C Squadron struggling with shell shock, or his colleague Major MacDonald trying to rebuild A Squadron – might have sounded nightmarish, it certainly was not by the standards of the British 2nd Army. During Goodwood, for example, the 7th Armoured Division had actually suffered significantly fewer cases of battle exhaustion than the fresher, supposedly more gung-ho 11th and Guards. Twenty-six men from the Desert Rats were evacuated for psychological reasons, sixty-eight from the Guards and eighty-two from 11th Armoured. If anything, the old sweats tended to stabilise the new soldiers rather than spread fear and bad practice among them, as Major-General Verney believed.

Among infantry divisions in Normandy, with their heavier role in face-to-face *bocage* fighting, the figures were higher still. The 15th Scottish Division had many more cases than the armoured ones, as did the 43rd Wessex Division which, during the first three weeks of its Normandy campaign, had sent 334 men to the battle exhaustion centre. The general view in the army was that these soldiers could not be dealt with harshly, and certainly not by firing squad as they had in the Great War. At the same time, they were wise to the idea that some might plead exhaustion in order to avoid the dangers of combat. Reviewing the Normandy campaign of VIII Corps, its senior medical officer Brigadier Glyn Hughes opined, 'It must be accepted that in the strain of modern war and now that the stigma and punishment for exhibiting fear has been largely removed cases of exhaustion will occur in such numbers as to present difficult problems to the Medical Services.' He noted the differences in the German army, and one evening discussed them with the recently captured Medical Officer of the 1st SS Leibstandarte Adolf Hitler Panzer Division. Those SS men no longer able to function because of shell shock were immediately weeded out and sent away, but in less serious cases 'the crime of disloyalty to his country and to the Führer pointed out to him and he was sent straight back to his duty'. There was implied menace in the use of the word 'crime', and certainly anecdotal evidence of German officers occasionally placing a gun to the head in order to ensure obedience.

By mid-August, increasingly positive reports about the progress of the war provided their own tonic for Crickmay and his squadron. The pounding of the Falaise pocket continued, and US troops were fanning out in western France as well as towards Paris. Crickmay envied them this 'swanning about', as they had called rapid advances in the desert days. The constant smashing that German forces were receiving, and their difficulties in resupplying men and machines, meant that divisions were breaking down into combat groups of battalion or even company size. As these formations withered, their ability to hold land was reduced and that of the Allied forces to advance increased.

By 21 August 5th Tanks was motoring eastwards towards the River Touques, where a crossing marked an important objective. In this new, freer situation the 11th Hussars were able once more to speed about in their armoured cars as they had in North Africa, discovering an intact bridge across the River Touques at the town of Fervaques. As the tank crews had moved off the plain of Caen at long last, they had noticed the landscape become more rolling and picturesque. They passed intact half-timbered Norman farms that had survived since medieval times. And among these hamlets they saw smiling faces, waves and people holding up their children to see the liberators. It lifted their spirits to escape the sullen, haunted stares of the few visible civilians around Caen, whose communities had been pounded to smithereens by the Allied bombers.

Fervaques sat at the bottom of a valley, with a steep rise just beyond it. There, some remnants of the 21st Panzer Division stood in defence. The 1st RB had crept to the edge of the town the night before, securing the bridge, but the situation was fluid. After months in which advances were slow and deliberate, the presence of the British at this place caught many German soldiers by surprise. 'A dispatch rider went flying past us and over the bridge to where 5th RTR were blocking the road,' said a Rifles officer. 'Sure enough, we heard a screech of brakes and having encountered the tanks he came speeding back, so we killed him.'

A Squadron of the 5th RTR was pushed down into the village to reinforce the riflemen. C Squadron, meanwhile, took up firing positions overlooking the town from its western side. One of their Cromwells was hit by a shell on its front, the round mortally wounding the driver. The crews knew that it was solid or armour-piercing shot, and reckoned the wooded ridge above the town on the other side was at least 2500 yards away. They lobbed some high-explosive shells in the general direction it had come from in case there were 88s in the woods, but the crews had the uneasy feeling that they were being targeted by a King Tiger.

Later that day there was a concerted attempt by German infantry to retake the town. A Squadron and two companies of

1st RB fought well together, calling in artillery and 'finishing off' those who survived the barrage. It was not yet three weeks since the fight at La Lande, but this time cooperation between foot and tank soldiers was impressive. At times reports came through that the British had been surrounded in Fervaques, but they got through the night with sufficient ease for many of the crews to tuck into calvados and get some sleep. Small parties of Germans or vehicles were in fact still moving about to the west of the River Touques. The speed of the British advance had caught them out, and during the 20th several German vehicles and forty of their soldiers had fallen into 5th RTR's hands as they travelled roads that they assumed were still safe.

Moving into Fervaques the next day, one of the B Squadron gunners remained anxious about a possible counter-attack, but found it hard to focus on the danger now that the people of the town had realised they had been liberated. 'We were engulfed literally by dozens of men and women climbing on the tank,' he wrote as he looked down the Cromwell's aiming telescope, waiting for a German tank to round the corner. 'My line of sight was continually being interrupted by delirious French men and women climbing on and off. We tried to order them off the tank but they seemed almost incapable of hearing us.'

The next key objective was the River Seine. By 29 August the 22nd Armoured Brigade was in Le Neubourg, south of Rouen and within striking distance of the river. News of Free French troops entering Paris on 25 August had reached the soldiers, and they had witnessed increasingly joyous scenes as they sped up the Norman roads. Hundreds of Germans had been taken and, included in the bag as they struggled back towards the Seine, dozens of Tigers and King Tigers that had broken down, run out of fuel or were too heavy to get across the remaining crossings. The Battle of Normandy was over. Of the German defenders –

around half a million in the ground combat units – nearly 300,000 were casualties, around 200,000 of them prisoners. The Allies had suffered 210,000 casualties during the eighty-day fight, a smaller number out of a considerably bigger total. While Monty had been castigated for slowness early on in the campaign, and for failing to meet the planned phase lines of his advance, the offensive overall, to Paris and beyond Normandy, had delivered its result slightly ahead of a schedule drawn up months before. Very little of the fighting equipment used in the German defence was successfully evacuated. Instead Hitler's troops lost 1500 tanks as well as armoured assault or anti-tank guns and 3600 aircraft in their abortive struggle.

The 7th Armoured Division was placed under the command of a new corps headquarters and by the end of August, as the first units crossed the Seine, objectives had been given that would carry these forces on beyond France and into Belgium. The Desert Rats had been ordered to take the city of Ghent, more than two hundred miles away. That distance was covered during the next five days – an average advance of forty miles per day, with some units actually motoring sixty or seventy miles on some days. This dizzy rush forward, an 'exploitation' or 'pursuit' in generals' language, was what tank forces were for, and the 7th Armoured took their opportunity with alacrity, blowing away the trials of the months since June in a cloud of exhaust and a thundering of tracks. For some of those old-timers in the 5th Tanks the turning of the tables on the Germans was complete, for they passed through places from which they had been tumbled by German panzer divisions in the summer of 1940. Even the legion critics of the Cromwell tank had to concede that it was fast and reliable enough to perform this mission excellently, unlike the Fireflies that struggled to keep up, throwing their tracks or blowing engines. This advance became known in British army legend as the Great Swan.

'In one place we halted for [a] while and the people brought us eggs, butter, bread and milk,' wrote Sergeant Wardrop, whose mood had been improved by a couple of brandies with breakfast. 'On the morning of the 3rd we set out again to hustle to a place called Bernaville where we had the usual rousing welcome of flowers, flags, wine, cognac and mademoiselles.'

Many vivid scenes that emphasised the changed fortunes of war planted themselves in the minds of the advancing soldiers. Along with French and then Belgian joy, there was the bewildered expression of thousands of German prisoners who fell into the bag. In one case, they had been lining up behind field kitchens for their breakfast when the British tanks appeared; in another, they simply drove into Allied columns and realised the game was up. Some were sullen to the last, others seemed delighted that their war was over. When time allowed, 'they were stripped of any watches, cameras, or binoculars they might have' by the tankies. The desire for loot increased as the magnitude of their triumph became clear. Motorbikes and staff cars were eyed covetously, even by Major Crickmay, and all manner of German weapons, stores and catering equipment were soon festooned from the tanks.

One subaltern in B Squadron felt that the buccaneering appearance of these war machines thundering along the French roads symbolised something deeper about the unit and its identity:

We called ourselves the Fighting Fifth. But I discovered the rest of the 7th Armoured Division called us the Filthy Fifth! No wonder with a mountain of bedrolls behind each turret, everything but the kitchen sink dangling from any available point of attachment and the officers dressed as if they were going to the races! . . . It wasn't a lack of discipline or good housekeeping. It was the ethos of the regiment.

During the early hours of 5 September the 5th Tanks reached its objective of Ghent, with C Squadron at their head. The city was evidently being held by a garrison of some size, but once dawn had come happy Belgians emerged to meet their liberators. Here as in other Belgian towns, members of the White Brigade or resistance proved to be vital sources of information. They reckoned the occupiers' morale was poor, and that they might surrender. Taking a local man and one of his sergeants with him, Crickmay walked forward with a white flag, approaching a German checkpoint on the main boulevard into town. The soldiers there agreed to take the British to meet their officers.

'We felt fairly exposed as we set out,' Crickmay admitted. 'However, my thoughts hovered between, Is this a lethal hoax?, and the possibility of the squadron capturing Ghent single-handed.' It was the sort of dashing deed that might win a man the DSO, after all. The Germans took their British guests, blind-folded, to a command post, where the British and their enemies eyed one another up:

> Rifle and Panzerfaust-toting Kraut soldiers standing around regarded us with interest. This was my first real encounter with these gentry – free and in their natural habitat so to speak. The unmistakeable tang of Teutonic cigarettes and gun oil hung heavy in the air.

Crickmay told them there were hundreds of British tanks at the gates of the city, and if they knew what was good for them they would pack it in. Once again the German officers suggested they needed a higher authority, so the commander of C Squadron soon found himself in a nearby château, where he came face to face with a perfectly dressed, jackboot-wearing, monocled German general.

Major-General Brun decided to stand on military protocol, perhaps hoping that he might profit by stalling for time. He told Crickmay that he would only surrender to a British general. It was here that Crickmay, who put so much effort into cutting a fine figure in a London club or Cairo hotel, could see that his youthful appearance, dirty tank overalls and meagre rank would not do the trick. So, accepting that others would appropriate the glory for the seizure of the city, he retraced his journey to the outskirts of Ghent.

Returning late in the afternoon to the checkpoint, Crickmay discovered that much had happened during his long absence. There had been German shelling during the day, scattering many of the civilian revellers who had surrounded their tanks. Crickmay and Lieutenant-Colonel Holliman formed a plan to hoodwink General Brun into thinking Holliman was a general too, and so could accept the surrender. When Brun appeared at the checkpoint at eight o'clock that evening Holliman attempted the subterfuge, but the game was given away by a British officer who called him 'colonel', prompting the German to walk out.

It was after midnight when at last the commander of 22nd Armoured Brigade met General Brun in a last attempt to talk sense into him. The British wanted to spare the medieval centre of the town, as well as its inhabitants, from destruction. They had all seen clearly enough what had happened to Caen and other places in Normandy. The meeting in the early hours of 7 September brought together senior men from both sides, one observing that 'all the British officers were very dirty and the Germans immaculate'. The brigadier in time delivered his threat that 'a decision to fight on would reduce the number of Germans in the next generation'. Brun asked for the others to withdraw and spoke to the brigadier in French for a few minutes. The German insisted that he was only trying to find an honourable path between his officers, who he considered defeatist, and his higher commanders whose orders to fight on were unrealistic. In the end, Brun left the negotiation without agreement.

The following day it became clear that the Germans had withdrawn from the old part of the city, retiring to an industrial area on its northern side, where a canal and some other obstacles made their position more defensible. The OC of C Squadron was soon wondering whether General Brun had tricked them all. Had he used a series of excuses about the British officers' lowly rank in order to buy himself the hours in which to redeploy his troops to a smaller, more defensible perimeter? Crickmay had his suspicions, and it was the thirst for a little glory on his own part, Holliman's and finally the brigadier's that had made the German tactic possible.

Seventh Armoured Division had performed prodigies during the Great Swan, not least in taking ten thousand German prisoners as it advanced hundreds of miles. During one twenty-four-hour period on the outskirts of Ghent 5th Tanks alone reported its bag at six hundred. Every man who had come through Normandy had found ways, during conversation or even their own late-night thoughts, to manage their hopes of survival and it all being over soon. Now many of them dared to think they could make it. They knocked back drinks, celebrating their escape from Normandy and toasting the dream of being home by Christmas. But after a week in which they had advanced at breakneck speed they settled down to a sobering task: how to dislodge a couple of thousand well-armed Germans from a built-up area in northern Ghent. Everyone in the battalion knew well enough that it could cost them dear.

21

BLOODIED BUT UNBOWED

The rush to Ghent had produced a degree of confusion on both sides. The 22nd Armoured Brigade had reached the city ahead of their infantry support in the Queen's Brigade, which made the tank crews wary about entering built-up areas where the enemy might approach them undetected. There was much dismounting – usually by commanders and lap gunners (the machine gunner who sat next to the driver in the hull of the Cromwell) – to peer around corners, cross bridges or talk to locals. The Germans for their part had been discomfited by the speed of the Allied advance. Detachments of men were trying to extricate themselves from areas the 7th Armoured Division had just swept through in order to rejoin their comrades in the northern part of Ghent. This produced many surprise meetings between British and German soldiers, some of which resulted in surrender and others sudden death.

On the evening of 6 September elements of B Squadron were patrolling a few miles south of the city. As night fell, one of its four sub-units, 7 Troop, found itself west of Gavere, a small town on the River Scheldt. This was Sergeant Charlie Bull's outfit. He had been campaigning since the outbreak of the war, and at twenty-nine was one of the older men still on tanks. One of the crewmen on his Cromwell felt the sergeant was 'a tough character, experienced and confident'. Bull presented very different faces to his troop and to those who knew him at home. His sisters regarded him as a Jack the lad with a taste in unsuitable women – none more so than Peggy, the eighteen-year-old he had married when on leave that February. He had a swagger that had become worse as he gained promotion in the army. In B Squadron, though, one officer described him as 'competent yet unassuming . . . he never raised his voice nor bullied his men'. It was as if he recognised that the success and status he had won in 5th Tanks required him to maintain a different standard of behaviour in uniform.

Bull had at various times commanded 7 Troop, but an officer, Lieutenant Eric Stevenson, was with them that night. Stevenson, a twenty-year-old Scot, had the necessary qualifications for the crewmen in that he was brave and 'willing to listen'. Many of the subalterns sent to the battalion from early 1944 onwards did not make the grade but, as Roy Dixon in A Squadron had discovered, those who did were the ones who were willing to lean on the enormous experience of their troop sergeants and drop any airs and graces they might have had about holding a commission.

With darkness enfolding the surrounding hamlets and a steady stream of rain coming down it was not easy to guard against being attacked by enemy soldiers on foot. The tanks were big, noisy vehicles from which it was hard to retain an awareness of one's surroundings. They did not have night-vision equipment, and the headphones all the crew wore made it hard to hear things, even when the tank's engine was not running. With numerous reports of German soldiers moving about, snipers taking pot shots at tanks and mortar bombs dropping on unsuspecting troops, Lieutenant Stevenson was afraid. He was keen to make contact with some infantry from the Queen's Brigade who, his squadron commander told him, were in the area. Spotting some lights up ahead, he dispatched a willing member of the Belgian resistance to investigate. The man soon returned to report that the people up ahead, in a ditch beside the road not fifty yards to their front, were Germans. Stevenson's crew opened up with the tank's two machine guns. Moments later a flare popped over them, an anti-tank gun opened fire and all hell broke loose.

The troop escaped this situation by speeding forward with its four tanks, out of the danger and closer to Gavere where the Queen's were waiting, according to messages coming across the radio. Of the Belgian resistance man, caught outside the tank when it happened, there was no trace. The infantry could not be found either, even when they reached the smaller part of the town which lay on the western bank of the Scheldt. What should they do? Sergeant Bull and Lieutenant Stevenson dismounted from their tanks. They had positioned the vehicles at each point of the compass since they had no idea where the next threat might appear from. They walked about the dark houses, straining their eyes in a vain search for any British infantry and were coming to the conclusion that they might be safer on the eastern side of the river. As they debated their move, a Besa machine gun on the lieutenant's Cromwell opened up. The two commanders ran back to their tanks. German infantry had been spotted marching bold as brass down the road they had just used to escape the ambush.

Once more 7 Troop sped forward, this time across the bridge. They took up defensive positions, using the houses of Gavere for concealment. The crews chatted nervously about what had just happened. The machine-gunner was sure he had hit a few of the Germans. Stevenson reported the situation to the squadron leader, Major Dennis Cockbaine, by radio. Not long afterwards the order came back: cross back to the western side of the river. Cockbaine was insistent – the Queen's infantry were there, the lieutenant *must* find them. After the two contacts they'd already experienced they knew the Germans were waiting across the water in some strength, but everyone in 7 Troop knew they would be better off operating together with their own foot soldiers. The tanks rumbled back across the bridge, Stevenson's followed by Bull's, the third Cromwell and the Firefly.

By the time they had got to the other side Sergeant Bull had dropped down into the turret. Finding a place to stop, crewmen pulled him out of the vehicle and attempted to treat him. The tank showed no signs of being hit, so they assumed that their sergeant was one more commander who had paid the price for keeping his head and shoulders out of the tank in order to see what was going on. Whether it was a bullet or a piece of shrapnel from a shell fired at the bridge that had pierced Charlie's chest, his life blood was pumping away. Some of the tankies lowered him down to street level, and local people guided them to a closed shop, where the stricken sergeant could be laid on the counter for treatment. The other crewmen could not dawdle with so many Germans around, so they quickly mounted up again, with the wireless operator taking command of the tank. Later, they would take the body to squadron HQ.

The troop passed the remainder of the night anxiously peering from the hatches of their tanks, trying to detect anyone creeping up on them while avoiding being claimed by snipers. In the morning, off to the west and close to the first contact, they could see German half-tracks and self-propelled guns moving off. The squadron refused 7 Troop permission to engage them and so Stevenson and the others watched the enemy vehicles head back north, having failed to break out eastwards across Gavere Bridge. In that sense they had fulfilled the task set for them by their OC, by denying the bridge to the enemy. In the daylight, Lieutenant Stevenson would discover that the Queen's had been in a wood off the main road, where Major Cockbaine had insisted they would be found, but for some reason they had not made their presence known when the lieutenant and Sergeant Bull had been searching on foot for them in the darkness.

Sergeant Bull was buried in a nearby cemetery. Local people provided a coffin and attended the service conducted by a Belgian priest. In death, Charlie Bull was claimed by the people of Gavere as the martyr who fell in their liberation and the bridge was subsequently named after him. He had survived the escape from 1940 Cherbourg, the airfield of Sidi Rezegh and the plains of Caen, but Charlie Bull would never return to his native Staffordshire. Whatever they thought of him back home, Bull had found a status and respect as a tank commander that he could not give up and, like Wardrop and the other long-serving NCOs, he had shunned safer posts. Several days later Major Cockbaine, the B Squadron leader, wrote to Peggy Bull, Charlie's teenage bride, explaining the circumstances of his death before continuing:

In the village there was an English-speaking priest who readily agreed to bury him in his church-yard on the top of a hill. This he did and with the Union Jack on his coffin Charles was given a burial which he so richly deserved. I tell you all this because it shows how the people are eager to help us. After the service the priest told us that later on the townsfolk will erect a granite and marble headstone as a token of their gratitude to one who fell defending them.

And we left the grave covered with flowers, a bunch from every family in the village and they promised that there will always be some flowers on the grave forever. We have since returned to the church-yard and have taken a photograph of the grave, and if you so desire we will send a copy of it later on. Charles was one of the good old timers of 'B' Sqn. He was loved by all, and never tried to exert his authority over anyone. He was always cheerful and his courage was of the highest order. His passing has indeed left a gap which will never be filled.

Bull's death touched a nerve in the squadron, even after the loss of so many men during its campaigns. The Great Swan and the arrival in Ghent had marked an escape from the grim murder of Normandy; spirits had soared and men had dared to hope that they might just come through it all unscathed. But in the days of mopping-up that followed, there came reminders that survival could not be taken for granted. Sergeant Bull's gunner summed it up: 'To come all that way and die near the end of the war was a bitter blow.'

On 9 September C Squadron felt a similar loss. The push to flush out the Germans in the northern part of Ghent had begun, but the British found their way blocked on the quayside of the canal behind which their enemy had withdrawn. There was a swing bridge across the waterway that the Germans had left open before destroying its motor. Under the direction of Captain Butler, the squadron second-in-command, a couple of soldiers from the Queen's had volunteered to paddle to a pier in the middle of the canal, upon which the bridge pivoted. When they got there they attached a heavy-duty rope to one end of the bridge and paddled back. Butler, who had watched from the canalside, then attached the rope to the front of his tank and directed it to reverse, pulling the bridge back into position.

This daring operation had been observed by Germans in the factories across the water, and they called in artillery fire that dropped on the quayside. While most of the British dived into cover Butler was cut down by shrapnel and, despite being rushed to hospital, died later that day. Just like Sergeant Bull, he left behind a young wife whom he had married a few months earlier. After his death, one of the crewmen in Butler's tank found his diary, and learned of that officer's daily struggle with his own fear. 'After breakfast I bailed out. I did not tell anyone I could not stand the strain,' Butler had written about an engagement back in June. 'I was worried about how I should fare in action again.'

The captain's boss, Major Crickmay, had found Butler withdrawn and difficult during the weeks since he had taken over the squadron but now he understood. Butler had forced himself on, despite being convinced that he was not going to make it. The diary had been the captain's place to confide the fears that so many of them felt. Butler had, like Crickmay, been serving since 1939, but his time had run out.

Among the veterans of the battalion, anger with the enemy that would deny them their safe return home was simmering. They had hardly been offering Jerry an easy time for the previous four years, but now many of them concluded, in the words of one B Squadron officer, 'that the only good German was a dead one'. If they could not see the futility of fighting on, better blast them to kingdom come.

A troop of tanks was able quickly to move across the bridge that had cost Captain Butler his life, where they found and engaged dozens of Germans with machine-gun fire. The following morning 9 Troop, including Sergeant Jake Wardrop, relieved the troop that had crossed into the industrial area, occupying defensive positions. The Germans had fired mortars at the British troops sporadically during the night, but with a new day they elected in the textbook Wehrmacht fashion to mount a counter-attack. At about eleven o'clock Wardrop and his troop commander noticed people moving at the windows of houses to their front. The sergeant pulled out some boxes of .50-calibre ammunition for the big Browning machine gun next to the commander's hatch of his Firefly. The number of mortar shells dropping among the factory buildings started to pick up:

> ... then the stupid pig-headed Boches infantry came at us marching across the open fields. I could see them distinctly, black against the grass with their big helmets and firing from the hip as they came. I looked across at Lt Crocker who grinned and pointed at them, rubbing his hands and a bit later when they were good and close we went to town with the machine guns. There was a scatter straight away, they dropped and started to crawl about on the grass but there was no cover and we kept firing and firing, it was great.

Some of the attacking force had avoided the killing ground of this open field, working their way towards the tanks behind a railway embankment, but as soon as they emerged into the open 'we cut them down at about a hundred yards'. The German counter-attack had been smashed by three tanks and a platoon of British infantry. Some time passed and they were reinforced by an additional troop, then their fourth 9 Troop tank arrived. Fresh infantry was moving through too.

Perhaps realising that these odds were impossible, and that dozens of their comrades had already been killed, some of the Germans who had gone to ground decided to surrender. Sergeant Wardrop dismounted from his tank, joining an officer of the Queen's Regiment to investigate reports of a white flag being waved from a railway signal box. Entering the box with guns drawn, they found three wounded soldiers. The fittest of them, the man who had been waving the flag, was led away by the Queen's officer as he went off to get assistance. Wardrop was left guarding the prisoners, one of whom he could see was bleeding out and close to death. The other man was slumped, groaning, having a long gash along his leg. When the soldier sent by the Queen's officer arrived he quickly surveyed the scene, then drew a Luger from the belt of one of the two wounded Germans and shot them both in the head. Wardrop had been through so much that he wasn't even that shocked. 'It might not have been a good thing to do but he did it and there is this much to be said for the action,' the sergeant wrote in his diary. 'A couple of stretcher-bearers might have gone to pick them up and been killed themselves.'

Returning to his tank, Wardrop could see that some of the Germans in front of his troop had also had enough. One of them fashioned a white flag, which he started to wave. The tankies beckoned the men, but the figures they could see standing in the grass would not come forward. Wardrop dismounted from his tank and walked over to Lieutenant Crocker's. The sergeant agreed to walk ahead in order to investigate the surrendering Germans.

'I was just going forward', Wardrop recounted, 'when just then the Boches started to lob more mortar, they dropped quite close and I picked up a splinter in my face. That settled it, I got back on the tank, gave Jimmy the word, and he chopped them down with the Browning.' White flag or no, the mortar fire had sealed the Germans' fate.

That night Wardrop found catharsis drinking with the troop in a local bar. He had his face bandaged by this time, 'and the civilians were coming from far and near to see the Scotsman who had killed a hundred Boches and got wounded fighting for "*la Belle Belgique*", such is the war'. There were young women there too, and friendships were formed. Some of the 5th Tanks men claimed to have bedded Belgians during these weeks of liberation, others even to have fathered children, but for most they were too drunk and exhausted to do anything more than sleep off nights like those.

During the days that followed there many more encounters with German stragglers and Ghent was secured. The Great Swan had carried them rapidly into a new environment – the Low Countries – and pitted them against a new enemy, or at least a different sort of enemy. The German troops in places like this were second-line, consisting of a curious amalgam of foreigners (such as the *Ost* or East European battalions), paratroopers, those removed from the eastern front due to sickness (the so-called 'stomach battalions') and youths flushed out of military training establishments and into ad hoc companies, as well as field units of the Luftwaffe and navy. They were armed with rifles, machine guns, mortars and ubiquitous anti-tank weapons that ranged from 75mm guns to Panzerfausts and the more capable Panzerschrek, or bazooka. Of the weapons hitherto dreaded by the tankie, too many Tigers and Panthers had been lost in Normandy for there to be any significant number on the road to Holland. Some StuGs or other self-propelled guns were encountered, and the anti-aircraft defences of the Low Country industrial centres yielded up plenty of 88mm flak guns. Tanks were still being lost to these weapons, but at a rate far below that in Normandy, and with the proportion accounted for by the hand-held anti-tank weapons rising from 6 per cent back in France to 34 per cent in the months ahead.

While the open fields and smaller panzer forces opposing them might have suggested that Allied armoured divisions could now dominate the battlefield, there were still some obstacles. The waterways and boggy ground of the Low Countries often channelled movement along roads or across bridges, making ideal ambush points. It also made route-denial easier for their retreating enemy, with mines, blown bridges or sluice gates opened to slow Monty's men down. This meant that infantry remained vitally important, and field engineers became more so.

In thrusting forward into Belgium, the Allied armour had encountered some of those difficulties that came with success – issues that would have been quite familiar to Rommel in 1940 or 1941. During the Great Swan they had advanced faster than new maps could be printed and delivered to them. They had also run out of fuel at times; the 7th Armoured Division needed seventy thousand gallons per day. There was a bigger logistical problem facing Montgomery and General Dwight D. Eisenhower, the American who had now taken over the supreme command of Allied armies. They had left their Norman supply dumps hundreds of miles behind them and urgently needed to switch their logistic routes through nearby ports such as Antwerp. But the Germans intended to sell these harbours dearly, having built major defences there. Even when forced out, they often destroyed facilities or scuttled ships in harbours to impede their use.

The combined effect of geography, German resistance and logistic strain was to slow the campaign down again. It did not help that tens of thousands of German troops on the coast had been allowed to escape by a British oversight. They became available to defend the river and canal lines that impeded the Allied path into the Netherlands.

On 17 September the 5th Tanks watched hundreds of aircraft passing overhead, many of them Dakotas towing Horsa and Hamilcar gliders. A vast airborne operation designed to shorten the war had begun. This air armada was carrying British and US airborne forces to seize a series of bridges, opening a route deep into the Netherlands. The 7th Armoured Division was not centrally involved in Operation Market Garden; the Guards Armoured had been given the vital task of pushing through by road to link up with the paratroopers. In the fighting that followed, unexpectedly large German counter-attacks prevented full success, though the operation did succeed in forcing the first two major water obstacles in the Allies' path.

While fierce battles raged around Nijmegen and Arnhem, the Desert Rats had begun to move forward once more, and 5th Tanks crossed the Dutch border on 22 September. They fought a series of mopping-up actions, dealing with Germans in farmhouses or bunkers and supporting British infantry and American paratroopers. It was not easy work, although in the steady rain and autumn gloom the foot soldiers had things much harder.

The 5th pushed on towards the River Maas, where they spent much of October near the town of Nistelrode, waiting for the advance to resume. 'To us who had travelled so far and fast then had to stagnate in a silly little place such as it was without even seeing a Boche was most tiresome,' thought Wardrop.

In B Squadron, meanwhile, spirits were even lower. Major Dennis Cockbaine, who had taken over as acting OC after his boss had been wounded on 3 August, was nudged aside by precisely the kind of 'fat pig' that Crickmay feared might appear at any moment and take over his own squadron. Major Pat Wood had assumed command of B Squadron on 1 October, after spending years in Moscow and at the War Office. He was a regular army officer who had been told that he would not keep his rank come peacetime demobilisation if he did not exercise a major's command at the front. Cockbaine had been a perfect fit for his old sweats. He had started the war as a trooper, before being commissioned in the Royal Gloucester Hussars and then moving on to the 5th Tanks. He was highly experienced, phlegmatic, courageous, straight-talking and, at twenty-four, of similar age to most of the squadron. Wood was ten years older, rode his subalterns hard, maintained a more aloof attitude to the men and drank heavily to boot.

By replacing an extremely popular OC with such a man, the powers that be had created a similar situation to that which had culminated in the sacking of Lieutenant-Colonel Dicker Wilson five months earlier. As complaints about Major Wood multiplied, nobody was more aware than Lieutenant-Colonel Holliman (who had replaced Wilson) that history might be about to repeat itself in terms of the battalion reserving the right to choose its own officers.

'I felt that the lives of the men were being put at risk under an inexperienced officer', wrote Lieutenant Stevenson, 'just to salvage his career in the army.' Wood baited the subalterns by insisting they take part in drinking games late into the night, one of which consisted of having to fall forwards without putting out hands to break the fall, another of sticking pins into their arms. One B Squadron lieutenant argued, '[Wood] simply could not or would not adapt to commanding a very battle-experienced squadron, made up largely of non-regular troops and officered entirely by non-regular officers.' The gradual replacement of old pre-war personnel in the battalion had by this point produced a situation where just three of the thirty-five or so officers in 5th Tanks were regular-commission men, the other thirty-two being citizens in arms.

As with Dicker Wilson, the commissioned class might have resented Wood deeply but they could not muster the will for mutiny. The squadron's NCOs, however, men like Pluto Ellis and Nippy Lyons, stood about next to their tanks muttering discontent as they sucked on their cigarettes and looked about to see whether they were being overheard. They wouldn't stand for it. So Pluto and the others organised a petition that was given to the Regimental Sergeant Major and, via him, to Gus Holliman. It said that the sergeants of B Squadron had lost all confidence in their OC and wanted another commander. Holliman decided to ignore the petition, for he could see what was at stake and he, after all, was the man who had posted Sergeant Emmin Hall away from the 5th RTR after he toppled Lieutenant-Colonel

Wilson. The colonel tried to buy time as he mulled how to deal with this new revolt. The rapid promotion of wartime meant that Wood was, in terms of his army seniority, ahead of every other man in the battalion – including himself – as CO. But allowing the major to remain in place acted as an anchor on B Squadron, holding it back.

With each week that passed, the temperature dropped and the battlefield froze along with the polders and canals. The British divisions followed the practice of previous centuries when commanders such as the Duke of Marlborough put their armies into winter quarters in the Low Countries. The 5th Tanks eventually fetched up in a place called Sittard, where an officers' mess was established in a grand country house and only a single squadron did duty at a time, manning the front-line outposts.

The disappointment that the war would continue into another year was well understood by Monty and the rest of the top brass. Too many hopes had been expressed over the previous months of it being over by Christmas for there not to be a deep sense of gloom. So the chain of command tried all kinds of ploys to give a couple of months of rest and to lighten the mood of its battle-weary divisions.

Monty turned up in person late in November to pin medals on the Desert Rats. Among those who smartened up for the investiture were Holliman, who received a DSO, as well as Major MacDonald, Lieutenant Garnett and Lieutenant Dixon, who all got MCs for their actions in Normandy. There were movie shows too – with the troops catching Laurence Olivier's *Henry V* among them – ENSA concert parties and all-ranks dances. The men tuned their tanks' 19 Sets to the US armed forces network and listened to the Count Basie Orchestra and Tommy Dorsey's band, and much drink was consumed by all. Leave passes to Brussels were given out freely, and many of the soldiers took their chance to convert the loot they had taken from German prisoners into cash for wine, steak and chips, and perhaps a night in the arms of a Belgian whore.

Arthur Crickmay busied himself with a needle and thread, tailoring his fur-collared winter coat, changing the buttons on his battledress and generally keeping up appearances. When Christmas finally came, he reported the day to his mother as 'sober but passed in a reasonable degree of comfort and in beautiful weather and hard ice'. Still, news of the German counter-offensive in the Ardennes reminded them of the unfinished nature of the war, and the futility of making merry in khaki. 'The square heads have produced a high-power comeback,' wrote Crickmay. 'One is only surprised that it did not come before.'

So for days the battalion occupied positions along a frozen, windswept front, 'listening on the radio to the Yanks being given a pasting'. The aim of this Ardennes offensive had been to reach Antwerp and cut off the British army. It was stopped after a couple of weeks' intense fighting, but just in case Hitler had something similar planned for them they had to remain on the qui vive. The long-brewing infantry shortage in the British army had now produced dramatic results. Despite the breaking-up of the 59th Division in order to send its men as replacements to others, there were so few that for weeks the 5th Tanks had to do infantry duty in front of their observation posts.

For many of them, carrying a rifle or Bren gun was a completely new experience and, crouched shivering in trenches in sub-zero temperatures, it was a thoroughly unwelcome one. Crickmay thought it horrible, but also overdue in the sense of giving the tankies a proper appreciation of what their infantry colleagues were going through. 'We became acquainted with trip wires, flares, field telephones, dug-outs, PIATs, mortars, "silent killing", piano wire and all the other paraphernalia of the infanteer,' he wrote to his brother, who was still serving as an army doctor in the Mediterranean, adding, 'We were all over-joyed to return to our ironclad monsters.'

The army knew it had thousands of people who had been serving for years and who were intensely frustrated that the war was not already over. It therefore announced a special form of leave, called Python, under which men like Major Crickmay and Sergeant Wardrop would be able to get home for a couple of weeks before campaigning resumed in earnest. It also allowed COs at the battalion considerable discretion in selecting people who they thought had become too weary or bomb-happy to be sent back to Britain on extended training courses, or indeed to transfer them out of the unit. At this time, for example, a couple of the B Squadron sergeants who had signed Pluto's petition against Major Ward went home for good. Indeed, Pluto himself was packed off to a training job and it was unclear whether this was at Holliman's behest or if the sergeant, who had come through Normandy in his Firefly without being knocked out, felt he was living on borrowed time.

So at this late stage of the war there was one final reduction in that repeatedly reduced bouillon of experience that fuelled the 5th Tanks and gave it such resilience in battle. There were still dozens of men like Jackie Garnett the adjutant, Nippy Lyons in B Squadron or Snowy Harris in C, who formed this hardened cadre. They had made a pledge to themselves and their comrades that they would fight to the bitter end. They would not give up on all those who still relied upon them, they would not forget the fallen, they had to see it through and they were quite ready to kill any German who got in the way.

The degree to which they had been changed by war came home to George Stimpson during a leave visit to Brussels. Rather than enjoying the food, drink and the warmth of central heating, 'Little George' missed Wardrop and the other friends he had shared so much with, feeling lonely and morose. 'I realised now more than ever that I was solely dependent on my old mates for companionship,' he wrote, adding, 'I was without doubt nothing more than a bloodthirsty fighter whose only interest in life was the next battle.'

For Jake Wardrop these pressures between the duty he had to do, his love of fighting and its toll on his own mind were becoming unbearable. He had noticed the unmistakeable signs of the jitters again during the late fighting in the Low Countries and had been boozing hard. He wanted it all over as soon as possible. With the battalion apparently stranded in the Dutch snows doing very little, he became increasingly irritated with the stupidity of it all. An attempt by a new troop leader to impose some organised relaxation on them produced an insubordinate outburst from the sergeant. Fed up, he put in a request to be transferred to Burma, where they might be more fighting. When he was ordered on a Cromwell training course early in November he refused to go. Jackie Garnett, as adjutant, told Wardrop that if he didn't go he would be refusing an order and would be put under arrest. The sergeant said he accepted that, and a little later that morning he was marched into the CO's office to be put on a charge.

When Holliman asked the sergeant why he was refusing an order Wardrop told him that they had done 'nothing useful since we arrived in Holland and that I objected to silly little officers who detailed me to play soccer on a Sunday afternoon'. The colonel asked him if he accepted that the generals running the war knew what they were doing. Wardrop chose to be tactful in his answer. Why on earth did he want to go to Burma? Both Wardrop and Stimpson had put in for a transfer there in search of more action. Holliman batted aside this plea, just as he waved away Wardrop's course. He sent him back to the squadron, promising that they would be in action again soon enough.

'He was a great man and I had the greatest respect for him as a leader and a man,' wrote Wardrop of Holliman. They were two of a kind, dauntless men of action who had driven themselves through countless dangers during years of war, and neither was ready to quit. It was their example and that of others like them in the battalion that would be needed to carry the war forward in 1945, into the heart of the Reich.

22

INTO THE REICH

By mid-January 1945 the 5th RTR and the rest of the 7th Armoured Division were shaking themselves out of their winter torpor. It was still horribly cold, and they moved about under a glowering, steel-grey sky. They had been warned off for another operation, pushing somewhat ahead of the outpost line they had maintained for weeks in order to clear enemy troops from a pocket of land between the Rivers Maas and Roer. It would carry them further east by a few miles, pitting them against an expected opposition of hastily thrown together German units, mines and anti-tank weapons. The process of inching closer to Germany was proceeding, but the soldiers all understood that a set-piece operation to force the Rhine still lay some way ahead.

Lieutenant-Colonel Holliman was in a better mood than many of his men. He had learned in December that his wife had given birth to a baby boy, and was looking forward to some leave and seeing his son for the first time. He had embraced with alacrity the usual series of tedious officers' conferences and meetings that preceded a major operation. In keeping with the desert custom of Griff talks to keep everyone in the picture, he had briefed the battalion in a local cinema on 16 January. Holliman knew well enough that the winter inactivity and promise of further months away from loved ones had been driving people mad, but he had confidence in the chain of command to produce a series of operations that would end the war soon.

On 21 January, late in the afternoon, the colonel headed off in a scout car to make a call on the Commanding Officer of 1st Tanks several miles away. When they were not far from their destination a shell dropped onto the little open-topped vehicle, killing Holliman and his driver instantly. His family were told that he had perished in action against the enemy, but the gloomy men who pieced together what had happened over the officers' mess dinner table in the days that followed didn't buy any of that. They knew that there had not been any fighting with the Germans in that vicinity at the time, but that some heavy guns of the Royal Artillery had been firing towards targets several miles away.

'We all believed', wrote one 5th Tanks officer, 'and it added to the pointless tragedy of losing so fine a man and so splendid a leader – that our CO had been killed accidentally by the premature airburst of one of our own shells.'

The operation pushed on, with troops of tanks farmed out to a number of different infantry brigades, including the commandoes. As commander of C Squadron, Arthur Crickmay didn't like handing over his tanks in these penny packets. It was 'always an unsatisfactory and dangerous situation'. His fear was that the infantry wouldn't have much idea how to use these machines properly, and the lieutenant or even sergeant commanding the tanks would not easily be able to resist unwise orders from superior officers in the infantry battalion they were attached to. Even so, the operations of late January and early February passed off without a major disaster, even if there was a steady stream of wounds caused by Panzerfausts and shrapnel.

With the Rhine-crossing operation looming, it was vital to find a new man to replace Gus Holliman. The army sent Lieutenant-Colonel Rea Leakey, a Kenyan-born twenty-nine-year-old with a war record similar to the impressive ones that Holliman and a few other RTR men chosen to lead battalions had notched up. Leakey had already won the MC three times when he reached 5th Tanks, and was a veteran of much desert fighting in 1st and 3rd RTR. During the Normandy battles he had been commanding the Churchill heavy tanks of 7th RTR.

On receiving the order to take command of the 5th, Leakey had pushed through the Dutch farmland in a scout car to find its Cromwells engaged and under enemy artillery fire in a snow-covered field. Taking his chances, the colonel leapt on the back of one tank only to have its commander shout at him, 'Get off this bloody tank, I am moving for cover!' That turned out to be Major MacDonald, the A Squadron OC who had been left in acting command of the whole battalion after Holliman's death. As the shelling stopped and calm was restored the two men began again, for MacDonald, being one of the two regular commission holders or members of the pre-war officer corps left in 5th Tanks, was the only person in the unit that Leakey really knew.

Leakey's impressions of the 5th RTR as it was beginning its final campaigns are worth noting because he can be considered a sympathetic critic – i.e. someone with a good knowledge of how other battalions worked, but who had a new commander's desire to improve it. The 7th Tanks, who regularly parcelled out their Churchills to infantry battalions, were also a seasoned outfit, but one built on a 'can do' attitude to pleasing their many customers. The 5th, on the other hand, acted more often as a complete battalion, tended to make its own rules, relied heavily on the experienced eye of its NCOs and revelled in its image of being the Filthy Fifth, a bunch of 'hairy-arsed barbarians'. Their new Commanding Officer observed that

[They] had seldom been long out of action throughout the war. Many were beginning to get war-weary, and they had certainly had their 'bellyful'. I soon noticed the difference between this regiment and the 7th. The 5th fought as hard as any and with a good deal of cunning; where the 7th would lose two tanks, they would lose one. Even so, I missed that 'urge to go' which the 7th never lacked.

Leakey soon pinpointed what he saw as the weaknesses in the officers' mess. He managed to fire Pat Wood, the widely disliked OC of B Squadron, and moved Captain Garnett out of the adjutant's job. Dispatching Wood and reinstating Dennis Cockbaine to run B Squadron brought the new boss acclamation. Of Garnett, a quiet legend in the 5th, Leakey wrote, 'Neither of us was good at reading and writing . . . one of us had to go.' In place of the grizzled pipe-smoking ex-ranker, Leakey brought the boyish Roy Dixon, who had won his MC in Normandy and had the appetite for the bumf or paper war that Leakey couldn't stand.

In trying to confront some of the battalion's recalcitrance, the new colonel ordered freezing early-morning PT sessions and a greater attention to dress and saluting. As operations picked up once more these measures were quietly forgotten and both the aggrieved old sweats and the new CO were able to consider themselves victorious.

*

For Sergeant Wardrop and Major Crickmay, there was a period of Python leave before the planned crossing of the Rhine. By 29 January Wardrop was on his way down to Calais, hitchhiking then taking a train. On board the ferry he found some 'stout men' from the 15th and 51st Divisions (both Scottish formations) and the jocks killed one whisky after another as the snowflakes flew past the windows. Wardrop's boat docked at Harwich and he got back home to Glasgow late on the 31st. He and his father talked long and honestly while the rest of the family slept upstairs. The days raced away, a great round of reunions with family and friends, sing-songs with his guitar and a wonderful cornucopia of alcoholic beverages. But by 8 February Wardrop was making his way back to the front, catching a train back to Harwich, deeply depressed that his leave was over. In the early morning his despair reached a peak. 'Cold, and miserable blue, and ready for the .38,' he jotted in his diary. The .38 was his Smith & Wesson revolver.

Boarding the ferry, Wardrop got a grip of his emotions. He had been through worse before, and he would get through what lay ahead. But that night he tossed and turned in his bunk: 'lie all night, and think, and think, my brain is doing ninety-five. I must get back [to the 5th] and get back again [home] – roll on.'

As for Arthur Crickmay's leave, it passed in a blur of good food, good wine and good company. He spent most of it in London, taking his cousin Diana to dances and forgetting about the war for a few precious days. At the Bagatelle they ate things that could only have come from the black market, and danced to the Latin rhythms of Edmundo Ros. Other members of the squadron, who had not been serving as long as Wardrop and Crickmay, made it at least to Brussels for a few days and the sybaritic pleasures that city was able to offer.

*

It was late March before the war moved to what many knew would be its final phase. The British had long been planning their assault on the Rhine under the codename Operation Plunder. Further south, the Americans had already found a way across the river when a German attempt to demolish the bridge in the town of Remagen failed and US troops were able to pour across. To the east, the Red Army was fighting through German territory and stretching for Berlin.

Britain's multi-phase plan involved a major airborne operation, to be followed by an assault crossing (by infantry) to link up with the paratroopers, and then a breakout. The 7th Armoured Division would not come into play until late on, after the engineers had constructed a heavy-duty Bailey bridge across the Rhine. The 5th Tanks entered Germany on 25 March, moving into a concentration area where final drills were carried out and Griff talks given. They crossed the Rhine two days later.

For the soldiers entering the Reich there were different views about how people would greet them. Of course nobody expected the shows of gratitude and open-hearted friendship they had experienced in Belgium and the Netherlands. 'There will be no brutality about a British Occupation', ordered the official handbook distributed to the men, 'but neither will there be any softness or sentimentality.' It warned about locals with hard-luck stories, telling soldiers not to be taken in: 'The German is brutal when he is winning and sorry for himself and whines for sympathy when he is beaten.' Particularly stern injunctions were given against 'fraternisation', a term that covered everything from being too friendly to a passing German to having sex with one.

For one small group within the battalion, this phase of the campaign carried particular anxieties. Half a dozen German-Jewish men – refugees who had come to Britain before the war – had been posted to 5th RTR. Other units within 7th Armoured

Division had the same arrangement. Some of them had been with the battalion all the way from the D-Day beaches and were well-integrated members of tank crews, often serving on the squadron commander's vehicle in case he needed help interrogating prisoners. They served under assumed, British-sounding names and the other members of the crews were determined to protect their Jewish comrades' aliases in the event of capture when, as one B Squadron man put it, 'they could expect a fate literally worse than death'.

Moving through the area of the airborne landing they saw broken-up gliders, dead Germans and brewed vehicles. They also beheld British paratroopers hanging lifeless from trees and were surprised by the bright colours of the silk parachute canopies draped across roofs and fields. Their enemy in this part of Germany was a similar mixture of scratch units with infantry weapons to those they had fought in the Low Countries, but there were some differences. Some surviving units of German paratroopers were deployed for home defence, as were some schools of particularly indoctrinated Nazi youth and SS cadres who were armed to defend their fatherland. While the threat that presented itself was similar, albeit perhaps tougher, the environment was subtly different in that 'now we could take nothing for granted' when civilians told them things.

'The breakout in Germany was even more hair-raising than the breakout after the big tank battles in Normandy,' wrote one B Squadron man. 'It was only a matter of time before the point tank caught it.' Major Cockbaine had told him and the rest of the squadron their mission was to 'bash on regardless', which they all understood to mean moving forward without the normal caution in order to exploit the disorganisation that forcing the Rhine defences had already sown. Speeding through German villages, they saw that many householders had hung out white flags. They wanted no more. Walking ahead of his tank soon after crossing the

Rhine, Sergeant Stimpson found an attractive woman walking beside him. She was a teacher and said to him in flawless English, 'How nice to see you, the war for us is now over.'

'On the faces of most of the civilians was a look of blank incredulity,' one cavalry officer wrote in his journal. 'Scores of wounded Germans, some with an arm missing, some one-legged, others with bandages over their heads limped and hopped to the roadside from the hospitals we passed, most of them silent and grim except for a few excited and a few sneering.'

The 7th Armoured advanced 120 miles during the first week of the breakout operation. That wasn't quite the Great Swan – this was the enemy heartland, after all – but it was still a cracking pace. While many Germans decided that their war was over, others came to a very different conclusion and were intent on resisting the invaders to the end. In one village the mayor, a staunch Nazi, took cyanide when the British entered his office. Elsewhere ambushes were set and boys with Panzerfausts or Spandaus waited to pot their own Tommy.

Sergeant George Stimpson, that diminutive legend of C Squadron, gained further notoriety in the battalion when he stopped on the outskirts of one village, sensing something was wrong. A circular road sign had been detached from its metal post and sat propped up against it. That struck him as odd, in such orderly communities. He ordered his gunner to tap a few machine-gun bullets through the sign. When they dismounted to inspect it they found they had shot a youth lurking in a foxhole behind the signpost through the head; he was holding a bazooka in his dead hands.

The general mood in the 5th Tanks dictated that it was better to lace a suspicious building with Besa fire or high-explosive shells through the window than to take a chance. Where organised resistance was encountered they called in some orbiting Typhoons or an artillery stonk.

With this rapid advance, Major Crickmay detected a change of mood in his squadron. 'Over the years of conflict the idea of ultimate survival was one that played little part in the average soldier's thoughts,' he wrote. 'It was now beginning to occur to many that survival was not only possible but probable.' Sergeant Wardrop had, as the battalion pushed across northern Germany, emerged from the angry funk that had engulfed him during that dull winter on the Dutch border. Glimpsing the light of victory at last, at the end of the long tunnel of war, he jotted in his diary: 'In great form these days. Everything is good.' This spirit made men more cautious, but it also fuelled a certain type of desperation among those who realised that the titanic struggle was coming to an end: they were not going to allow some diehard Nazi to stop them going home. When dealing with German hold-outs there was little mercy on either side.

Four days after the breakout battle Lieutenant Ted Zoeftig, commanding a troop in A Squadron, was ambushed in his Cromwell tank. It was early morning and they were nearing a town called Vreden. Zoeftig was unsure about pushing forward because of signs of enemy activity and wanted to deploy infantry into the town. 'No, you're late,' said Lieutenant-Colonel Leakey over the radio net, 'you've got to go on.' So they drove forward and moments later an anti-tank round hit the turret, showering metal around its inside and leaving Zoeftig concussed and disorientated. Bailing out, he rolled onto the ground beside the tank. Looking about, he saw that some infantry who had been riding on his tank had disappeared. Machine-gun fire started and Zoeftig realised that the Germans were trying to kill him and the rest of the bailed-out crew. Rounds were zipping overhead, just inches above him, 'and the tracer from their machine-gun bullets were coming over . . . catching my tank suit on fire'.

Lying there wounded, his clothes smouldering, Zoeftig was then assailed by several German paratroopers who had rushed up to his Cromwell. They rained blows on him, using their gun butts as clubs. But for one paratrooper who intervened, 'they would have killed me'. He was taken away and interrogated with further violence before being put in hospital. Moving through Vreden, Zoeftig glimpsed scores of Germans lined up for inspection, carrying hand-held anti-tank rocket launchers. He and one of his surviving crewmen were among the last members of 5th RTR to be taken prisoner during the war. They were freed a few days later when Allied forces overran the hospital. Their experience, though, gives some idea of the ferocity of these final battles.

With German forces under assault from the west, south and east, they were rapidly disintegrating. The battalion continued its rush forward, crossing the Dortmund–Ems Canal by an intact bridge on 4 April. This was about one third of the way between the Rhine and the division's final objective, Hamburg. Dozens of prisoners were being taken as well as much loot. A couple of days later, and thirty-five miles further east, they found themselves approaching the town of Sulingen. The squadrons had piled up on the verges beside the road because of reports of German armour in the town. As minutes became hours, senior officers grew frantic at the lack of progress. At this point Trooper 'Glynn', one of the German-Jewish soldiers serving with C Squadron, returned to tell his boss, Major Crickmay, that the local *Gasthaus* or pub had a working telephone. Glynn returned to the place, telephoning the mayor of Sulingen and pretending to be a panzer commander who had lost his unit: were they in Sulingen? The mayor told him that there was only one tank in the town, and it had broken down. Just before the delayed column moved off, Glynn came up on the battalion's radio net to ask Lieutenant-Colonel Leakey if there was anything else they needed to know from the mayor. Before he could give a serious answer, Arthur Crickmay piped up, with the entire battalion listening, 'Ask him what's on at the pictures.'

As any old campaigner could have attested, the gap between laughter and fear could often be measured in seconds. While many of the infantry battalions had already suffered significant casualties on the push into Germany, by the morning of 8 April C Squadron could reflect that it had got off mercifully lightly. Since entering Germany, two men had been wounded. Indeed, since the start of Operation Plunder, just two men of the 5th RTR as a whole had been killed (both in B Squadron) although there had been several wounded. Now, however, they encountered more serious resistance.

As they advanced into the industrial communities south of Bremen they entered an area defended by the 2nd Marine Division and some SS units. The 'marines' were in fact a couple of thousand base personnel and teenage cadets from a naval academy. Nonetheless, they had been heavily armed and in places had taken over the flak guns used to defend the area from air attack. It was also to become clear that many of these lads were prepared to defend the area to the last extreme.

In a village called Barrien C Squadron again used its German interpreter to arrange the surrender of forty enemy soldiers. On they went to the next place, Brinkum. Pushing forward to the outskirts of the village the tanks came up against a wood. The light was almost gone and Snowy Harris's tank from 9 Troop was taking the point position, at the head of the column, when the crump of a Panzerfaust broke the calm. The anti-tank round had hit the hull of his Cromwell near the back, making a mess of the engine and kindling a fire that soon took hold. Harris and his crew bailed out, which was when the Germans raked them with Spandau fire.

This ambush triggered a heavy response from C Squadron and accompanying infantry from 1st RB. They plastered the woods with high-explosive shells and laced it with thousands of rounds from their machine guns, but the enemy held firm — they were soon discovered to be an SS detachment several dozen strong. A full-scale infantry attack on the woods was planned for the next day. It was a wretched night for Jake Wardrop, knowing that his troop sergeant and close friend's tank had been hit and left behind in enemy territory. He wrote in his diary, 'Snowy is bazooka'd. I hope he is alright.' This futile resistance from the Boche was driving him mad. That afternoon Wardrop had seen one of the young SS men being brought in as a prisoner of war; his anger had boiled over at the German and he had beaten him up. On the same afternoon another old-timer, a sergeant in B Squadron, had been killed when he went forward to take a German surrender. The same thing happened again on 9 April with a lieutenant from C Squadron: he was shot through the head by a sniper while taking prisoners.

By the evening of 8 April it was clear to Wardrop that Harris had been killed. When the squadron leaguered up for the evening he and Sergeant Stimpson sat together in the darkness, drinking a few beers. They recalled the names of all the C Squadron men who had been with them in that evacuation from Cherbourg harbour nearly five years earlier, and who had since been killed.

This latest casualty was particularly hard for them, but of course it was a bad blow to the squadron as a whole for Harris, the heroic-looking character chosen for the cover of *Picture Post*, was in many ways the archetypal tank commander. Major Crickmay wrote a letter of condolence to Snowy's wife Kathleen. He did so with a heavy heart, feeling that he had already penned too many of them and that it was hard to explain why someone had fallen when the end seemed so close. When it came to such messages he felt angry with himself for not being able to find better words, writing to his mother, 'I'm afraid letters of sympathy appear cold-blooded even to me on re-reading but I cannot bring myself to produce false sentiment or the usual sort of clichés.' However, the phrases Crickmay chose for Mrs Harris were better judged than he could have hoped, because she wrote back:

> I feel very relieved by the heartening words and praise of character that you gave him. It is very comforting to know that he died as he did and the more so to know that at the time of his death he had earned the right to a recommendation for gallantry. I feel more proud of him than ever. Later on my little boy (of 6 years) will know and understand how his Daddy died, for I shall preserve your letter with such nice expression for his reading a few years hence.

On 10 April the 5th Tanks were still moving about the countryside south of Bremen, encountering pockets of resistance. They were ordered to support the 53rd Welsh Division in clearing operations. Each squadron was parcelled out to a different battalion, and within those the individual troops given to infantry companies. It was not something the tankies liked doing. Pushing across the River Weser near the town of Hoya another wood, a forest almost, lay in front of them. The officers of the 6th Battalion Royal Welch Fusiliers, who were running the operation, did not expect the wood to be contested. Nevertheless, they decided to push companies through on two parallel routes, each with a troop of tanks for added punch. Wardrop was with one column, Stimpson with the other. The tanks wanted the infantry to walk ahead but they rode on the armour instead, since it was felt safe to do so and they were under pressure to advance.

At length Wardrop's Firefly reached a crossroads in the woods. Tall, dense avenues of trees stretched away in four directions. The commanders were just checking their maps and some infantry had dropped off the vehicles to have a look around when all hell broke loose. Panzerfausts were fired at the tanks and machine-gun fire sprayed on the Fusiliers who rode them. Wardrop's Firefly was hit by one of the anti-tank rockets and the crew bailed out. It was a bad decision because the vehicle would later be discovered to be driveable, and the men were safer in it than out. On reaching the ground Wardrop had been shot in the legs by machine-gun bullets. Many of the Fusiliers had been hit too. The tank behind them was burning. Someone tried to clamp field dressings to Wardrop's wounds. Several men already lay dead around the tank, and the German fire sweeping the forest track was ricocheting off its hull. Those who could ran for it, leaving Wardrop in a ditch with only his revolver for protection. The troop's sole surviving tank also pulled back.

Hearing of the disaster, Sergeant Stimpson later asked Major Crickmay if he could go into the woods to find Jake and the others. The OC agreed, as long as everyone on Stimpson's tank was a volunteer. There was no shortage of them, so they drove gingerly into the dark woods in their Cromwell. 'The two tanks were still and quiet and there were bodies of British soldiers everywhere,' reported Stimpson. 'I found Jake's body at the side of his tank.' Stimpson boarded the Firefly and succeeded in starting it. He brought it back to the squadron that night, and recovered his dead friend's diary from where it had been left on the vehicle. Four members of 5th Tanks had been killed in the action, and five were missing. Six of the Welch Fusiliers had also lost their lives; three limped back wounded and another fifteen were missing. They and the five captured tank men were sent back by the Germans to Rethem, a town several miles to the south-east.

The loss of both Harris and Wardrop, veterans who had been through so much yet perished so near the end, reverberated through the battalion. While Harris had been a taciturn character and was unfamiliar to some people in other squadrons, Wardrop was known throughout. He could bring alive any shindig with his guitar and songs, and everyone knew the one-time stalwart of the boxing team was one of the hardest men in the 5th Tanks. Sergeant Emmin Hall, who was by that stage of the war serving in another unit nearby, made his own inquiries about what had happened, writing to Wardrop's sister in Glasgow:

> I know what a shock it must have been for his Mother, it was a bitter shock to us too, for if any one deserved to come home it was [Jake]. A better, braver, or truer pal has never yet been born he didn't have a single enemy in the Regt ... he was better than any man alive and I was pleased to call him pal. He has been taken from us, but we shall all meet again.

Hall and Stimpson agreed that Wardrop had probably been found by the Germans lying in his trench. They believed he might have fired his revolver until he was killed, or maybe he had simply been shot out of hand. In any case, Sergeant Stimpson had discovered the fatal wound to Jake's chest and later buried him. 'Little George', as Wardrop had called Stimpson, was the last member still alive of the close-knit trio who had faced a court martial in Egypt four years earlier. Stan Skeels, Jake's boxing buddy, had died off Salerno. As for that wild, dangerous, charmer Wardrop, he had left a trail of friends of many nationalities along the line of the 5th RTR's long drive from Egypt: there was Pasquale in Tripoli, who had invited Jake to his native Capri; Simone, whose address he had taken in Tunis; and Lulu in Ghent, who had kept him sane through that last winter. He had made so many plans for 'after the war'. But on a cold April night all those hopes were interred with the corpse of a twenty-nine-year-old sergeant from Glasgow, buried by Little George in the sandy soil of northern Germany.

*

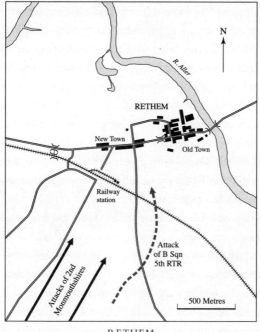

RETHEM

At Rethem on 11 April the advancing British encountered heavy resistance. It was to be the last significant battle of the war for 5th RTR, fought in support of the 53rd Division once again. The town's importance derived from a crossing over the River Aller that could not easily be bypassed. Rethem's outlying villages had been fortified and the area around the railway station provided a natural line of defence, since the line ran on an embankment that offered both cover and excellent fire positions.

Around the town were numerous weapons pits manned by five to six hundred members of the 2nd Marine Division. They had been well equipped with weaponry including machine guns, mortars, Panzerfausts and anti-tank guns. It was a unit of these marines that had ambushed Jake Wardrop's column in the woods. Additionally, near Rethem, a train mounting five 105mm anti-aircraft guns had been deployed on a siding near the station. The 105mm flak was a big brother to the 88 – highly accurate and quite deadly. The train and some 75mm Pak40 anti-tank guns dominated the western approach to the town. Roads had been cratered to channel movement into certain ambush routes, and many buildings were barricaded , with Molotov cocktails at the ready. The key bridge, to the backs of those German defenders, had been rigged with explosives for demolition. A and B Squadrons of 5th Tanks were given orders to mount an attack in support of the 2nd Battalion, The Monmouthshire Regiment, on this formidable objective.

Moving up on the afternoon of 11 April the mood among the British troops was ugly. It all seemed so pointless, for one thing. Comparing the strength of resistance they encountered with other battles he had fought in northern Germany, one member of B Squadron commented, 'Here they were even more fanatical, as the young boys threw away their lives for a lost cause.' Rumours were going around that fifteen or so of the Welsh soldiers had been murdered by the Germans after surrendering. This proved to be untrue, but undoubtedly inflamed feelings. They all knew, too, that good men had been lost in the days before, trying to take prisoners.

Advancing towards the outskirts of town a Cromwell gunner in 8 Troop looked through his sights as the ground opened out in front of them into fields with haystacks; 'we spotted Germans in the open, not dug in, behind the hay and took them out'. Machine guns had been used on this first group, but before long they had to deal with anti-tank guns. The British crews were so experienced that they were able quickly to use a complex technique. The loaders fused 75mm high-explosive shells on delay and the gunner carefully aimed at a point just in front of the target. When the shell was fired it glanced off the ground, activating the fuse, and exploded over the heads of the enemy soldiers as an airburst. Round after round was fired at the heavy guns on the railway, glancing off the ground in front, exploding over the Germans' heads. Manoeuvring around the end of the train, one troop leader was heard to thank God that the guns were pointing in another direction, at which point some diehard Germans who had survived the earlier bombardment trained one on the officer's tank and opened fire. The shell hit the ground just in front of them, triggering several British tanks to open up in response, obliterating the gun crew.

As the tanks moved about, brassing up any sign of resistance, white flags and raised hands began to appear. 'No quarter was given,' asserted a member of B Squadron, adding, 'We had heard that members of the Queens [*sic*] had been taken and shot – everyone believed it and we responded in kind.' There would be no prisoners. Signs of surrender were ignored as the tanks' machine guns chattered away into the twilight. As darkness fell the attack had secured the station area but had not penetrated Rethem itself. What was more, dozens of British infantry had been killed in an area just short of the railway. The tank men, who had pushed forward without their infantry cover to silence the German weaponry on the railway embankment, were shocked by these losses, considering the 2nd Monmouths to have gone forward in much the same fatal, cavalier way as the Essex Regiment men they had worked with in Normandy. After their failure to fight their way into the town itself, the Monmouths and B Squadron's armour fell back. They needed to rearm, since a couple had fired off their entire load of high-explosive shells and machine-gun bullets.

Back at HQ, Lieutenant-Colonel Leakey had been on the radio, talking to higher commanders about Rethem. The attack would be renewed in the morning, since the capture of the town and its bridge were deemed to be vital.

Early the next day, 12 April, Leakey decided to recce Rethem in person and took off in his scout car. It was a bright, crisp morning, and he was in high spirits. Spotting Major Crickmay, he invited him to join the trip. The two officers were listening intently to the radio and scanning the horizon as the armoured car barrelled along. Eventually the driver remarked, 'Blimey Sir! I have not seen so many dead Germans lying around for many a day.' Their eyes took in a scene of devastation. The corpses of naval cadets were interspersed with empty ammunition boxes, spent casings and smashed equipment. Crickmay, whose squadron, unlike the other elements of 5th Tanks engaged at Rethem, had taken prisoners the previous day, was disturbed by the sight of so many dead teenagers. But these grim surroundings had distracted them from something just as important. 'We had driven through the main defensive position on the outskirts of town,' recorded Leakey. 'The Germans had gone.' They pushed a little further and called in the remainder of C Squadron to occupy Rethem. Leakey meanwhile decided it was time to announce this unexpected triumph to divisional headquarters. Instead of sounding grateful, the staff officer on the radio told Leakey that the previous night Montgomery had tasked hundreds of RAF bombers to obliterate the town, and that they would be arriving over the target within the hour.

Leakey raced off in his scout car, heading for divisional HQ and leaving Crickmay and the rest of C Squadron in Rethem. As the CO went he had to negotiate three German villages that had not yet been cleared. His scout car screeched to a halt outside the command tent with just fifteen minutes to go until the aerial bombardment began. The RAF bombers were running in to the target. Despite the rudimentary communications between ground troops and strategic bombers, and the incomprehension of one layer of obtuse staff officers after another, the strike was called off with minutes to spare.

Later, back in the centre of Rethem, the tankies watched the

Welsh infantrymen following in their tracks trudge through the town. There had been some grumbling from the foot soldiers about the lack of support from the tanks being a reason for their heavy casualties on the previous day. The 5th RTR felt that the opposite was true, and that the 2nd Monmouthshire Battalion was a callow formation that had paid heavily for its poor leadership. Spotting the infantry unit's CO, Leakey could not stop himself calling out, 'We have taken your town for you.'

The surviving German defenders of Rethem (estimated at a third of the six hundred men given the task of holding it) had slipped across the Aller at night, blowing the vital bridge. It was estimated by the defenders that seventy-three of the naval troops had been killed, along with fifteen civilians. About 120 of the armed Germans were taken prisoner, evidently surviving the fury of those who had attacked on 11 April. During the two days of fighting, from Wardrop's death to his squadron entering the town, 230 members of the two Welsh infantry battalions they were supporting had become casualties too: a heavy price indeed. Why had the men and boys of the 2nd Marine Division fought so hard compared to so many of their disheartened compatriots who were brushed aside during the rush across Germany? One captured officer said that the navy had wanted to show the Wehrmacht how well it could defend the Fatherland, suggesting an outbreak of service tribalism as Hitler's forces went to pieces.

In the days that followed Rethem, reported Crickmay, 'there was a growing euphoria in the air, the adrenalin flowed strongly as we gathered in the spoils of war'. He had picked up a huge Mercedes staff car – and why not? The loot seemed proportional to the man's position in the chain of command. A troop leader had hoisted a Zundap motorcycle onto the back of his tank, and humble troopers had German officers' binoculars or watches.

The riflemen of 1st RB were reckoned to be particularly expert at this game. A report over the radio that some Germans were coming in under a white flag was followed by a correction saying it was some RBs returning from patrol, the leader of whom was carrying a snow-white goose rather than the sign of surrender across his shoulders. 'Once we were in Germany, "Operation Plunder" was a clear hint as far as we were concerned,' said one of the Rifles officers in I Company. 'One of my soldiers went in for anything for his wife – I saw him making up parcels of clothes to send her.'

As they pushed on towards Hamburg they were surrounded by the sights, sounds and smells of the disintegrating Third Reich. Thousands of forced labourers from the occupied countries freed themselves and started for home before anyone could declare an end to hostilities. There were Dutchmen heading west, and Poles east. Prisoners of war were also waking to find their guards had disappeared, leaving the gates open. One Russian joined a Cromwell crew in 5th Tanks. Across on the eastern flank of the crumbling Nazi empire hundreds of thousands of prisoners had been set trudging westwards during the bitter winter. These Death Marches included concentration-camp prisoners and also thousands of Allied servicemen who had been used as forced labour in East Prussia and Poland.

Men captured at Sidi Rezegh in 1941, like Corporal Harry Finlayson of A Squadron, or in Normandy less than one year before, such as Trooper Bill Chorley of C Squadron, were among the small figures, freezing and starving, trying to survive the last great drama of their war. Not all did: a fellow member of Chorley's crew disappeared on the march, never to return home.

Even in late April, as the 7th Armoured Division secured the outskirts of Hamburg, there were odd people firing anti-tank rockets or lobbing grenades at them. There was a pause of a couple of days on the outskirts of that great port city before the order came that the authorities there had surrendered. The end of the battalion's war was just one more day's drive away.

23

JOURNEY'S END

By late April 1945 the 7th Armoured Division was speeding across northern Germany with orders to prevent the escape of enemy forces northwards into Denmark. Elsewhere the Red Army was fighting its way into Berlin and the Americans had gone far to the south, where there was talk of Nazi last stands in Bavaria and Czechoslovakia.

The great convoy that snaked across the Soltau plain, brushing aside resistance with bursts of machine-gun fire or high-explosive shells, was nearing the end of an epic journey. Fifth RTR's tanks were laden with all manner of comforts picked up along their odyssey: frying pans from Normandy, Dutch cast-iron stoves and German motorbikes. Major Crickmay's three-litre Mercedes purred along, having been painted up with army tactical signs and designated the squadron commander's staff car.

People had been picked up too – a few members of the Belgian and Dutch resistance serving as interpreters, the Russian tank driver Tamarov and several members of the battalion liberated from a prison camp at Fallingbostel on 16 April. These included four men who had been captured after the ambush in which Sergeant Wardrop had been killed, and who told of being beaten by their captors. There were other prisoners recovered too, including Trooper Bill Chorley, another C Squadron man, who had been taken at Villers-Bocage in June 1944. He had survived a Death March from Poland and weighed just six stone. In time, the battalion's North African prisoners started coming in too, men like Corporal Harry Finlayson, captured at Sidi Rezegh more than three and a half years ago. Like many taken during those early months of the desert war, his PoW odyssey had carried him through a succession of camps in Italy, Germany and Poland. He had avoided a Death March by faking an injury to his knee, which got him a train ride westwards instead.

Nearby, soldiers from the 11th Hussars discovered Bergen Belsen concentration camp. Rumours soon spread through the division about the appalling treatment of the inmates and the reality of the Final Solution.

Even as they neared the Elbe, at the mouth of which was their objective of Hamburg, they encountered resistance. Major Crickmay and his wireless operator had a narrow escape when a Panzerfaust flew just behind them, a tank was hit by an 88 a couple of days later and the commander of a Honey in the Recce Troop, wounded by an anti-tank rocket on 24 April, had to finish off its firer with his revolver. Inexorably, though, the miles were covered to Harburg on the other side of the waterway from the great port.

On 29 April German officers had appeared from their lines with a white flag to discuss terms for the surrender of Hamburg.

The Nazi state had broken up. Divisions were disbanding into knots of dazed individuals, forced labour freeing itself from its shackles and German communities cutting their own deals to save themselves from further destruction. At the highest level the Allies were trying to negotiate surrenders with senior commanders. A few days after their initial contacts with the garrison commanders and city authorities in Hamburg, the 7th Armoured Division launched a phased operation to secure the city. The 1st Tanks took the main bridges over the Elbe and on the 3 May the 5th RTR and other elements of the division crossed.

As so often with the Desert Rats, the 11th Hussars had been in for a quiet shufti first. 'The first thing that struck us was the incredible tidiness of the place,' wrote one of their officers. 'The streets were absolutely clear, the telephone lines and tramwires were in perfect order … the German clearance organisation must have been brilliant. But all the same the damage was terrific. Not single houses but whole streets were flat.'

Trundling across in his armoured vehicle, 'I well remember looking down at that bridge and noticing that explosive charges were ready to drop it into the mighty river', wrote Lieutenant-Colonel Leakey. Sighting the great buildings that marked the outskirts of Hamburg proper, Arthur Crickmay atop his Cromwell wondered why such a fuss had been made about the RAF's bombing of the city. But as they grew closer still, 'we realised they were all empty shells'. The advance was held up for a time because the B Squadron troop leader driving into the city got lost. When at last the squadron rumbled into the square in front of Hamburg's post office, the OC of B Squadron's Cromwell threw a track with a great screeching of metal and clattering of cobblestones. The driver reported to his boss in the turret, 'Well sir, that's that.' The tank, reckoned to be only one of three in the battalion that had motored all the way from the D-Day beaches – a distance of more than two thousand miles, including the twists and turns that the fighting had forced them to adopt – would go no further.

Reaching the main square, Major Crickmay found the city police force drawn up for inspection, awaiting his command. Having fought his way across the thousands of miles from Cairo, Crickmay couldn't quite believe it when a heel-clicking German police commander accepted his order to carry on about their normal duties with a '*Jawohl, Herr Major!*'

Positions were taken up around the Westminster Bank (the British company had established it during the city's happier days as a hub of Baltic trading) by C Squadron while other elements of the 5th RTR and 7th Armoured Division established themselves around the city. It was shortly after arriving that a limousine under escort by a swarm of Royal Military Police outriders was seen coming through the city. Peering into the back of the car, Crickmay's wireless operator Corporal Bob Lay spotted Admiral Doenitz. As others realised who it was, the effect was electric: 'That could only mean one thing. And we didn't know what to do, so we all threw our berets in the air ... When we saw that we knew that was the end.'

Doenitz, who briefly served as Führer following Hitler's suicide, signed a formal surrender agreement with Montgomery at Lüneberg Heath, to the south of Hamburg, the following day.

At the city's Hotel Streits, Lieutenant-Colonel Leakey, his second-in-command and some officers from the Queen's walked in to find a full dinner service under way in the dining room. Some customers were shooed away as the city's new burghers, caked with grime from their drive across Germany, walked in, sat at the starched tablecloths and ordered the best meal any of them could remember having in years. For a time it was decided to let the soldiers use Reich Marks, and some of them had great bundles of the money packed into spaces in their tank turrets. They had picked it up from German soldiers and vehicles, and had been using it for such tasks as lighting cigarettes. Suddenly the notes were treated with more respect.

The order had come down to the 5th RTR on 3 May to observe a ceasefire. As one of the Firefly crews was clearing its guns, parked on a Hamburg street, a single shot was accidentally fired, hitting Trooper Cyril Duckett, who was working at the front of the tank. He died of his wounds. The battalion had become used to burying its men where they fell – they were subsequently reinterred in cemeteries. So Trooper Duckett was consigned to the earth in the back garden of a Hamburg house, the last member of the battalion to die in the war. It was a bitter end to the long campaigns of his squadron. The following morning they discovered some flowers and a note on his grave. It had been left by a German woman, a mother, who wrote that her own son had also fallen in the war not so long before.

During the following days the battalion was moved out of central Hamburg and VE Day was formally marked on 8 May with Verey lights fired into the night sky and impromptu parties across the 2nd Army. Lieutenant-Colonel Leakey wasted little time in giving the men what was effectively their last Griff talk, on the subject of 'looting and fraternisation'. There was, he ordered, to be none of either, and in particular told them to get it out of their heads that anything that looked like German state property could simply be carted away. The Reeperbahn, Hamburg's notorious red-light district, was placed out of bounds.

Each soldier began to reflect on victory and his own survival. For Arthur Crickmay, during that first night in the city, he laid his bedding on the manager's desk at the Westminster Bank and at last 'slept at peace with the world'. C Squadron threw a big party at which all of the old favourites were sung, from 'A Famous Battalion' to the 'Old Eighty-Seventh'. Their OC joined in the singing and many remembered Jake Wardrop, who had strummed his guitar so memorably at squadron gatherings across North Africa and Europe. At one point a show of hands was called for: who here was at Alamein? Around ten of the seventy-five men present raised their arms.

B Squadron had a big party too. At first the OC could not understand the subdued atmosphere. 'Perhaps we were a bit inhibited', wrote one of his troopers, 'thinking of all our dead comrades and who should have been there, and still only half believing it was over and nobody was going to kill any of us in the morning.' As the night wore on their reticence was drowned by copious amounts of alcohol; they sang until the small hours and collapsed senseless in their tents. They too had survived.

In June a formal service of thanksgiving was held by the 5th Tanks. There were hymns, prayers and an address, the proceedings concluding with Rupert Brooke's poem 'The Soldier', the one that begins, 'If I should die, think only this of me'. A roll of honour was produced, listing the eighty-four members of 5th RTR killed between D-Day and the end of the war. This was the price paid during the final eleven months of fighting, but the full list of men lost by the battalion could not be compiled at that time because of the inadequacies of army book-keeping.

My own research shows that 224 members of 5th RTR were buried in British military cemeteries, having fallen during 1939 to 1945. When one deducts a couple who died in Italian PoW camps and adds several men listed as missing but who perished in unknown places, the total number killed in action or died of wounds is around 240. The worst period of the war for the battalion was the Normandy battles of June to September 1944, when it lost fifty-three men in combat. Its biggest losses of tanks occurred during the Gazala battles, notably the engagement of 2 June 1942, a period of chaotic fighting in which forty-nine men were killed.

The record of the dead, although sobering, remained less than that of the infantry that fought through the same battles with them. Undoubtedly, those who went into battle inside an armoured carapace were safer because of the large number of bullets and other bits of metal flying across the battlefield that could not harm them. When the 1/5th Queen's tallied up how many of their original twelve hundred troops had survived and were still serving with the battalion at the end of the war, it came to just ten men. They had also served in 7th Armoured Division but their war had been significantly shorter than 5th RTR's, since the Queen's Brigade only joined the Desert Rats in August 1942. The tankies understood only too well how right those Great War veterans had been years earlier in telling them to avoid the infantry. 'I am sure that if we had joined the infantry I would not have been alive to see the end of the war,' wrote Sergeant Stimpson.

How many men had gone all the way through the war in 5th Tanks? It was not more than twenty-five or thirty. However, when one adds soldiers who had been serving in other RTR battalions in 1939 or those who had started in the 5th Tanks, been posted away and then come back, the number who had fought all the way through is close to forty or fifty, out of around 730 serving on VE Day. That included three officers – Rea Leakey, Deryck MacDonald and Arthur Crickmay, all subalterns at the start of the war – and a couple of regular NCOs who were commissioned during the conflict, one them being Lieutenant Jackie Garnett.

It is possible to trace the fate of all 194 officers who belonged to 5th RTR through the war: twenty-one were killed while serving with 5th Tanks (some others lost their lives with different units later); nine were taken prisoner or went missing never to be found; and thirty-three were wounded in action but survived the war (this figure does not include those who were wounded but subsequently fell into the killed or captured category). Most of those who left the battalion were simply posted to other units, having seen too much action, had been rejected by their men or were sent elsewhere in the Royal Armoured Corps.

The churn among Other Ranks was not as high, but many (like Charlie Bull or Emmin Hall) did move between Royal Armoured Corps units, which complicates the business of tracing them. Since there is no definitive list of those who were in 5th RTR, it is harder to be categorical about what became of them than is the case with their officers. In fact, when tracing the fortunes of the 1st/95th Rifles or the 23rd Royal Welch Fusiliers for earlier books, it was easier to find out what happened to men serving in 1809 and 1775 because there were proper pay lists with all their names. The Second World War tank battalion, in contrast, was a collective that received countless drafts of new recruits and deliveries of fresh armour, a revolving door for men and material in which much was never properly recorded. There were six major rebuilds of 5th RTR: after France in 1940; in May/June 1940 following evacuation from Tobruk; early in 1942 after Operation Crusader; just before El Alamein (i.e. after the disasters of the Gazala battles of that summer); the Shakers Wood period early in 1944; and following the losses at La Lande in August 1944. My research suggests that something like 2200 Other Ranks served in the battalion during 1939–45, giving a combined figure with officers of about 2400.

Of this total, as we have seen, around 240 fell in battle. The number of men who became prisoners of war was eighty to ninety. The number wounded could be estimated at around 1100 (this would include men subsequently killed or captured, as well as those who returned to duty or were declared unfit for further service). It was a grim record, but not as sanguinary as that of many infantry battalions, let alone that of Hitler's smashed panzer divisions. The relatively high chance of surviving in 5th RTR, despite the many battles it fought, may be seen as a token of success in its tactics, the skill of its commanders and the Allies' use of firepower as well as superior numbers to overwhelm their enemies.

Such was the fighting record of the 7th Armoured Division that it was selected to take part in a victory parade in Berlin in July 1945. The 5th Tanks had been trying to put itself back onto a peacetime footing, with increased attention to regulation dress, more saluting and the like when the prospect of this move set them bulling up their tanks with fresh paint. In the end, despite the hours of elbow grease, 5th RTR was one of the elements in the division told they could not be spared to go to Berlin. There was a good deal of moaning but the reputation of the Filthy Fifth, something they usually revelled in, had finally caught up with them.

In that same month demobilisation began and the first soldier from the battalion was sent home. It would take many months for all of them to be processed out, but even as early November 1945 one of the old-sweat NCOs returning from a course reported the unit was 'unrecognisable' from its wartime self. The hardware was changing too, with Comet and Centurion tanks arriving in Germany. These were generally reckoned to be quite superior to the Cromwell and Sherman. The Comet had seen limited service before VE Day but the arrival of such a high-quality vehicle at this stage seemed like another distinctly British example of industry and officialdom getting their act together just too late.

Along the way, during years of road marches, tank battles and training, they had forged an extraordinary record as a fighting force. The 5th RTR's great advances – at the start of Operation Crusader in 1941, pushing on to Tunis in 1943, during 1944's Great Swan to Ghent and the final dash to Hamburg – were comparable in rates of advance to any feat by German Panzer divisions. Yet somehow a myth was accepted by many analysts or historians that British armoured divisions were never quite the equal of their enemy. This version of events requires many victories to be ignored and repeated reference to the disasters. So the debacle of Villers-Bocage on 13 June, when a British armoured battalion was mauled by a few Tiger tanks, is held up as a definitive example of British failure, yet the drubbing the Germans received the following day is rarely explored. While Rommel's brilliance in conducting his Gazala offensive in the summer 1942 is rightly admired by armchair generals, few chose to analyse his utter defeat by the 8th Army at Alam Halfa in 1942 or the Medenine battle of 1943. He would have understood only too well that in the fluid business of armoured warfare, the margin between defeat and victory was often wafer thin, the ebb and flow of battle frequent.

Compared to their German foe, it is true that in the British officer corps there was more of a culture of blame, outspokenness and individualism. This had been a fact of life since the earliest days of the institution, with eighteenth-century generals indulging in recriminations over any disaster, often taking to print with their accusations in sharp exchanges of pamphlets long after the guns had fallen silent. There was plenty of this in the Second World War too, with rivals angrily magnifying one another's setbacks and diminishing their successes. Commanders trying to defend themselves in this backbiting atmosphere had to develop a playbook of excuses, among which the inferiority of British tank design or the failure of tactics were but two. This distinctively Anglo-Saxon fondness for accusation produced countless historical debates after the war, but the two most famous of these disputes concerned the claim by some that the 8th Army was already poised for victory before Montgomery's arrival in Egypt and whether he badly mishandled the Normandy battle. It also resulted in bitter arguments about the purpose of armoured forces before, during and after the war. It generated a welter of words between blame-trading generals that has provided fuel to those who wish to argue that the tank arm of the British army was never quite up to the German one.

Yet the record of the 5th Tanks, as one of the long-serving battalions of the most celebrated armoured division, suggests a force that was equal to and in some respects more successful than its enemy. The armoured division had been conceived largely as an instrument for the exploitation of success or for counteracting the enemy's breakthroughs. When performing in this role the Desert Rats' tally of success was quite extraordinary. While exact figures for the number of prisoners lost by 5th RTR to the figure taken do not exist, we have a pretty good general idea and it is quite clear that during the Second World War as a whole the battalion captured something like one hundred enemy soldiers for each PoW of its own. The ratio for equipment such as trucks or artillery pieces destroyed or captured is not as pronounced, but is still very much in its favour. On tank losses the figures for 1944–5 suggest somewhat higher losses than they inflicted – a ratio of perhaps three of theirs to each two German panzers.

Of course, vanquished German generals had their own list of excuses – usually that the massive material superiority of the Allies and the weight of aerial firepower as well as artillery was irresistible. Their assertion, keenly adopted by their admirers in the countries of their one-time adversaries, was that episodes like Operation Goodwood in July 1944, in which the Royal Armoured Corps took heavy losses, demonstrated the inferiority of Allied tank forces and tactics more widely. Yet if Allied firepower had really been a decisive factor, Goodwood would have gone very differently, since scores of 88mm and other anti-tank guns that lined the German positions would have been neutralised by the awesome bombardment that preceded the British advance. Instead, these units survived largely intact and the British paid the price of a frontal armoured assault across a narrow front on heavy defences in open ground. This was demonstrated time and again on the Eastern Front, where the Red Army in particular was willing to accept large sacrifices in armour for limited advances. Perhaps what the high cost of Goodwood represented more than anything else was a desire on the part of British commanders that the armoured corps should take the lead, whatever the cost, after weeks in which the infantry had suffered heavy losses around Caen for limited gains.

The most credible estimate is that only around one hundred of the fifteen hundred German tanks and assault guns or tank destroyers lost in Normandy were accounted for by Allied aircraft. The Allies' superiority in artillery probably did produce a more marked effect in that the range of the weapons allowed fire to be concentrated from a wide area onto a decisive part of the front, something far less easy to do with the superior number of tanks. Goodwood, in any case, showed both the dangers of concentrating armour in the same way and the limitations of the Allies' artillery force against dug-in troops.

There are, among the litany of narratives used to explain unpleasant reverses or futile sacrifice, some that cannot be argued with. It is true that German tank production could not match that of the UK and US, let alone the Soviet Union. Yet the evolution of warfare during this conflict, including the wider availability of automatic firearms, hand-held anti-tank weapons and better mines, meant that by the latter years of the war a pronounced enhancement of forces was required in order to overwhelm a skilfully conducted defence. This was just as plain during costly German counter-strokes in the Ukraine or Normandy as it was with Allied thrusts. Of course Germany was out-produced and overwhelmed by its adversaries in the end, but that was a feature of grand strategy and Hitler's disastrous choices.

The inferiority of the medium-velocity 75mm gun mounted on British and American tanks to its German equivalents is another empirical fact – it can be demonstrated by studying ballistic tests of their comparative penetration of armour. It can also be seen in the context of wider debates about the offensive versus the defensive. Having worse tank guns didn't trouble the British too much when they were on the defensive, but was definitely a handicap during offensive operations, notably the long weeks of fighting in Normandy. The British, though, did find a partial answer in their excellent seventeen-pounder gun, something that allowed the veteran commanders of the 5th Tanks to knock out many a Panther and even the odd Tiger during the last year of the war. In order to overcome these technical hurdles they also had to improvise tactically and improve coordination between arms, something they did well.

There is one more area where the differences between the adversaries cannot be denied, and it is a good deal more subjective than the business of tank production or armament. It concerns the fundamental element of this story: the human component of the 5th Royal Tank Regiment and quite a few other British battalions or regiments that had a similarly long and distinguished record during the war. In their training, discipline and ideological indoctrination (or lack thereof) they were fundamentally different from the German or Soviet soldier. Of course, there were similarities with the US forces as well as those of Britain's Empire and Dominions. However, the British were in a category of their own in sharing a bitter folk memory of senseless slaughter in the Great War, a lively sense of class division and a boisterous tradition of free speech, including complaint. These factors made successful leadership harder, as well as the resort to coercion or ideology. The insubordinate or frightened British soldier could not be marched in front of a firing squad, sent to the head of an advancing penal battalion or reminded of his duty to give all for his Fatherland. He had to be treated with care, his small part in the war explained often by his officers, and it was through love of his comrades that he came to accept he might easily die in a blazing metal tomb.

The challenge of leading men forward in an army in which, to quote one senior British doctor in Normandy, 'the stigma and punishment for exhibiting fear has been largely removed', was enormous. There were times when men of the 5th Tanks fled – for example during the desert flaps or at Villers-Bocage – but these represented very short periods in more than five years of near relentless combat, a period exposed to danger that only a tiny proportion of units in any army of the Second World War were asked to endure. That this was achieved with the British soldier made the achievement all the more remarkable.

It would be wrong to sentimentalise the men that emerged from this alloy of old regular-army tank soldiers and citizens called up in time of war. They were hard men, quite ready to kill without hesitation when circumstances demanded it. There were times when they dispatched enemy soldiers trying to surrender, fired shells through the windows of houses where they thought snipers might lurk or machine-gunned enemy tank crews as they bailed out. At times, too, they thwarted their superiors' orders because they did not believe in the missions they had been asked to perform. In short, they were soldiers seasoned by combat who often fought by their own rules.

Of course the battalion that first went into action at Saint-Valéry-sur-Somme in May 1940, or El Agheila in April 1941, was quite different in thinking from the one that ended up in Hamburg in May 1945. New tactics were learned, often the hard way, more reliable tanks acquired, and – most importantly – the methods of leadership shifted quite dramatically. An older generation of aloof officers was displaced by men in their twenties, who were far better able to talk to their young soldiers. The RTR was never particularly fond of the spit and polish, or the occasional resort by non-commissioned officers to physical coercion that typified the 1930s garrison army. During the war these methods, even in so far as they had been used, were forgotten. The 'Shitty Fifth' enjoyed its reputation as one of the scruffiest battalions in the army.

The qualities of toughness, initiative and determination that were distilled within the battalion had produced a very rare type of unit by the end of the war. It was inevitable that as men were demobilised it would change. But enough men stayed on to guarantee that the hard-won lessons of the war were not forgotten. This meant protecting tank battalions as the rest of the army demobilised.

Even as the guns fell silent, the senior officers of the Royal Tank Regiment in the 21st Army Group were gathering, exchanging views, anxious about the future. They had endured many slights at the hands of senior men from other branches of the army during the war and feared that, just like the 1920s, a conservative army establishment would soon cut the tank upstarts to the quick. The formation of the Royal Armoured Corps had been a shotgun wedding with the cavalry. When it had happened, on the eve of war, the RTR had operated most of the army's tanks and had the lion's share of experience in armoured warfare. Very few of the men who knew about armoured vehicle maintenance or keeping a squadron of tanks in formation across country belonged in 1939–40 to cavalry regiments. This was a feature of Britain's late decision in the 1930s to re-arm and mechanise its horse soldiers more than anything else. By 1945, most tank-equipped battalions in the British army belonged to the cavalry, they had accumulated plenty of knowhow and there was no chance of them trying to regain their role on horseback. The Royal Tanks officers were particularly anxious, since they believed the greater number of cavalry officers and their higher social status would give them a distinct advantage in the promotion or spending battles ahead.

In May 1945 those officers, including the likes of Major-General Pip Roberts, Mike Carver, who was commanding an armoured brigade, and the battalion COs such as Lieutenant-Colonel Leakey, signed a joint letter to their Colonel Commandant, the titular head of the RTR family back in England. It warned:

Cavalry units have gained their position and knowledge at the expense of the RTR officers and units who taught them, and there is undoubtedly a feeling that the prop on which they depended can now be dispensed with ... it has become clearly apparent that a struggle between the cavalry and ourselves is now taking place.

The following month a conclave of RTR officers met in an annexe of the War Office in London. It was agreed that the regiment needed a new figurehead in order to defend its interests during the uncertain times that lay ahead, and Field Marshal Montgomery was that man. It was a measure of the respect that Monty had for the RTR that he accepted this role, and its implied role as chief of the tribe, despite being an infantryman. Montgomery had himself encountered plenty of snobbery during his rise through the army, and had regarded the RTR as more professional than the cavalry. Upon taking up his new role the field marshal wrote to the men of the regiment, noting that ever since being given RTR headgear on the eve of Alamein, 'I have proudly worn your beret and your badge ever since that day'. Its battalions, he wrote, 'have fought magnificently in every theatre ... the regiment has made a great name for itself'.

While memories of the war were fresh and Monty was patron the RTR managed to hold its own. Its demobilisation, from fielding a peak of twenty-three battalions down to a peacetime eight regular units was fair. Yeomanry regiments (i.e. reserve cavalry) were all placed back in reserve and that unusual wartime expedient, the Guards Armoured Division, soon returned its men to an infantry role. Over time, however, traditional army politics reasserted themselves, and while the RTR should have had little difficulty maintaining its role during the long years of Cold War, the cuts fell each time a little more heavily on it than the cavalry. In 1970 5th Royal Tank Regiment was disbanded.

What became of the men of the 5th Tanks, that 'Famous Battalion' which had given so much during the war? Of the six put in the spotlight at the beginning of this narrative, Charlie Bull and Jake Wardrop were killed in action. Brian Stone, the culture-loving young officer seriously wounded and taken prisoner in 1942, lived life to the full despite the loss of his leg. He worked as a journalist in Palestine during the crisis that culminated in Israeli independence, before returning home to pursue the academic life. He became an authority on poetry and a founder member of the Open University, raised a family and died in 1995.

As for Arthur Crickmay, he managed to obtain a regular commission and remained in the army after the war. 'The war took a hell of a lot out of him,' says one cousin, 'he was quite a diffident man to start with, and he became even more so.' Crickmay left the army in the late 1950s, returning to architecture and construction, the trade he had trained in before the war. He too raised a family, passing away in 1998.

Of the other officers mentioned here, some got on extremely well in the peacetime army. Richard Ward, that glory-hunting OC of A Squadron in the desert, became a general and Governor of Hong Kong. Both Rea Leakey and his young adjutant Roy Dixon also became generals. The RTR's greatest success, though, was to prove to be Mike Carver of the 1st Tanks, who became a field marshal and, as Chief of the Defence Staff in the 1970s, the professional head of the UK armed forces.

Jackie Garnett, the officer promoted from the ranks, remained in the armoured corps for many years after the war. As a man for whom 'the army was his whole life', he did not adapt well to peacetime or his eventual departure from it in 1968. Soldiering transformed Garnett from the son of a miner to an officer and winner of the Military Cross. During the Korean War he was in action again, commanding a squadron of the 5th RTR. Faced with civilian life, Garnett did not cope well. His marriage broke up, he hit the bottle and finally, in 1975, took his own life.

Emmin Hall, the sergeant who had challenged the hierarchy in Shakers Wood and got his CO sacked, was never allowed to return to the 5th Tanks despite many requests to do so. After the war he worked as a long-distance lorry driver from a base back in his native Warwickshire.

Gerry Solomon recovered well from the wounds he sustained in Normandy and after working in a couple of training jobs took off as soon as demobilisation allowed him to. He returned to Ipswich where he worked as a newsagent, raised a family and, at the age of ninety-five, spent many hours explaining to this author the intricacies of life in the 5th RTR.

All of those that survived were haunted by the memory of the hundreds who did not. The sacrifices of this one battalion were, after all, simply a drop in the ocean of worldwide slaughter that raged for six years. The survivors of the 5th Tanks would not have claimed themselves to be an elite, nor would I on their behalf. Instead they were an example, one of the bodies of men expert in armoured warfare who had to pay with their blood for the consequences of Britain's slowness to rearm and Germany's investment in its armoured forces.

The true cadre of the Royal Armoured Corps as Britain went to war in 1939 consisted of around about a dozen regular units. Most of them belonged to the Royal Tank Regiment by virtue of their longer experience with armoured vehicles, but some of the newly mechanised cavalry regiments might also be counted in this number. Much of the regular cavalry at that time retained its horses and the reserves, in the shape of yeomanry regiments, were largely clueless about tank warfare.

It was the men of 5th RTR and those other regular units that formed the essential capital for what lay ahead; the transformation of the British army into a mechanised force while it was engaged daily in a battle with an adversary that had already mastered that form of warfare. During the early years of the war the output of British industry – horribly unreliable, poorly designed tanks – did more to hinder than help in this struggle. The human factor, throughout this story, was paramount.

The farming-out of experienced men to newly formed units and the acceptance of hundreds of untrained people within battalions like the 5th Tanks were the process by which knowledge and experience were disseminated. It was a trick that could only be performed once, for by the end of the war the entire Royal Armoured Corps was both mechanised and experienced. The men who had served as apostles for this new form of warfare were by that time dead, spent or trying to hold on as the army demobilised. Whatever the setbacks along the way – and there were plenty – the British army could not have emerged victorious from the western desert or Normandy without an effective tank force.

George Stimpson, one of the 5th RTR's sergeants, was one of the select few dozen in the unit who fought through the Second World War in tank crews from its first day to its last. He was lost in reflection as he walked down to the banks of the River Elster near Hamburg in May 1945. He sat on the bank, unlaced his boots and took off his socks. It was at the moment that he dipped his aching feet into the waters that he realised their long odyssey was over. Their journey involved mastering machines and cooperating with all the other elements of the 'orchestra of war' that was the armoured division. It was at heart, though, a triumph of ordinary men, against long odds, in the darkest of times.

NOTES

Abbreviations

BTM	Bovington Tank Museum
Cheeseman	Ernest Cheeseman, 5th RTR, interview with the Imperial War Museum. IWM interview 18516
Crickmay	Papers of Arthur Crickmay
DAK	*Deutsches Afrikakorps*
IWM	Imperial War Museum
Lay	Bob Lay, 5th RTR, author interviews, 2010–12
LHA	Liddell Hart Archive, King's College London
NA	The National Archives, Kew
Solomon	Gerry Solomon, 5th RTR, author interviews, 2010–12
Stimpson	George Stimpson, 5th RTR, unpublished memoir
Storer	Syd Storer, 5th RTR, unpublished memoir in the BTM archives
Wardrop	Papers of Jake Wardrop
WD	War Diary

Chapter 1: A French Farce

1 *'our emotions had been torn to bits'*: Cheeseman. This IWM interview is the source of much good detail on the scene, including the strawberries.

2 *had literally gone to pieces*: The battalion WD at the NA gives details of the different parties and course of this short campaign. NA, WO 167/449.

2 *a small party of volunteers was moving among the vehicles*: Including R. Green, 5th RTR. Interview with Bovington Tank Museum. BTM, E2004.1637.

4 *'if she did not find the keys . . . '*: Stimpson. This account contains the best detail

of the march to Cherbourg.

4 *'My soldiers were of a high standard . . . '*: Carver, *Out of Step*.

5 *Hall was the product of unhappy family circumstances*: I am grateful to Emmin Hall's daughter, Margaret Roe, for sharing her written private memoir and personal reflections.

5 *Wardrop . . . had joined the 5th in 1937*: See Forty (ed.), *Jake Wardrop's Diary*.

5 *'cat-like eyes'*: Lay.

5 *'I never ever had a meal cooked by the army . . . '*: Cheeseman. Stimpson confirms that the army cooks never caught up with them.

5 *He had joined the army not long after*: Information on Charlie Bull comes from his letters, privately published by his family, and his nephew David Bull.

6 *Lieutenant Brian Stone, a 5th Tanks reservist*: Stone, *Prisoner from Alamein*, contains most details and quotes from him included here. Some additional information is found in his obituary, *Independent*, 4 March 1995.

7 *just one of the British commanders claiming a kill*: For a detailed account of Saint-Valéry, see WO 167/449. The lone successful commander was Sergeant Marsden, who was awarded the Military Medal for this action.

7 *Gerry Solomon had volunteered for the tanks*: Solomon.

9 *Lieutenant Arthur Crickmay, having joined*: Crickmay.

10 *'The officers of the Royal Tank Corps . . . '*: Carver.

10 *Tank production and design had been run down*: See Leland Ness, *Jane's World War II Tanks and Fighting Vehicles: A Complete Guide* (London: HarperCollins, 2002), for much useful data on tank production as well as technical details of the vehicles themselves.

11 *The balance of power, as it applied to the tank forces*: Harris, *Men, Ideas and Tanks*.

Chapter 2: Arrivals and Departures

12 *Trooper Gerry Solomon reported*: Solomon.

13 *'I didn't want to get into the infantry'*: Ibid.

15 *up the hill from the camp to Admiral Robert Hamilton's house*: Brenda MacDonald (née Pitt), one of those nieces, author interviews, 2011–12. Mrs MacDonald was the source of much useful information about Thursley and the 5th RTR's officers.

15 *'They were all very stressed . . . '*: Ibid.

16 *afternoons at the Guildford Lido*: This emerges in one of Charlie Bull's letters home.

17 *Starting in 1936, the army decided . . .* : See Harris, *Men, Ideas and Tanks* and Liddell Hart, *The Tanks*. Brigadier George Davy suggests in his memoirs that the 7th Hussars had begun a mechanisation trial in Egypt in 1929.

17 *'the principles of training in field operations . . . '*: Quoted in Harris.

18 *still much use of Tank-Corps terminology*: Indeed Harry Finlayson, 5th RTR (1936–41), still soldiered on using terms such as 'private' and 'company' when I interviewed him in 2011–12. Among those soldiers who came into

the war later, after the formation of the RAC, this use of language was distinctly less marked.

18 *'from a high and mighty corps to a regiment'*: Cheeseman.

18 *'We didn't like the cavalry . . . '* . . . *Stories abounded of RTR men . . .*: For example from Cheeseman, Finlayson and Solomon. The terms 'donkey bashers' and 'donkey wallopers' persist in corners of the RTR to this day.

19 *'shit and efficiency'*: Stimpson.

20 *built to a strength of fifty-two tanks*: 5th RTR WD, NA, WO 166/1406.

21 *During the tactical debates of the inter-war years*: Sources such as Harris and Liddell Hart reflect on these. The LHA provides an extensive archive on these matters, including the letters of many tank corps pioneers, including Percy Hobart.

23 *'cost millions of lost man hours'*: MacLeod Ross, *The Business of Tanks*.

25 *'I pointed out Dumbarton Rocks . . . '*: Wardrop.

25 *'I was full of the spirit of adventure'*: Solomon.

Chapter 3: The Desert

26 *'Trussed up like a mummy'*: Crickmay. Memo on first year of the war, a candid account written during his sea passage to Burma at the end of 1941.

28 *'we never dreamt how far we should eventually go . . . '*: Ibid.

29 *'The chief discomforts are a lack of water . . . '*: Crickmay. Letter home, dated 21 September 1940. Crickmay's letters provide much of the detail about his experiences, including leave visits to Cairo.

30 *'I sometimes think we are the legion of the lost . . . '*: Ibid.

30 *'dirty, filthy, smelly'*: Cheeseman.

30 *'I didn't like it at all. . . '*: Harry Finlayson, 5th RTR, interview with the author.

31 *'wogs', 'darkies' and 'gippos'*: These terms emerge in many 8th Army accounts. Wardrop, for instance, uses 'wogs' several times, although it appears from his diary that he bears little ill will towards the Egyptians, compared to some of his comrades.

31 *'The horse still prevailed as the ruler . . . '*: Brigadier George Davy, memoir.

32 *'Each day we bought six bottles . . . '*: Wardrop.

32 *The 5th handed its A9 tanks over to the 3rd*: 5th RTR WD, NA, WO169/1414.

33 *'a festive atmosphere'*: Wardrop.

34 *The 1939 Army Tank Brigade Training Instruction*: The source of much information about Hobart and other early tank pioneers. A copy is in file 9/28/67 at the LHA.

35 *Hobo and others borrowed one of Nelson's terms*: For hostile views of Hobart and his influence, see Harris, *Men, Ideas and Tanks*, or Griffith, *World War II Desert Tactics*.

36 *'We drove around to avoid the enemy shelling . . . '*: Quoted in Delaforce, *Churchill's Desert Rats 2*.

37 *to his delight Trooper Solomon was moved*: Solomon.

38 *the Battalion Technical Officer had been sent off to Cairo*: 5th RTR WD, NA, WO169/1414. The BTO, Major Southon, left his own papers to BTM.

38 *'by the time we did move off the desert was horribly empty'*: Cheeseman.

39 *they were leaving seat cushions*: Ibid.

39 *Many of the A13s were by this time approaching two thousand miles*: 5th RTR WD, NA, WO169/1414.

40 *Of the fifty-three tanks on the regiment's books*: Southon Papers, BTM.

40 *'hitherto undreamed-of possibilities'*: Liddell Hart (ed.), *The Rommel Papers*.

41 *'The plan for defence was impracticable . . . '*: Unpublished memoir, Crickmay.

Chapter 4: First Blood

44 *'If I am going to get killed, I will be wearing the Tank Corps beret'*: Stimpson. This is also a very good source on the fight at Ajdabiya.

44 *'a beer and the whiff of a barmaid's apron was all it took'*: Harry Finlayson, 5th RTR, author interviews. He was another member of the boxing team.

45 *'Although I could have managed quite well without the incident . . . '*: Wardrop. The section on the Amirya incident and court martial was edited out of Forty and other published editions, presumably because it showed Wardrop triumphing over the army hierarchy.

45 *Some time after four o'clock the commander of their brigade*: Details of the action are drawn from 5th RTR WD, NA, WO169/1414, which includes a substantial memo on the fight from Lt-Col Drew, and from the German side the DAK WD, which is extensively quoted in Jentz, *Tank Combat in North Africa*.

46 *'The crews were sat on top of their tanks . . . '*: Stimpson.

47 *'stand by to open fire at eight hundred yards'*: 5th RTR WD, NA, WO169/1414.

47 *a battalion of seventy Panzers*: The 2nd Battalion of 5th Panzer Regiment, made up according to Jentz of eighty tracked vehicles: ten Mk I panzers, twenty-two Mk IIs, thirty-eight Mk IIIs and ten Mk IV's. I have not counted the Mk I variants in my figure since they were command vehicles without effective anti-tank armament.

47 *'hair raising'*: Solomon. His tank had been one of half a dozen A Squadron vehicles grouped with armoured cars from the King's Dragoon Guards that had been involved in a night action before C Squadron's fight. He says they had not realised at the time that they were fighting Germans rather than Italians.

47 *'the quickest, deadliest duffy . . . '*: Wardrop.

49 *The Germans reported losses of three tanks*: Jentz, quoting DAK WD.

49 *Some had died but most were captured*: The figure of twenty-three comes from the 5th RTR WD. It actually took years for the army to establish what had become of the men lost that day. One, for example, had been captured but later died in captivity in Italy. Eight to ten of the twenty-three were killed or died quickly of their wounds; the remainder were captured.

50 *'So that every man understands . . . '*: Rommel is quoted by the DAK WD in Jentz.

50 *the 90th Light*: This division was not formed under this name until November 1941, but served initially as the 'special purpose division', made up of a handful of infantry and support units.

51 *Kampfgruppe Ponath, formed on 3 April*: Details from the WD of 8th Machine Gun Battalion, reproduced in Forty, *Afrika Korps at War*, vol. 1.

55 *of fifty-three tanks, just two were left*: Drew's report detailing what happened to the battalion's tanks is attached to the 5th RTR WD.

56 *'among some of the most exasperating and unpleasant . . . '*: From his memo on the first year of operations. Crickmay.

56 *Dozens of tanks had broken down*: The German workshop report quoted by Jentz suggests forty-four Mk IIIs broke down on this march.

Chapter 5: Egyptian Summer

58 *Old desert hands reckoned that during these winds . . .* : Crickmay, for example.

59 *'I suppose the whole of the MEF passed through the place . . . '*: Wardrop.

59 *James Cagney in* The Bride Came C.O.D.: The diary of Mel David, a fitter in A Squadron of 5 RTR, is particularly good on films and other down-time activities such as card games. I am grateful to Ashley Rossiter for giving me access to it.

60 *a certain Lieutenant-Colonel Bernard Montgomery*: The story is told in Hamilton, *The Full Monty*.

60 *Sisters Street was Alexandria's destination for men*: Cheeseman.

60 *'I realised that I was cut out to be a drunkard . . . '*: Stimpson. He is very open about aspects of soldiers' leave-time behaviour that others prefer not to dwell upon.

61 *Crickmay's leave life was sufficiently well organised . . .* : These details emerge in letters home. Crickmay.

61 *'You can't imagine what it means . . . '*: Letter dated 9 June 1941, Crickmay.

62 *'in the midst of so much order, counter order, and disorder'*: The Downing Street report on these events, complete with Churchill's foreword, is in the NA: CAB 66/17/32.

63 *the PM had convened 'Tank Parliaments'*: Some interesting references to these occur in Alanbrooke, *War Diaries 1939–1945*.

63 *They would be joined in this brigade by the 3rd Tanks*: Numerous sources including Delaforce, *Churchill's Desert Rats*, who also has details of the Battleaxe disasters.

65 *On 21 July the 5th received the first of its new tanks*: 5th RTR WD.

66 *If they didn't crank the engine for ten minutes to circulate the oil*: Eric Smith, 5th RTR, IWM interview 28675. Smith, who drove in A Squadron, was a good friend of Gerry Solomon, who also remembers the peculiarities of driving the Honey.

66 *By 21 September the 5th Tanks*: 5th RTR WD.

66 *'It was beautifully cool, absolutely lovely'*: Solomon.

67 *The Americans sent representatives from the companies*: MacLeod Ross, *The Business of Tanks*.

70 *'I am sitting inside the tank writing this . . . '*: Letter dated 31 October 1941, Bull family.

71 *'This will be a tank commander's battle . . . '*: Davy, memoirs.

Chapter 6: Crusader

73 *They moved off at six that morning*: 5th RTR WD.

74 *a sound like ripping paper as they passed*: Lay.

74 *yellow and green tracer streaking*: Stone, *Prisoner from Alamein*.

75 *When the 7th Armoured Division swung around*: The narrative here is the product of many sources, including general accounts of the desert war such as by Carver, Neillands or Delaforce, but one interesting primary one is 'An Account of the Operations in Libya 18th November to 27th December 1941', the official divisional after action report, signed off by Major-General Gott early in 1942, in file 15/11/11 (Hobart Papers) in the LHA.

76 *'As we came in sight of the airfield . . . '*: Davy memoirs.

76 *'memorable scene'*: Among the many valuable items in the Crickmay Papers is his annotated copy of Davy's account.

76 *a blow that caused even a commander of Erwin Rommel's skill*: See Kriebel, *Inside the Afrika Korps*. Kriebel was Chief of Staff of the 15th Panzer Division. See also Liddell Hart (ed.), *The Rommel Papers*.

77 *'We had no experience of battle . . . '*: R. Goodwin, 2nd RGH, quoted by Delaforce, *Churchill's Desert Rats 2*.

78 *'he had absolutely nothing on at all . . . '*: Solomon. The knocking-out of Lt Moss's tank is an incident for which I had the benefit of two living eyewitnesses (Solomon and Harry Finlayson, who was in the same troop) as well as documentary sources such as the War Diary.

79 *. . . each tank had fired an average*: Stone.

80 *the 90th Light Division*: It was still designated differently, as the special purpose division.

81 *So the push northwards by 6th Tanks*: Their ride to destruction was one of the definitive 'Balaklava charges' of the war. Davy and Crickmay are the main sources for this passage.

82 *'Arthur, put away your maps'*: Crickmay's annotations on Davy's memoir.

83 *'My God, what a shock'*: Watt, *A Tankie's Travels*.

83 *'To see them sometimes reminded me of battleships'*: Letter dated 10 January 1942, Bull family. This is the most revealing of Charlie Bull's letters home, many of which somehow evaded military censorship.

84 *lying dead in the shape of a cross*: Watt.

84 *'My tank was hit and the driver killed instantly'*: Cyril Joly, 3rd RTR, in his book *Take These Men*.

84 *'We went storming up to these tanks . . . '*: Forty (ed.), *Jake Wardrop's Diary*.

85 *'You've never seen such a balls-up'*: Harry Maegrith, 3rd RTR, quoted by his colleague Robert Crisp in *Brazen Chariots*.

85 *had its radio antenna shot off*: Harry Finlayson, 5th RTR, author interviews. Harry argues he had been promoted to sergeant in the field two days before this happened, but as the army did not record this fact I have referred to him throughout as corporal.

86 *'closed in and gave them the charge'*: Wardrop.

86 *But the Germans had exacted a heavy price*: Kriebel.

86 *Hall withdrew but soon realised something was wrong*: Some audio recordings of Hall were passed to the BTM, catalogued as E2004.1636, after the war by his family. His daughter Margaret also has them transcribed.

88 *'At this moment I was just getting out of the tank . . . '*: This and other details of Hall's odyssey come from the BTM recording.

89 *there had only been two occasions during the war that he had cried*: Hall told Bill Green, a journalist, this after the war. He gave Green much information, some of which was included in an article for the April 2001 issue of *Medal News*. There is a copy in BTM.

89 *On the 24th they hit an enemy infantry column*: 5th RTR WD.

90 *'Up at four o'clock . . . dragged on my boots . . . '*: Stone.

90 *'Orders were never necessary'*: Joly.

91 *'at all costs'*: 5th RTR WD.

91 *'flapped a bit at first as I put my hand to my face . . . '*: Letter dated 10 January 1942, Bull family.

92 *'went to pick this thing up . . . '*: Solomon.

94 *when the final reckoning was done*: Carver uses these figures in *Dilemmas of the Desert War*.

94 *'the enemy had consistently appeared to have . . . '*: Ibid.

94 *'In the end'*: Kriebel.

95 *'the first real battle of the war'*: John Bolan, 6th RTR, IWM sound archive interview 22117.

95 *'I felt a close bond . . . '*: Joly.

95 *'I cannot think how the Delsons . . . '*: Letter dated 10 December 1941, Crickmay.

95 *lost twenty-seven men, with a great many more wounded or captured*: 5th RTR WD, plus information from the Commonwealth War Graves Commission.

Chapter 7: New Year, New Broom

96 *'We went into a rather small street corner bar'*: Stimpson.

97 *'It's very gloomy here without the chaps . . . '*: Letter dated 28 December 1941, Crickmay.

98 *'I feel perhaps the fact that we suffered no casualties . . . '*: 5th RTR War Diary.

99 *'the handsomest man outside films'*: Stone, *Prisoner from Alamein*.

100 *'The German will not commit himself to tank v tank battle . . . '*: 7th Armoured

Division, 'An Account of the Operations in Libya 18th November to 27th December 1941', LHA.

101 *'like going from wood to steel at sea'*: Pip Roberts, letter to Basil Liddell Hart dated 12 February 1954, LHA, file 9/28/48.

101 *the Grant needed six or seven men*: In addition to the crew functions I have listed, there was a hull machine-gunner too. The 5th Tanks appear to have operated their Grants with four rather than five men in the hull, six in total.

101 *The 5th RTR's Grant crews would soon decide . . .* : Lay.

103 *'the Americans were infinitely more jealous . . .'*: MacLeod Ross, *The Business of Tanks*, which is also the source of information about the stepping-up of production at the Chrysler Tank Arsenal. MacLeod Ross was the British officer overseeing UK orders there.

104 *'After nightfall, as we were fully rested . . .'*: Stone.

104 *'hadn't got time for civvies in the army'*: Solomon.

104 *'very strict, a hard man . . .'*: Eric Smith, 5th RTR, IWM interview 28675.

105 *'Dickie saw your fire . . .'*: Solomon.

107 *'At 20:30 hours I ordered Operation Venezia . . .'*: Liddell Hart (ed.), *The Rommel Papers*.

Chapter 8: Disaster in the Cauldron

108 *At half past seven the order came through*: 5th RTR WD, NA, WO 169/4508.

109 *With the weight of reports now suggesting*: Carver, *Dilemmas of the Desert War*, is good on the British army's dawning realisation of what was going wrong.

109 *The 4th Armoured Brigade's tanks*: 4th Armoured Brigade WD, NA, 169/4216.

110 *'Drive towards the sun!'*: Eric Smith, 5th RTR, IWM interview 28675. Smith was serving in the A Squadron transport packet at the time.

110 *'the leading enemy tanks had halted . . .'*: Roberts, *From the Desert to the Baltic*.

111 *He also learned that the 8th Hussars . . .* : 5th RTR WD.

112 *'feelings on getting my orders were mixed'*: Major R. E. Ward, 'A Desert Adventure', article in BTM library.

113 *'reported that they had captured 200 enemy MET . . .'*: 4th Armoured Brigade WD.

114 *Sergeant Hall of C Squadron heard Uniacke*: Emmin Hall, 5th RTR, interview in BTM, E2004.1636.

114 'We began firing . . .': Ibid.

115 *'Our commander gave the order to bail out . . .'*: Stimpson.

116 *'I ran and ran as fast as my legs could carry me'*: Brian Taylor, 5th RTR, author interviews 2011–12.

117 *only one had made it back to their leaguer*: 5th RTR WD.

118 *'this set back in the Regt seemed to have a demoralising effect . . .'*: Harry Ireland, 5th RTR, unpublished memoir, BTM.

118 *put down by some to its vehicles being too spread out*: For example by General Lumsden. Mentioned in Agar-Hamilton and Turner, *Crisis in the Desert*.

118 *'I was closed down but looking through the periscope . . . '*: Forty (ed.), *Jake Wardrop's Diary*.

120 *'and told him the set was duff'*: Ibid.

120 *'nobody in their right mind wanted to be . . . '*: Lay.

120 *'In my opinion [4th Armoured Brigade] . . . '*: Frank Messervy, letter to Basil Liddell Hart, LHA, file 9/28/33.

121 *'Most of us were suffering from chronic exhaustion'*: Stone, *Prisoner from Alamein*.

122 *'I was in contact with these fly-by-night . . . '*: Ibid.

123 *'for every one of my "Africans". . . the high point of the African war'*: Liddell Hart (ed.), *The Rommel Papers*.

123 *'a staggering blow'*: Alanbrooke, *War Diaries 1939–1945*.

123 *'we have been out-gunned, out-manoeuvred . . . '*: Ireland.

124 *'more German tanks than they knocked out of ours'*: Roberts.

124 *Sergeant Hall's tank might have survived fourteen hits*: See Hall and Wardrop. Also, in a post-war letter, Roberts told Basil Liddell Hart that one tank had survived twenty-five hits: LHA, file 9/28/48.

Chapter 9: The Price of Failure

126 *It was eight o'clock in the morning, and Captain Brian Stone*: Stone, *Prisoner from Alamein* is – not surprisingly – the main source of this account. Some other details have been drawn from the 5th RTR WD and general sources.

130 *'Gun blown to buggery'*: This is from one of the tapes Hall made after the war, but is not in the BTM audio recordings. It comes from the memoir compiled by his daughter, Margaret Roe, which includes much material transcribed from the tapes.

130 *It was a fate that had already consumed scores*: The task of determining exactly how many 5th Tanks soldiers became prisoners of war during the desert war is not easy. The War Diary does not itself give comprehensive figures or name many of them. However, a collation of information from various sources suggests that by the summer of 1942 some sixty or seventy men in the battalion had been captured.

131 *'I received water from them . . . '*: These men are quoted in Bramall (ed.), *The Desert War 1940–1942*.

132 *'We were kicked and slapped . . . '*: Harry Finlayson, 5th RTR, author interviews, 2011–12.

132 *'We were not looked after well'*: Brian Taylor, 5th RTR, author interviews, 2011–12.

Chapter 10: The Tide Turns

134 *Lieutenant-Colonel Walter Hutton*: See the August 1994 issue of *Tank* magazine for his obituary.

135 *In this sense, the 5th Tanks was different from most regiments*: '5th Bn Royal Tank Regiment Battle Drill', dated November 1942, is a fascinating distillation of

their tactical procedures at this time. It includes a section on the regimental net. BTM.

136 *'We all had great faith in him . . . '*: Lay. Bob Lay later became a 'squadron operator', so his views on radio communications are particularly valuable.

136 *'The lads would have done anything for him . . . '*: Forty (ed.), *Jake Wardrop's Diary*.

138 *'I keep getting away with it'*: Hutton, quoted by Solomon.

138 *'he was almost apologising for us . . . '*: Ibid.

140 *Roberts was visited by Lieutenant-General Montgomery*: I have relied on Roberts's account of Alam Halfa in the LHA, but it is repeated in much the same words in his book *From the Desert to the Baltic*.

140 *circulating a secret memo*: The memo survives in 22nd Armoured Brigade WD, NA, WO 169/4251.

141 *Hutton met Churchill and was observed speaking to him*: Wardrop.

142 *'Now I can see the enemy myself through my glasses . . . '*: Roberts memo, LHA.

144 *'Before we start firing we lose a tank'*: 2/Lt Richard Tryon, 4th CLY, quoted in Delaforce, *Churchill's Desert Rats 2*.

144 *'Now everyone opened up'*: Storer. Storer's work is the most impressive and detailed of the 5th Tanks typescript accounts at Bovington, many of which were produced for circulation in the authors' families. Storer, like Crickmay, had endured the early battles of the desert war in 6th RTR, but by the time of Alam Halfa had been transferred to the 5th.

144 *'Here they come, Five, hold your fire . . . '*: Wardrop.

145 *'between ten and twelve o'clock we were bombed . . . '*: Liddell Hart (ed.), *The Rommel Papers*.

145 *The 4th Armoured Brigade, sweeping along in its Honeys*: Both Rommel and Delaforce allude to the effect of these actions.

146 *'We had heard of a change in command'*: Storer.

146 *'It is impossible to exaggerate the difference . . . '*: Geoffrey Waterson, 5th RTR, whose memoir appears on the BBC WW2 People's War website.

147 *'in the minds of many, as far as armour is concerned . . . '*: Roberts memo dated 15 September 1942, 22nd Armoured Brigade WD.

148 *'Only those who have experienced a similar decision . . . '*: Stimpson.

148 *In the plan they rehearsed . . .*: The 5th RTR and 22nd Armoured Brigade WDs contain a wealth of information about the planning.

149 *The Italian Folgore Parachute Division*: This information comes from intelligence assessments in 22nd Armoured Brigade WD.

149 *'The German Afrika Korps and the Italian Libyan Army . . . '*: 5th RTR WD.

151 *'the "Baker" tank of our troop . . . '*: Storer.

151 *'I didn't think Paddy would be doing much smoking . . . '*: Wardrop.

153 *'the Italians must have felt all hell had been let loose . . . '*: Roberts quoted in Delaforce.

154 *'The 5th were a regular battalion . . . '*: Waterson.

155 *'What do you think of the 8th army now . . . '*: Letter dated 16 November 1942, Bull family.

Chapter 11: The Drive to Tripoli

156 *'The bugle had blown and we couldn't stop!'*: Forty (ed.), *Jake Wardrop's Diary*.

157 *At one point they were to convert to the new Sherman tank*: 5th RTR WD, which in 1943 becomes WO 169/9365.

158 *'If it goes on like this . . . '*: Liddell Hart (ed.), *The Rommel Papers*.

159 *turkey, pork, vegetables and beer*: 5th RTR WD. Wardrop, Storer and others describe the festivities.

159 *'Home on the Range'*: Bob Lay, 5th RTR, produced a 'Desert Songs' pamphlet with these and other lyrics.

160 *Wireless operators much preferred the Sherman*: See, for example, Storer.

162 *The 5th Seaforths in the Highland Division*: See Borthwick, *Battalion*.

162 *'snipe shoot'*: The WD describes it as such. The '5th Bn Royal Tank Regiment Battle Drill' at BTM gives a good working definition of the term.

162 *carrying boot polish and Blanco*: Delaforce, *Churchill's Desert Rats*.

163 *'The drill and turnout by the 5th R.T.R. was perfect . . . '*: Geoffrey Waterson, 5th RTR, memoir on BBC WW2 People's War website.

163 *'I felt a large lump rise in my throat . . . '*: Alanbrooke, *War Diaries 1939–1945*.

163 *'After the war, when a man is asked . . . '*: Churchill's speech has been reproduced in many places, among them Delaforce.

164 *Quite a few of those who heard Churchill's words*: For example Waterson.

164 *'I was pleased because I'd changed gear long enough'*: Wardrop.

Chapter 12: The Finishing Line

166 *he kept up a steady stream of reports to his brigadier*: Quite a few survive in the 22nd Armoured Brigade WD for 1943, NA, WO 169/8903.

166 *'His aim at all times has been to kill Germans . . . '*: Citation for G. Thomson's MC, *London Gazette*, 25 November 1943.

167 *'He didn't suffer fools . . . '*: Mike Jeffrey, 2nd RGH, author interviews, 2011.

167 *Ward did not like the Crusader when it first appeared . . . :* Indeed, Mike Jeffrey says that Ward unilaterally swapped his Crusaders for the 2nd RGH's Honeys at one point when two squadrons met in the desert. Ward, it seemed, had bowed to the inevitable by early 1943.

167 *anything up to twenty-two Crusaders*: 5th RTR WD for 1943, WO 169/9365.

169 *From around ten in the morning shells started to drop*: Ibid.

170 *'crazy bugger'*: Solomon.

170 *'The traffic carried on, bullets pinging around them . . . '*: Brian Taylor, 5th RTR, author interviews, 2011–12.

171 *It was on 6 March 1943 that the attack finally came*: The accounts in Liddell Hart (ed.), *The Rommel Papers*, 22nd Armoured Brigade WD and Delaforce, *Churchill's Desert Rats 2* were all useful.

171 *'They just let the tanks come on . . . '*: Solomon.

171 *The 1st RTR claimed eleven of those kills*: 22nd Armoured Brigade WD.

172 *'A great gloom settled over us all'*: Liddell Hart (ed.). The German general, like Napoleon in Egypt in 1799, knew the value of escaping a doomed army far from home.

172 *'With the light tanks sent out in advance . . . '*: Ibid.

175 *'If they happen to run out of ammo . . . '*: Forty (ed.), *Jake Wardrop's Diary*.

176 *'They were big lads, over six foot . . . '*: Solomon.

176 *'a Tiger tank appeared on top of a ridge . . . '*: Lt-Col Michael Carver, 'Report on Operations 6–9th May', part of the 22nd Armoured Brigade WD.

177 *Opening up with 75mm high-explosive shells . . . *: 5th RTR and 22nd Armoured Brigade WDs.

178 *'it was all very moving'*: Solomon.

178 *'Carry yer bag, mate?'*: Wardrop has these details.

178 *'We have taken today approx 5000 [prisoners of war] . . . '*: 22nd Armoured Brigade WD.

179 *'we had quite a lot to drink . . . '*: Forty (ed.).

179 *'we missed a lot of loot . . . '*: Bill Chorley, 5th RTR, letters home, shared with me by his son Bruce Chorley.

180 *'Over and over again I was with the boys . . . '*: Stone, *Prisoner from Alamein*.

181 *'Yet again this officer has shown outstanding . . . '*: Ward's DSO citation is in NA, WO 375/25.

181 *'the performance of this regiment . . . '*: WO 375/25.

182 *'very big stuff'*: Roy Dixon, 5th RTR, author interviews 2010–12.

183 *he unceremoniously sacked Hutton*: My account relies upon Wilson, *Press on Regardless*.

184 *'as he passed I could see that he was crying . . . '*: Wardrop.

184 *'it was a terrible day for the battalion . . . '*: Storer.

184 *'The Fighting Fifth is ready . . . '*: The poem is reproduced in Forty (ed).

184 *'So for miles in the desert they travelled . . . '*: Bob Lay, 'Desert Songs' pamphlet.

Chapter 13: Into Italy

187 *'a bit pleased with itself'*: Unpublished memoir, Crickmay.

188 *'at last getting a little publicity after three years . . . '*: Letter dated 26 May 1943, Crickmay.

188 *'like a shot-putter'*: Unpublished memoir, Crickmay.

188 *'like a great white fish'*: Solomon.

189 *'Why did he do it? . . . '*: Unpublished memoir, Crickmay.

189 *much thought to the type of fighting they would face in Italy*: The 22nd Armoured Brigade WD for 1943, WO 169/8903, has details of training exercises conducted in Libya, including plans for advance in 'enclosed country'.

191 *'Whenever I see a squadron roaring across . . . '*: Letter dated 6 March 1943, Crickmay.

191 *'I am not even sure that I want to go to 6th RTR . . . '*: Letter dated 21 June 1943, Crickmay.

191 *his soldiers would regard him as unusually close*: Lay.

192 *'pale-skin type'*: Wardrop. Wardrop uses this phrase about Wilson in notes about the 5th's COs that were left out of his published diary. His excoriation of Wilson is quoted later by me in more detail (see page 232). In this same passage, Wardrop says Wilson was known as a 'yellow belly' from the 'November business', i.e. Operation Crusader.

194 *'On a single road with ditches and trees . . . '*: Unpublished memoir, Crickmay.

195 *'we had to use our ingenuity to improve . . . '*: Ron Maple, 5th RTR, quoted in Wilson, *Press on Regardless*.

195 *Scafati turned into a nerve-racking, day-long fight*: Well described by Delaforce, *Churchill's Desert Rats 2*.

196 *The following day, 29 September*: Daily details from 5th RTR WD, WO 169/9365.

196 *'All the tanks which have been lost . . . '*: Wilson's long account of the Italian campaign is in a letter to the CO of 6th RTR, included in the unit's WD.

197 *'The greeting by ecstatic, jubilant . . . '*: Unpublished memoir, Crickmay.

197 *'The local inhabitants are just ghastly'*: Wilson, letter to CO, 6th RTR WD.

197 *'We've got a tame hen on the tank'*: Letter dated 19 October 1943, Bull family.

199 *decided there was nothing for it but to go forward on foot*: Details of the raid come from Crickmay's MC citation, WO 373/4. Perhaps typically for someone of his generation, he does not refer to the incident in his private memoir of the war.

202 *'come up to within the ten-mile range of the set'*: Wardrop. This story exists in a few different forms. It is recounted by Edward Wilson in his history, *Press on Regardless*, and by Norman Smith, also of 5th RTR, in his book *Tank Soldier*; they attribute different words to Doyle, but with a similar message. This quotation comes from an unpublished passage in Wardrop's notebooks. Since his note was written in late 1944, much closer to the event that Wilson or Smith's accounts, I have used Wardrop's formulation.

203 *Lieutenant-Colonel Wilson's order was therefore ignored*: Stimpson. Wardrop also refers to the steel helmets order in the unpublished section of his diary.

203 *'excessive cheeriness'*: Letter from Maj A. Cox dated 31 July, Crickmay.

Chapter 14: Homecoming

206 *'They were banging with spanners and crowbars . . . '*: Solomon. Wardrop and others also describe the homecoming evocatively.

207 *'food ration card for appropriate number of days . . . '*: 22nd Armoured Brigade WD.

207 *They tied the knot on 24 February 1944*: Information, including wedding certificate, Bull family.

207 *With Deryck MacDonald*: Brenda MacDonald, author interviews, 2011–12.

209 'a smashing attack of the blues . . . ': Forty (ed.), *Jake Wardrop's Diary*.

210 'I want to make sure . . . ': Wardrop. The letter, dated 1 November 1943, was written before he left Italy. It is not included in Forty's edition of his diary.

211 'Some of us . . . ': This was Captain R. T. Chesterfield, who had been serving since Tobruk in 1941. The quote comes via his son, from a private memoir.

211 'Several non-commissioned officers . . . ': Carver, *Out of Step*.

212 'Our first impression of it . . . ': Forty (ed.).

213 *Reliability had indeed been designated the principal quality*: See Buckley, *British Armour in the Normandy Campaign 1944*.

214 *had poor HE capability*: High-explosive rounds were developed for these anti-tank guns but they were rarely fielded.

214 *the 5th Tanks had practised a technique*: The 22nd Armoured Brigade WD records a demonstration of this technique by 5th RTR.

215 'If they are to be effectively and quickly dealt with . . . ': Ibid.

220 'None of the men in the "Skins" had seen action . . . ': Smith, *Tank Soldier*.

220 *This 'gripping', as the old sweats called it*: Tom Schofield, 5th RTR, author interviews, 2011–12.

221 *When an American GI was found drowned in King's Lynn*: Ibid.

221 'I was almost always in my office until 22.00 hrs . . . ': Unpublished memoir, Crickmay.

222 'the only cheers came from the officers': Schofield. Smith, *Tank Soldier*, also gives a negative account of Monty's Griff talk. Wardrop and one or two others offer a less jaundiced view of his reception.

Chapter 15: The Revolt

223 'Screaming Willy': Lay.

224 'He had repeatedly proven himself to be . . . ': Hall's citation in the NA, WO 373/26.

224 *It was generally reckoned that he was in charge*: Lay.

225 'The spirit of the battalion was second to none': Hutton wrote this in the foreword to Forty (ed.), *Jake Wardrop's Diary*.

225 'No Leave, No Second Front': Gerry Solomon, among others, recalls this.

225 *the 5th was known to be 'bolshie'*: Tom Schofield, 5th RTR, author interviews, 2011–12. Some veterans baulk at the use of the word 'bolshie', which clearly had stronger connotations in 1944 than it might now, but Schofield used it unprompted when we spoke.

226 *more than a thousand soldiers Absent Without Leave*: According to Brigadier James Hargest, military observer with XXX Corps, NA, CAB 106/1060.

226 'Some of the old desert men suggested [Wilson] might meet with an accident . . . ': This remarkable claim is made by Norman Smith, B Squadron, in his memoir *Tank Soldier*.

226 'Dicker Wilson simply wasn't up to the job': Roy Dixon, 5th RTR, author interviews, 2010–12.

226 *His decision . . . one Sunday*: Lay and Schofield.

227 *'a slur on all we had done so far'*: Lay.

227 *Sergeant Emmin Hall, however, refused*: Good written sources on what happened are Edward Wilson's book *Press on Regardless*, and Bill Green's article on Emmin Hall in the BTM.

228 *the requirements of duty and gratitude meant supporting his CO*: This becomes clear from Crickmay's letters.

228 *'Many, probably most, were unhappy . . . '*: Wilson, *Press on Regardless*. Wilson was a subaltern in B Squadron at the time.

228 *'got things moving'*: Lay.

230 *On 4 May the thunderbolt finally fell on Shakers Wood*: 5th RTR War Diary for 1944, WO 171/867.

230 *'You will be sorry to hear my colonel and 2 i/c have both got the sack . . . '*: Letter dated 26 May 1944, the one really candid expression of views on the subject in the Crickmay Papers.

230 *known throughout the RTR as Gus Holliman*: In *Out of Step*, Carver writes touchingly about his friendship with Holliman. Details also from Wilson, and Holliman's obituary in *Tank* magazine (August 1994).

231 *day passes for a final trip to London*: 5th RTR WD.

232 *as he left 5 RTR's camp, he had cried again*: Bill Green.

232 *'Fat, rather short, frightened, blusterer . . . '*: Wardrop. His candid notes on his various COs were, perhaps unsurprisingly, excluded from the published editions of his diary.

Chapter 16: Into the Hedgerows

234 *It was the middle of the day on 7 June*: 5th RTR WD, Norman Smith, *Tank Soldier* and others give accounts of the landing.

235 *'the little ships of our squadron plunging along . . . '*: Unpublished memoir, Crickmay.

235 *'So much for D+1 . . . '*: Ibid.

236 *Coming up a gentle rise*: 5th RTR WD and Solomon.

238 *distance of sixty yards*: There were different marks of this weapon, but the one introduced early in 1944 had a sixty-metre range.

238 *'I've had it in a big way'*: Roy Dixon, 5th RTR, author interviews, 2010–12.

239 *contested by the Panzer Lehr Division*: The essential reference for the German side of these battles is Zetterling, *Normandy 1944*. I have also used Lefèvre, *Panzers in Normandy*.

240 *'I . . . looked down into the turret . . . '*: Dixon. Also of interest is Jarymowycz, *Tank Tactics*. Jarymowycz's main focus is the Canadian and US armoured forces, and he takes a generally dim view of British leadership and tactics in Normandy.

240 *the 1st Battalion of Rifle Brigade . . . were beaten back by the Germans*: The fight for 'Essex Wood' is described in 5th RTR WD, 22nd Armoured Brigade

WD, Delaforce, *Churchill's Desert Rats 2* and Jacquet, *Tilly-sur-Seulles*.

241 *'They did not seem to have a great deal of idea . . . '*: Forty (ed.), *Jake Wardrop's Diary*.

241 *'They appeared to be very new, and too spick and span . . . '*: Storer.

242 *'It was some tank and no mistake'*: Forty (ed.).

243 *had gone from having eighty-six combat-ready tanks to just twenty-three*: Zetterling.

243 *Montgomery had been obliged to give artillery and armour a major role*: See Buckley, *British Armour in the Normandy Campaign*.

244 *16 per cent of the 2nd Army's strength but 71 per cent of its casualties*: Ibid.

244 *'the need for more infantry was felt time and again'*: This comes from a memo on the first week's fighting appended to the 22nd Armoured Brigade WD, WO 171/619 , as Appendix Y NA.

Chapter 17: Villers–Bocage

245 *The morning of 13 June presented*: There are many accounts of Wittman's action, including Lefèvre, *Panzers in Normandy*, and a couple of others originally published in French under the After the Battle imprint. *Churchill's Desert Rats 2* by Patrick Delaforce and Neillands are also very useful.

248 *The 5th Tanks were second in the 22nd Brigade's order of march*: 22nd Armoured Brigade WD.

248 *'but heart-breaking and frightening . . . '*: 'Ibby' Aird, 4th CLY, quoted in Delaforce.

249 *A couple of surviving Yeomanry Fireflies and infantry crewing*: According to Schneider, *Tigers in Normandy*, two were disabled by Fireflies and two by six-pounders. This suggested that up to five Tigers were lost in Villers-Bocage on 13 September: Wittman's vehicle and four from Mobius's company. However, it is possible that a couple of machines from the latter company were recovered damaged and recorded in the returns cited by Zetterling (in *Normandy 1944*) as being out of action but repairable.

249 *'nightmare'*: Porter, *1st SS Panzer Corps at Villers-Bocage*.

250 *Sergeant Jake Wardrop, commanding his Firefly*: Forty (ed.), *Jake Wardrop's Diary*.

250 *'I discovered then that I was having some difficulty . . . '*: Ibid.

251 *The troop leader had fled his tank*: The exact story of which tanks were abandoned in working order had to be assembled from several different sources, including Wardrop and the account of Bill Chorley, 5th RTR, in BTM. The 5th RTR WD appendix on casualties in north-west Europe itemises vehicles and people lost, specifying who was on which crew, as well as which vehicles were abandoned at Villers-Bocage despite being undamaged by enemy fire.

251 *Another commander, Lance Corporal Stainton*: Chorley. He was one of the men captured.

252 *the 4th CLY had lost twenty-five tanks*: This is the breakdown given in the 22nd Armoured Brigade WD.

252 *'Where did you leave the tank, sir?'*: George Stimpson, 5th RTR, letter to

Patrick Delaforce, in the latter's papers at the IWM. Stimpson suggests here and in his memoirs that this conversation took place about a fortnight after they arrived in Normandy, i.e. one week *after* Villers-Bocage, but there is no evidence to support this in the WD and other sources. Rather, the abandonment of Allen's tank is recorded at Villers-Bocage in the unit WD.

253 *By the afternoon a full-scale battle was in progress*: I used many descriptions of the Battle of the Box, including from Wardrop, Storer and Lay, and from Delaforce and Neillands, quoting other protagonists.

254 *'Whaddya want? A Serenade or an Obligato?'*: Unpublished memoir, Crickmay.

255 *'Be prepared to engage with the 95 [howitzers]'*: Wardrop, from notes he wrote about the various COs that were not included in Forty or other published editions.

255 *'. . . SS men they were, all washed and shaved . . .'*: While the SS Heavy Tank Battalion did have a small number of infantry with it, Wardrop's attackers were more likely Wehrmacht soldiers from the 2nd Panzer Division.

255 *'confident that we could hold the position . . .'*: Carver, *Out of Step*.

255 *anything up fifteen of 101st Heavy Battalion's Tiger tanks*: Returns cited by Zetterling. In terms of the detail of how nine of these vehicles came to be destroyed, accounts such as Schneider, *Tigers in Normandy*, suggest that five or six Tigers may have been lost in and around the village on 13–14 June. Three more Tigers of the 3rd Company, 101st Heavy Tank Battalion were destroyed by aerial bombing near Évrecy on 15th. While the latter incident would not be considered by some as part of the 7th Armoured Division's battle, in my view it is fair to do so, since this company was part of the concentration of German assets designed to counter the British push, even though the Desert Rats had pulled back by that time.

256 *'Right that's it. Let's go'*: Unpublished memoir, Crickmay.

256 *'The enemy attack was completely smashed'*: Ibid.

256 *were dispatched to the Pioneer Corps*: Eric Smith, 5th RTR, IWM interview 28675.

257 *'should have been court-martialled had he not been captured'*: Roy Dixon, 5th RTR, author interviews, 2010–12.

258 *'The idea of a massed weight of armour . . .'*: From Hinde's Appendix Y to 22nd Armoured Brigade WD, WO 171/619.

258 *Brigadier Peter Pyman, an RTR officer*: See Buckley, *British Armour in the Normandy Campaign 1944*.

259 *'We have nothing to fear from the Panther . . .'*: Ibid.

259 *'dismal failure'*: Hargest's illuminating dispatches from the front are in the NA, CAB 106/1060.

259 *'A great deal of their failure is due to the retention . . .'*: Hargest is quoted, for example by Buckley, as a critic of the Royal Armoured Corps in general but, as this passage makes clear, it was the cavalry he had no time for.

260 *These remarks . . . conformed to the views of many of the RTR officers*: See Carver, *Out of Step*, on his argument with General Horrocks.

Chapter 18: Pluto's Tiger

263 *'It was a regular thing that he would do . . . '*: Tom Schofield, 5th RTR, author interviews, 2011–12.

263 *'Short, stocky, with black hair . . . '*: Smith, *Tank Soldier*.

263 *'a sturdy chap like a little bulldog, tough'*: Harry Ireland, 5th RTR, unpublished memoir, BTM.

263 *the Panther's frontal armour could be pierced at seven hundred yards*: The 22nd Armoured Brigade WD for July–December 1944, NA, WO 171/620, says the demonstration happened on 10 July 1944.

264 *'Please convey to all ranks my great satisfaction . . . '*: Ibid, entry dated 17 July.

264 *They had lost more men killed and wounded than the Allies*: See Badsey, *Normandy 1944* or Buckley, *British Armour in the Normandy Campaign 1944* for accounts of the relative losses in Normandy and the failings of German strategy. Zetterling, *Normandy 1944*, offers the counter-point.

264 *This idea was communicated down through the chain of command*: While some of Monty's critics argue that this 'strategy' was an *ex post facto* rationalisation of poor British progress, it is clear that British troops had been briefed to this effect, at least by late July. For example, in a letter dated 16 August 1944 Crickmay reflects on pinning the Germans down while the Americans go 'swanning about'.

266 *German generals had placed three divisions*: See Lodieu, *Operation Goodwood* and Daglish, *Operation Goodwood* for two highly detailed accounts of the battle.

266 *The German divisions in question had already taken many beatings*: Zetterling.

267 *Major-General Roberts had made representations*: Roberts, *From the Desert to the Baltic*.

267 *'Bloody well get a move on or you will be sacked!'*: Leakey, *Leakey's Luck*. This happened during the fight for Hill 112, the bully in question being Major General G. I. Thomas of the 43rd Division.

268 *one company of Tigers was caught by the bombing*: See Lefèvre, *Panzers in Normandy*, for photographs of this.

269 *It was around half past nine that things started to get tougher*: Lodieu gives a good sense of the timings.

269 *there was not enough space to deploy his units*: Roberts.

270 *'The turret was blazing well'*: Geoffrey Waterson, 5th RTR, memoir on BBC WW2 People's War website.

270 *'tanks brewing up with flames belching . . . '*: Jack Thorpe, Fife and Forfar Yeomanry, quoted in Daglish.

271 *'None of us was looking forward to the morning . . . '*: Bill Close, 3rd RTR, quoted in Lodieu.

271 *'We had gone about a thousand yards . . . '*: Forty (ed.), *Jake Wardrop's Diary*.

272 *As they moved on Soliers*: I have relied on the written accounts of Norman Smith, Syd Storer and Geoffrey Waterson in B Squadron, as well as interviews in 2011 with Tony Crassweller, 1st RB, who was commanding one of the two infantry platoons on the day.

274 *'their shots flying just over the top of the Firefly's turret'*: Smith.

274 *'on the assumption that a Tiger tank commander . . . '*: Ibid.

275 *While there would be conflicting claims*: Harry Ireland, Pluto's gunner, actually claimed to have knocked out three Tigers, but German records give the lie to this. The 22nd Armoured Brigade WD also carries the claim of three Tigers. Schneider, in *Tigers in Normandy*, says that Tiger 231 of the 101st Heavy Tank Battalion was knocked out near Bourguébus, and although he confuses the date (saying it was the 20th rather than the 19th) this was almost certainly Pluto's Tiger. Interestingly, Schneider also credits 5th Tanks with knocking out a Tiger during the fighting of the late afternoon or early evening of 18 July, and there is some evidence from the memoir later produced by Harry Ireland that they may also have accounted for this vehicle. While this is probably true, in my view it cannot however be credited to the 5th Tanks as unambiguously as the one on 19 July.

275 *around 213 of the 'lost' British tanks . . . were actually destroyed*: 21st Army Group Royal Armoured Corps Equipment States, NA, WO 205/112. The 213 figure is actually for all tank losses during 17–20 July. Since some other forces in the Army Group were engaged elsewhere during these days the actual number lost during Goodwood was probably around two hundred.

276 *Casualty figures for Goodwood give the lie*: VIII Corps Medical Services WD, NA, WO 177/342.

276 *Many in the 5th Tanks blamed Monty*: The anger was still evident talking to Bob Lay and Tom Schofield more than sixty-six years later.

276 *'Going to the 5th Tanks had probably saved my life'*: Schofield.

276 *'Perhaps the 11th Armoured were too gung ho . . . '*: Tony Crassweller, 1st RB, author interviews, 2011–12.

277 *they were actually safer in them*: WO 205/112 shows that, up to 21 July, 493 or 35 per cent of the British Shermans being used in Normandy had been destroyed in action, as opposed to 81 or 23 per cent of the Cromwells – a significant difference. Some of this can be explained by the fact that the main user of Cromwells, 7th Armoured Division, had been taken out of the battle line at times, whereas Sherman-equipped brigades were constantly supporting the infantry. However, it was recognised by British army operational analysis (described, for example, in Buckley, *British Armour in the Normandy Campaign 1944*) that the Sherman was more likely to burn when struck by enemy fire, a fact attributed by research to its ammunition stowage arrangements. Hits to the Cromwell, in other words, were less likely to ignite its ammunition. The British vehicle's lower profile also made it a less conspicuous target and its greater speed could also help its survival, as Jake Wardrop had discovered when his Sherman Firefly was hit. Eric Stevenson, 5th RTR and Mike Carver 1st RTR, were among the minority who argued the Cromwell was the better machine, rejecting the received wisdom of the 1944 tank park.

277 *The Orne bridgehead was too small*: Unpublished memoir, Crickmay.

277 *'For the first time we had the feeling to have failed'*: Freiherr von Rosen, quoted in Daglish.

278 *The crowd of crews hanging about*: Eric Stevenson, 5th RTR, arrived in the echelon at this time. Correspondence with the author, 2011–12.

278 *'Anybody is liable to crack'*: Forty (ed.).

279 *'It will be a great luxury . . . '*: Letter dated 6 July 1944, Crickmay.

279 *'The war here is a good deal less attractive . . . '*: Letter dated 16 August 1944, Crickmay.

Chapter 19: The Fifth's Dark Hour

280 *'press on regardless'*: Both Delaforce and Neillands record the atmosphere of pressure in their Desert Rats histories.

282 *Lieutenant Tony Crassweller from I Company*: Author interviews, 2011–12.

282 *3 Troop under Lieutenant Roy Dixon pulled up*: Roy Dixon, 5th RTR, author interviews, 2010–12.

282 *'If you wanted to move fast . . . '*: Ibid.

283 *4 Troop had made its way to Point 138*: 22nd Armoured Brigade WD.

284 *Lieutenant-Colonel Holliman fed B Squadron into La Lande*: 5th RTR WD. The accounts of Syd Storer, Harry Ireland and Norman Smith describe the action from B Squadron's perspective.

285 *Lance Corporal Shute, had moved on foot*: Details from Shute's Military Medal citation in the NA, WO 373/50.

286 *'I've tried everything I can to get you out . . . '*: Harry Ireland, 5th RTR, unpublished memoir, BTM.

287 *'I thought, This is it, and just prayed'*: Norman Smith, *Tank Soldier*.

287 *'signs of the jitters'*: Solomon.

287 *'I'd got a sergeant who'd gone bomb-happy . . . '*: Eric Smith, 5th RTR, IWM interview 28675.

288 *'What do you think, Smudger? . . . '*: Ibid.

288 *'hell-for-leather'*: Norman Smith.

288 *'We all walked around to see who was there . . . '*: Forty (ed.), *Jake Wardrop's Diary*.

289 *seven were dead for sure, twenty-three wounded and eight missing*: 5th RTR WD.

289 *'For Christ's sake slow down!'*: Solomon.

290 *During that period the corps had 2141 men killed*: VIII Corps Medical Services WD, NA, WO 177/342.

290 *50 per cent became casualties while inside their vehicles*: Buckley, *British Armour in the Normandy Campaign 1944*, citing War Office records.

290 *'The place seems to be a model . . . '*: Brigadier James Hargest, NA, CAB 106/1060.

291 *On 17 August forty new soldiers arrived*: 5th RTR WD.

292 *'The infantryman can find opportunities for lying low . . . '*: Verney in Neillands.

293 *He pointed out that the 1/6th Queen's, the worst-hit*: Verney, in a letter to Basil Liddell Hart, LHA, file 29/6/55.

293 *'When the moment came for them to form up . . . '*: Ibid.

294 *'Once you were on your feet'*: Tony Crassweller, author interviews, 2011–12.

294 *'suffered far higher casualties than they should have'*: Verney, letter to Liddell Hart.

294 *'the infantry soldier is regarded by our own troops . . . '*: Intelligence summary of LXXXIX Corps, translation in Verney Papers, LHA, file 4/1-6.

295 *August 1944 was to prove the division's worst month*: Desertions statistics, 21st Army Group Adjutant General's Dept WD, NA, WO 171/182.

296 *'shit hot'*: Tom Schofield, 5th RTR, author interviews, 2010–12.

296 *'Skins in the lead again until they meet . . . '*: Norman Hewison, 1st RTR, quoted in Delaforce, *Churchill's Desert Rats*.

Chapter 20: Breakout

299 *'I've been a major for ten days . . . '*: Letter dated 16 August 1944, Crickmay. The preceding paragraphs are based on his letters throughout the war.

299 *only a minority were Alamein veterans by this time*: Lay, plus analysis of the WD and other sources.

300 *'had been around a bit'*: Forty (ed.), *Jake Wardrop's Diary*.

300 *'he was not overly familiar . . . '*: Bob Lay, who remains friendly with Crickmay's family to this day.

300 *He was the fifth OC to lead C Squadron*: Following Majors Maunsell, Burt and Adams, and Captain Messent.

300 *struggling to keep his fear under control*: A couple of photocopied pages of Butler's diary, describing these feelings, were contained in a letter from Gordon Johnson, 5th RTR, to Patrick Delaforce. The pages are now with Delaforce's papers in the IWM.

300 *the twitching in his leg or shaking of his hands*: All described in Wardrop's extraordinary diary.

302 *Lieutenant Baker, had lasted just a few days*: Gordon Johnson, 5th RTR, letter dated 11 October 1993, Delaforce Papers IWM.

302 *'That worm Lt Hedges . . . '*: Forty (ed.).

302 *The army medical guidelines for dealing with 'battle exhaustion'*: See VIII Corps medical standing orders in WD, WO 177/342.

302 *'unit Medical Officers are reminded . . . '*: Ibid.

303 *Some . . . were found easier jobs*: The weekly return of officers attached to the 5th RTR WD gives details of 'officers quitting the unit'.

303 *7th Armoured Division had actually suffered significantly fewer cases*: Casualty returns in WO 177/342.

303 *Among infantry divisions in Normandy*: Ibid.

304 *'It must be accepted that in the strain of modern war . . . '*: This is from a Quarterly Report from Brig Hughes appended to the WD, WO 177/342.

304 *'the crime of disloyalty to his country . . . '*: Ibid.

304 *By 21 August 5th Tanks was motoring eastwards*: 5th RTR WD, Delaforce, *Churchill's Desert Rats 2* and Neillands.

305 *'A dispatch rider went flying past us ... '*: Tony Crassweller, 1st RB, author interviews, 2011–12.

306 *'finishing off'*: Wardrop. Storer and Norman Smith, among others in 5th RTR, also describe Fervaques.

306 *'We were engulfed literally by dozens of men ... '*: Smith, *Tank Soldier*.

307 *nearly 300,000 were casualties*: Zetterling, *Normandy 1944*, breaks this down into 198,000 missing/prisoners, 67,000 wounded and 23,000 killed. Zetterling ridicules figures from Badsey, *Normandy 1944*, claiming 440,000 casualties out of one million Germans fighting in the battle for Normandy. Zetterling's methodology, in using German military primary sources, is undoubtedly more sound, which is why I have adopted his figures. However, some caveats are necessary. A figure of one million could be applied to all of the German armed forces elements fighting in the western front (i.e. France, Belgium and the Netherlands). Zetterling's estimate for 'ground combat elements' (i.e. army, SS and Luftwaffe field troops with a specific ground combat role) in the western command is 880,000. Similarly, his 500,000 for Normandy excludes most Luftwaffe and naval units in northern France. While detailed work would need to be done on naval and air force casualties, it is likely that counting these in would bridge some of the gap between Zetterling's total casualty estimate of nearly 300,000 and Badsey's of 440,000.

308 *'they were stripped of any watches, cameras ... '*: Tom Schofield, 5th RTR, author interviews, 2011–12.

308 *'We called ourselves the Fighting Fifth ... '*: Eric Stevenson, 5th RTR, from his privately published memoir, *A Kick Out of Life*.

309 *'We felt fairly exposed as we set out'*: Crickmay gives an extensive account of the Ghent affair in his unpublished memoir.

310 *'a decision to fight on would reduce the number ... '*: Brigadier Mackeson's account is appended to the 22nd Armoured Brigade WD.

311 *wondering whether General Brun had tricked them all*: Unpublished memoir, Crickmay.

Chapter 21: Bloodied but Unbowed

313 *'a tough character, experienced and confident'*: Henry Hadwin, 5th RTR, correspondence with the author, 2010–11.

313 *'competent yet unassuming ... he never raised his voice nor bullied his men'*: Eric Stevenson, 5th RTR, correspondence with the author, 2011–12.

313 *'willing to listen'*: Bob Lay, among others, gives this qualification.

314 *Stevenson's crew opened up with the tank's two machine guns*: This account rests in part on Stevenson's privately published memoir, *A Kick Out of Life*, as well as our correspondence.

316 *'In the village there was an English-speaking priest ... '*: The letter was retained by the family and was shared with me by David Bull.

317 *'To come all that way and die near the end ... '*: Hadwin.

317 *Under the direction of Captain Butler:* Wardrop observed this.

318 *one of the crewmen in Butler's tank:* Gordon Johnson, Delaforce Papers, IWM.

318 *found Butler withdrawn and difficult:* Unpublished memoir, Crickmay.

318 *'that the only good German was a dead one':* Edward Wilson, in *Press on Regardless*, uses this phrase to describe the attitude of some in the 5th RTR during the final months of war.

319 *'... then the stupid pig-headed Boches infantry ...':* Forty (ed.), *Jake Wardrop's Diary.*

320 *'It might not have been a good thing to ...':* This episode appears only in Wardrop's manuscript diary, having been edited out of the published version.

320 *claimed to have bedded Belgians:* Amorous adventures punctuated Norman Smith's memoirs, just as Wardrop seemed able to find booze pretty much anywhere.

321 *the proportion accounted for by the hand-held anti-tank weapons:* Buckley, *British Armour in the Normandy Campaign 1944.*

322 *the 7th Armoured Division needed seventy thousand gallons:* Delaforce, *Churchill's Desert Rats 2.*

323 *crossed the Dutch border on 22 September:* 5th RTR WD.

323 *Wood was ten years older, rode his subalterns hard:* These contrasts were highlighted by Eric Stevenson and Wilson, both B Squadron subalterns who served under the two very different OCs.

324 *'I felt that the lives of the men ...':* Stevenson, *A Kick Out of Life.*

324 *'[Wood] simply could not or would not adapt ...':* Wilson.

325 *Among those who smartened up for the investiture:* 5th RTR WD lists them.

325 *catching Laurence Olivier's* Henry V: Unpublished memoir, Crickmay.

325 *Count Basie Orchestra and Tommy Dorsey's band:* Tom Schofield, 5th RTR, author interviews, 2011–12. Norman Smith also writes about their liking of big bands, and indeed Brussels brothels.

326 *'sober but passed in a reasonable degree of comfort ...':* Letter dated 27 December 1944, Crickmay.

326 *'The square heads have produced ...':* Letter dated 2 January 1945, Crickmay.

326 *'listening on the radio to the Yanks ...':* Wardrop.

326 *'We became acquainted with trip wires ...':* Letter dated 27 January 1945, Crickmay.

327 *Pluto himself was packed off to a training job:* The 5th RTR WD for 1945, WO 171/4711, reveals the attempts of the battalion subsequently to get Sgt Ellis back, once a different CO was in charge.

328 *'I realised now more than ever that I was solely dependent ...':* Stimpson.

328 *'nothing useful since we arrived in Holland ...':* Forty (ed.).

Chapter 22: Into the Reich

330 *Lieutenant-Colonel Holliman was in a better mood than many:* Holliman family, author interview.

331 *he had briefed the battalion in a local cinema on 16 January*: 5th RTR WD for 1945, NA, WO 171/4711.

331 *'We all believed'*: Wilson, *Press on Regardless*.

331 *'always an unsatisfactory and dangerous situation'*: Unpublished memoir, Crickmay.

332 *The army sent Lieutenant-Colonel Rea Leakey*: Details from *Leakey's Luck*, which he wrote with George Forty. One of Leakey's three MCs was the Czech award.

332 *'Get off this bloody tank, I am moving for cover!'*: Ibid.

333 *'hairy-arsed barbarians'*: Smith, *Tank Soldier*.

333 *'[They] had seldom been long out of action . . . '*: Leakey and Forty, *Leakey's Luck*.

333 *Leakey brought the boyish Roy Dixon*: Roy Dixon, 5th RTR, author interviews, 2010–12.

334 *'stout men'*: Wardrop. This was not part of Forty's published account.

334 *'Cold, and miserable blue . . . '*: Ibid.

334 *a blur of good food, good wine*: Unpublished memoir, Crickmay.

335 *The 5th Tanks entered Germany on 25 March*: 5th RTR WD.

335 *'There will be no brutality about a British Occupation'*: This pamphlet was reissued by the National Archives, Kew, in 2006 as 'Germany 1944: A British Soldier's Pocketbook'.

335 *Half a dozen German-Jewish men*: They are written about by Wilson and Smith, and Bob Lay has discussed them with me. 1st RTR, for some reason, had many more of these Jewish refugee soldiers, and started to receive them in the desert.

336 *'they could expect a fate literally worse than death'*: Smith.

336 *'The breakout in Germany was even more hair-raising . . . '*: Ibid.; also the source of the preceding quote.

337 *'How nice to see you, the war for us is now over'*: Stimpson.

337 *'On the faces of most of the civilians . . . '*: Richard Brett-Smith, 11th Hussars, quoted in Delaforce, *Churchill's Desert Rats 2*.

337 *took cyanide when the British entered his office*: Delaforce.

337 *Sergeant George Stimpson, that diminutive legend*: Wilson.

338 *'Over the years of conflict the idea . . . '*: Unpublished memoir, Crickmay.

338 *'In great form these days . . . '*: Diary entry for 3 April, Wardrop.

338 *'No, you're late'*: Ted Zoeftig, 5th RTR, author interviews, 2010–11.

339 *'Ask him what's on at the pictures'*: The story is told by Wilson, and by Crickmay in his unpublished memoir.

340 *just two men of the 5th RTR as a whole had been killed*: 5th RTR WD.

341 *'Snowy is bazooka'd . . . '*: Wardrop.

341 *'I'm afraid letters of sympathy appear cold-blooded . . . '*: Letter dated 20 September 1944, Crickmay.

342 *'I feel very relieved by the heartening words . . . '*: Letter from Kathleen Harris, Crickmay.

342 *At length Wardrop's Firefly reached a crossroads*: The account of Wardrop's demise relies on George Forty's edition of the diary (which contains Stimpson's letter) and Sgt Emmin Hall's letter to the family in Wardrop's papers, which

was shared with me by Jeff Simpson.

343 *'The two tanks were still and quiet . . . '*: George Stimpson, 5th RTR, quoted in Forty (ed.), *Jake Wardrop's Diary*.

343 *Six of the Welch Fusiliers had also lost their lives*: There is much useful and authoritative detail on this incident and the subsequent battle at Rethem in Russell, *No Triumphant Procession*.

344 *'I know what a shock it must have been . . . '*: Letter from Emmin Hall, Wardrop.

346 *'Here they were even more fanatical . . . '*: Storer.

346 *This proved to be untrue, but undoubtedly inflamed feelings*: The story of the 'massacre' even made it into *The Times*, on 17 April 1945, and the *Illustrated London News*. Russell's book successfully unpacks and demolishes the myth.

346 *'we spotted Germans in the open . . . '*: Joe Cannon, 5th RTR, account of Rethem in BTM.

346 *loaders fused 75mm high-explosive shells on delay*: Ibid.

347 *'No quarter was given'*: Anonymous member, 5th RTR, author interviews. Both Wilson and Smith from B Squadron say in their written accounts that prisoners were not taken at Rethem. I explored the meaning of this with an additional source, who had been present during the fighting. Under condition of anonymity he made clear to me that Germans who tried to surrender were killed. He is the source of the following quote too.

347 *Leakey decided to recce Rethem in person*: Leakey and Forty.

348 *'Blimey Sir! I have not seen so many dead Germans . . . '*: Ibid.

348 *Crickmay . . . was disturbed*: Unpublished memoir, Crickmay.

349 *'We have taken your town for you'*: Stimpson.

349 *the navy had wanted to show the Wehrmacht*: Russell, who also provides the 230 casualties figure for the two Welsh battalions.

349 *'there was a growing euphoria in the air . . . '*: Crickmay.

350 *'Once we were in Germany . . . '*: Tony Crassweller, author interviews, 2011–12.

350 *a fellow member of Chorley's crew disappeared*: Bill Chorley, 5th RTR, memo, BTM.

Chapter 23: Journey's End

351 *all manner of comforts picked up along their odyssey*: Norman Smith mentions this in *Tank Soldier*, as does Crickmay in his memoir and Tom Schofield, 5th RTR, in author interviews, 2011–12.

352 *Trooper Bill Chorley, another C Squadron man*: Bill Chorley, 5th RTR, memo, BTM.

352 *a Panzerfaust flew just behind them*: Lay.

352 *On 29 April German officers had appeared*: 5th RTR WD.

353 *'The first thing that struck us was the incredible tidiness . . . '*: Brett Smith, 11th Hussars, cited in Delaforce, *Churchill's Desert Rats 2*.

353 *'I well remember looking down at that bridge . . . '*: Leakey and Forty, *Leakey's Luck*.

353 *'we realised they were all empty shells'*: Unpublished memoir, Crickmay.

353 *'Well sir, that's that'*: Smith.

354 *'That could only mean one thing . . . '*: Lay.

354 *At the city's Hotel Streits*: Leakey and Forty.

355 *a single shot was accidentally fired, hitting Trooper Cyril Duckett*: Gordon Johnson, 5th RTR, letter in Delaforce Papers, IWM.

355 *VE Day was formally marked on 8 May*: Delaforce and Neillands describe the celebrations across 7th Armoured Division.

355 *'slept at peace with the world'*: Unpublished memoir, Crickmay.

356 *Around ten of the seventy-five men present raised their arms*: Lay.

356 *'Perhaps we were a bit inhibited'*: Smith.

356 *a formal service of thanksgiving was held by the 5th Tanks*: The order of service is in BTM.

356 *My own research shows that 224 members of 5th RTR*: The key data in this regard is a list compiled for me by the Commonwealth War Graves Commission.

357 *When the 1/5th Queen's tallied up how many*: Delaforce.

357 *It was not more than twenty-five or thirty*: This is a rough estimate based on anecdotal evidence from interviews. RTR historical sources suggest one dozen members of 5th RTR who had fought all the way through the war were assembled for the Berlin Victory Parade in 1945. I have not, however, been able to find a list of their names.

357 *That included three officers*: There is greater certainty about the path of 5th RTR's officers because most of the Weekly Returns of Officers survive, attached to the various files of the 5th RTR WD in the NA. Deryck MacDonald, although he went away to 6th and 7th RTR for a few months in 1942, and a couple of training courses, is the only officer who could reasonably have claimed to have served in the battalion from the start of the war to its end.

357 *the fate of all 194 officers*: This is my work based on the weekly returns, WD and all of the accounts consulted in this study. The figure of 194 includes all the RTR cap badge men but not the attached ones such as the medical officer and padre.

358 *the 1st/95th Rifles or the 23rd Royal Welch Fusiliers*: For my books *Rifles: Six Years With Wellington's Legendary Sharpshooters* (London: Faber, 2003) and *Fusiliers: Eight Years with the Redcoats in America* (London: Faber, 2007).

358 *who became prisoners of war was eighty to ninety*: Once again some imprecision is inevitable. It is possible to make a definitive list solely of those taken during the last year of the war, 22 men. We know from the WD that twenty-five officers and men went missing during November 1941, probably the worst single month of the war for captures. Of course some of those who were listed missing either returned to the battalion or turned out to be dead.

358 *wounded could be estimated at around 1100*: This extrapolation is based on an estimate of just over five wounded men for each one killed in action, a

synthesis from several sources notably the table of battalion figures for the Canadian Armoured Corps in Jarymowycz, *Tank Tactics*. This provides total figures for the numbers of casualties and killed in action for every Canadian armoured unit in the war.

359 *'unrecognisable'*: Storer.

361 *the battalion captured something like one hundred enemy soldiers*: In the Tunis fighting alone, 5th RTR captured several thousand Axis troops. When one adds episodes in Ghent and the drive across Normandy it exceeds ten thousand. In one sense this figure has little meaning, for these episodes of German collapse were the product of an Allied machine of which 5th Tanks was just a part, but equally the men taken by the Germans in France 1940 or the Gazala battles of 1942 are rightly counted against the British, and the overall message, that the 5th RTR took far more prisoners than it lost, is the significant point.

361 *The ratio for equipment . . . destroyed or captured*: The striking thing in the WD is the number of transport vehicles and artillery accounted for during the 7th Armoured Division's great advances. This tends to confirm the view of the armoured division as an instrument of exploitation or annihilation, and undermine the view of it as an anti-tank formation.

362 *around one hundred of the fifteen hundred German tanks*: Zetterling, *Normandy 1944*.

366 *'I have proudly worn your beret and your badge . . . '*: Montgomery's speech to the RTR, *Tank* magazine (May 1945).

369 *one of the 5th RTR's sergeants*: The story is in Wilson, *Press on Regardless*.

BIBLIOGRAPHY

Agar-Hamilton, J. A. I. and L. C. F. Turner, *Crisis in the Desert: May–July 1942* (London: Oxford University Press, 1952)
————, *The Sidi Rezegh Battles, 1941* (London: Oxford University Press, 1957)
Alanbrooke, Field Marshal Lord (ed. Alex Danchev and Daniel Todman), *War Diaries 1939–1945* (London: Weidenfeld & Nicolson, 2001)
Badsey, Stephen, *Normandy 1944: Allied Landings and Breakout* (London: Osprey, 1990)
Beale, Peter, *Death by Design: British Tank Development in the Second World War* (Stroud: History Press, 2009)
Borthwick, Alastair, *Battalion: A British Infantry Unit's Actions from El Alamein to the Elbe, 1942–45* (London: Baton Wicks, 1994)
Bramall, Field Marshal Lord (ed.), *The Desert War 1940–1942* (London: Sidgwick and Jackson, 1992)
Buckley, John, *British Armour in the Normandy Campaign 1944* (New York: Frank Cass, 2004)
Carver, Michael (Field Marshal Lord Carver), *Out of Step: Memoirs of a Field Marshal* (London: Hutchinson, 1989)
Carver, Michael, *Dilemmas of the Desert War: The Libyan Campaign 1940–1942* (Stroud: History Press, 2002)
Close, Bill, *A View From the Turret: A History of the 3rd Royal Tank Regiment in the Second World War* (Bredon: Dell & Bredon, 1998)
Crisp, Robert, *Brazen Chariots: An Account of Tank Warfare in the Western Desert, November–December 1941* (London: Frederick Muller, 1959)

Daglish, Ian, *Operation Goodwood* (Barnsley: Pen and Sword, 2004)

Delaforce, Patrick, *Churchill's Desert Rats: From Normandy to Berlin with the 7th Armoured Division* (Stroud: Sutton, 1994)

——————, *Churchill's Desert Rats: 7th Armoured Division in North Africa, Burma, Sicily and Italy* (Stroud: Sutton, 2002)

D'Este, Carlo, *Decision in Normandy* (London: Harper Collins, 1983)

Forty, George (ed.), *Jake Wardrop's Diary: A Tank Regiment Sergeant's Story* (Stroud: Amberley, 2009)

Forty, George, *Afrika Korps at War: 1. The Road to Alexandria* (Shepperton: Ian Allan, 1978)

Griffith, Paddy, *World War II Desert Tactics* (Oxford: Osprey, 2008)

Hamilton, Nigel, *The Full Monty: Montgomery of Alamein, 1887–1942* (London: Penguin, 2002)

——————, *Monty: Master of the Battlefield, 1942–1944* (London: Hamish Hamilton, 1983)

——————, *Monty: The Field Marshal, 1944–1976* (London: Hamish Hamilton, 1986)

Harris, J. P., *Men, Ideas and Tanks: British Military Thought and Armoured Forces, 1903–1939* (Manchester: Manchester University Press, 1995)

Hills, Stuart, *By Tank into Normandy: A Memoir of the Campaign in Northwest Europe from D-Day to VE-Day* (London: Cassell, 2002)

Horrocks, Brian, *Corps Commander* (London: Sidgwick and Jackson, 1977)

Jacquet, Stéphanet, *Tilly-sur-Seulles* (Bayeux: Heimdal, 2008)

Jarymowycz, Roman Johann, *Tank Tactics* (London: Lynne Rienner, 2001)

Jentz, Thomas L., *Tank Combat in North Africa: The Opening Rounds – Operations Sonnenblume, Brevity, Skorpion and Battleaxe* (Atglen: Shiffer, 1998)

Joly, Cyril, *Take These Men: The Campaign of the Desert Rats from 1940 to 1943* (London: Constable, 1955). Joly's book is sometimes described as a 'novelised' account of the desert war, but he served at Sidi Rezegh with 3rd Tanks and suggests in his foreword that only the names of those in his unit have been changed.

Kriebel, Colonel Rainer, *Inside the Afrika Korps: The Crusader Battles, 1941–1942* (London: Greenhill, 1999)

Leakey, Rea and George Forty, *Leakey's Luck* (Stroud: Sutton, 1999)

Lefèvre, Eric (trans. R. Cooke), *Panzers in Normandy* (London: Compass, 1983)

Liddell Hart, B. H. (ed.), *The Rommel Papers* (London: Collins, 1953)

——————, *The Tanks: A History of the Royal Tank Regiment and its Predecessors*, 2 vols (London: Cassell, 1959)

Lodieu, Didier, *Operation Goodwood* (Paris: Histoire et Collections, 2008)

MacLeod Ross, G., in collaboration with Major-General Sir Campbell Clarke, *The Business of Tanks, 1933 to 1945* (Ilfracombe: Arthur H. Stockwell Ltd, 1976). This book is the source of much useful information including

British tank design, manufacturing methods, American techniques and technical specification.

Neillands, Robin, *The Desert Rats: 7th Armoured Division 1940–1945* (London: Weidenfeld & Nicolson, 1991)

Porter, David, *1 SS Panzer Corps at Villers-Bocage: 13 July 1944* (London: Amber Books, 2012)

Roach, Peter, *The 8.15 to War: Memoirs of a Desert Rat* (London: Leo Cooper, 1982)

Roberts, G. P. B., *From the Desert to the Baltic* (London: Kimber, 1987)

Russell, John, *No Triumphant Procession* (London: Arms and Armour, 1994)

Schneider, Wolfgang, *Tigers in Normandy* (Barnsley: Pen and Sword, 2011)

Smith, Norman, *Tank Soldier: The Fight to Liberate Europe 1944* (Lewes: Book Guild, 1989)

Stevenson, Eric, *A Kick Out of Life* (Exeter: Librario, 2008)

Stone, Brian, *Prisoner from Alamein* (London: H. F. & G. Witherby, 1944)

Verney, Gerald L., *The Desert Rats: The 7th Armoured Division in World War II* (London: Hutchinson, 1954)

Watt, Jock, *A Tankie's Travels: World War II Experiences of a Former Member of the Royal Tank Regiment* (Bognor Regis: Woodfield, 2006)

Wilson, Edward, *Press on Regardless: The Story of the Fifth Royal Tank Regiment in WWII* (Staplehurst: Spellmount, 2003)

Zetterling, Niklas, *Normandy 1944: German Military Organisation, Combat Power & Organisational Effectiveness* (Winnipeg: Fedorwicz, 2000)

Acknowledgements

This book would have been quite impossible without the help of a good many people who were so generous in guiding me on the road to publication. Of course there were the former 5th Tanks officers and soldiers who communicated with me by letter, phone, email and face to face: Roy Dixon, Harry Finlayson, Henry Hadwin, David Hargreaves, Bob Lay, Tom Schofield, Gerry Solomon, Eric Stevenson, Brian Taylor, Irwin Thornton and Ted Zoeftig. Relatives of those who had served were also vital in pinning down letters, memoirs and the like: David Bull, Richard Chesterfield, Isabelle Abu Hejleh, Mariam Abu Hejleh, Jeremy Holliman, Les Huett, Gill Johnson, Brenda MacDonald, Eyre Maunsell, Margaret Roe, Ashley Rossiter, David Ryder, Jeff Simpson, Susan Smethurst, Carl Stimpson and Richard Watkins. Deryck MacDonald, who served in A Squadron for much of the war, eventually commanding it, was the best single source of photographs. I am grateful to Brenda MacDonald, his widow, and Carl Stimpson for supplying images for this book. Quite a few members of the wider Royal Tank Regiment fraternity also gave freely of their help, including George Forty, Michael Jeffries, David Leakey, Stephen May, Terry Price, Tony Uloth, Mick Wilby and Peter Vaux. Among the non-RTR veterans who assisted were Tony Crassweller, Patrick Delaforce, David Dent and David Stileman. Many academic or professional experts on armour also went out of their way to advance my research, including David Fletcher, Martin Langford, Ian Paterson, William Spencer and David Willey.

Shortly before publication a pair of television documentaries based on the research for this book aired on BBC 2. Making these was a pleasure in itself but also turned up some final gems for this account. Among those who worked with me to bring the 5th Tanks' story to television screens were Graham Cooper, Dominic Crossley-Holland, Martin Davidson, Alex Mason and Francis Whately. Special thanks are due to George Entwistle, who gave the TV 'Tankies' their initial impetus.

As for the book, thanks are due to Jonathan Lloyd, my inde-fatigable agent, as well as the team at Little, Brown: Zoe Gullen, Zoe Hood and Tim Whiting. Inevitably, though, the ultimate gratitude must be expressed to my wife Hilary, as well as children Isabelle, Maddy and Sol. They held their nerve while this panzer of a project rampaged through what should have been family time.

Index

Mark Urban is Diplomatic and Defence Editor for the BBC's *Newsnight* and the author of the Number One *Sunday Times* bestseller *Task Force Black*. His previous books *Rifles* and *Fusiliers* were ground-breaking histories of earlier campaigns told through the lives of men in those regiments. He held a gap-year commission in the 4th Royal Tank Regiment and subsequently served in the Territorial Army. As a television journalist Mark has covered many of the world's conflicts during the last twenty-five years. He lives in London with his wife and children.